Audels
DO-IT-YOURSELF
ENCYCLOPEDIA

Audels

DO-IT-YOURSELF ENCYCLOPEDIA

ILLUSTRATED EDITION

VOLUME 2

*Comprehensive How-To Series for
the Entire Family...containing
material from the Illustrated
Do-It-Yourself Encyclopedia...written
in simple language with full step-by-step
instructions and profusely illustrated*

Theodore Audel and Co., N. Y.

How-To Guide To Screw Sizes

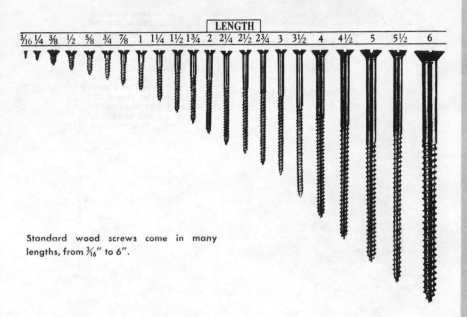

| ³⁄₁₆ | ¼ | ⅜ | ½ | ⅝ | ¾ | ⅞ | 1 | 1¼ | 1½ | 1¾ | 2 | 2¼ | 2½ | 2¾ | 3 | 3½ | 4 | 4½ | 5 | 5½ | 6 |

Standard wood screws come in many lengths, from ³⁄₁₆" to 6".

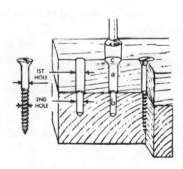

1ST HOLE
2ND HOLE

Pilot holes for screws Hole "a" is for the shank, hole "b" for the threaded or root section of the screw and hole "c" is used for countersunk flathead screws.

Sketch and table from "Tool Guide" courtesy of Stanley Tools.

Sizes Of Bits Or Drills To Bore Holes For Wood Screws

NUMBER OF SCREW		1	2	3	4	5	6	7	8	9	10	12	14	16	18
BODY DIAMETER OF SCREW		.073	.086	.099	.112	.125	.138	.151	.164	.177	.190	.216	.242	.268	.294
		5/64-	3/32-	3/32+	7/64+	1/8	9/64-	5/32-	11/64-	11/64+	3/16+	7/32-	15/64+	17/64-	19/64-
FIRST HOLE	TWIST DRILL SIZE	5/64	3/32	7/64	7/64	1/8	9/64	5/32	11/64	3/16	3/16	7/32	1/4	17/64	19/64
	AUGER BIT NUMBER							3	3	3	3	4	4	5	5
SECOND HOLE	TWIST DRILL SIZE		1/16	1/16	5/64	5/64	3/32	7/64	7/64	1/8	1/8	9/64	5/32	3/16	13/64
	AUGER BIT NUMBER												3	3	4

Although power tools make the job easier, there are many handymen who prefer to make their furniture with hand tools. Unless you are fairly skilled with tools, you will find that contemporary pieces are the simplest to make. Most cutting is along a straight line and corner joint construction is kept simple. On the other hand, period furniture involves intricate cutting and shaping, and some of the work cannot be done without a lathe and other power tools.

In the plans on the following pages, you will find some simple and some involved projects. Every plan can be modified to meet your requirements and your skills. Should you wish to make changes, re-read the basic primer section and make modifications accordingly.

But before you start on any project, remember that good furniture making involves:

1. accurate and careful workmanship

2. use of good woods and attractive grains, unless the pieces are to be painted

3. proper finishing—this cannot be rushed if you wish to obtain a craftsmanlike result.

Collect your tools, materials, plans and . . . good luck!

Planter-Coffee Table

This attractive coffee table, 24″ by 48″, is made of fir plywood and rests on four ¾″ hardwood dowel legs. It is easy to make with ordinary hand tools.

The tools you need are: rule, square, hand saw, center punch, drill, bits, countersink bit, brace and screwdriver bit, expansion bit, ex-

Materials Needed

1 Top	24 "x48"	¾" plywood
2 Side aprons—Part C	3⅝"x50"	¾" hardwood
2 End apron—Part A	3⅝"x24"	¾" hardwood
2 Cleats—Part D	¾"x48"	¾" hardwood
4 Legs—Part B	¾" hardwood dowels 15" long	

No. 10 flat and round head screws, 1¼" long; sandpaper

pansion bit or jig saw, keyhole saw or coping saw.

Follow the accompanying step-by-step instructions and you'll be able to make this unusual planter-coffee table in a single evening.

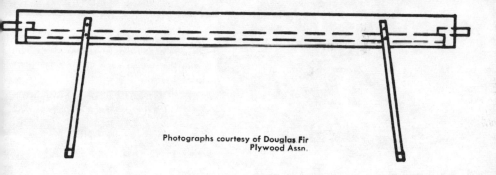

Photographs courtesy of Douglas Fir Plywood Assn.

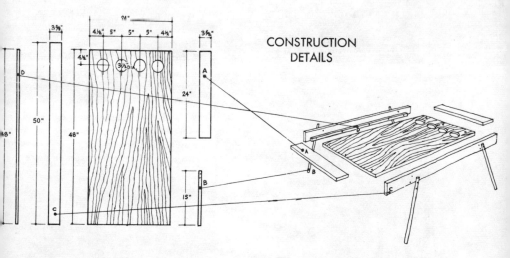

CONSTRUCTION
DETAILS

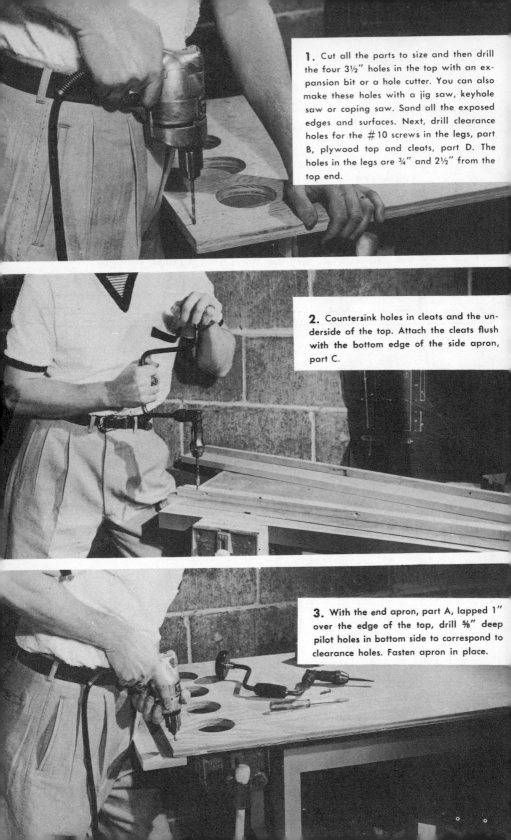

1. Cut all the parts to size and then drill the four 3½" holes in the top with an expansion bit or a hole cutter. You can also make these holes with a jig saw, keyhole saw or coping saw. Sand all the exposed edges and surfaces. Next, drill clearance holes for the #10 screws in the legs, part B, plywood top and cleats, part D. The holes in the legs are ¾" and 2½" from the top end.

2. Countersink holes in cleats and the underside of the top. Attach the cleats flush with the bottom edge of the side apron, part C.

3. With the end apron, part A, lapped 1" over the edge of the top, drill ⅝" deep pilot holes in bottom side to correspond to clearance holes. Fasten apron in place.

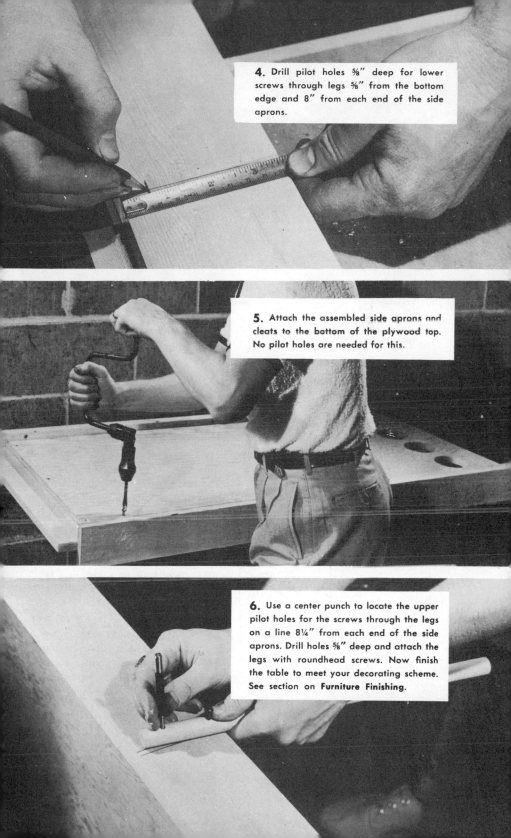

4. Drill pilot holes ⅝" deep for lower screws through legs ⅝" from the bottom edge and 8" from each end of the side aprons.

5. Attach the assembled side aprons and cleats to the bottom of the plywood top. No pilot holes are needed for this.

6. Use a center punch to locate the upper pilot holes for the screws through the legs on a line 8¼" from each end of the side aprons. Drill holes ⅝" deep and attach the legs with roundhead screws. Now finish the table to meet your decorating scheme. See section on **Furniture Finishing.**

Play Table for Children's Room

If you have an old table about
and want to convert it to a play table
for your youngsters, or you'd like to
build one from scrap, here's a novel
idea. Use rubber tiles over the surface and band the edge with an aluminum or chrome metal trim.

The resulting play table is as
durable as it is attractive. Pounding
and rolling of wheels won't damage
the rubber, which also helps to
muffle the sound of energetic play
activities. Crayon marks, paint and
ink are easily cleaned from the rubber tile surface.

If you wish to make this table
from scratch, make the top out of
¾" plywood cut in circle form, 36"
to 48" in diameter. The top rests on
a base made of 2x2 wooden legs and
a frame of 1x4's so that the top is
14" above the floor. See *Furniture
—Basic Primer* for leg joint details.

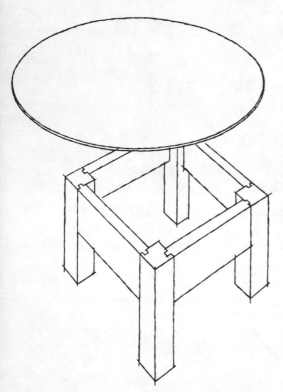

Basic construction plans for table.

End or Bedside Table

Sketches courtesy of Douglas Fir
Plywood Assn.

This unusual table with a glass top and lower storage compartment can be built with ½″ pipe legs or with attractive plywood legs. It is easy to make out of ¾″ fir plywood, a 44″ strip of ¼″x1″ hardwood and a piece of plate glass 24″x25½″.

The only tools you need are: a hand saw, rule, square, hammer, center punch, nail set, drill, bit and screwdriver.

Follow the step-by-step instructions and you'll find that you can make this table in a few hours.

1. Cut all the parts to size as noted in the materials list. Sand all surfaces and edges. Then glue and nail the bottom and shelf, part E, to the plywood back.

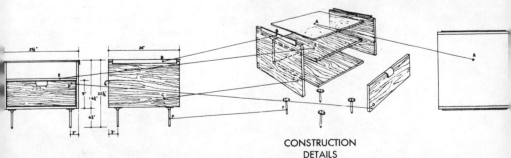

CONSTRUCTION
DETAILS

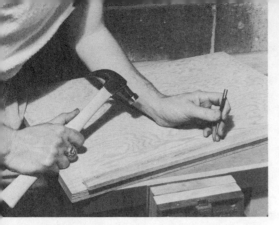

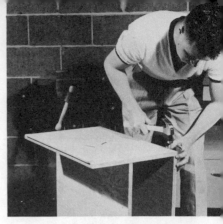

2. Set the hardwood retaining strips, part B, so that they project ¼" past the top edge of the sides, part C. Secure in place with glue and brads.

3. Next, glue and nail the sides so that they line up with the front edges of the shelf and bottom pieces. Set nails and brads; fill holes before finishing.

4. Fit the door in place between the bottom and the shelf. Center-punch to locate the holes for the hinges in the bottom and then attach the door with a piano hinge.

5. Drill a hole for a friction or bullet catch into the top edge of the door. Drive the catch into place. The handle is made of a piece of leather 3" wide and 5" long.

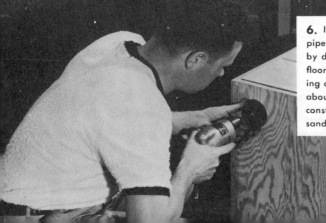

6. If you wish to use pipe legs, attach pipe flanges 3" from front, sides and back by drilling holes for screws. To protect the floors, insert dowels into the bottom opening of the pipes so that the dowels project about ⅛". For other types of legs, see leg construction details which follow. Now sand all surfaces and finish.

Materials Needed

1 Plate glass top—Part A	¼"x24"x25½"	
2 Retaining strips—Part B	1 "x22"	¾" hardwood
2 Sides—Part C	16 "x24"	¾" plywood
1 Door—Part D	8 "x24"	¾" plywood
1 Back	8¼"x24"	¾" plywood
1 Shelf—Part E	24 "x24"	¾" plywood
1 Bottom	24 "x24"	¾" plywood

1 piano hinge 24" long, with screws; 4 Pipe legs ½"x6½", with flanges and screws; I Friction catch; 6d finishing nails; brads; glue; sandpaper.

LEG DETAILS

There are several different types of legs you can use with this piece of furniture as well as others shown in this section. These legs can be made of ¾" plywood or, if you wish, 1" hardwood stock.

Note the accompanying illustrations showing the leg details. Cut the parts to size indicated, smooth all surfaces and edges. You can use the plywood edge tape, if you wish, or fill the end grain and paint the entire leg—black blends in well with contemporary furniture.

Alternate leg details.

HANDLES YOU CAN MAKE

While you can purchase any of a large variety of handles in a hardware store or lumber yard, there are many unusual handles you can make yourself. Here are just a few; maybe these will spark your own ideas.

Leather handle is made of a piece 3" wide and 5" long. Glue one end around a dowel, ½" in diameter. To attach the handle, you can cut a slot in the door or drawer front or else notch out a piece 3" wide and ⅛" deep. The back of the leather is fastened with glue and small roundhead screws.

Sketches courtesy of Douglas Fir
Plywood Assn.

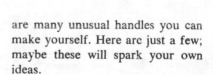

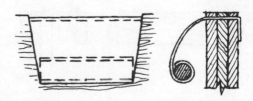

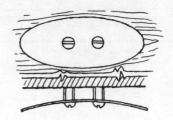

A piece of elliptically shaped brass can be fastened with bolts through thin brass tubing to make a modern pull. Smooth all metal edges and use brass bolts or paint the bolt heads black.

A piece of leather, 3" wide and 9" long, can be shaped into a loop to act as a drawer or door pull. Two roundhead screws with washers directly beneath the heads fasten leather to drawer or door.

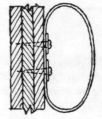

A wooden ball, available in many sizes in specialty lumber yards, makes an attractive pull. A screw is countersunk in the wooden ball to hold it fast to the forward surface of the door or drawer. Wooden balls are also available in hardware stores; these use a bolt to fasten in place.

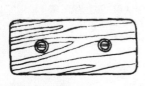
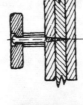

Wooden trim and moldings also make unusual pulls. Here are two types which can be used when making furniture.

Photograph courtesy of Douglas Fir
Plywood Association.

Make Your Own Ping-Pong Table

Here is a ping-pong table which is a welcome addition in any recreation room. Because of its simple construction and assembly, it can be taken apart and stored in a small space. It can also be taken outdoors and used on the patio or terrace in warm weather.

If you don't go in for ping-pong, you can make this table for general utility about the home. It is very handy as an extra serving table both indoors and outdoors.

All you need is a single piece of ¾″ plywood, 5′ by 9′, or you can make the top out of two pieces, 60″ x 54″ joined with a piano hinge on the underside. For the base, you need a 4′x8′ sheet of ¾″ or ⅝″ plywood.

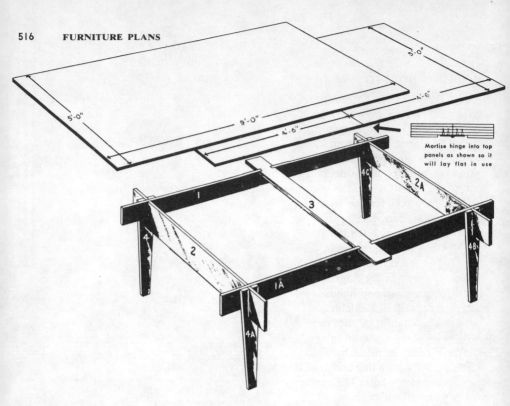

Mortise hinge into top panels as shown so it will lay flat in use

Detailed view of the table parts and assembly. Note sketch showing how hinge is mortised into underside of top when this part is made of two separate pieces.

Sketch courtesy of Douglas Fir Plywod Association.

Layout of table frame parts showing how they can be cut out of a single 4'x8' sheet of ¾" or ⅝" plywood.

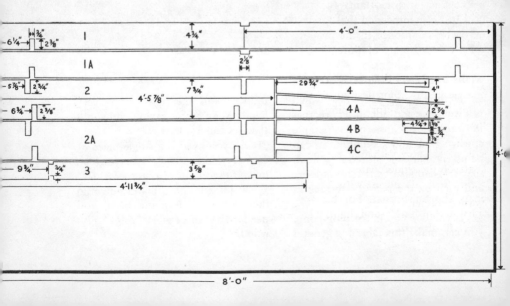

CUTTING HOW-TO

1. The top may be made from one piece—a 5'x9' plywood panel—or two pieces 5'x4' 6" hinged in the center. A hinged top, of course, will require less storage space. If you hinge the top, see hinge detail diagram.

2. The pieces for the base may be cut from one 4'x8' panel (as shown) or from one 8'x30" panel.

3. On one of your panels, carefully mark the frame pieces to dimensions shown in the diagram, and cut them with a sharp handsaw or power equipment, if available.

4. The notches in the various panels should be accurate in width. They can easily be made by drilling a hole at the bottom line and sawing each edge into the hole. The corners can be trimmed with a chisel.

5. Sand all edges. You are now ready to finish the table.

FINISHING HOW-TO

1. Apply two coats of exterior enamel undercoater. The initial or prime coat is important; for this coat it is recommended that the undercoater be thinned in the proportions of one quart of pure linseed oil per gallon of paint.

2. Brush on one coat of exterior enamel in any color desired. Green is recommneded for a ping-pong table.

3. Be sure to paint the underside of the top with one or more coats of the undercoater.

4. Seal all edges with undercoats and finish coat. For best results in finishing, sand lightly between finish coats.

FOR GENERAL USE INSIDE

1. For a light stain finish to retain natural beauty of wood, apply a resin sealer, followed by a stain coat, then a flat or gloss varnish as a wearing surface.

2. Seal the underside of the top with one or more coats of the resin sealer.

3. Finish all edges with sealer and other coats.

ALTERNATE INTERIOR FINISH

1. Apply coat of interior undercoater, followed by a coat of interior paint.

2. Apply one or more coats of the undercoater to the underside of the top.

3. Finish all edges with undercoater and finish coat.

FOR PING-PONG TABLE

1. The ping-pong table top should be painted in dark green color, in a flat, thin, nonreflecting paint.

2. One procedure for achieving such surface would be to apply a coat of lacquer sanding sealer, followed by a flat green pigmented lacquer. Edges would be finished, of course, and the underside of the top should have one or more coats of the sanding sealer or other protective coating.

ASSEMBLY—The base may now be assembled as pictured in the sketch. The simple lock joints hold the base rigid without the use of any fastenings. It may be readily taken apart and stored until needed again.

Drop-Leaf Table-Cart

This ingeniously designed serving table-cart can be used as a buffet table, a tea table, movable bar or a dining table for two. When not in use, it adds a decorative note as a side table in a finely furnished room.

As planned here by designer Russel Wright, power tools are needed to cut the miters and grooves. The setting of the blind dowels calls for a certain amount of skill. However, these plans can be modified if desired—just re-read the basic primer section and you will find easier ways to do the same job.

No matter which method you choose for the construction, you will be able to build a beautiful and useful table of which you and your family will be proud. As designed by Mr. Wright for the series of Famous Designer Plans, the table is made of Weldwood African Mahogany plywood with legs of solid mahogany and a drawer bottom of green Micarta or laminated plastic. You can, of course, use any other hardwood-veneered plywood you like.

Photograph courtesy of United States
Plywood Corp.

Here are the basic plans together with the materials you will need to make this striking table-cart.

Front and side views showing construction details on this drop-leaf table-cart.

Sketch courtesy of United States
Plywood Corp.

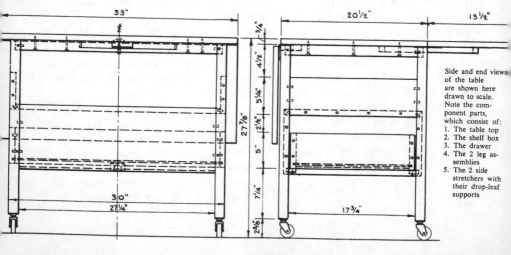

Side and end views of the table are shown here drawn to scale. Note the component parts, which consist of:
1. The table top
2. The shelf box
3. The drawer
4. The 2 leg assemblies
5. The 2 side stretchers with their drop-leaf supports

	Materials Needed
TOP	1 center 33"x20½"x¾" plywood good-2-sides 2 leaves 33"x13½"x¾" plywood good-2-sides
LEGS, SHELF BOX, AND FRAME	4 legs 24⅝"x1⅜" solid mahogany 2 side stretchers 27¼"x1⅜" x⅜" solid mahogany 2 end stretchers 17¾"x1⅜"x¾" solid mahogany 2 side panels 27¼"x9"x¾" plywood good-2-sides 2 end panels 17¾"x5⅜"x¾" plywood good-2-sides 1 shelf 28½"x19¼"x¾" plywood good-2-sides 2 drop-leaf supports 14⅞"x3"x¾" plywood 2 drawer-slides 27¼"x1⅜"x½" maple or other very hard wood 1 center tie 17¾"x2"x1" maple or other very hard wood
DRAWER	2 sides 28½"x5"x¾" plywood 2 ends 17⅝"x5"x¾" plywood 1 bottom 29"x16⅝" ¹⁄₁₆" Micarta bonded to ⅛" hardboard
OTHER MATERIALS	4 4" hinges with ⅝" screws to fit 4 Bassick casters No. 9439-SC-RP with clear plastic wheels 2¼" carriage bolts, 1¾" long, with nuts and flat washers Presto-Set glue Mahogany veneering strips for edges 1 qt. Satinlac, wood filler, sandpaper, and fine steel wool (00) Contact Cement.

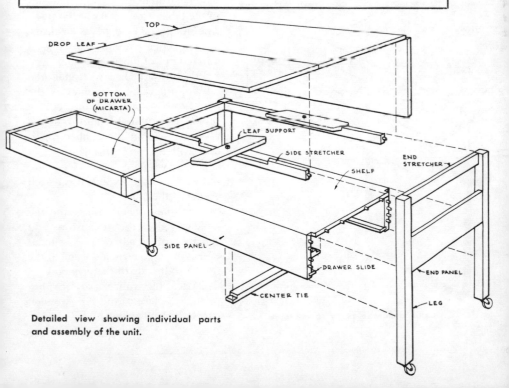

Detailed view showing individual parts
and assembly of the unit.

Photograph courtesy of Rubber Manufacturers' Association.

Pink Elephant Coffee Table

This rubber-topped coffee or cocktail table with a pink elephant and butterfly inserts should be a special inspiration for a weekend project because resilient rubber is easy to cut into any pattern. Furthermore, the rubber top is easy to clean and won't be harmed by spilled drinks.

Make the base for the table out of a piece of ¾″ plywood and attach two cleats, out of 1x4, to the underside about 1″ from the ends of the table. Use #9 flathead screws 1½″ long, and blue, to fasten cleats.

The edge around the table is mitered out of hardwood stock, ½″ x1½″, and attached with glue and 6d finishing nails. Counterset the nail heads. Note that this edging should extend above the top of the plywood so that the rubber top is flush with the top of this trim.

The wrought iron legs are screwed into the 1x4 cleats at each corner of the table.

Cut the rubber inserts for the table as well as the rubber top. You can use roll goods or tiles, whichever is more convenient. Cement the rubber to the top of the plywood.

After the rubber surface has dried in place, sand all wooden edges and apply a finish.

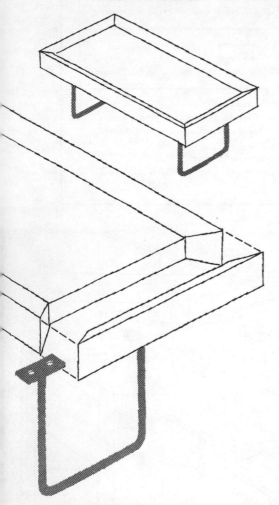

Detailed plans for pink elephant table.

Drop-Leaf Coffee Table

You needn't have an elaborate workshop to make this striking coffee table. The shelf provides convenient storage and the two hinged sides lift up to provide additional surface space when needed.

It was designed by Freda Diamond out of rift oak plywood and topped with black Micarta.

Materials Needed

4'x4' ¾" plywood panel (choice of wood up to you)	40 2" No. 10 flathead wood screws for shelf and legs
1 pair of 3" hinges for the butterfly supports	8 1½" finishing nails
2 pairs of 2" hinges for the drop leaves	Plastic resin glue
6 1" angle irons for attaching the table top	⅟₁₆" Micarta panel 30"x60"
	1 qt. contact cement and applicator
16 ¾" No. 6 flathead wood screws for the 2" hinges	1 qt. Satinlac
12 ¾" No. 8 flathead wood screws for the 3" hinges	Fine steel wool (Number 00)
	Furniture paste wax
12 ¾" No. 6 roundhead wood screws for the 1" angle irons	Spackle and oil color for making Swedish putty—or wood veneer for edge banding
	4 "Domes of Silence"

Sketch courtesy of United States
Plywood Corp.

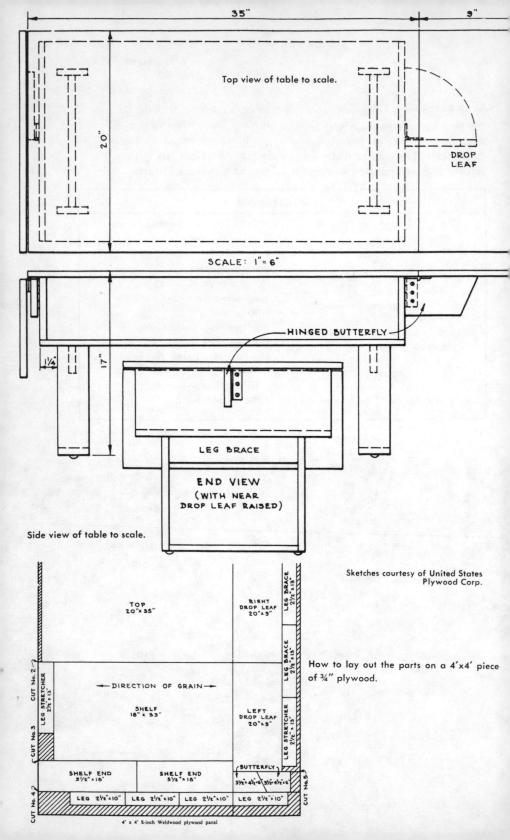

35" 9"

Top view of table to scale.

20"

DROP
LEAF

SCALE: 1"= 6"

HINGED BUTTERFLY

1¼" 17"

LEG BRACE

END VIEW
(WITH NEAR
DROP LEAF RAISED)

Side view of table to scale.

Sketches courtesy of United States
Plywood Corp.

TOP
20"x 35"

RIGHT
DROP LEAF
20"x 9"

LEG BRACE
2½"x 13"

LEG STRETCHER 2½"x 13"

CUT No. 2

CUT No. 3

←DIRECTION OF GRAIN→

LEG BRACE
2½"x 13"

How to lay out the parts on a 4'x4' piece
of ¾" plywood.

SHELF
18" x 33"

LEFT
DROP LEAF
20"x 9"

LEG STRETCHER
2½"x 13"

SHELF END
5½"x 18"

SHELF END
5½"x 18"

BUTTERFLY
3½"x 4½"x 6" 3½"x 4½"x 6"

CUT No. 4

LEG 2½"x10" LEG 2½"x10" LEG 2½"x10" LEG 2½"x10" LEG 2½"x10"

CUT No. 5

4' x 4' ¾-inch Weldwood plywood panel

Stacking Cabinets

Here's a novel and sensible idea in the way of cabinets. These stacking cabinets of fir plywood are finished in bright decorator colors. Used separately or stacked on top of one another, they fit into almost any room in the house.

To make the cabinets:

1. Cut the top and bottom out of ¾" plywood to size—11¾"x 23".

2. Cut dadoes or grooves for sliding doors as shown in the detail sketch. You can use the alternate technique with ¼" quarter-round and ¼" square stock or any of the methods shown in the basic primer.

3. Drill four holes, ½" in diameter, through bottom and top for legs.

4. Cut two sides out of ¾" plywood to size—11¾"x11¾".

5. Cut two doors out of ¼" plywood to size—11⅝"x10⅝". Drill finger-grip holes as shown in sketch. These holes are 1" in diameter.

6. Rabbet the top and bottom edges of the sides to receive top and bottom of the cabinet.

7. Cut four legs out of ½" hardwood dowel; each should be 15⅞" long.

8. Cut back panel out of ¼" plywood to size—11"x23".

To assemble the unit, it is necessary to sand all edges and surfaces smooth and then:

1. Glue and nail one side to the top, bottom and back.

2. Insert two of the legs and fasten to the side as shown in the detail sketch using a #8 roundhead screws 1" long.

3. Slide doors into grooves.

4. Attach the other side to the top, bottom and back with glue and nails.

5. Slip the other two legs through the pre-drilled holes and fasten the side.

Materials Needed

EACH CABINET

Top, bottom and ends: 2'x3', ¾" plywood

Back, sliding doors: 2'x2', ¼" plywood

Legs: 5½' of ½" dia. hardwood dowel rod

1 Doz. 1" No. 8 roundhead wood screws; glue; 4d, 6d finishing nails

(if alternate door detail is followed); door guides: 8' of ¼" quarter-round; door guides: 4' of ¼" square stock.

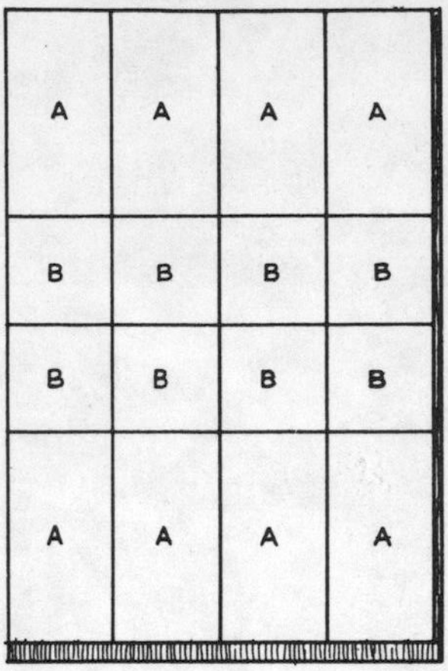
A A A A
B B B B
B B B B
A A A A

¾'' x 4'-0'' x 6'-0'' PLYPANEL A-D
(MATERIAL FOR 4 CABINETS)

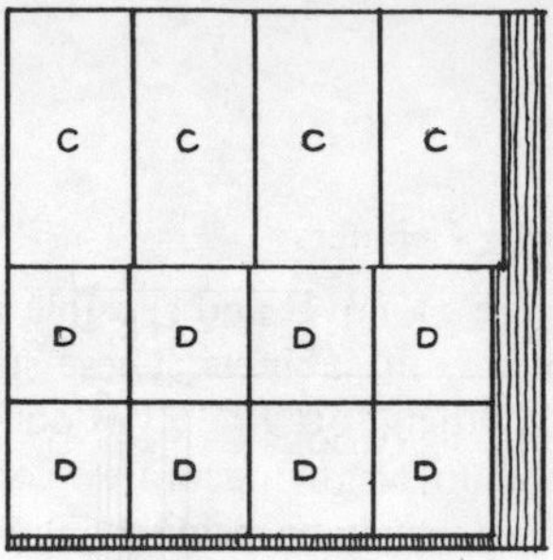
C C C C
D D D D
D D D D

¼'' x 4'-0'' x 4'-0'' PLYPANEL A-D
(MATERIAL FOR 4 CABINETS)

How to cut the basic parts for four cabinets out of 1 sheet of 4'x6' plywood ¾" thick and a 4'x4' sheet of ¼" plywood. Part A is top and bottom, 11¾"x23"—part B the sides, 11¾"x11¾"—part C the back, 11"x 23"—and part D the sliding doors, 10⅝"x 11⅝".

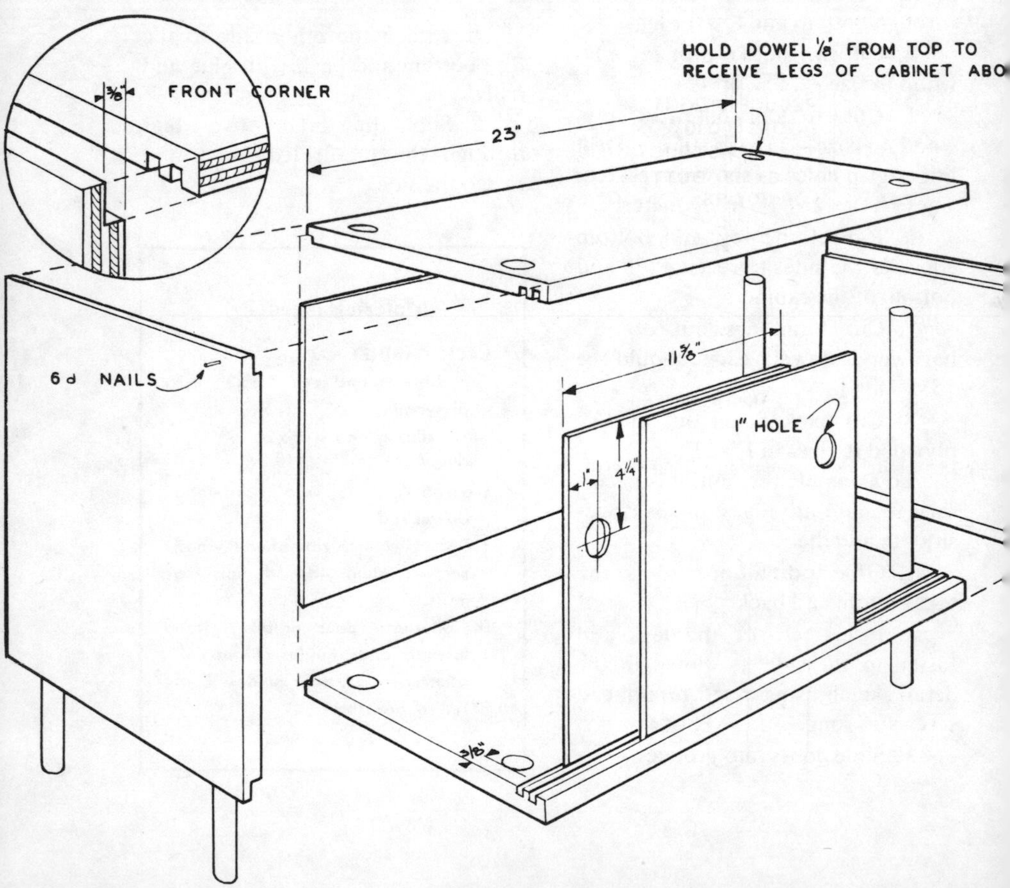
HOLD DOWEL ⅛" FROM TOP TO
RECEIVE LEGS OF CABINET ABO
FRONT CORNER
⅜"
23"
6d NAILS
11⅝"
1" HOLE
1"
4¼"
⅜"

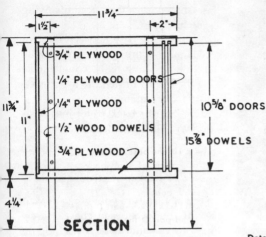

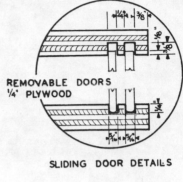

3/4" PLYWOOD

1/4" PLYWOOD DOORS

1/4" PLYWOOD

1/2" WOOD DOWELS

3/4" PLYWOOD

11¾"

11"

10⅝" DOORS

15⅝" DOWELS

4¼"

11¾"

1½"   2"

SECTION

Sectional or end view of the cabinet.

REMOVABLE DOORS
1/4" PLYWOOD

SLIDING DOOR DETAILS

Details for cutting grooves for the sliding doors in the top and bottom of the cabinet.

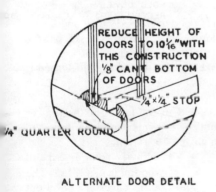

REDUCE HEIGHT OF DOORS TO 10 1/16" WITH THIS CONSTRUCTION
1/8" CANT BOTTOM OF DOORS
1/4" x 1/4" STOP
1/4" QUARTER ROUND

ALTERNATE DOOR DETAIL

Alternate plan for making sliding doors.

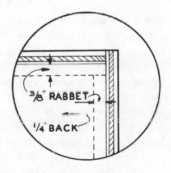

3/8" RABBET

1/4" BACK

BACK CORNER DETAIL

Details for joining back.

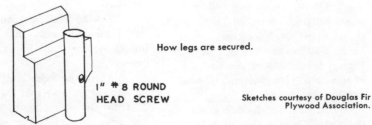

How legs are secured.

1" # 8 ROUND
HEAD SCREW

Sketches courtesy of Douglas Fir
Plywood Association.

Buffet Storage Chest

Simplified contemporary design has created this striking combination buffet and storage unit which is made of fir plywood and painted iron legs. The slope-front drawers are ideal for storing linens and flatware and the top of the unit is perfect for serving light buffet meals.

For this unit you will need a 24"x30" piece of ¼" plywood, one 4'x4' and one 4'x8' panel of ⅜" plywood and one piece of ¾" plywood 48"x54", plus 2½' of 2x4, 2½' of 1x2 and 38" of ⅝" steel rod.

1. Cut the parts as noted in the accompanying material list and shown in the detail sketches.

2. Fasten the drawer guides to the inside surface of the two sides of the chest. Use glue and 1" brads for the job.

3. Attach the divider guide to the underside of the top of the chest as shown in the accompanying sketch.

4. Set the base between the two sides and secure in place with glue and 6d finishing nails, countersinking the heads. Fasten the top as well in the same manner.

5. Set the back panel into position with glue and brads.

MAKING THE DRAWER

These unusual drawers are easy to make and can be used in any piece of furniture you design as well as this buffet storage chest. Here's how to cut and assemble a sloping front drawer:

1. Cut the bottom out of ⅜" plywood to size—28⅜" wide and 22⅞" deep.

2. Cut two sides out of ⅜" plywood to size—3" high and 20⅞" long. Next, cut the bevel on the front of each side as shown in the sketch; the top of the side piece is 19⅞" long and the bottom is 20⅞" long.

3. Cut the back for the drawer out of ⅜" plywood to size—3" high and 26¾" long.

4. The drawer front is cut out of ¾" plywood; it is 4"x28⅜". The top and bottom edges are bevel cut with a saw or plane as shown in detailed sketch. Next, cut a rabbet along each edge—1³⁄₁₆" wide and ¼" deep.

5. Set the back between the two sides and join with glue and 1" brads, forming butt joints at each corner.

6. Place the sides and back on the drawer base so that the back is 2" from the rear edge of the base and a ⁷⁄₁₆" space is left on each side.

Fasten in place with glue and 1″ brads.

7. The front of the drawer is mounted last. It is fastened with glue and 6d finishing nails into the sides and the base of the drawer.

8. Sand all edges smooth so that the drawer slides freely back and forth on the guides attached to the sides.

Front and side views of the unit.

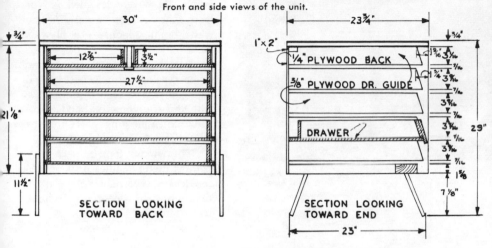

SECTION LOOKING TOWARD BACK

SECTION LOOKING TOWARD END

Detail view of the drawer face.

Detailed view of the construction of the chest. Note that rubber crutch tips are used on the ⅝″ steel rod legs to prevent marring the floor.

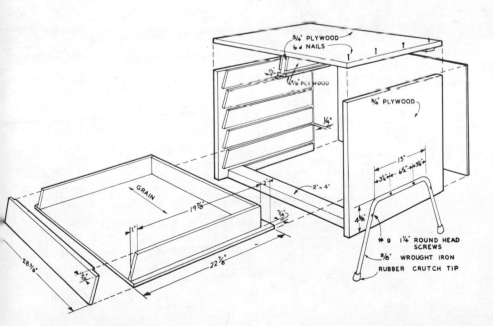

Base and Wall Cabinets

These attractive units can be built individually as separate wall and base cabinets or used in pairs as shown in the accompanying photograph. These were designed by Norman Cherner to be cut without waste from standard-size plywood panels.

It is best to use glue with another type of fastener—screws or nails—to make secure joints. You will find C-clamps or hand screws valuable in holding parts together while the adhesive is drying.

The units shown here have painted metal handles. It is possible to use any type of handle you find fits into your decorating scheme.

Photograph courtesy of Douglas Fir Plywood Association.

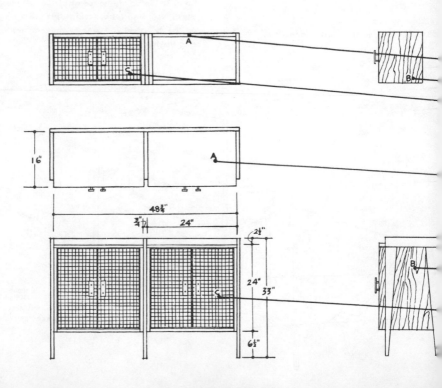

Materials Needed

BASE CABINET

1 Top (A)	16"x24"	¾" plywood
1 Back	22½"x22½"	¾" plywood
2 Sides (B)	16"x23¼"	¾" plywood
1 Bottom	16"x22½"	¾" plywood
2 Doors (C)	11"x22¼"	¾" plywood
Legs	¾"x4"x14'	fir, pine or hardwood
2 Side aprons	¾"x3¼"x14"	fir, pine or hardwood
1 Back apron	¾"x2½"x50¼"	fir, pine or hardwood, if

cabinets are built in pairs; if only one cabinet is constructed, back apron is 25½" long.

2 handles; 2 piano hinges 22" long, with screws; 2 friction catches; 6d finishing nails, screws, glue, sandpaper; 4 furniture glides ½" size.

HANGING CABINETS

1 Top (A)	12"x24"	¾" plywood
1 Back	12½"x24"	¾" plywood
1 Bottom	12"x24"	¾" plywood
2 Ends (B)	12"x14"	¾" plywood
2 Doors (C)	11¾"x12¼"	¾" plywood
1 Spacer	12"x14"	¾" plywood

2 handles; 2 piano hinges 12" long, with screws; 2 friction catches; 6d finishing nails, glue, sandpaper.

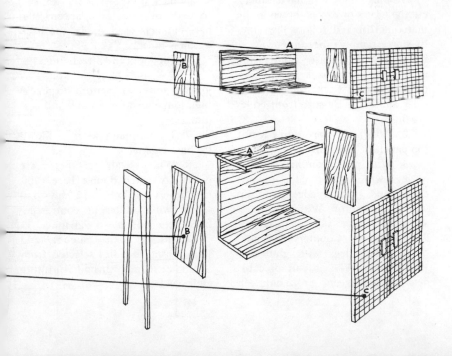

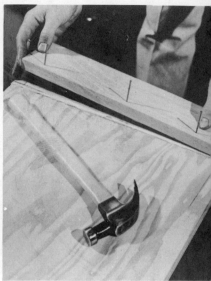

For addition handles, as well as leg construction details, see plans for the end or bedside table earlier in this section.

To make these unusual cabinets, cut the pieces to size as shown in the materials list and follow this step-by-step assembly procedure:

1. Assemble base cabinet by nailing bottom to back panel; sides to bottom and back; top panel to sides and back. Be sure front edges are flush.

2. Attach side aprons to edge of top panel, ¾″ forward of rear edge.

3. With pencil, outline location of legs with tapered edge toward center and straight edge lined up with end of apron. Within outlined area, drill cabinet side for three #9 flathead screws. Countersink inside.

4. Attach legs with glue and 1¼″ screws. When a pair of cabinets is used as one unit, only six legs and three side aprons are required. Clamp cabinets in alignment and attach to middle pair of legs with glue and screws. Fasten single back apron ¾″x2½″x50¼″ to ends of three side aprons. On base cabinets used singly, the back apron is ¾″x2½″x25½″.

5. Fit doors and attach hinges

6. Assemble hanging cabinet by joining top and bottom to back; then join ends to top, back and bottom.

7. Fit and hang doors as shown for base cabinet.

8. When wall cabinets are paired to match double base cabinets, insert a ¾″x12″x12″ plywood spacer with similar or contrasting finish between the two wall units.

9. Install door catches and stops. Install handles selected from alternate details. Install furniture glides on legs.

This combination unit, made of walnut plywood and black Micarta, is used for the bar top and for alternate leaves of the screen. It is a high-style furniture piece designed by Edward Wormley.

Unusual Screen-Bar

Edward Wormley, one of the great innovators in contemporary furniture design designed this screen-bar as a high-style piece of furniture. The bar stands 6' high and it may be used from the front or rear. When not in use, it is covered by a handsome screen made of alternate panels of hardwood-veneered Weldwood plywood and Micarta. It can be made of other woods, of course.

The bar is designed with built-in lights that cast a soft glow down on the stemmed glasses which hang from racks on each side of the bar.

As planned here, the bar requires five 6' brass piano hinges which run the full length of the screen. They are especially attractive when light is reflected from the long brass strips, but for economy's sake, you may prefer to use a less expensive hinge technique. You can substitute several butt hinges, but decide upon which one you like and can afford before cutting the parts.

Here are the basic working drawings together with a materials

Materials Needed

2 4′x6′¾″ plywood panels (good-2-sides)
1 4′x6′¾″ plywood panel (good-1-side)
1 4′x8′1/16″ Micarta
3¼″x½″x4′6″ solid stock for the drawer and glass racks
¼″x½″x10′6″ solid hardwood for drawer slides and glass frame
12″x12″x⅛″ hardboard panel
10⅝″x34⅜″x⅛″ white flash opalescent glass
2 20″ 60-watt Lumiline lamps with 4 mounts
1 ½″ toggle switch
10′ of No. 16 insulated wire
5 6′x1¼″ (open) continuous brass hinge
1 3′x1¼″ (open) continuous brass hinge
2 gross ⅝″ No. 5 oval-head brass screws
1 gross ½″ No. 5 oval-head brass screws
50′ of ⅛″x¾″ edge banding or wood veneer
14 single-pin ¾″ "Domes of Silence"
2 quarts Satinlac
8 ¼″ adjustable shelf pins
3′ ¼″ dowels
3′ ⅜″dowels
½ gross 1¼″ No. 10 flathead wood screws
2 polished brass pulls for drawer and door
1 magnetic door catch

list. The more advanced handyman can build this unit from these plans following the techniques of construction given in the basic primer and elsewhere in this section.

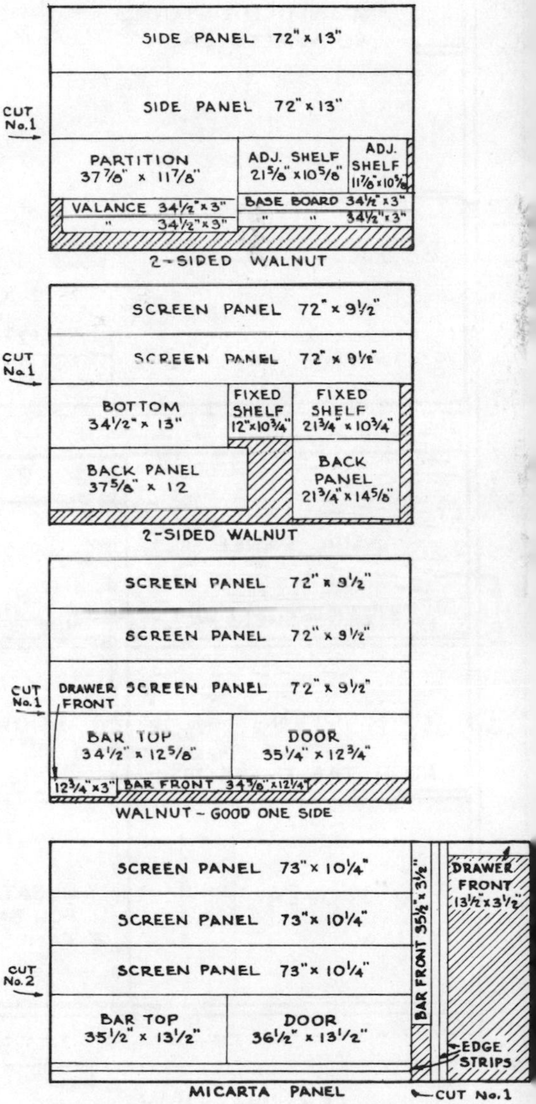

Plans for cutting the basic parts out of plywood and plastic laminate.

Front and side views of the screen-bar.

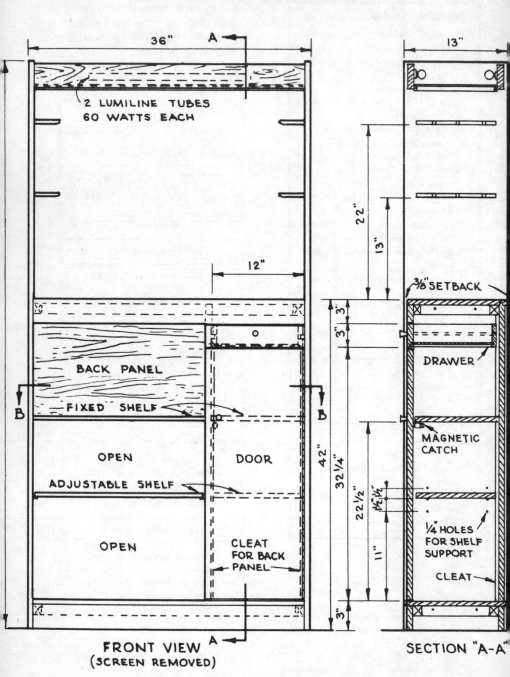

FRONT VIEW
(SCREEN REMOVED)

SECTION "A-A"

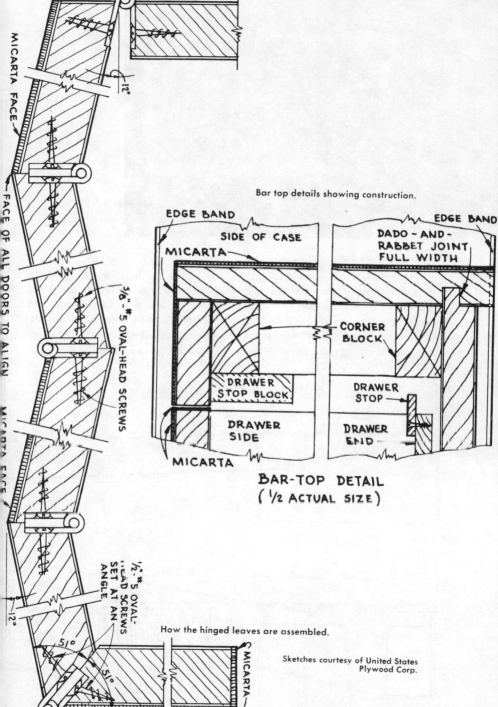

MICARTA FACE

FACE OF ALL DOORS TO ALIGN

MICARTA FACE

12°

5/8" #5 OVAL-HEAD SCREWS

1/2" #5 OVAL-HEAD SCREWS SET AT AN ANGLE

12°

51°

51°

MICARTA

Bar top details showing construction.

EDGE BAND

SIDE OF CASE

MICARTA

EDGE BAND

DADO - AND - RABBET JOINT FULL WIDTH

CORNER BLOCK

DRAWER STOP BLOCK

DRAWER STOP

DRAWER SIDE

DRAWER END

MICARTA

BAR-TOP DETAIL
(1/2 ACTUAL SIZE)

How the hinged leaves are assembled.

Sketches courtesy of United States
Plywood Corp.

Contemporary Desk

This attractive contemporary desk is made of fir plywood and pieces of hardwood and pine. There are several types of legs and drawer pulls which can be used; see earlier suggestions on legs and pulls in this section.

To make the unit, cut all parts as noted in the materials list. Sand all edges and surfaces smooth and you're ready to assemble the unit. Remember, all joints, except for the center apron and leg rails, are glued and nailed.

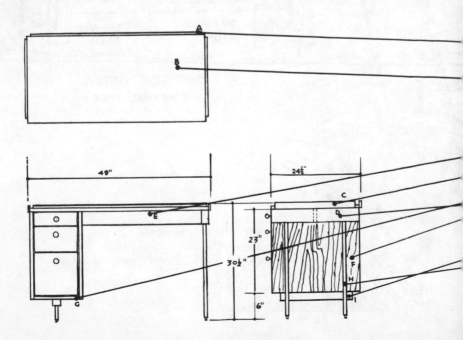

Materials Needed	1 Back strip (A)	1½"x46"	½" hardwood
	1 Top (B)	2'x4'	¾" plywood
	2 Side strips (C)	1½"x22"	½" hardwood
	1 Leg rail (D)	3⅝"x24"	1⅝" fir or pine
	1 Leg rail (I)	2"x20"	1⅝" fir or pine
	1 Center apron (E)	3⅝"x32¾"	1" fir, pine or hardwood
	1 Cabinet bottom (G)	12"x24"	¾" plywood
	2 Cabinet sides (F)	23"x24"	¾" plywood
	1 Cabinet back	12"x22¼"	¾" plywood
	2 Legs (H)	¾"x29"	Steel pipe (not threaded)
	2 Legs (J)	¾"x6"	Steel pipe (not threaded)
TOP DRAWER:	1 Front	3⅝"x11⅞"	¾" plywood
	1 Back	2⅜"x10⅞"	¾" plywood
	2 Sides	2⅜"x22"	½" plywood
CENTER DRAWER:	1 Front	6⅜"x11⅞"	¾" plywood
	1 Back	5⅛"x10⅞"	¾" plywood
	2 Sides	5⅛"x22"	½" plywood
BOTTOM DRAWER:	1 Front	12"x11⅞"	¾" plywood
	1 Back	10¾"x10⅞"	¾" plywood
	2 Sides	10¾"x22"	½" plywood
	3 Drawer bottoms	11⅞"x22"	½" plywood
	6 Runner strips	¾"x¾"x22"	plywood, pine or hardwood

3 drawer handles; 4 angle braces 2", with screws; 4 crutch tips, or hardwood dowels, for ends of legs; 9 flathead wood screws; 2½" and 3½" brads; 6d and 4d finishing nails; glue; sandpaper.

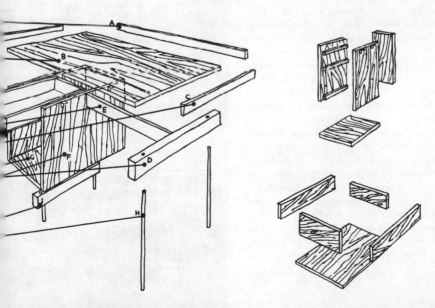

Sketches courtesy of Douglas Fir Plywood Assn.

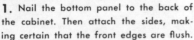

1. Nail the bottom panel to the back of the cabinet. Then attach the sides, making certain that the front edges are flush.

2. Measure down $2\frac{15}{16}$", $9\frac{3}{8}$" and $21\frac{1}{16}$" from the top edge of the cabinet to locate the upper surface of each of the three drawer runners on each side. Exactly $\frac{1}{16}$" clearance is left above and below each drawer front. The ends of the runners, $\frac{3}{4}$" from the forward edge of the cabinet, act as drawer stops.

3. Drive pipe legs into tight holes drilled into leg rails. Drill and countersink cabinet bottom on centerline for three #9 flathead screws $2\frac{1}{2}$" long. Fasten the rail with glue and screws. Drill the cabinet side and countersink inside for two #9 flathead screws $2\frac{1}{2}$" long into the end of the center apron.

4. Drill and countersink $1\frac{5}{8}$"x$3\frac{5}{8}$" leg rail for two #9 flathead screws $3\frac{1}{2}$" long into the center apron. Attach two angle braces to the side of the cabinet and two to the leg rail. It is best to assemble the desk upside down on a bench or floor. After the cabinet, center apron, legs and angles are assembled, slide desk top into position, bottom side up, and screw angle braces to underside of the top.

5. Use 6d finishing nails through top into edges of the cabinet, center apron and leg rail. Attach $\frac{1}{2}$"x$1\frac{1}{2}$" back and side strips to the edge of the top with glue and 1" brads. Assemble all drawers by joining the back, bottom and sides to the front panel. Attach handles to drawers and set them in place in the desk. Counterset all nail heads, fill with wood putty and you're ready to finish the unit.

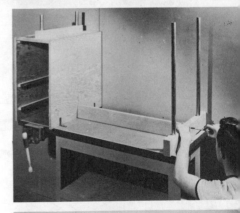

Photographs courtesy of Douglas Fir Plywood Assn.

Decorative Storage Chest

Peter Hunt, probably the out-standing American authority on decorative peasant art, has designed this handsome storage chest which has dozens of purposes around the house. It can serve as a window or fireside seat and is readily moveable for it has easy-rolling ball casters in each leg.

It is easy to construct and the painted decorations can be applied even by those who have had no previous experience in doing such work. This chest was made of maple plywood but you can use any type of wood you wish.

Although the plans for this decorative chest were prepared by Mr. Hunt for distribution by United States Plywood Corporation and its dealers, here is a complete list of materials and working drawings for the more advanced handyman to follow.

Materials Needed

4'x8'¾" lumber core plywood
4'x4'⅜" Novoply panel
48—1½" No. 10 flathead steel screws
12—1⅛" No. 10 flathead steel screws
4—¾" ball-casters
1 box 1" finishing brads
Presto-Set glue
36' ½"x¾" No. 8432 pine parting strips
(for nailing strips)
10' ¾" No. 8610 flat screen molding
10' ¹¹⁄₁₆x3½" No. F402 clam-shell base molding
10' ⁷⁄₁₆"x¹¹⁄₁₆" No. 8422 shoe molding
2 black hammered butt-strap hinges, with ¾" wide butts
1 slotted brass stay hinge for lid
2' ⅜" dowels for screw-hole plugs
4—1½" No. 6 flathead steel screws for hinge butts
2 good-grade camel's-hair brushes Nos. 10 and 11
4 tubes of oil colors—red, green, blue, yellow, and white
½ pint turpentine
½ pint clear varnish
paste wax
Satinlac

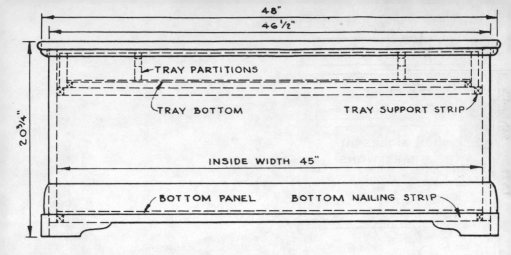

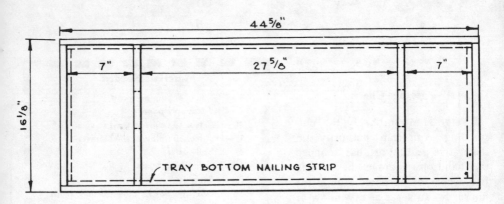

How to lay out the pieces for cutting.

Front and side views of the chest plus a top view showing basic dimensions and assembly of parts.

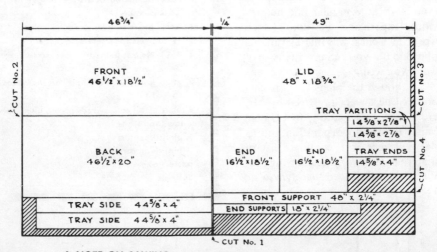

A NOTE ON SAWING

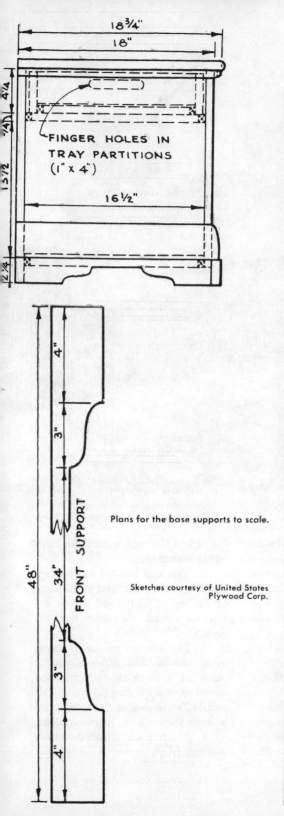

18¾"
18"
4¼"
¾"
15½"

FINGER HOLES IN
TRAY PARTITIONS
(1" x 4")

16½"

2¼"

48"
4"
3"
34"
3"
4"

FRONT SUPPORT

Plans for the base supports to scale.

Sketches courtesy of United States
Plywood Corp.

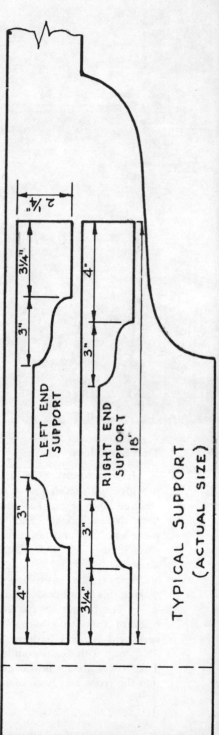

2¼"
3¼"
3"
LEFT END
SUPPORT
3"
4"

4"
3"
RIGHT END
SUPPORT
3"
3¼"

18"

TYPICAL SUPPORT
(ACTUAL SIZE)

Twin Bunk Beds

Photograph courtesy of United States
Plywood Corp.

Here is a furniture built-in which provides two beds in a room for two children and yet makes the most floor space available. Each bed is made as a unit and fastened to the studs in the wall with 4″ flathead screws.

Here is the basic how-to for making this twin bunk bed unit:

1. The frames for the beds are made of 1x6's with butt joint corners held by #9 flathead screws 2½″ long with heads countersunk. Two braces are set into dadoes cut into the front and back of the bed frame and fastened in the same manner as the corners.

2. You can use No-Sag springs under a mattress or else set a piece of ⅜″ or ½″ plywood across the top and rest a foam rubber mattress on it.

3. The storage cabinet is made as a built-in. The exposed side is made of a piece of ½″ plywood nailed to cleats on the floor and wall and 1x2's are used to form the sides and top around a ¾″ plywood door.

4. The entire unit rests on a base made of 1x2's.

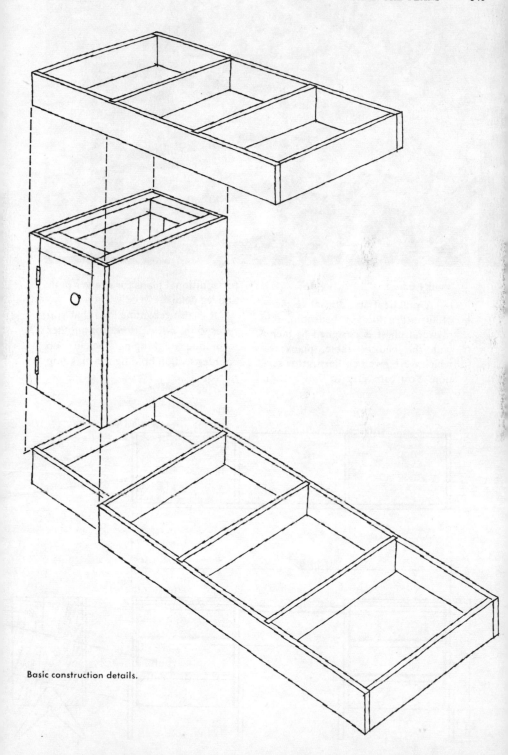

Basic construction details.

Vanity Chest

A practical and attractive piece of furniture for any bedroom, this plywood chest is designed to blend with the bedside table, plans for which were given earlier in this section. You can refer to that section for additional plans for drawer pulls and leg details.

It is also recommended that you refer to the *basic primer* for another technique of hinging the lift up counter section holding the make-up mirror.

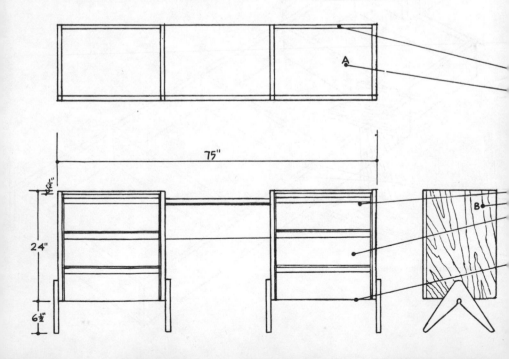

Materials Needed

ONE CHEST ONLY

1 Top (A)	16"x24"	¾" plywood
2 Sides (B)	16"x24"	¾" plywood
1 Bottom	14"x24"	¾" plywood
1 Back	22¾"x24"	¾" plywood
3 Drawer fronts	7½"x23⅞"	¾" plywood
6 Drawer sides	6½"x14¼"	¾" plywood
3 Drawer backs	6½"x22⅜"	¾" plywood
3 Drawer bottoms	14½"x23⅞"	¾" plywood
4 Drawer runners	¾"x¾"x14"	fir, pine or hardwood
3 Facing strips	¾"x¾"x24"	fir, pine, or hardwood
1 Facing strip	½"x¾"x24"	fir, pine, or hardwood
2 Retaining strips for drawer bottoms	½"x½"x20"	fir, pine or hardwood

4 Furniture glides, ½" sizes
6d and 4d finishing nails, screws, glue, sandpaper.

VANITY

1 Top	16"x24"	¾" plywood
1 Front	7⅝"x24"	¾" plywood
2 Sides	6⅞"x15¼"	¾" plywood
1 Back	6⅞"x22½"	¾" plywood
1 Bottom	15¼"x24"	¾" plywood
1 Facing strip	¾"x¾"x24"	fir, pine or hardwood
1 Piano hinge	24" long, with screws	
1 Mirror	14"x22", with clips or glue to fasten to underside of top.	

6d and 4d finishing nails, screws, glue, sandpaper.

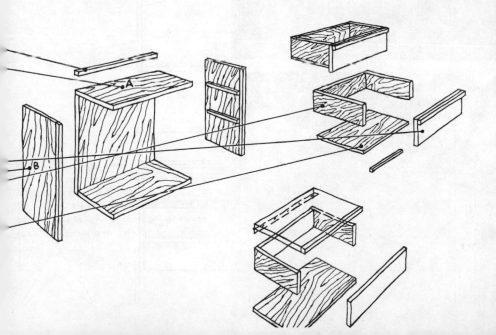

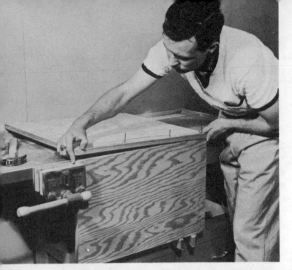

Photographs courtesy of Douglas Fir
Plywood Assn.

1. Nail back of chest to bottom. Be sure edges align perfectly.

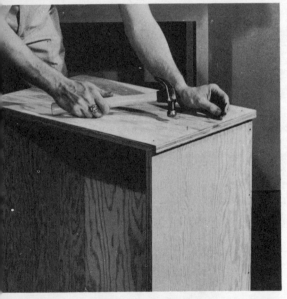

2. After sides are attached flush with back and bottom panels, install top by nailing first through top into back and then through sides into top. (Sides project ½" past top and ¾" past front edge of bottom panel.)

3. Screw two runners onto each side to give three equal spaces (a trifle over $6\frac{13}{16}$") for drawers. (Bottom drawer slides on bottom panel—not runners.) Apply ¾" square facing strips to edge of side and top panels, and ½"x¾" strip along rear edge of top panel.

4. On leg edges, mark location of chest bottom 6½" from floor and outline leg location centered on chest. Drill side panel on centerline 1" below apex of leg for No. 9 flathead screw. Countersink inside.

5. Assemble vanity sections by nailing two sides to back; bottom to sides and back; and front to sides and bottom. Attach hinges to top and back panel. Apply facing strip to forward edge of top.

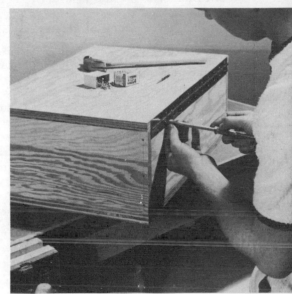

6. Construct drawers by nailing sides to back; front to sides; and bottom panel to sides and back. Upper edge of drawer front lines up with upper edges of sides. On the top and center drawers, ½" square strips prevent thin ¼" drawer bottoms from sagging. (Do not add to lower drawer; the chest bottom supports drawer and strip would keep it from closing.) After painting, suspend vanity between chest sections by driving two No. 9 flathead screws 1¼" long in each side. Mirror may be attached to underside of top with clips or glue.

Furniture Repairs, Glued

Furniture usually comes apart because of dampness in the atmosphere or in the wood itself; because moisture gets into the joints when the piece is washed and this dissolves the glue; because in a dry, hot atmosphere, the wood shrinks and the glue dries out; or because some part is not plumb with the rest of the piece, or does not fit properly, and the strain breaks the glue.

The parts to be reglued will hold together only when they are completely free from the old glue, paint, and other surface covering; when the wood is dry and the pores are open; when the parts to be glued are close-fitting, with all surfaces touching each other; and when they are held together tightly until dry (about 1 to 24 hours, depending upon the type of glue).

Tools and Supplies

Select from the following list what you need for your own gluing job.

Glue—Most glues are good but many are not moisture resistant and few are waterproof. The urea resin glues that come in powder form to be mixed with water are strong and moisture resistant, and do not dry speedily. Cements of various type are not as a rule so strong as woodworking glues. Other furniture glues which you can use include casein, white polyvinyl liquid (which does not stain and generally won't mar the surface finish), as well as hide and fish glues. For absolutely waterproof gluing, a resorcinal resin glue is best, but it is also excellent for ordinary furniture repairs because it fills gaps successfully, which most glues won't do.

Clamps—Several clamps of different sizes to hold glued parts together. If you cannot get clamps, use:

Rope to hold large joints together; a new clothesline is good.

Cord to hold small joints together; heavy fish line or sash cord is good.

Spikes, clothespins, or round 5" sticks; these are to use with rope or cord to make tourniquets.

Large rubber bands cut from an old inner tube.

Vise.

Claw hammer.

Hard-rubber tip to put over the end of the claw hammer; tips used on the end of canes or crutches will serve. A piece of leather over a wood mallet or a paper pad may be used instead.

Brace and bit, or hand-drill and straight-shank drills for making holes in wood.

Coping saw or other small saw.

Sharp jackknife.

Sandbag—In size about 5"x8", and three-fourths full of dry sand.

Board— In size about 1"x8"x 12" to use on top of sandbag.

Dowel sticks to replace missing or broken rungs or old rungs.

Dowel pins—Spiral or grooved pins, from ⅜" to ⅝" in size, to mend dowel joints.

Sandpaper — Medium and coarse.

Newspaper—These keep the table clean and make good pads to use under clamps or rope.

Shears to cut paper and cloth.

Rags to wipe off the glue.

Vinegar to wash off hide or liquid fish glue.

Small stick of soft wood to make wedges.

Preparation for Gluing

Sometimes a part of a piece of furniture may have been put in the wrong way or in the wrong place; it may crack, break, or pull apart.

To prevent this mistake, mark the parts of each loose joint with the same numbers or letters before they are taken apart, so they may be put together again quickly and in the same places. Then pull all the loose pieces apart.

Those that do not pull out easily, gently knock apart by tapping with the rubber-tipped claw hammer. Do not force them, or some part may crack or break.

Most joints that are already tight may be left that way; when it is necessary to open a tight joint, try working hot vinegar into it to dissolve the glue; this will work if hide glue was originally used, which is likely to be true in the case of old furniture.

Be sure all the old glue is entirely cleaned off. Gently scrape or chip off the thickest parts, being careful not to remove any wood. Then wash off with hot vinegar every bit of glue that remains; this quickly dissolves hide glue without injuring the finish.

Open the pores of the wood to allow the glue to enter freely, either by dipping the parts to be glued in warm water and letting them dry thoroughly, or by laying them on top of a warm radiator or stove, or in the sunshine until they are warm.

When the parts are clean and thoroughly dry, put all of them together again to test them for proper fit. If they fit closely, they are ready to be glued. If an end that goes into a hole fits a little loosely, then glue

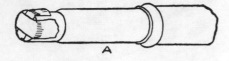

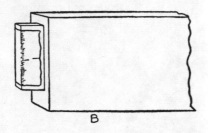

Strips of soft, cotton cloth, if glued over ends a little small for holes, will make a tight joint.

one or two strips of cotton cloth over the end until it fits snugly into the hole or use a gap-filling glue such as resorcinol resin or casein; or glue in a dowel or a piece of wood the right size and shape and, when it is dry, bore a new hole in it of the correct size. This is always done when the hole is much too large.

Gluing Parts Together

Have all materials, tools, and glue laid out ready to use. Lay all parts in place as they are to be re-assembled, having numbers or letters matching. That is, for a chair, lay the right legs and rungs at the right side of the seat, the left ones at the left side, the front pieces in front, and the back ones behind the seat.

Because some glues set quickly, the parts of the furniture to be glued should be in place and braced before the glue sets.

Have the furniture and the glue at room temperature if the room is warm, because cold wood and cold glue, except casein glue, may not hold well. Rub the glue well into the pores of the wood with a stiff brush, covering all surfaces to be joined, and press the pieces in place. Freshly glued pieces should be held tightly together until the glue has set hard. Of the various types and sizes of clamps, select the ones that force the parts together the best. If clamps cannot be had, use a rope or a stout cord and with a spike or round stick make a tourniquet to draw and hold the parts closely together. Always protect the wood and finish from damage by using soft wood pieces or thick pads of paper under clamps or the ropes where they touch the furniture.

Immediately after all of the parts have been glued and clamped, wipe the glue from the finish while it is still soft. Use a stick cut to a smooth chisel-edge to clean around the joints and small places, and then wipe the rest of the surface with a clean damp cloth. Let the piece remain until the glue is dry (about 24 hours unless a fast-setting glue has been used). See *Adhesives.*

How To Clamp or Tie Joints Together

Find in which direction pressure is needed before putting on the clamps or rope. Always put the greatest pressure right on or near the parts being glued together. Have the clamps or tied ropes directly over or near the joint or break, to draw the pieces close together and to hold them there until the glue has dried.

Sometimes it is necessary to use two clamps or to tie two pieces of rope, one on either side of the part being glued, to get enough pressure to draw the parts together. To hold the rung tight, place the clamp on the legs directly over the place where the rung enters; or if rope is used, pass it around the two legs at the point where the rung enters. If a rung is being glued on the other side of the chair at the same time, place a second clamp or rope in the same way.

When a loose chair back or the top of a chair is being glued, pass one end of the rope down the front and under the seat and tie it to the other end that comes over and down the back. Make the tourniquet at the front of the chair. Two ropes, one at each side of the back and tied in the same way, are better than one. If the two ropes slip off the top of the back after they are tied, hold them together with the cord.

Dowel Joints

A dowel or pin that holds a furniture leg in place sometimes breaks, leaving one or both ends in the holes. Bore the dowel out of the hole with a brace and bit, or a hand drill with straight-shank drills slightly smaller than the diameter of the dowel. Never bore beyond the depth of the dowel because the hole may become too deep or the bit in some cases may go through to the other side. Usually you can tell when to stop because boring through the hardwood dowel is slower than bor-

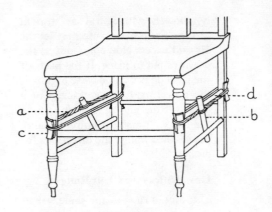

A rope and tourniquet hold the glued parts together: a, rope; b, tourniquet; c, pad to prevent marring; d, glued rung.

Sketch from Cornell Extension Bulletin #684, "How To Glue Furniture" by Charlotte Brenan Robinson.

ing through the soft wood of the furniture. With a small chisel or penknife, chip and force out what remains of the dowel, but do not cut the hole any larger. Wash out the glue with vinegar. Then select a new dowel that fits the hole snug-

ly. Dowels with spiral or straight grooves are best because they let the air and excess glue come out as the dowel is put in place. If the parts of the joint do not come close together, the dowel may be too long. Cut a piece off the end of the pin, round the cut with a sharp knife or sandpaper, then follow the directions for gluing.

Dowel Sticks for Chair Rungs

If an old rung of the same size as the broken or missing one cannot be found, a dowel stick may be used to replace the broken rung. Select one of the same diameter as that of the rungs already on the chair. To get the length, measure the distance between the legs and add the depth of the two holes into which the dowel stick will be glued; then cut it off. At each end of the new rung make pencil lines completely around the stick to mark the depth of the holes. With a sharp knife cut straight down and deep into the pencil lines. Put the rung into a vise with one end toward you. With a sharp knife, or a chisel and hammer, and working away from you, shave the dowel, cutting straight back from the end to the deep cut, then test to see whether it is the right size for the hole. Keep cutting all the way around if necessary, until the end fits the hole snugly. Then trim the other end of the dowel. Round off both ends slightly with a sharp knife or with coarse sandpaper. If the end is long for the depth of the hole, cut a little piece off and round the end again. Clean all old glue out of holes in the legs with warm vinegar; glue the new

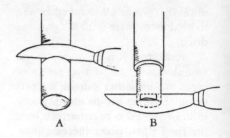

Cutting the ends of a new dowel. A, cut around the dowel on the pencil line; B, shave the end of the dowel to fit the hole snugly; cut away from you with a knife or a chisel and hammer.

rung in place as directed.

If an ornamental turned rung is missing, sometimes a similar one of the right length can be purchased at a second-hand shop.

Simple Breaks

Simple breaks on legs, rungs, spindles, and arms that are diagonal or lengthwise of the piece may be glued; those broken straight across the short way or across the grain, and table tops, need special tools and skill to repair them.

A new break may be ready to glue and brace together immediately. An old break that has been glued before, must first be washed out to remove the glue and then reglued as directed.

Because there is likely to be great strain where the back legs are fastened to a chair seat, those places may need to be made more secure. After the glue has dried, put a long slim screw through the leg and the seat. Countersink this screw, cover the head with matching wood or water putty, and paint it, or apply matching shellac stick, so that the place will not show.

Small Cracks

Cracks such as those at the ends of table leaves can be glued. Gently force the crack open with several small wedge-shaped pieces of soft wood. With a hammer gently tap the point of the wedges into the crack, one at a time, beginning at the edge of the leaf, until the crack is opened far enough to receive the glue. Be careful not to split the crack farther. Work the glue in with a slim stick or small brush. Remove the wedges and clamp the crack together tightly.

Veneer

Small pieces of loose veneer and blisters may be glued in place. Lay the loose piece of veneer face down on a flat surface and scrape off the glue. Do not wet the veneer. Then apply the glue to the furniture but not to the veneer. Lay the veneer in place, add a paper pad, and clamp it down, or lay the sandbag on top of it. Be sure the bag covers and holds in place all parts of the piece of veneer. If necessary, put a flat board, with weights on it, on top of the sandbag.

With the point of a sharp knife, cut a slit at the side of the blister where the veneer is still glued. Be sure to follow the grain of the wood. Hold the slit open with the knife, fill the blister with warm vinegar, and let it stand for several hours to dissolve the glue. Remove any vinegar that remains, and let the blister and the surrounding wood dry thoroughly before adding glue. Then work plenty of glue under the blister and clamp it down or lay the sandbag on it. If the sandbag is not heavy enough to hold the veneer flat, put a board with a weight on top to hold it down.

Chips and Small Pieces

Chips and small pieces can be treated like loose pieces of veneer, but the glue should be brushed on both the chip and the place where it goes.

Furniture Upholstery Repairs

Upholstered furniture consists basically of a frame, strip or cleat webbing, padding, and cover. Some furniture also has spring upholstery. Repairs needed on upholstered furniture generally include recovering, replacement or redistribution of padding, replacement or refastening of webbing, and regluing, reinforcing, or replacing frame parts. With spring construction, replacing, anchoring, and retying springs may also be necessary. Loose cushions may also be repaired.

Recovering

Replace the entire cover if the covers on seat, back, or arms are torn, soiled, or worn beyond repair.

Even with fairly new furniture it is usually impossible to match new material to worn or faded fabric, so all sections must usually be recovered when one is damaged.

Procedures for recovering upholstered furniture vary with furniture design, but the following general procedure applies to almost all types:

1. Remove old cover carefully, taking out all tacks.

2. Using the old cover as a pattern, cut a piece of new material to approximate shape and size.

3. Smooth out and replace any lumpy or torn padding and lay new cover in place, making certain all four sides have the same amount of surplus material.

4. Tack center of opposite sides, stretching the material lightly but firmly. Do not drive tacks all the way in. Work from center to edges, stretching material evenly. If wrinkles develop, remove tacks and work the wrinkles out. Note how the old covering was folded and fitted at corners and around legs and arms. If this was satisfactory, fit the new cover the same way. When covering fits smoothly, drive tacks all the way in.

5. After covering is tacked to the side of the frame, cover tack heads with an edging or gimp. Fasten gimp with large-headed upholstery nails spaced about 2″ apart.

Replacement or Redistribution of Padding

Padding of tow, cotton batting,

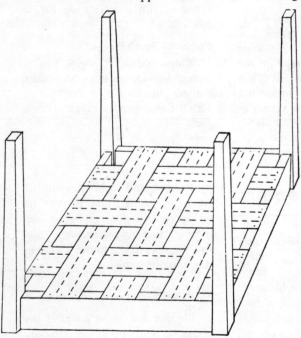

Attaching webbing to framework of a stool.

excelsior, or moss is used over the springs in the case of spring construction, or on the webbing in the case of padded construction. When padding shifts or becomes lumpy, remove the cover and redistribute or replace the padding. To replace padding;

1. First, remove all old padding and tack a piece of burlap smoothly over the entire surface to be padded.

2. Spread padding evenly over the burlap, forming a compact cushion about 1½" thick.

3. Cover this with a second piece of burlap or muslin, tacked down securely, and place a 2" layer of cotton batting on top. Pull off surplus cotton around the edges; do not cut the cotton since this will make a ridge under the cover.

4. Tack a cambric cover over the frame bottom to keep padding from working through to springs or webbing and falling out.

5. Replace cover as described previously.

Repairing Frame

Tighten loose frame joints with glue blocks, pins and screws, or angle irons. Repair any frame damage.

Repairing Webbing

Check strip or cleat webbing for signs of wear or breakage whenever cover is removed. Replace damaged webbing and refasten loose strips. To insure that webbing will hold securely, double it over at the ends to give tacks more gripping power, tighten, and tack so stress is at right angles to tack length. Run webbing in two directions, at right angles to each other. Closing the entire bot-

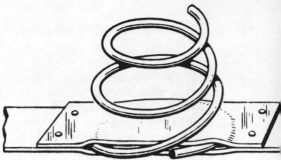

Tying spring to webbing.

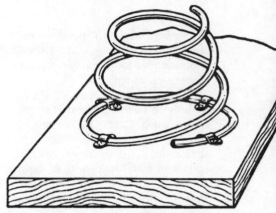

Fastening spring to metal strip.

Fastening spring to wood cleat.

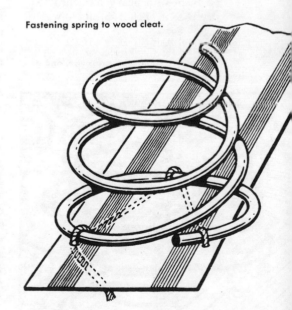

tom with webbing is not necessary, but too much webbing is better than too little. If springs are to be anchored to webbing, space the webbing to support spring bases. Similarly, anchor metal strips or wood cleats securely and space them for springs.

Adjusting Springs

Springs may shift, bend, or become damaged otherwise. Re-anchor and retie loose springs; replace those that are damaged.

Springs are usually attached differently on webbing, on metal strips, or on wood cleats. Fasten spring bases to webbing with heavy flax cord about 1/8" in diameter. Anchor springs to metal strips with clamps. If clamps loosen, rerivet them. Fasten springs to wood cleats with staples or metal straps and nails.

After springs are anchored, retie them with heavy flax cord like that used to anchor springs to webbing:

Springs tied lengthwise, crosswise, and diagonally.

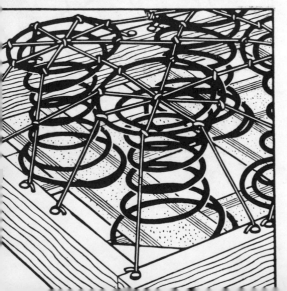

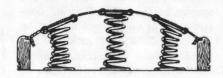

Springs tied in place.

1. Nail cord to the center of one side of the frame. Pull it over the top of the springs to an opposite anchoring nail. Allow enough cord to tie two double half hitches to each spring and cut to this length.

2. Bring cord up to the top of the first coil spring and tie it with a double half hitch to the nearest rim of the first spring. Before drawing the knot tight, pull spring down to shape the seat or back. Continue to opposite side of the top on the same spring and tie it.

3. Continue in like fashion, tying two points on each spring and finally anchoring cord to nail on opposite side of frame. Run cords in both directions (side to side and front to back) at right angles to each other, until all springs are tied in two directions.

4. Tie springs diagonally in the same manner, beginning at one corner of the frame and anchoring cord on the opposite corner.

5. Repeat with cord at right angles to the first set of diagonal cords. Tie this cord to spring with two double half hitches and also tie it to the other three cords at their junction in the center of the coil. Each spring is now tied in eight places and the crossing cords are also tied together.

6. Replace padding.

Glass

Glass—How To Buy It

A homeowner can get a lot for his money or a little when he buys glass for windows, doors or partitions. But if he knows which glass will do what, and how to buy it, he won't pay double or triple prices for plate glass when he could have used heavy sheet glass, nor will he waste money by ordering glass by the sheet when he could have used a case.

Window glass, also called *sheet glass,* is the most commonly used in the house. In fact before glass walls and picture windows were used it was usually the only kind. It comes in two thicknesses, single strength and double strength; and in two qualities, A and B.

Grades A and B differ only in the number of small defects and waves. However, the difference is not ordinarily noticeable, and many dealers don't even stock A quality because they do not believe that it is worth a 25% premium.

Whether to use single or double strength depends mainly on window size. A good rule to follow is to use double strength for anything over about two feet square. How large can double strength glass be? If winds don't exceed 70 m.p.h., double strength glass may be used in sizes up to 38″x48″, or 34″x72″.

The next price jump to crystal sheet or plate glass is very sharp. If you want a window wall consider

Economical way to buy window glass is by the case. This way it is much cheaper and easier to handle. Except in very large sizes, a case contains approximately 50 square feet—for example, eight 24″x36″ sheets.

the possibilities of working it out using the indicated dimensions of double strength instead of plate glass. This can be most attractive and at about one-fourth the cost. Go right across the room with 30″x72″ double-strength glass placed vertically. The distance of approximately 30″ to the floor can be plain wall or used for built-in bookcases, cabinets or ventilating louvers.

Case Lots

Buying window glass by the case is one way to save money. Glass by the case doesn't cost much more than half as much as by the sheet. It's also easier to handle. At economical prices you can afford to use glass liberally in anything you build or remodel or enclose. And, buying by the case does not mean

Plate glass top finishes this table handsomely. To order glass for rectangular one, dimensions are enough. An irregular shape should be traced on sheet of stiff paper.

Inside, looking out—Note the frost-free double glass window at left with pair of ordinary plate glass units. Inset shows the sealed air space that is built into double-glazed units, providing valuable heat insulation and preventing condensation.

you're stockpiling it for years to come. Usually a case of window glass is whatever number of sheets comes nearest to totaling 50 square feet. Cases of very large sheets contain 100 square feet.

Crystal sheet, which is heavy window glass of good quality, is the economical thing to buy when the opening is too big for double strength.

Plate glass, which is polished to optical perfection, may be ⅛" thick or for a big view window, ¼" thick. If you have a long-distance view through your window, you will need plate glass. Otherwise you can use crystal sheet; for short distances you will never notice the slight waviness.

For plate and usually crystal sheet, in sizes too big for you to handle and too expensive for you to risk breaking, you must figure on

Heat-absorbing plate glass makes wind-break for terrace of seashore home. Panes of this type, slightly tinted, filter out sun's infrared rays.

paying a higher installed price, which includes an expensive labor cost.

Heat-absorbing plate glass, while no substitute for air conditioning, does screen out approximately 29% of the sun's heat. It is used in west windows of seaside homes, as well as in car windows. It costs about 2½ times as much as regular plate glass.

Obscure glass is used where you want light but no visibility. For example, a wall of it might be just the

Use patterned glass wherever light without transparency is desired. There are many patterns; wide and narrow corrugations, stipples, ribs and diamond designs.

thing for a basement recreation room where part of the basement is used as a garage or workshop. For this you would need the thick kind, say ⅜". Thinner figured glass serves for entrance panels, cupboard doors and shower enclosures.

Transparent mirror glass is often used for one-way vision in entrance doors. Ready-made it is extremely expensive, but a glass dealer who makes mirrors can usually prepare it for you at about half the price.

Insulating glass is the modern, superior replacement for ordinary windows plus storm sash. Like any insulation, it usually pays for itself over the years in fuel savings as well as comfort. It consists of two or three panes sealed in units, with air spaces between the panes. A typical double glazed unit has two sheets of ¼" plate glass with a ½" air space between. Originally all insulating units were made of plate glass, but it is now made in window glass as well. Unless you need large windowpanes, you can save about one-third by using the window glass kind.

Glass Blocks

In the long list of building materials, glass blocks rank as one of the most versatile. They can be used for exterior as well as interior walls or for partition walls that do not go entirely to the ceiling.

Glass blocks provide light plus privacy. They come in many sizes and shapes and there are special blocks made to control the sun. Furthermore, glass blocks are easy to maintain and special units are available to provide ventilation through glass block walls.

Glass blocks can be installed within a wooden frame or in a bed of mortar. Once you understand how to set glass blocks in mortar—

a project you might want to undertake to replace an existing basement window with glass blocks—then you will be able to handle glass blocks within a frame inside the house. Literature on interior framing of glass blocks is readily available from glass block manufacturers.

Glass blocks make an attractive entrance to a contemporary designed home.

Photograph courtesy of Pittsburgh Corning Corp.

Glass blocks are an ideal way of enclosing the lower half of a porch with louver windows used above. Exterior lighting illuminates the porch at night as the light shines through the glass blocks.

Light and privacy are assured in this glass block wall bathroom. A window is set into the glass block wall for ventilation.

It's possible to get more light in the kitchen by adding a glass block wall above the kitchen sink work area.

Here glass blocks are used to add wall space between the two rooms. The large archway is made narrower by adding translucent walls.

Photograph courtesy of Pittsburgh Corning Corp.

How To Work with Glass Block

The proper mortar materials and mix are important whether for laying bricks or glass blocks.

The proper mortar materials are Portland cement, hydrated lime, sand, water, and waterproofing compound. The addition of an integral waterproofer of the water-repellent type is an added measure to insure watertight joints. Manufacturer's specifications concerning the use of this material should be followed very closely. Where a waterproof masonry mortar is used, no additional waterproofer should be added to the mix. For better results, accelerators and antifreeze compounds should not be used.

ACCURATE MEASUREMENT

The accurate measurement of materials is important. Generally a 1–1–4 mortar mix is satisfactory. However, reasonable variations from the mix are permitted and allowable limits are covered by manufacturer's specifications.

MORTAR CONSISTENCY

The consistency of the mortar mix has a direct bearing on the strength and weather-proofness of the joints. Since glass blocks have no suction like bricks, the mortar must be drier . . . it should not flow or have too much slump. Too wet a mix makes it extremely difficult to get proper alignment of block joints, and cleaning time is greatly increased. The mix should be not too dry, not too wet, but just right. Here is a good thing to remember: Do not re-temper mortar after the initial set has taken place.

1. The sill is cleaned of dirt or foreign materials. The next step in preparing the opening to receive glass blocks is the application of a heavy coat of asphalt emulsion to the sill . . . only to the area to be covered by the mortar bed joint. The emulsion must be dry before the mortar is applied. This generally takes two hours.

2. Check the dimensions of the opening, then mark off the spacing for the courses of block at the jambs and sill. Glass block sizes are modular. This modular coordination with other building materials makes it easy for the mason to lay out his work. Proper marking of courses eliminates any need for fudging joint thickness in the last courses laid. Where practical, story poles can be used for joint spacing.

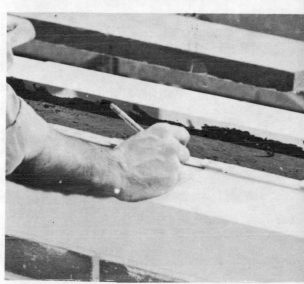

3. For panels of glass block over 25 square feet in area, expansion spaces are required at the side jambs and heads of the openings. To prevent mortar bridging the expansion space, strips of expansion joint material are placed at these points and held by gobs of asphalt emulsion on the back of the strip. The first strip must be placed tight against the sill, and as the panel goes up, additional strips are placed. If desired, these strips can be applied for the entire panel prior to the blocks being laid. The expansion strips are 4⅛" wide, 25" long and ⅜" thick.

4. The careful preparations show di
dends as you set the first block in place
the mortar bed joint. After the block h
been set, pieces of cardboard cut from 1
glass block carton dividers are placed b
tween the sides of the block and the cha
Wood wedges are sometimes used for t
purpose, but by using cardboard, exc
mortar which would have to be remov
later, cannot get into the chase.

5. To insure plumb and level work, we
to a guide line. A block is set in the m
dle of long panels to prevent line sag.

The accurate squareness and thickn
of all glass blocks helps you get a plu
level job with good joint alignment.

Note rubber crutch tip on the maso
trowel. This avoids any possibility
chipping the glass when the mason to
the block to get alignment of joints.

6. To insure weather-tight joints all b
and head joints should be full of mort
Full joints can be obtained by sligh
crowning the mortar.

To get a full joint at the corners
the blocks, the mortar should be cut
square at the ends . . . as it is placed
the block. The heavy application of g
on the mortar bond coating preve
slippage of the mortar from the block.

. When you furrow the bed and head
int mortar, voids are caused. Driving
in often forces itself into these voids.
hese voids or channels in the mortar
ints provide an easy passage for any
ater which has penetrated through cracks
the face of the joint. The final result is
leaking panel. Remember, don't furrow
ortar joints.

We all know that a full mortar joint
necessary to keep water out. Here is
hat happens if you furrow the bed and
ead joint mortar. The block in this pic-
re has been removed from the panel.
e the void caused by furrowing . . . it
ill provide an easy passage for water.

. Properly crowned mortar joints are
own in photograph 6. With the mortar
ightly crowned, a full joint will be ob-
ined without voids. This will result in a
ater-tight panel.

Here is what happens when the head
int mortar is not furrowed.

Look at the mortar on the edge of this
ock taken from the panel. The full im-
ession of the key-lock edge profile on
is block shows that the joint was full.

. Wall ties are placed In horizontal joints
the panel according to building code re-
irements. Generally, the spacing is every
" regardless of block size.

Wall ties . . . 1) Should be used im-
ediately below and above openings in
nels . . . 2) Should not bridge expansion
aces . . . 3) Should lap minimum of 6"
hen more than a single length is used
. 4) Should not touch glass. To avoid
s . . . lay half bed joint . . . press wall
in place . . . complete bed joint. Wall
s are welded galvanized wire mesh 8'
ng, 2" wide with cross wires spaced
ery 8".

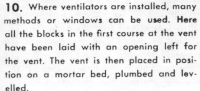

10. Where ventilators are installed, many methods or windows can be used. **Here** all the blocks in the first course at the vent have been laid with an opening left for the vent. The vent is then placed in position on a mortar bed, plumbed and levelled.

As these units are generally small, no expansion space is required and mortar is tamped solidly between the vent and blocks. Wall ties are used in the joints at the sill and the head of the ventilators.

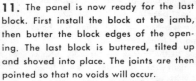

11. The panel is now ready for the last block. First install the block at the jamb, then butter the block edges of the opening. The last block is buttered, tilted up and shoved into place. The joints are then pointed so that no voids will occur.

12. Final appearance and weather-tightness depend on the care with which you tool the joints. The joints should be concave and smooth to provide best protection against water penetration. Pressure on the tool reveals joints which are not full; these joints should be tuck pointed as tooling progresses.

13. Cleaning should be done before the mortar reaches its final set. If proper mix and amount of mortar are used, cleaning will be simple: fiber brush to remove excess mortar, a rag to clean the surfaces.

14. The final result of care in selection and preparation of materials, and of good masonry workmanship is strong weather-tight joints.

Note the smooth concave mortar joints which reveal the block edges as sharp, clean lines.

15. Free movement of the panel with support against wind loads is provided by tightly packed oakum between the chase and panel. A space should be left for calking.

16. The final step in the installation is the calking of the panel perimeter. When this is done, the panel will withstand satisfactorily the weather and wind loads to which it will be exposed over the lifetime of the building.

PANELS OF GLASS BLOCK 35 SQ. FT. OR LESS

In this type of construction the maximum area is 35 square feet with maximum width 5' and height 7'. The general practice is to use an expansion space at the side jambs of all glass block panels. However, for small panels as illustrated here the blocks can be mortared in solid at the side jambs. It is necessary, however, to keep a finger space between brick withes about ¾" deep. This allows the mortar to key in at jamb and secure panel.

Glass block panels, regardless of area or size, are nonload bearing and require space at the head to take care of expansion and lintel deflection.

PANELS OF GLASS BLOCK BE- TWEEN 25 AND 100 SQ. FT.

Where it is desirable to show the full face of the block panel, chases cannot be used for lateral support. Proper support can be obtained by using wall anchors if the area is not over 100 square feet and neither panel dimension is over 10'. The wall anchors should be spaced 24" apart—and occur in the same joint as the wall tie. To permit free movement of the panel, the anchors are crimped or bent in the expansion space. As a space for calking must be provided, a standard expansion strip is easily cut to 3" width to be inserted between the anchors with gobs of asphalt emulsion. Local code authorities in some areas may restrict the use of wall anchor construction.

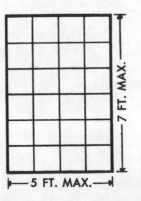

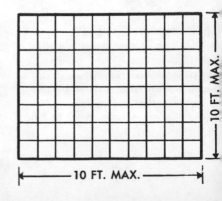

Glass Cutter

This tool is used to cut glass to size. Usually, a glass cutter has a small rotary wheel or diamond set in the handle.

There are also glass cutting bits for drilling holes in glass. These special bits require the use of a lubricant while cutting. It is best to make a 'well' or 'dish' around the spot to be drilled by using putty to form the walls. Then pour a little turpentine or oil into the 'dish' to lubricate the bit while it is cutting through the glass.

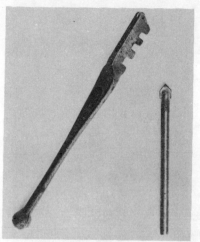

On the left is a glass cutter most frequently used by the handyman. On the right is a glass drilling bit to make holes in glass.

Glass Cutting

While you can usually buy glass cut to size, there are times when it is necessary to cut the glass yourself. When you watch an expert cut glass, it looks easy enough. Well, here's how to cut glass like an expert.

All you need is a quality glass cutter, a straightedge and some lubricating oil.

It is essential that the glass be perfectly clean. Wipe the surface off with a clean cloth for any dirt or a film over the glass will prevent the glass cutter from making a uniform cut. Now follow the simple step-by-step procedure.

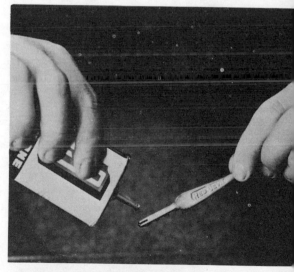

1. Lubricate the wheel of your glass cutter using any household oil, such as 3-in-One. This lubricating of the wheel reduces friction between the glass and the edge of the wheel.

2. Here's how to hold the glass cutter correctly. The right way is between the first and second fingers with your thumb on the under side of the handle. Do not squeeze too hard.

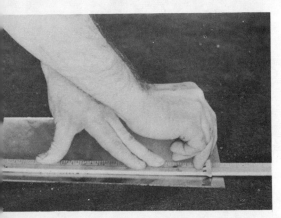

3. Rest the glass on several sheets of newspaper or a piece of felt. If you use a yardstick as a straight edge, moisten the bottom so that it won't slip on the glass. Gently, but firmly, press the cutter to the glass, holding it upright. Start about ⅛" from the edge farthest from you. Make a straight, even and continuous stroke across the whole surface and off the very edge of the glass.

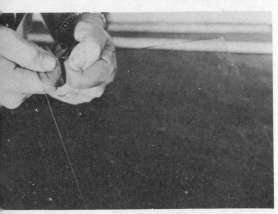

4. To break the glass, hold it firmly on opposite sides of the cut line. Then give a quick bending motion away from the cut. Keep your fingers and thumbs as close to the cut line as possible. Be careful . . . hold firmly. Always break right after cutting so that the cut does not get "cold."

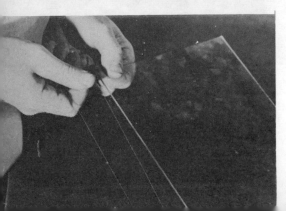

5. Here's what not to do! This shows how hesitation during cutting stroke leaves an uneven spot. This causes the break to curve from the straight line. An even, firm, positive cutting stroke avoids this result.

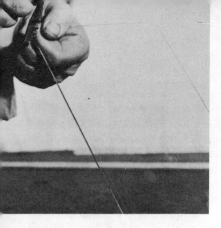

6. The slots in the end of the glass cutter are used for breaking off narrow strips. If you have to break off a narrow strip, hold the glass in one hand and the cutter in the other. A firm movement will separate the glass at the cut. Tapping the underside of the glass, immediately after making the cut, may make the glass separate more easily.

Fancy Glass Cutting

Once you have learned how to cut a straight line, you might feel adventurous and try some fancy glass cutting. Free-form lines and circles are not too difficult if you have the proper tools and knowledge. There are available circle cutters for glass which will cut circles from 2" to 24" in diameter.

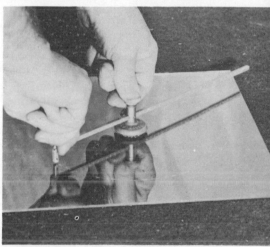

1. A circle cutter is used in the same manner as a regular cutter. Set the glass on a proper base and place the rubber suction cup in the exact center of the circle. Swing the cutter around but do not overlap at the end of the circle. Hold the glass in your hands and press with your fingers to impress the circle right after cutting so that the etched line won't get "cold."

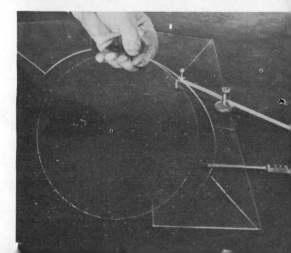

2. The glass surrounding the circle must be cut with a regular cutter to free the circle. Make several straight cuts from the circle to the edge of the glass and then break away the circle.

Photographs courtesy of Red Devil Tools.

Glass Tinting

To prevent sun glare, as well as reduce the heat from the sun, you can buy a clear, invisible plastic to wipe on the glass of your automomile windshield. It comes in several different colors, and may be used not only for the car, but on the screen of the television set and in cases where special colorful window effects are desired. The plastic coating dries in about half an hour; it leaves no streaks on the glass, and does not wash off.

A quart of this material covers about 50 sq. ft. of glass; with it comes a special applicator and manufacturer's directions for its use.

Glazier's Chisel

This is a wide but thin chisel. It is used for removal of window trim and molding.

Because of the thin blade, it is usually possible to remove the trim or molding with this chisel without any appreciable damage to the painted surface.

It can also be used for removal of the shoe mold of the baseboard or even crown molding along the ceiling without marring the surfaces.

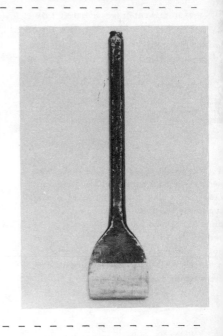

A glazier's chisel.

Glazier's Points

These are small, flat, triangular metal pieces which are used in addition to putty to hold the glass window pane in place. For information on the way they are used, see the section on *Glazing—Windows*.

Glazing— Windows

It's easy to replace a broken window pane.

Photograph courtesy of Libbey . Owens . Ford Glass Co.

A broken windowpane can be replaced without much difficulty. It is usually advisable to remove the sash which contains the broken pane, especially an upstairs window and lay it on a flat surface such as table or workbench, although if the window is on the ground floor, the pane may be replaced with the aid of a stepladder.

Materials Needed

You will need: chisel or jackknife for removing putty and for driving in glazier's points; putty knife; rule to measure size of glass needed; small flat paint brush; glass cutter (if you intend to cut glass); yardstick or steel square; glass of the same thickness as the broken pane; glazier's points; putty; raw linseed oil to soften the putty and be

used as a primer; and matching paint for the putty after it has hardened. Good putty suitable for ordinary household use can be made by mixing the best grade of whiting and pure raw linseed oil, or may be obtained already mixed from hardware and paint dealers.

Removing Old Glass and Putty

Broken glass should be removed from the sash and the old putty chipped off with a chisel or jackknife. Glazier's points should be pulled, and the wood where the new glass is to rest should be scraped well with an old jackknife or similar tool. The wood should then be given a coat of thin paint or linseed oil to act as a primer and prevent the oil in the putty from being absorbed by the wood and the putty from drying out and crumbling.

Measuring for New Glass

Measure accurately the size of the needed glass and give the dimensions to the hardware or paint dealer, letting him cut the pane to the proper size, if you prefer not to cut the glass at home. All four sides from wood to wood in the sash should be measured and $\frac{1}{8}''$ to $\frac{3}{16}''$ deducted to allow for expansion and irregularities. Measuring the four sides is advisable because some sashes are not true and do not form a perfect rectangle. Most of the window glass stocked by dealers is designated as "double strength clear American."

Setting Glass

A thin coat of putty, about $\frac{1}{16}''$ thick, should be spread on the rabbet or groove in the sash for the glass to rest in, and the pane placed in the sash. Care should be taken to have the putty evenly distributed so that unfilled gaps will not appear between the sash and the glass. By pressing gently on the glass to imbed the edges of the pane in the putty, the pane can be made watertight and the cushion of putty thus formed will reduce the possibility of cracking the glass when glazier's points are put in.

1. To protect your hands, wear gloves when removing the broken pieces of glass. This is best done from the putty side.

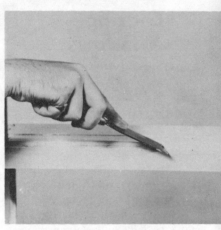

2. Use an old chisel to remove any old putty. If it's hard, you can use a soldering iron to soften the putty or else tap the chisel lightly with a hammer, or preferably with a mallet.

3. Use a rule or a steel tape to measure rather than a cloth tape. Measure the exact height and width of the opening on the outside of the sash.

Glazier's points are small, flat, triangular metal pieces used in addition to putty to hold the glass in place. They should be laid on the glass, about three or four to a side, on the long sides first, and forced into the sash with the side edge of a chisel or screw driver by sliding the tool over the surface of the glass. If the glass is still loose after the points have been set, remove those which do not fit well and replace them, pressing the glass more firmly against the bed of putty during the process.

Use of Putty

Putty is usually purchased in a can with a lid which provides an airtight seal. To prepare the putty for use, it should be kneaded on a nonabsorptive surface such as a glass plate until the mass is pliable. Putty that remains in the can after use may be kept for some time by pouring a thin film of linseed oil over it to keep it pliable and by placing waxed paper or foil immediately on top of the oil as a seal. Upon removing the waxed paper or foil, and kneading the putty, it will again be ready for use.

For application to the sash, a small piece of putty should be rolled out between the palms of the hands to form a pencil-shaped roll. The rolls should then be laid end to end on the glass where it abuts the sash, one side at a time. The putty should

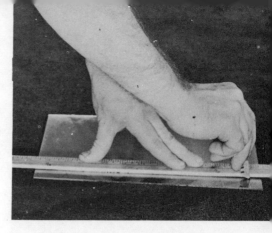

4. Buy the glass cut to size or cut it yourself. It's best if the pane of glass is ⅛" to 3/16" smaller than the vertical and horizontal measurements of the window.

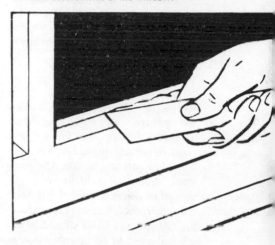

5. Before inserting the new glass, apply a thin layer of putty in the rabbet of the sash where the glass will rest. Apply with a putty knife.

6. Lay the glass in putty bed and press against sash. Then drive or press glazier's points into wood. Use three or four to a side, starting with a long side.

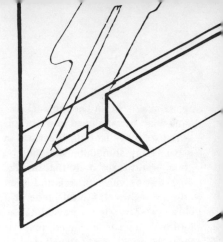

Photograph courtesy of Red Devil Tools.

Sketches courtesy of Libbey.Owens.Ford
Glass Co.

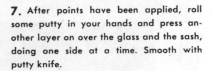

7. After points have been applied, roll some putty in your hands and press another layer on over the glass and the sash, doing one side at a time. Smooth with putty knife.

8. This is the way the smoothed putty should look against the window pane. A portion has been removed in this sketch so that you get a cross-sectional view. Finally, paint the surface.

be pressed down firmly but gently with a putty knife, drawing it along the sash from one end to the other. To lessen the danger of breaking the glass by strong pressure, the putty should be soft and pliable. The putty knife should be held at an angle, guided by the glass and sash, to form a smooth bevel. Excess putty spreading beyond this bevel should be cut off and used to fill any depressions that have occurred. Care should be taken not to spread the putty far enough over the surface to show on the inside of the window. The same procedure should be followed for the other sides of the sash.

Putty stains may be removed from the glass with a cloth moistened with turpentine or gasoline. After a day or two, when the putty has hardened, it should be painted to match the window sash.

Metal Sash

Most metal sash are constructed so that the glass may be replaced with little difficulty. There are many kinds of metal sash, however, and the steps to be taken may vary to some extent. The manufacturer usually issues instructions for using his particular product, which should be followed. In case of an emergency, where no such information is at hand, one of the following methods may be used:

The tools and materials needed are screw driver, putty knife, and small flat paint brush; double-strength glass or plate glass; putty made of whiting and white lead; and enough paint of the same color as the sash for covering the top coat of putty.

Some windows are glazed on the outside, while others are glazed on the inside of the sash. In either case, the old putty and broken glass should be removed and the metal sash scraped clean where the new glass is to rest. If wire spring clips were used to hold the glass, they will have to be removed before the glass can be taken out. The new glass should then be imbedded in putty to prevent it from being in direct contact with the metal. The putty should be spread over the metal where the glass is to rest and the glass pushed firmly into place so that putty fills every crevice. The glass can then be fastened tightly with wire spring clips, placed in the holes which have already been bored through the sash. When the glass is thus firmly secured, putty may be applied in the same manner as for wooden sash. After the putty has thoroughly hardened, it should be painted the same color as the sash.

In some other types of metal windows, the broken glass may be taken out by unscrewing and removing the metal beading or glazing strips and scraping the old bedding putty from the sash. The new glass can then be imbedded in putty, as described in the foregoing. When it has been placed, the metal beading or glazing strips should be refastened tightly against it. These strips will form a neat frame around the glass, which is usually held in place by brass screws.

See *Glass Cutting*.

Glides, Casters and Rests

Glides are metal, plastic, or rubber plates, discs or cushions used under the legs of furniture to protect the floor. They are needed to prevent indentations in resilent flooring materials, scratching, staining and sometimes indentation of wooden floors and the flattening of carpets and rugs.

Casters are wheel or ball-bearing units used to make furniture easily movable. They are attached to the bottom of the leg in place of a glide.

Rests serve the same function as glides but are not attached to the furniture. They are placed under the furniture leg between it and the floor.

Photograph courtesy of Robert Brady Co.

Adjustable casters and glides have been gaining in popularity because it has been realized that many of our furniture faults—sticky drawers, doors that refuse to stay

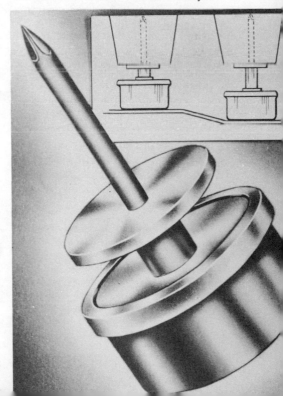

closed, etc.—are caused by uneven settling of the furniture on uneven floors.

The symptoms of uneven floor troubles are an everyday experience to most people. Without stretching one's memory, we can vividly recall the wobbly restaurant table with a wad of paper or matchbook shoved under a leg, a wobble-dancing washing machine, a sticky door or drawer, that wobbly TV set partly on and off the rug. All of these are in need of controlled support, and we probably blame the manufacturer for making faulty furniture when the underlying cause is uneven floor condition.

Why are there so many uneven floors? The answer is that even the best floors will wear unevenly or settle unevenly. What makes floors settle and become uneven? Underground water, leaky water mains, weathering of building materials, traffic vibrations, earth tremors all have a part in creating uneven floors. Articles placed on such floors either wobble or settle.

Wobbling jars mechanisms of motorized equipment. Appliances, TV sets and phonographs serve better without this jarring.

When furniture settles on uneven floors, their frames are twisted out of line. This causes doors and

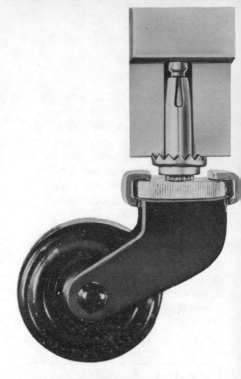

This modern caster with on-the-spot finger adjustment for easy leveling on uneven floors is designed for use on TV sets, washing machines and other household furniture.

This tiltable base glide is designed for use on heavy pieces where slope or worn spots on uneven floors would cause one edge of the glide to dig into the floor covering. Tiltable feature prevents bends of the stem by assuring broad supporting surface on glide base regardless of floor conditions.

Photograph courtesy of Adjustable Caster Co.

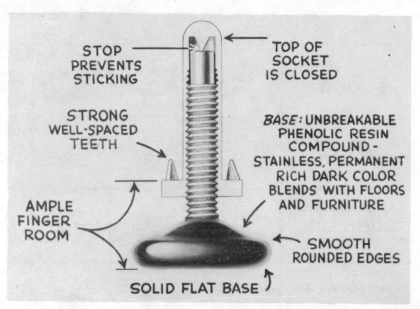

STOP PREVENTS STICKING

TOP OF SOCKET IS CLOSED

STRONG WELL-SPACED TEETH

BASE: UNBREAKABLE PHENOLIC RESIN COMPOUND - STAINLESS, PERMANENT RICH DARK COLOR BLENDS WITH FLOORS AND FURNITURE

AMPLE FINGER ROOM

SMOOTH ROUNDED EDGES

SOLID FLAT BASE

Sketches courtesy of Adjustable Caster Co.

How an adjustable glide as well as caster works: threaded section inside outside sleeve enables finger-tip adjustment for height.

Here are several types of glides and rests. The one in the upper left is designed for use with metal tubular furniture. After it is inserted into the tube, the parachute washer expands and prevents it from coming loose. On the right (top and bottom) are rests designed for round and square furniture legs.

1- LEG UNSUPPORTED - CRACK CLOSED (BEFORE SETTLING)

2 - SETTLING LEG OPENS CRACK -

3 - GLIDE SUPPORTED LEG - *CRACK CLOSED!*

FLOOR				
WOOD				
LINOLEUMN, CORK OR PLASTIC TILE				
ASPHALT TILE				
CARPET & RUGS THICK PILE				
CARPET & RUGS SHORT PILE				
FLAGSTONE OR CERAMIC TILE				
MASONRY OR TERRAZZO				

ASTER TO USE

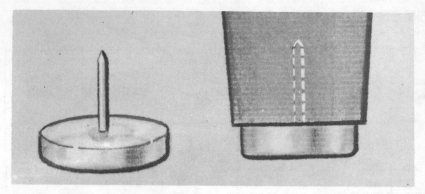

Clear plastic is sometimes used for glides.
The button type with a nail in the center
is hammered into the chair leg.

drawers to rub. If they rub hard
enough, they stick and cannot be
closed or locked. Unclosed furniture doors and drawers invite dust.

Furniture is frequently moved
around in the home so that it is subjected to settling anew each time it
is moved. These frequent settlings
over a period of time result in loosened glue joints.

Photograph courtesy of Plastiglide Mfg. Corp.

It is plain that a modern caster
and glide with controlled support
helps to protect furniture and equipment placed on uneven floors. The
old concept of protecting floors
from furniture legs is now supple-
mented by the important idea of
protecting valuable pieces from uneven floors.

Another way to protect floors from metal
tubular furniture is by means of special
glides or crutch tips, which fit over the
metal.

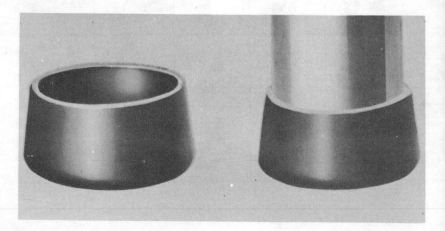

How-To Guide To Wood Joints

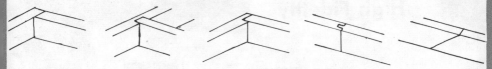

Typical wood joints frequently used when joining two pieces of wood (left to right): butt, dado, rabbet, tongue-and-groove and scarf.

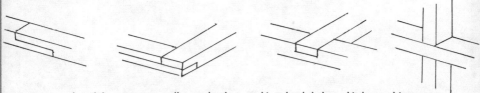

Lap joints are generally used when making bookshelves, kitchen cabinets, easels and similar projects. Among the various types of lap joints are (left to right): half lap, end lap, middle lap and cross lap.

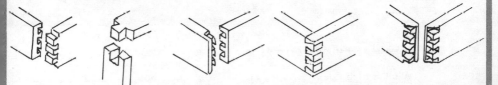

Dovetail joints are used by the skilled craftsman in construction of fine furniture, particularly drawers. Among the dovetail joints are (left to right): lap dovetail, single-through dovetail, stopped-lap dovetail, multiple dovetail, and blind dovetail.

Miter joints are used principally for picture frames and screens but can also be used for furniture, window sash and doors. Here (left) is the typical corner miter joint and (right) a beveled miter joint.

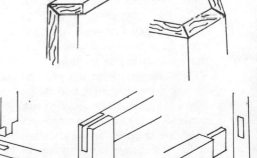

Mortise-and-tenon joints are also used frequently by skilled craftsmen. They are used for furniture that will be subject to hard usage. Here are some typical mortise-and-tenon joints (left to right): through mortise, stub mortise, open and blind mortise.

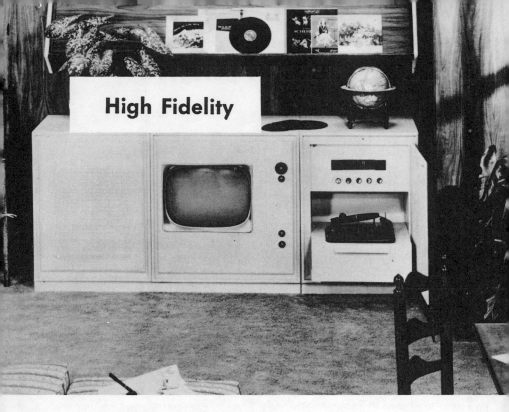

High Fidelity

What is high fidelity? As we apply it to home music systems, it is just about what the two words would imply: the reproduction of speech and music with as much realism and faithfulness to the original performance as is technically possible. There is no such thing as perfection in the reproduction of sound, but during the past few years improvements have been made which can best be described as startling.

How do we achieve this prodigious thing we call high fidelity? It comes of applying new and rigorous standards of performance to objects which are in appearance very similar to those commonplace items in the American home—the radio and the phonograph. There are also high-fidelity television sets and the tape recorder.

For almost three decades, the consumer bought radios with his eyes. Cabinets were fancy, dials were impressive, and the sound they produced, considered as an afterthought if at all, was barely intelligible. A few individuals, mainly engineers and musical hobbyists, knew what good reproduction can be, and constructed systems for their homes which astonished those who heard them. But until a few short years ago, when the long-playing microgroove record appeared on the market, the total of high-fidelity home radio-phonograph systems in the country was negligible. True, the number was growing every year. But there is no doubt that these wonderful discs sparked an amazing revival in the public's interest in listening to music at home. In the face of the competition of television, which monopolized the publicity until recently, a number of small manufacturers have been quietly building home reproduction equipment which has such intrinsic superiority to the conventional products it resembles that it has caused many to sit up and take note. Suddenly, high fidelity has been discovered by the entire electronics industry.

The incentive to develop a concert atmosphere at home is stronger than ever. The long-playing record has made a new source of uninterrupted diversion available to all. Tape recordings have long been used in making records and by broadcast stations for repeating programs. Now, several companies are introducing to the consumer market pre-recorded musical programs on tape. New developments in the technology of manufacturing tape recordings would indicate that this new medium of home entertainment may someday rival the long-playing record.

The Nature of Musical Sounds

For those willing to make the journey through the technical side of "Understanding High Fidelity" by Louis Biancolli, music critic, and Lester H. Bogen, member of the Audio Engineering Society, what follows is offered as a helpful guide.

Where necessary, analogies will be made that may seem over-simple and perhaps not completely parallel. Sound is a phenomenon of nature that does not always yield to ready-made definition or facile illustration. We take its presence for granted, but we seldom consider what it is.

Sound is largely a matter of vibrations moving through the air. It is important to stress "air," rather than space, because sound needs an "elastic" medium such as air to be able to travel at all. Sound cannot exist in a vacuum. Put another way, sound is a disturbance of molecules along its route of progression.

Now, it is the function of the ear to receive these vibrations and convert them into messages which the brain interprets as sound. The ear is so constructed that such vibrations, to be heard at all, must be of a certain minimum intensity. They must also be heard at a certain rate of repetition. The number of such cycles of repetition that occur in one second is known as the frequency of the sound. This accounts for the phrase "cycles per second." It is these frequencies that account for the pitch of a musical note.

Low frequencies (slow rates of repetition) determine a low note and high frequencies a high one. The highest frequency audible to humans is perhaps 20,000 cycles per second, and the lowest around 20. The majority of people, however, cannot hear well over the entire range, especially in the upper registers (over 15,000 cps).

Suppose we examine some of the advantages of high fidelity over other music systems by a comparison of their merits in reproducing the tone of brass instruments. These produce a characteristic sound in addition to the fundamental note played on them. This whirring sound results from a turbulent rush of air out of the bell or horn of an instrument like the trombone. It is located in the higher frequencies, not very loud, but very definite. The sound—or noise, if you will—is audible to the concert-goer. It is another mark of identification, one might say, of the brass instrument. It is lost in ordinary reproduction, but conveyed through high fidelity as another lifelike detail of realism.

The measure of the ability of a system to transmit all frequencies is known as frequency response.

Wide range frequency response is the most dramatic and widely publicized feature of the high-fidelity system, but equally important is the reduction of distortion. It is necessary to understand this clearly because, as much as anything else, it demonstrates the superiority of high fidelity over any other mechanical medium.

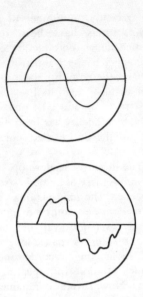

Distortion—Top: typical undistorted waveform. Bottom: typical distorted waveform.

Sketch courtesy of David Bogen Co., Inc.

Let us recall what we said before that a musical tone is a combination of the basic note and a web of surrounding sounds called harmonics. If the proportion between these is altered, the shape and quality of the tone resulting alters too. This means that the reproduced tone is not quite what was played on the instrument or uttered by the human voice. Distortion manifests itself usually by the generation of spurious harmonics which cause a slurred effect on what would otherwise be described as a sharply defined tone. High fidelity has reduced this harmonic distortion (as it is called) to an absolute minimum. Tests have shown that nerves grow fatigued from over-exposure to distorted sound reproduction.

How high fidelity adds realism

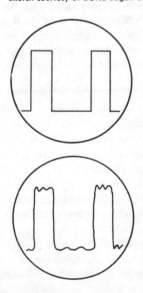

Transient Response—Top: good response to transients. Bottom: poor response to transients.

may also be seen in a study of certain percussion effects. Drums and other instruments of the percussion family produce sharp, staccato sounds. The picture of these sounds can be caught by an instrument called the oscilloscope. This is a device used by engineers to measure and examine electrical currents and percussion instruments appear on the oscilloscope as a succession of sheer walled plateaus, separated by flat plains. The effects take this form because the energy which produces them is enclosed in a very short interval of time. Both the sounds and the electrical impulses they give rise to are called transients. When properly reproduced, these effects are part of the realistc picture of "live" music. When they are not reproduced, the critical listener misses them. Sensitive response to these quick bursts of energy—or transients—is another achievement of the high fidelity system. It is one more clean, sharp, natural detail in the truthful picture of sound.

Distortions in Sound

Here, through the use of photographs, it is possible to show what is meant by distortion in sound. Your eye can see the differences easily, whereas, in sound, the untrained ear cannot detect the difference unless it is pronounced.

1. This print is good reproduction—it is similar to listening to recorded or broadcast music that sounds as if you were there with the orchestra.

2. This photograph is the visual equivalent of distorted narrow

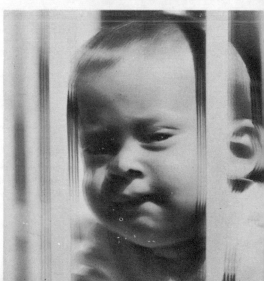

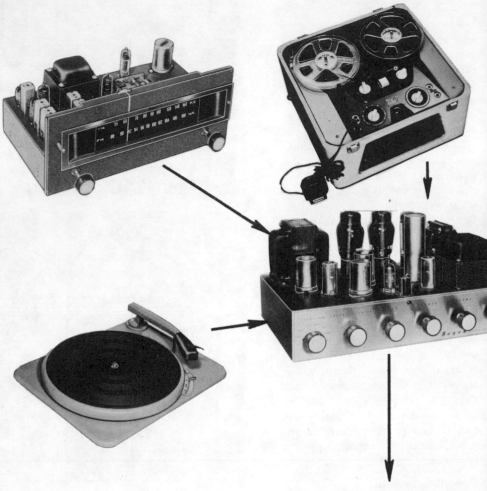

Speaker Enclosure

Photograph courtesy of Karlson Associates, Inc.

These are the components of a typical Hi-Fi system: the AM-FM tuner, record player and tape recorder feed their electrical impulses to the amplifier, which feeds electrical impulses to the speaker (inside of an enclosure) which converts them into sound waves.

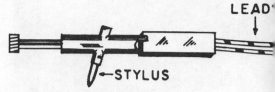

LEAD

←STYLUS

range reproduction. Notice the lack of gradation and the harsh effect.

3. This print represents the effect of poor transient response.

Elements of a High-Fidelity System

The word "system" is chosen advisedly to describe the high-fidelity hook-up. It is a system in which everything functions towards the one goal of absolute tonal naturalness; in which every component plays an equal and indispensable part. It is a system, in short, which has strength and quality only to the degree that each unit does its work in close technical harmony with the others. Before examining these separate units in detail, let us take a quick view of the complete system and notice how it differs from the conventional radio or phonograph-radio combination. A typical high-fidelity system begins, of course, with a phonograph player or tape recorder-player and a radio tuner. The electrical impulses put out by these units are fed into an amplifier. This, in turn, operates a loudspeaker unit in a suitable acoustical enclosure.

Cartridges

How does the cartridge work? Let us recall that the phonograph record is a storehouse of musical reproduction. When the original recording is made, the impulses which constitute the performance inscribe —or "graph"—on the disc a mechanical picture of the sounds produced by the performers. The record we play is a reproduction of the

The cartridge converts the signals engraved in the phonograph record into electrical energy and transmits them to the amplifier. The crystal cartridge is one of the methods of accomplishing this.

original disc. It contains the same "graph" made by the original impulses. When the record rotates on the turn-table, the phonograph needle—or stylus—is drawn through the grooves. As it moves from side to side, it is guided by the pressure exerted by the walls of the grooves.

To make use of the signals engraved in the phonograph record it

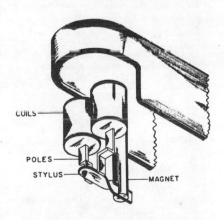

COILS

POLES

STYLUS

MAGNET

The magnetic cartridge, despite its added cost and the extra amplification required, is frequently preferred because the added compliance of the stylus means less wear on the records and a more nearly exact reproduction.

Today, many radio tuners and amplifiers are attractively designed in individual cases so that they need not be hidden in large cabinets with the other components or built into a wall unit. All you need is a convenient bench, shelf or table top on which to rest the tuner and amplifier. A single pair of wires to the speaker in its enclosure from the amplifier is all the wiring necessary.

Photograph courtesy of David Bogen Co., Inc.

is necessary to convert them to electrical energy, so that they may be amplified to operate the loudspeaker. The phonograph cartridge is the device which does this. The two most popular are known as the crystal and the magnetic. The crystal cartridge operates on a principle many hi-fi owners will recall from their high school physics, known as piezo electric effect. Certain materials, among them crystals of Rochelle salts, will produce tiny electrical currents if pressure is properly applied to the crystal. Connect a phonograph needle to a piece of this material and you have the phonograph cartridge. The magnetic cartridge performs the same function, but in a different way. Here the change from mechanical to electrical energy is made on the same principle that gives us the electrical generator.

A crystal cartridge is generally less costly, and some, using man-made crystals known as ceramics often give surprisingly good performance. But neither, it is felt, approaches the quality of the magnetic cartridge. It is therefore to be preferred, despite the added cost and the ' extra amplification needed by the signals produced by the magnetic type.

Another important factor to be considered in the choice of a cartridge is the compliance of the stylus assembly. This is the measure of the ease with which it responds to the sideways pressure exerted by the groove walls in order to produce the sounds we hear. The better cartridges are so constructed as to exhibit high compliance and, consequently, their use results in less wear on the records, as well as a more nearly exact reproduction.

This brings us to the subject of the needle or stylus. While this would seem to be contradictory, it has been found that the harder the needle the less damage it does to the record. Ordinary steel needles tend to wear out of shape after relatively short use. Once this happens, the needle may act as a chisel and cut into the sides of the record

While a speaker can be mounted in an enclosure, located in a section of the room away from the tuner, amplifier and changer, you can mount the speaker on a baffle board, which is attached to the book shelves. In this way, you can add a Hi-Fi system—speaker in the book shelves and tuner and amplifier on a bench or table top—without adding another piece of furniture in the room.

groove. Two or three playings with the needle in this condition may suffice to spoil the disc. On the other hand, a hard needle, one made of precious stones such as sapphire or diamond, will retain its shape over a longer period and thus spare the record early wear. A diamond stylus naturally costs considerably more than either a sapphire or steel-pointed needle. However, it lasts many times longer, and because it does, it is actually cheaper in the long run. One has only to remember that each record represents an investment of several dollars. The rest is simple arithmetic.

Record Players

To some extent, the type of records you now own, or plan to own will dictate the type of reproducing device your high-fidelity system will feature. If you prefer to play all speeds and find changing records by hand a nuisance, the answer to your needs is an automatic record changer. If you plan to play only LP records you may choose a manual transcription turntable.

Manufacturers have for years made available automatic changers requiring a minimum of effort for the playing of all-speed records. Not all record changers are of the same quality, however. A perfect record player would revolve the turntable in complete silence without any fluctuation in speed. Its turntable would be level at all times. The arm

which supports the needle should be light, but rigid, and mounted on bearings which cut friction to a minimum. Unfortunately, the conventional record changer is not capable of such perfection.

A slight fluctuation in speed, referred to by engineers as wow, is known to affect the pitch to some degree, and accordingly the quality of the music being reproduced. A noisy motor or set of gears will pass unwanted sounds through the amplifier and loudspeaker. Record changers found on conventional equipment usually have inferior car-

tridges and needles as well. The result is a clouding or blurring of the music, especially in low-register passages.

In order to minimize these defects, more care must be given to both the design and manufacture of the unit. Recognizing this, several manufacturers have introduced high-fidelity record changers which are available with a selection of high quality cartridges. These cost slightly more, but pay for themselves by increasing the life of the records played on them. There are also manual players which, in point of tech-

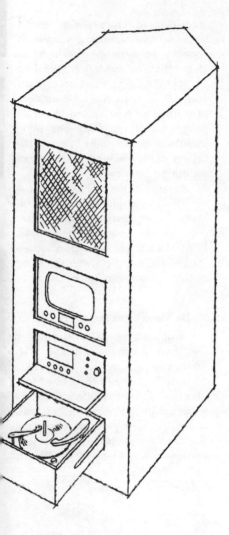

A pull-out drawer mounted with phonograph slides is used to house the turntable in the bottom of this corner music
wall. See Built-ins and Furniture for how-
to details. The tuner and amplifier are
mounted on a shelf behind a drop door
just over the turntable and the TV set
slides into an opening left for it in the
wall. This makes it easy to remove the set
for servicing. The folded horn is attached
to the wall and fits above the TV set.

nical performance, can meet all features of a record changer at considerable economy. There is often no
loss in convenience because most
single records are meant to be
played on both sides. This is particularly true of LP recordings.

A good transcription turntable,
because it is larger, heavier, and
more precisely tooled to sensitive
responses, will be used by the per-
fectionist. Driven by a sturdier
motor, such a turntable eliminates
noise and reduces speed fluctuations
(wow) to an almost inaudible minimum. The tone-form is longer than
the one usually seen on a changer,
has an easier side movement, and
leaves next to no trace of wear on
either the record or the stylus. Excellent turntables have been designed to operate at all three speeds.
They will handle records of any type
or size.

Tape Recorders

To understand how a tape recording is made, we must apply the
theory of the magnetic cartridge to
the old high school physics experi-
ment involving a permanent magnet
and a quantity of iron filings. If we
lay a sheet of paper over the two
ends of a permanent magnet and
sprinkle iron filings on top of the
paper, the filings will orient themselves so as to produce a graphic reproduction of the magnetic field between the poles.

Magnetic recording tape is made
by coating a base of either plastic or
paper with millions of very fine
particle of iron oxide. When the tape
is passed through a magnetic field
the particles tend to become mag-

netized themselves in proportion to the strength of the field. The recording head of the tape recorder is an electro-magnet, i.e., one whose magnetism varies both in strength and polarity with that of the electric current which energizes it. If the energizing current is a reproduction of a sound wave, we can see then that the magnetizing of the particles will follow a pattern which is a magnetic reproduction of the same sound. That, reduced to essentials, is tape recording.

Playback is achieved by passing the now magnetized tape over another head which, as it happens, is constructed in the same manner as the recording head. The variations in the magnetic field of the tape—which were caused by the recording head—produce an electrical current in the playback head. This current, amplified and properly equalized, is used to produce sounds in the same manner as the electrical current produced in the magnetic phonograph cartridge described earlier.

All that is necessary to re-use a tape that has been previously re-corded is to erase the magnetic image which it carries, and this is done by an erase head which re-aligns the iron oxide particles into an approximation of their original (prior to recording) condition. Most modern tape recorders are so designed that recording and playback are accomplished automatically with the erasing feature only in use during recording.

Because of the limitations of the recording and playback head, recorded tapes also require equalization, as do phonograph records. While the amount and type of equalization are not the same, the same general techniques are used to achieve it.

Radio Tuners and Receivers

Broadcasting in this country uses two systems—AM and FM. These initials stand for "Amplitude Modulation" and "Frequency Modulation." The latter offers infinitely wider frequency response, besides a superior filtering out of static and noise. Development in FM was proceeding apace when World War II

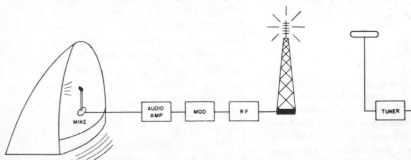

Schematic diagram of AM or FM radio broadcasting and reception. Those who insist upon getting the most out of a broadcast, frequently use a separate tuner to pick up the signals and convert them to audio frequency, and a separate amplifier which strengthens the signals so that they can drive the loudspeaker.

broke out and slowed it down. The number of FM stations is still small as compared to AM outlets. However, keener practical interest in FM has developed recently in radio circles because of growing public awareness of its superiority over AM. Many stations now broadcast simultaneously on AM and FM, and of course the sound portion of TV broadcasting is conveyed through Frequency Modulation. But most of the advantages of FM sound for TV are lost because the audio section of most TV sets is no better than that of a conventional radio.

Both types of radio broadcasting may be picked up by relatively simple, though different, receivers. However, those who insist on getting the most out of a broadcast must go one step further. To be able to pick up and hear the station in satisfactory clarity is one thing. The ordinary receiver will do that. But to respond to the finer subtleties and sensitivities of broadcast music, the receiver must contain special mechanical and electronic refinements. That, in turn, means more components to the system and added circuits, necessarily increasing the size of the unit. The receiver in many deluxe systems is therefore divided into 3 units to make installation easier. One is the tuner which actually picks up the signals and converts them to audio frequency. Another is the amplifier which increases the strength of the signals so that they can drive the loudspeaker, and the third, often combined with either of the first two, is the preamplifier.

Performance Characteristics of Radio Tuners			
Characteristic	Excellent	Good	Comments
Sensitivity	FM—5-10 microvolts, 30 db quieting AM—10 microvolts	10-25 microvolts 25-30 microvolts	This is usually expressed as a ratio of signal strength in microvolts to the amount of quieting or reduction in noise.
FM Drift	±25 KC, after a minute warm-up period	±50 KC, after a minute warm-up period	This is a measure of the ability of a tuner to keep tuned-in on the program.
Distortion	0.5% harmonic	1% harmonic	This is a measure of the fidelity of the tuner. It is expressed in terms of the output signal which the tuner feeds to the amplifier.
Hum level	60 db, below standard signal output	50 db, below standard signal output	This is a measure of the ability of the tuner to eliminate interference from its own power supply.

Data courtesy of David Bogen Co., Inc.

Like every other component in a typical high-fidelity system, the tuner is engineered to the finest precision. It is manufactured to feed into the amplifier signals that are almost the exact facsimile of those broadcast by the station. The distinctive features of high-fidelity radio reception may be summarized as follows:

1. *High sensitivity*—This is essential when amplifying a weak signal in order to provide the same strength and clarity that can be achieved with a strong signal.

2. *High selectivity*—A good tuner will be capable of separating two closely spaced stations so as to eliminate interference between them.

3. *Fidelity*—With a good tuner this may be achieved in two ways: a) by amplifying the handling signals without distortion; b) by accommodating the full range of frequencies transmitted by the broadcasting station.

Further considerations to bear in mind about tuners are these: The tuning should "stay put," that is, the tuner must be free from drift after tuning. Such drift is virtually impossible on a high quality tuner. A safeguard against it is known as automatic frequency control (AFC), a feature of many popular tuners. This consists of electronic circuits which prevent wavering and at the same time correct inaccurate tuning by the operator; thus tuning to stations is much easier.

Reduction of noise is another accomplishment of the high-fidelity tuner. To begin with, the tuner must have a noise limiting device as part of its design. Further, the tuner must be sensitive enough to amplify the signal to a point where this noise limiting mechanism will operate. A tuner which lacks sufficient sensitivity may bring in weak stations but fail to eliminate noise and static. Sensitivity is particularly important in suburban and fringe areas. If the FM tuner does not eliminate background interference, this will be much more conspicuous in a wide-range system than in a conventional narrow-range radio receiver.

A low hum level is still another feature of the high-fidelity tuner. Hum is a term used to describe the effect which household electric current can have when it interferes with the program. It would be particularly troublesome on a high-fidelity system for a very simple reason. Hum occurs at the frequency of the alternating current in the power line (60 cycles and its first harmonic, 120 cycles). Even with loudspeakers reproducing the lowest frequencies, a good tuner will keep the hum so low as to be negligible as a source of distraction.

It might be asked how ordinary radio sets function at all in view of their severely limited design. The answer, of course, is that the conventional receiver picks up only a small portion of the wide range of frequencies contained in the orignial program. Most of the hum, noise, and static is outside this band. So a radio set of the ordinary kind is spared a good deal of unpleasant distortion. There is a very simple way of showing the inferiority of the conventional product and, by the same token, the superiority of the high-fidelity technic. That is to play the conventional radio through a high-fidelity amplifier and loudspeaker. The inadequacies of the radio will be as clear as day.

Amplifiers

To understand the role of the amplifier, we start with the fact that electrical impulses are generated by the radio tuner, phonograph, or tape recorder. These impulses, as a rule, are too weak to be of any practical use. Vibrations must be produced in the loudspeaker which can be heard. To achieve this, tremendous amplification is required.

Here we see the difference in the range of tone correction provided by the high-fidelity tone controls (bass and treble) as contrasted with the limited action afforded by the single knob (tone control) used on conventional equipment. The solid lines show maximum deviation possible from the mid-position or zero correction setting. Top: control range with two controls, usually used with high-fidelity equipment. Bottom: single control knob range.

Sketch courtesy of David Bogen Co., Inc.

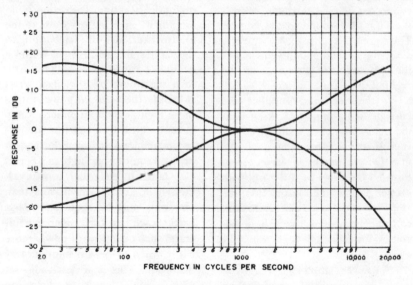

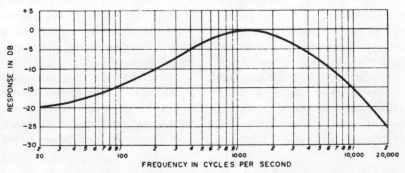

To explain in detail how the audio amplifier works is much too ambitious an undertaking for this exposition. Perhaps the easiest way of grasping the idea is to remember that the British call vacuum tubes (which make up the heart of the amplifier circuit) "valves." The use of the tube as an electronic valve gives the engineer the ability to magnify small currents. Consider the action of your foot upon the gas pedal of your car. A very slight pressure causes the motor to exert a large amount of power upon the wheels. This happens because the pedal is connected to a valve which controls the flow of gasoline to the engine. The engine does the work of moving a 3 to 4 thousand pound vehicle, but the movements of your foot do the regulating.

In the electronic amplifier, the current to be amplified, known as the signal, is applied to the circuit in such a manner that it controls the flow of a much larger current through the tube. In this case, with proper design and construction, the response of the large current to control can be so sensitive that it becomes an enlarged replica of the signal.

A power amplifier, moreover, must do its job of amplification without in any way marring or altering the electrical reproduction of the performance. Music, it will be remembered, covers a frequency range from 40 to 15,000 cycles. An adequate amplifier must achieve this range without serious distortion or omission of sound values. In the amplifier of a high-fidelity system

the extended frequency response insures in the performance an abundance of minute detail and shading unavailable to the set containing a conventional amplifier.

Amplifiers are usually rated according to the power they deliver to the loudspeaker with a specified amount of harmonic distortion. The lower the amount of such distortion, the better the output of the amplifier. Ordinary radios are rated at 10% distortion. This is the standard figure used by the radio and television industry in assessing vacuum tubes. Compare that figure with high-fidelity rating. Distortion in an amplifier delivering ten watts to the loudspeaker, measured according to the same standards, is held within a negligible range of less than ½ % to a maximum of 3%. Ten watts is merely the nominal power rating of a high-fidelity amplifier. Many have reserves of power that can accomodate loud passages in a symphony requiring as high as 15 and 20 watts of electrical power, although at average levels less than one watt may be required. It has been shown that the human ear tolerates such quantities of power more easily when there is a minimum of distortion. This is why a radio set with a high degree of distortion sounds uncomfortably loud when compared to a hi-fi system which may be playing at the same or a higher intensity level.

Amplifying the electrical signals produced by a tuner or phonograph is only one of several functions performed by the amplifier. Ordinary volume control is of course found

Corner Music Center

Here is a corner music center that houses all the necessary components in a striking cabinet. It is easy to decorate and becomes the focal point of this handsome room setting.

Look at what you can get into a cabinet that takes about 4′ of space along each of the two walls: the TV set is mounted in the center and directly below it between two hinged doors are the tuner and amplifier. In the cabinets on either side are space for record storage on the open shelf in the center and a speaker enclosure at the bottom. In the drawer of one side cabinet is a record changer and in the drawer of the other cabinet is a tape recorder. See **Built-ins** and **Furniture** for the how-to details.

Photograph courtesy of Armstrong Cork Co.

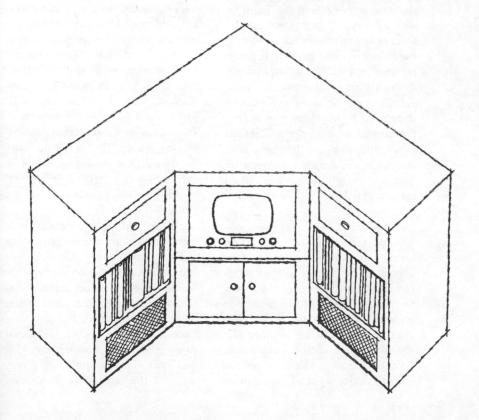

on every radio and phonograph. Besides this, however, high-fidelity systems incorporate more flexible controls that provide satisfaction over a much wider range of listening conditions. A high quality music system includes ways of providing record equalization through specially designed networks, tone controls, or both.

Record equalization, we will recall is a method of restoring the tonal balance of a recording to a close facsimile of the original performance. Such equalization, however, is valid at only one particular listening level. To enhance the beauty of the performance it is necessary to compensate for the special characteristics of both the room in which the system is located and the speaker and enclosure that are being used. This added flexibility is made possible in high-fidelity equipment through a set of controls that individually raise or lower the relative strength of high and low notes being reproduced by the system. Conventional equipments, if they have tone control at all, usually achieve it by means of a single knob, which, when turned, cuts either high or low frequencies.

Everyone knows that the acoustics of a room produces an effect on sound reproduction, just as the acoustics of a concert hall partly determines the effectiveness of a performance. Therefore, it is easy to understand the need for flexible tone controls. There is still another factor, however, and that is the actual level of intensity, what is ordinarily called "loudness," at which we listen

to music. This too has a decided effect on the fidelity of sound reproduction. It is a peculiarity of the human ear that, when exposed to sounds at various levels of intensity, it does not hear them all equally well. When listening to loud sounds, the ear registers well over its entire range. Listen to these same sounds at much lower levels. What happens? A considerable amount of the bass register, and to a lesser extent the treble, is lost to us. Now, since hearing and loudness are really subjective matters, we have a problem here.

The difficulty is introduced by the fact that the ear is not a good judge of "loudness." Assume that you're driving along on a summer's day and you have the volume of your car radio adjusted so that you can hear comfortably while you are doing 40 or 50 miles an hour. Have you ever noticed what happens when you stop for a red light, or if you happen to close the windows? The radio suddenly seems to be playing louder. That is because under the original conditions it had to overcome a considerable amount of background noise to attract your attention.

When you go to a concert in a large hall the orchestra is generating a large amount of acoustical energy. But, because even the best behaved audience makes some noise, you are much less conscious of the actual loudness at the live performance than you are when you listen to a reproduction in your home. Unless your home conditions are very unusual, the background noise level will be considerably lower. This seems to be one of the reasons why people often listen to music at home at lower than concert hall level. When you adjust the volume control of your home music system to a setting which you consider to be a satisfactory equivalent to the loudness of the original performance, you are usually playing it at a much lower intensity level.

This explains, incidentally, why some early high-fidelity addicts insisted on playing their equipment at very high volume levels which made other wince. Luckily, this is one situation in which you can now have your cake and eat most of it too. That is, it is possible to play recordings at comfortable levels of intensity and at the same time to compensate for the deficiencies of the ear. A good set of tone controls can be used for this purpose simply by advancing the bass control as you diminish the volume and by adding a lesser amount of treble boost at

the same time. Some manufacturers also feature what is known as compensated volume controls. These automatically increase the bass content of the audio signal as the volume level is turned down.

To achieve the same effect with a greater degree of precision, there has been developed a new device known as the "Loudness Contour Selector." Depending upon the level desired, the selector is set at one of the positions corresponding to the compensation required. More precise adjustments are then made through the volume and tone controls also provided in the high quality units which incorporate this device.

Loudspeakers

The loudspeaker is to radio what the receiver is to the telephone. The principle involved is pretty much the same. Just as the same electrical impulses enter both systems, so the same vibrations, translated into

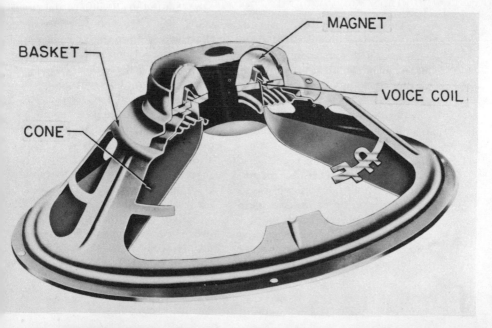

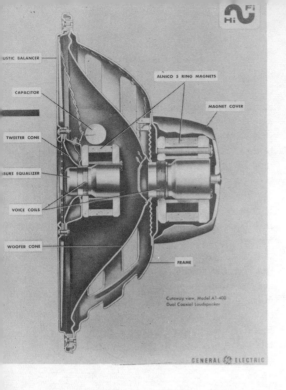

ACUSTIC BALANCER

CAPACITOR

TWEETER CONE

PRESSURE EQUALIZER

VOICE COILS

WOOFER CONE

ALNICO 5 RING MAGNETS

MAGNET COVER

FRAME

Cutaway view, Model A1-400
Dual Coaxial Loudspeaker

HiFi

GENERAL ELECTRIC

Cutaway view of a coaxial speaker showing tweeter and woofer.

music or words, pass through the radio loudspeaker on the one hand and the telephone receiver on the other..

Flowing through a coil of wire, these electrical impulses produce what is called a magnetic field. A second magnetic field is caused by a magnet. Because of the interaction of these fields the wire will move, if it is flexibly suspended. Let us now assume the current flowing through the wire is the electrical reproduction of a musical note and that the wire is attached to a diaphragm. The motions of the wire will cause the diaphragm to vibrate and these movements will set the air in motion, thus producing corresponding sound waves. Thus, the loudspeaker is a device for converting electrical

energy into mechanical energy. This, in turn, reaches us as sound.

The wire which is connected to the amplifier and receives from it the electrical impulses to be converted to sound waves is known as the voice coil. The magnetic field which interacts with that of the voice coil is produced by a permanent magnet. This is made of a special steel alloy containing aluminum, nickel, and cobalt, known as Alnico. The diaphragm operated by the voice coil is usually constructed on a cone of specially-treated paper and is designed to be light, but strong and tough.

Quality, again, is of paramount importance in the selection of a loudspeaker for a high-fidelity installation. The nominal size of the cone is alone no guarantee of quality. Often a well designed 8″ loudspeaker will produce better results than a 10″ or 12″ speaker of inferior design. For example, the performance of the loudspeaker depends on the interaction of the two fields mentioned above. The more effectively the two are brought into contact, the better the operation. One way to achieve this is through careful design and construction of both the coil and the magnet. Another factor is the precise alignment of the two units so that the coil is properly centered. It is important, also, to have a large and properly shaped magnet to achieve the powerful magneic field that is a requirement of high fidelity. Comparison of weight of the magnetic material used in conventional units and high-fidelity speaker often shows differences of pounds to ounces.

To capture the low notes of the organ or contrabass, otherwise known as the "bull fiddle," a powerful loudspeaker is needed to generate large movements of surrounding air. The voice coil must be capable of moving back and forth over a much longer path than that required for musical notes in the middle registers. To set these large masses of air in motion for the proper reproduction of rich low notes two things are essential—a large cone, or driving surface, and a a large and powerful magnet.

A note of caution must be injected at this point. This heavier equipment, while ideal for the reproduction of low notes, is less effective for high notes. Large cones tend to respond sluggishly to the short staccato pulses which generate the upper tones of the scale. To capture these high frequencies best a light and rigid diaphragm and a delicate and quick-acting voice coil are required. For the fastidious music-lover no one loudspeaker unit will meet both tests to perfection. Hence the recent trend towards divided units, with two or more separately handling the low and high frequencies.

It is not suggested that this multiple system has replaced the single unit. Far from it. And it should be stressed that a well-designed single unit will prove a better investment than a poorly-designed double unit. For one thing, it can later be utilized in a more extensive multiple speaker system, should the owner decide the time has come to improve his equipment. Actually, the very first step in improvement—that is,

from any mass-produced "set" loudspeaker to the most modest priced high-fidelity speaker—can be far more dramatic and breathtaking than any later one.

One method of splitting the frequencies without a complete double unit is to employ two driving surfaces, one a metal diaphragm and the other a paper cone, connected to one voice coil. These are so mechanically designed that the diaphragm reacts to the high notes and the cone to the low.

In the multiple speaker system each unit can be separately mounted or two or three can be mounted coaxially, and systems are now sold in which the audio spectrum is divided into two, three, or four bands. There are many ways of designing a speaker system even after the number of bands to be handled has been decided, On the low frequency end, for example, several methods are possible for achieving the large

A 12" loudspeaker for high fidelity reproduction.

A dual coaxial speaker for full range sound reproduction.

Photographs courtesy of General Electric

notes a special speaker designed for reproducing only the higher frequencies. Equally picturesque is the designation for a loudspeaker designed to operate only at the lower frequencies: woofer.) Improvements at both ends of the frequency spectrum can later be made without discarding the initial equipment.

Enclosures

In selecting the loudspeaker or loudspeakers for a high-fidelity system, it is essential to have in mind exactly where it is to be housed. The nature and location of the enclosures cannot be separated from an intelligent choice of speaker. Here again the superior virtues of a high-

The "1221" speaker has a wide range of sound coverage.

cone area required. Loudspeakers as large as 18" in diameter are commercially available. Electrically connecting a number of loudspeakers is also a possible method. Common arrangements for the more ambitious systems involve two 15" speakers, two or more 12" speakers, or a whole array of smaller units. For the middle and upper regions both cone speakers and small horns are used. Since upper notes are highly directional, it is necessary to incorporate a device for dispersing them, so that a broad area may be covered.

In the choice of a loudspeaker one or two other considerations should be weighed. If a moderate initial investment is intended, with hopes of future improvement, it is advisable to select a 12" co-axial unit, or a 12" single radiator speaker with separate tweeter. (Among audiophiles the word tweeter de-

fidelity installation become apparent.

Let us recall that the loudspeaker produces its effect by virtue of the back-and-forth movement of the diaphragm setting the air in motion. This motion, in the case of low notes, radiates out in the same way that ripples do from the splash of a pebble in a calm pond. Now, if the wave produced by one inward movement of the cone should reach the front of the loudspeaker just as the cone was moving to the front in the act of generating another sound wave, there would be the risk of impeding the formation of this second wave. To prevent this, a barrier must be set up around the loudspeaker to lengthen the path of the low notes. In that way, the opposite movements of air generated by the rear of the cone will not reach the front and cancel out the sounds. Enclosures which are designed merely

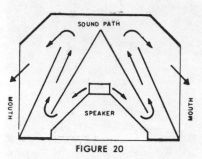

FIGURE 20

A folded horn is a complex speaker enclosure which helps to produce and emphasize the base tonal qualities and enriches the higher tones as well. See **Folded Horn**.

to separate front and back radiation of the loudspeaker are referred to as baffles. Such devices are known as infinite baffles when the above mentioned path is long enough to prevent any cancellation of low notes. This is achieved by mounting the speaker on a very large board or in the wall of a room, or if the baffle is completely enclosed.

These are the simplest forms of loudspeaker enclosure, and are quite effective if properly designed and constructed. However, the diameter of a baffle large enough to prevent loss of low notes must be several

A bass reflex speaker enclosure. The center sketch shows the opening made for the speaker itself and the port below. The sketch on the right shows how the enclosure operates to enhance the bass response.

Photograph and sketches courtesy of Jensen Mfg. Co.

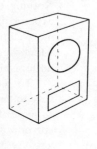

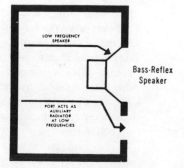

Bass-Reflex Speaker

LOW FREQUENCY SPEAKER

PORT ACTS AS AUXILIARY RADIATOR AT LOW FREQUENCIES

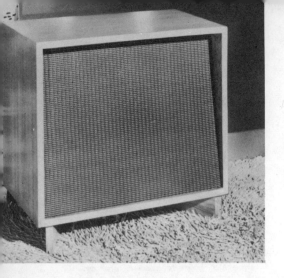

The speaker enclosure aids materially in the truthful reproduction of sound. The enclosure is usually designed for use with specific types or makes of speakers. This unit, 24" wide, 23" high and 14" deep is used to house an 8" speaker and tweeter, assuring undistorted reproduction from 36 to 16,000 cps.

yards. This makes apparent the defects of the type of commercial radio console cabinet in which the loudspeaker is contained in an open-backed enclosure barely large enough to accommodate it.

It is not generally realized that air confined in a small, rigid container is not readily compressed. Thus, if we try to solve the baffle problem by enclosing the rear of the loudspeaker in a small box, without providing any means of relief for the pressure which builds up within it, the speaker diaphragm encounters a resistance to its largest movements. This resistance overcomes the force exerted by the voice coil and physically distorts the cone. The effect on reproduction can be very objectionable.

To improve speaker performance, several enclosures have been designed to meet this need for venting in a small cabinet. The oldest and most commonly used of these is the bass reflex or phase inverter cabinet.

An 8" speaker can be housed in a bass reflex cabinet of only 1½ to 2 cubic feet. Satisfactory results can be achieved with a 12" speaker by enclosing it in a minimum volume of 6 cubic feet. For a 15" speaker 7½ to 8 cubic feet of volume will achieve the best results. This volume, proportional to the size of the loudspeaker is required to prevent the compression effect described above.

Man's ingenuity being what it is, loudspeaker enclosures of smaller size have lately been designed which produce startlingly good results. Most of these are similar to the bass reflex and employ the principle of the Helmholtz resonator developed in the 19th century—which goes to prove that there is nothing really new under the sun. But for perfectionists there is nothing to compare with the results achieved by a true infinite baffle, which to the engineer means housing the speaker in a structure of formidable proportions or in a wall separating two rooms. Nothing, that is, except the use of an exponential horn—a device even more cumbersome and complicated, which does for the low notes what nothing else can.

To see why this is so, consider that to produce low notes we have to generate large movements of the surrounding air. For a simple loudspeaker to achieve such results is almost impossible because it is so

Where space is limited, it is still possible to obtain faithful reproduction of sound and quality bass and treble reception through the use of specially designed small speaker enclosures. This small unit, contains two speakers and a tweeter with a range of 45 to 16,000 cps.

small compared to the volume of air which it is attempting to set in motion. But if in front of the loudspeaker we place a tube which flares out in a certain manner, the tube, known as a horn, acts as a coupling between the loudspeaker and the air, and more than doubles its efficiency. The performance of horns is determined by the rate at which their cross section increases, known as the rate of flare, and the area of the aperture from which the sound finally emanates. Horns designed for tweeters are short and small, but to reproduce a 60 cycle note, the horn must have an aperture of 10

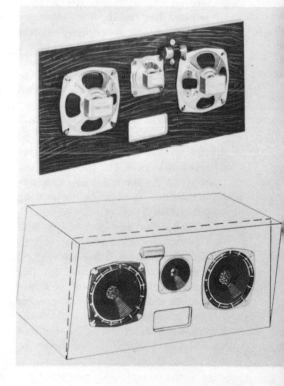

Here is a view of the actual unit without the decorative grille front, showing the two 6" speakers and the tweeter mounted in the center.

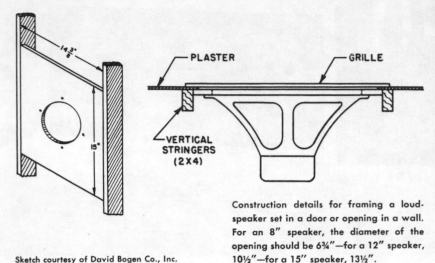

PLASTER

GRILLE

VERTICAL
STRINGERS
(2 X 4)

14 3/8"

15"

Sketch courtesy of David Bogen Co., Inc.

Construction details for framing a loudspeaker set in a door or opening in a wall.
For an 8" speaker, the diameter of the
opening should be 6¾"—for a 12" speaker,
10½"—for a 15" speaker, 13½".

square feet and a length of 4' to 8'.
Obviously not many people are so
interested in high fidelity as to desire an object of this size in their
homes. But again, the engineers
have been able to improve matters
somewhat. Taking advantage of the
fact that low notes tend to ooze
around corners with ease, they have
designed what are known as folded
horn cabinets of reasonable size. If
you happen to have a spare corner
in your listening room, a horn type
cabinet can produce extremely re-
warding sounds. The trick is that the
walls of the room act as extensions
of the horn, and take over where the
cabinet leaves off.

Whatever the size, shape, and
type of enclosures you use, high fidelity can only be achieved by good
construction. This means, for one
thing, that cabinets should be firmly
built, braced and padded to prevent
internal reflections. The walls of the
speaker cabinet should be made of
wood not less than ⅝" in thickness.

One inch or more is preferred for
large enclosures. This will prevent
the sides of the enclosure from com-
peting with the loudspeaker cone as
a source of sound.

How To Conduct a Listening Test

It may seem presumptuous to
offer suggestions on how to go
about listening to equipment immediately after telling you that the
subjective factor plays such a large
part in selection of components for
a high-fidelity home music system.
But the human ear is fallible—and
notorious for its bad memory. It is
very difficult to compare sounds unless there is a good deal of difference
between them, or unless you hear
them almost simultaneously. This
would indicate the necessity for
making choices on the basis of direct comparisons, known in engineering circles as A-B listening tests.

Fortunately, it is not necessary
to trundle your old radio console
down to the hi-fi dealer's showroom

The angles speakers disperse sound evenly throughout the room. The three speakers are mounted at a 7° angle from the perpendicular. This lengthens the reflected sound path by directing it around the cabinet and breaks up direct back-wave reflections between the back of the cabinet and the speakers. It also tilts the sound waves up toward the ears of the listener.

Sketch courtesy of Permoflux Corp.

in order to hear the difference between it and a high-fidelity system. The impact of hearing high-fidelity sound for the first time is so startling that the differences will be obvious. It is in the selection of individual components, and in the comparison of one high-fidelity system with another that the actual listening tests become profitable.

In order to best evaluate the equipment which you audition, you should proceed in a logical manner. The best method is to start from your own ears and work backwards; that is, decide on a loudspeaker first. If you have an idea of how much you want to spend for your entire system, use as a rule of thumb that the cost of the loudspeaker and its enclosure should be at least equal to the cost of the amplifier. If you plan to buy a separate speaker enclosure be sure that you listen to the speaker in that enclosure or in one which closely approximates it. If you are planning to use a console cabinet be sure that the loudspeaker you are evaluating is housed in a cabinet which approximates the dimensions of the enclosure of your console.

Ask that the speakers you wish to consider be connected to a high quality amplifier and program source (tuner, tape recorder or record player). For your first test listen at a level somewhat higher than that at which you ever expect to operate the system in your home, and note which of the speakers sounds best to you. Then repeat the tests at a lower loudness level. If the speaker you preferred on the first test does not sound as well to you the second time, ask that the various controls of the amplifier be adjusted to see if they will compensate for the difference. When you have made your selection, this loudspeaker should be used for listening tests of the other components you plan to purchase.

This is how critical listening to high fidelity should proceed. First select a phonograph or tape recording of a musical selection which has a wide range of frequencies. High-fidelity salons usually have a number of such records on hand for demonstrating the equipment. When listening at high levels try to detect such things as distortion, overhang, and acoustic feedback. We have already described distortion, and it manifests itself in sounds which are distinctly muddy and unpleasant to the ear. Overhang is a name we give to lack of crispness as the result of poor transient response. It is particularly noticeable on percussion instruments when, for example, you cannot separate the sound produced by the impact of stick against drumhead from the rumble which accompanies it.

Play a good recording containing high frequency sounds such as triangles, flutes, etc. and turn up the treble control so that you can hear the scratch in the record (or back-

ground hiss if you are listening to FM). Check the dispersion of your loudspeaker by walking back and forth in front of it and notice where the efficiency of reproduction of these high frequencies begins to drop off. A good high-fidelity loudspeaker should be able to disperse high frequency sounds so that you can get satisfactory results when you are so much as 45° off the axis of the speaker. This is important, because normally you may not be able to place your loudspeaker so that you will always have it facing directly at you, and the greater the angle of dispersion of the high frequency portion of the speaker, the more flexible can be your installation in the home.

The first comparison of amplifiers should be conducted at high level. But it is at moderate and low levels that the action of the individual controls for tone, loudness, equalization, etc. meet the real test. If the amplifier you are considering incorporates refinements which appear to be of doubtful value, you have the opportunity to assess them under conditions which are close to those under which you will actually listen at home. Notice particularly the effect of the various controls at all three levels. When your system is installed you will probably operate it at varying levels, depending upon the number of people in the room at any one time, the acoustics of the room, and the program material. Even though you may normally lean toward reproduction on the quiet side there may be times when you feel like turning it up.

Note what happens to low notes

when you advance the bass tone control. Be certain, of course, that the record you are using contains passages which employ the bass instruments such as the string bass or the bass drum. The organ is also excellent as a test of bass response at high level. Are the real low notes being increased or is the tone control merely raising the lower middle frequencies? The tympani and the string bass in an orchestra usually play a tune. If after listening to several records, the bass always seems to strike the same note the chances are your loudspeaker is at fault.

Notice the way the record equalizer operates, if one is incorporated in the amplifier, and try it on several records of different manufacturers. Do not be perturbed if simply setting the equalizer does not provide complete satisfaction. Tone controls are meant to be used.

Next try listening to a record or an FM program (live) featuring a male voice. Naturalness in speech reproduction is a critical test for high-fidelity systems. A man's voice is to be preferred because it gives a better test of the smoothness with which the loudspeaker and amplifier reproduce the bass passages. Notice also whether or not the sibilance in speech is reproduced. When we talk, certain sounds, notably those making use of the letter S, are accompanied by a hissing sound known as sibilance. Insufficient loudness compensation results in a tone which has a "thin" sound. The full tonal range of the performance at high level is missing. You can dramatize this simply by turning from high level to low level without

The closet door installation has much to recommend it, particularly in rented quarters. The original door can be removed and stored, and replaced by an inexpensive door on which the complete music system is mounted. Only a hole for the speaker is cut for the door. The tuner-amplifier and changer are mounted on shelves attached to the inside of the door. With the door closed, the clothes give excellent acoustic absorption.

Sketch courtesy of Federal Purchaser

Audible Frequency Range For Music, Speech and Noise

frequency in cycles per second

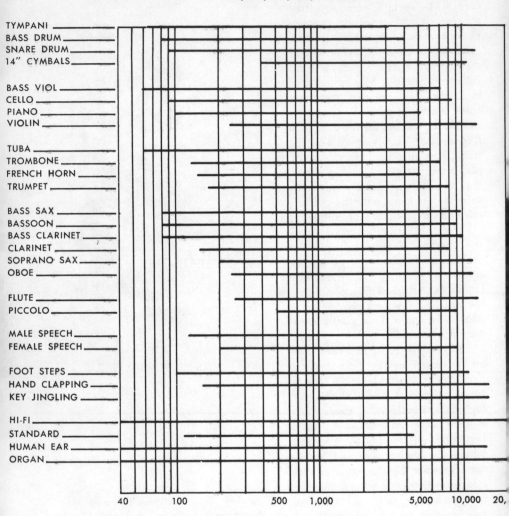

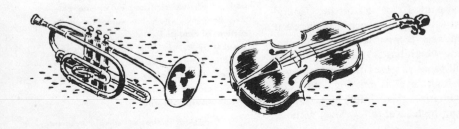

introducing any compensation at all, and then attempting to add compensation as required.

When checking built-in loudness controls be sure to try several records of different manufacture. Aside from the normal manufacturing variations in the production of records, different manufacturers record at different sound levels. The continuous-acting "compensated" loudness control used on some equipment is difficult to adjust for this variation because it is designed on the assumption that the signal fed into the amplifier is constant. Often it can be proved, by listening to phonograph records, that this is not the case. On AM radio reception, the variation in signal level of different stations is even greater. One solution to the problem is the Loudness Contour Selector described earlier. This device provides separate control of input signal and compensation, so that a wide range of variation in recording or radio program level can be accommodated.

With the choice of loudspeaker and amplifier out of the way, it becomes a simple matter to evaluate tape recorders and record players. Performance requirements imposed upon them are determined by the equipment through which they are played, as discussed previously.

The conditions for radio reception at your location must be taken into account when selecting a tuner. However, assuming that these do not dictate the purchase of an ultra-sensitive tuner, you should consider primarily convenience of operation

and listening quality when the unit is played through the rest of the system. Notice particularly the ease with which you can tune in on various stations. If you live in a metropolitan area check to see whether or not it is possible to hear separately stations which are close together on the dial. If the tuner includes a built-in preamplifier, the audio features should be tested in the same manner as suggested for amplifiers.

Demountable Music Wall

Here's an inexpensive fir plywood built-in that makes sense for music lovers. Instead of letting the components—radio tuner and amplifier, TV, record changer, record storage cabinets—clutter up the room, all are grouped together in one compact and efficient music wall.

Simple, interchangeable fir plywood "boxes" hold the radio tuner and amplifier, changer, TV, records and even have space for books. The speaker for the entire system is housed in a large "box" placed at the end of the music wall.

Materials Needed:		

FIR PLYWOOD

Number	Size and Grade	Where Used
2 panels	4'x8'x¾"— Interior A-A	Movable tops and sides, when these are visible from both sides
1 piece	4'x4'x¾"— Interior A-A	
3 panels	4'x8'x¾"— PlyPanel A-D	Bottoms, sides and backs where only one side is visible; TV front, speaker front, etc.

LUMBER

Size	Quantity	Where Used
1x2	12'	Speaker unit, radio, TV
2x4	30'	Legs, frame

HARDWARE AND MISCELLANEOUS

Item	Quantity	Where Used
Extension arms	3 pairs	Hold lid of radio, record player and speaker
12"x12" acoustical tile	1	Underside of record player lid
Fabric	as needed	For speaker cover and TV air vent
28½"x16½" asbestos sheet		Radio lid
Semi-concealed cabinet hinges	3 pairs	Lid tops

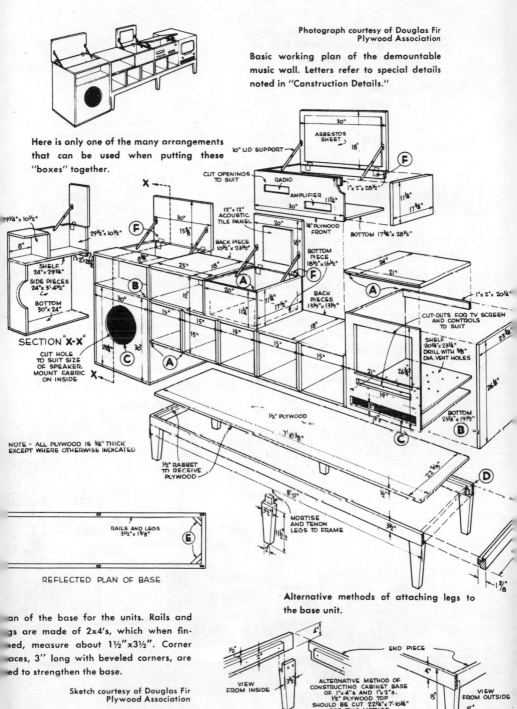

Photograph courtesy of Douglas Fir Plywood Association

Basic working plan of the demountable music wall. Letters refer to special details noted in "Construction Details."

Here is only one of the many arrangements that can be used when putting these "boxes" together.

NOTE – ALL PLYWOOD IS ¾" THICK EXCEPT WHERE OTHERWISE INDICATED

SECTION "X-X"
CUT HOLE TO SUIT SIZE OF SPEAKER. MOUNT FABRIC ON INSIDE

REFLECTED PLAN OF BASE

Alternative methods of attaching legs to the base unit.

...an of the base for the units. Rails and
...gs are made of 2x4's, which when fin-
...ed, measure about 1½"x3½". Corner
...aces, 3" long with beveled corners, are
...ed to strengthen the base.

Sketch courtesy of Douglas Fir Plywood Association

Construction details for the unit. The letters are references made in the basic construction sketch of the entire unit.

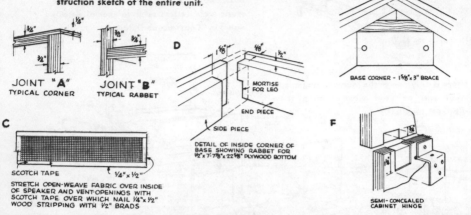

JOINT "A"
TYPICAL CORNER

JOINT "B"
TYPICAL RABBET

D

MORTISE
FOR LEG

END PIECE

SIDE PIECE

DETAIL OF INSIDE CORNER OF
BASE SHOWING RABBET FOR
½" x 7-7/8" x 22 5/8" PLYWOOD BOTTOM

BASE CORNER - 1 5/8" x 3" BRACE

F

C

SCOTCH TAPE   ¼" x ½"

STRETCH OPEN-WEAVE FABRIC OVER INSIDE
OF SPEAKER AND VENT-OPENINGS WITH
SCOTCH TAPE OVER WHICH NAIL ¼" x ½"
WOOD STRIPPING WITH ½" BRADS

SEMI-CONCEALED
CABINET HINGE

Music and TV Center

With this compactly planned high fidelity music and TV center, you can have the best in listening enjoyment without clutter or inconvenience. Record storage is planned for 12″, 10″ and 6″ records plus record albums. The controls for the various components fit nicely into the design and are handy to get at.

The TV set has been placed on

an easy-to-make turn-table mounted on window rollers so that the set can be revolved around 180°, providing a clear, head-on view of the screen through a full half circle.

The entire cabinet fits against a wall or it can be incorporated in a storage wall, either ceiling height or free standing. The speaker construction is the result of exhaustive research by General Electric sound engineers. The fabric for the speaker enclosure is mounted on a frame that is held in place simply by. four spring catches for easy access to the speaker.

The unit can be stained or painted (see *Finishing—Plywood*) or it can be covered in laminated plastic, such as Formica or Micarta, or in vinyl plastic, like Boltaflex or Naugahyde.

Materials Needed:		
Number	**Size and Grade**	**Where Used**
4 panels	4'x8'x¾" — Interior A-A	Top, sides, bottom, partitions and shelves
2 panels	4'x8'x¼" — Interior A-A	Back, record partitions, mountings
LUMBER		
Size	**Quantity**	**Where Used**
1x1	26'	Speaker frame, separators for mountings, stringers, nailing pieces
1x2	2'8"	Changer slide mountings
1x3	11'	Speaker cover frame
2x3	25'	Base support
¼"x⅝"	33'	Edging strip for face of cabinet
¼"x½"	13'8"	Edging for shelves and dividers
¼"x¼"	10'6"	Beading for outside of frame for speaker covering
HARDWARE		
Item	**Quantity**	**Where Used**
Door pulls	4	Drop door, cabinet door and changer drawer
1'5" Piano hinge	1	Drop leaf door on changer
Semi-concealed hinges	2½ pair	Doors and drop leaves
Spring catches	4	Speaker covering enclosure
Lid supports	1 pair	Record changer drop leaf
"C" type slides	2	Changer drawer
Window rollers	3	TV turntable
Copper tubing, 1⅝" diameter with flange attached	3'	Axis for turntable and lead for wiring
Fabric	6 sq. ft.	Speaker enclosure face

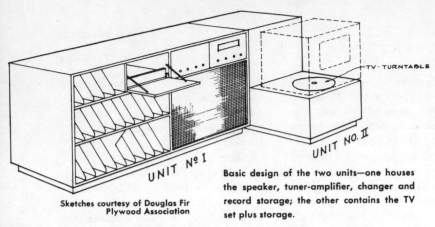

UNIT Nº 1

UNIT NO. II

TV· TURNTABLE

Sketches courtesy of Douglas Fir
Plywood Association

Basic design of the two units—one houses
the speaker, tuner-amplifier, changer and
record storage; the other contains the TV
set plus storage.

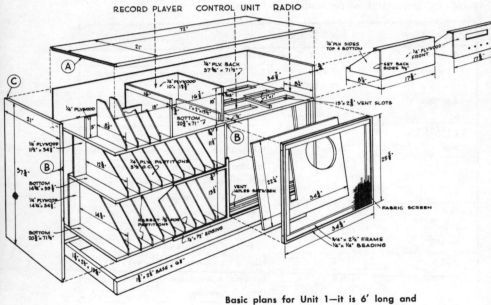

RECORD PLAYER   CONTROL UNIT   RADIO

Basic plans for Unit 1—it is 6' long and
21" deep with ample storage for a good-
sized record collection.

Detail plans for the changer drawer and
drop leaf door.

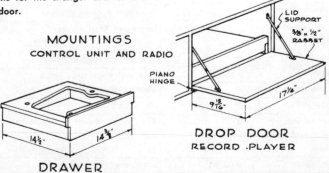

MOUNTINGS
CONTROL UNIT AND RADIO

PIANO
HINGE

LID
SUPPORT

3/8" x 1/2"
RABBET

DROP DOOR
RECORD PLAYER

DRAWER
RECORD PLAYER

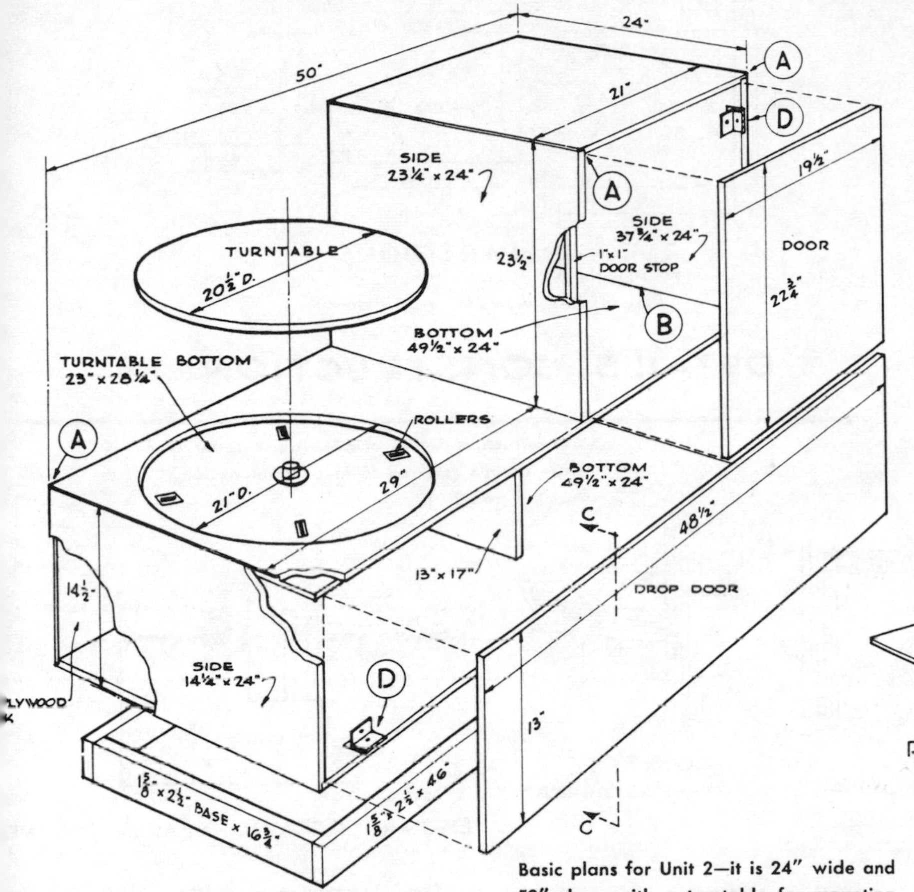

24"
50"
A
D
21"
SIDE 23¼" x 24"
19½"
A
SIDE 37¾" x 24"
TURNTABLE
20½" D.
23½"
1"x1" DOOR STOP
DOOR
22¾"
B
BOTTOM 49½" x 24"
TURNTABLE BOTTOM 23" x 28¼"
ROLLERS
A
29"
21" D.
BOTTOM 49½" x 24"
C
48½"
13" x 17"
14½"
DROP DOOR
SIDE 14¼" x 24"
D
13"
1⅝" x 2½" BASE x 16¾"
1⅝" x 2½" x 46"
C

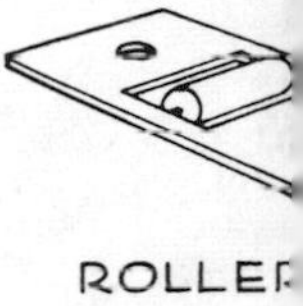

ROLLER

Basic plans for Unit 2—it is 24" wide and 50" deep with a turntable for mounting the TV set plus a storage cabinet in the back of the unit.

Details of speaker enclosure—mounting of baffle board or screen.

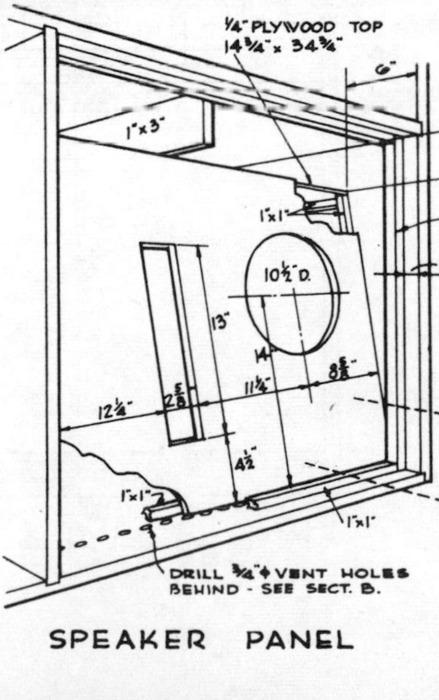

¼" PLYWOOD TOP 14¾" x 34¾"
6"
1" x 3"
3"
1"x1"
1"x1"
1"
10½" D.
13"
14"
8⅝"
12¼"
2⅝"
11¼"
A
4½"
1"x1"
1"x1"
B
DRILL ¾" ϕ VENT HOLES BEHIND - SEE SECT. B.

SPEAKER PANEL

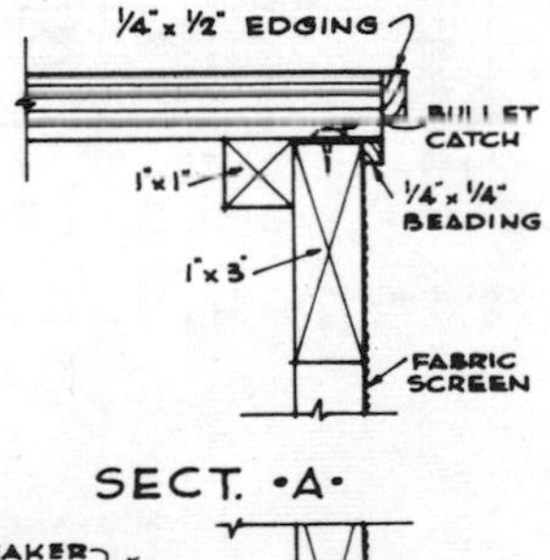

¼" x ½" EDGING
BULLET CATCH
1"x1"
¼" x ¼" BEADING
1" x 3"
FABRIC SCREEN

SECT. •A•

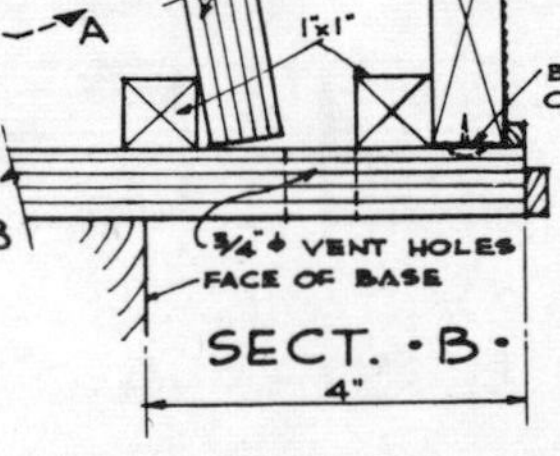

SPEAKER PANEL
1"x1"
BULLET CATCH
¾" ϕ VENT HOLES
FACE OF BASE

SECT. •B•

4"

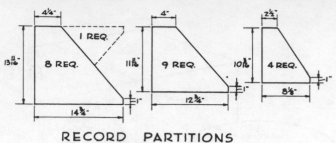

RECORD PARTITIONS
¼" PLYWOOD
Patterns for dividers for record storage.

DETAILS CONSTRUCTION

Construction details of basic parts. Letters
are details referred to in basic plans for
units 1 and 2

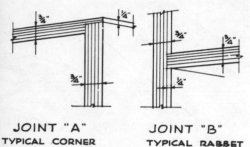

JOINT "A"
TYPICAL CORNER

JOINT "B"
TYPICAL RABBET

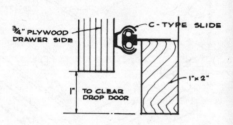

DETAIL - RECORD PLAYER DRAWER

Sketches courtesy of Douglas Fir
Plywood Association

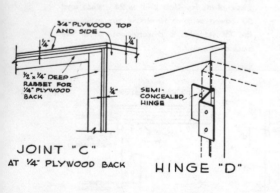

JOINT "C"
AT ¼" PLYWOOD BACK

HINGE "D"

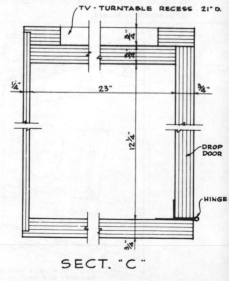

SECT. "C"

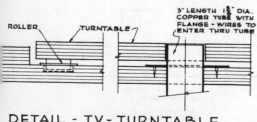

DETAIL - TV - TURNTABLE

Stereo and Hi Fi

Audio engineers have spent many years in the development of the illusion of depth and perspective in sound reproduction. Stereo is now developed to the point where the average homeowner can easily put the components together or even build his unit from kits.

Stereophonic sound comes from two Greek words meaning solid sound. This term describes the apex in high fidelity listening. In stereo sound reproduction, two separate channels are used to transmit the sound waves through the speakers. Your two ears collect these sound waves, and the mind interprets them. With an efficient and effective system, it is possible to duplicate the actual "live" sound, just as if you were present listening to the orchestra.

The current stereo systems are far advanced from the early systems introduced by Bell Telephone Laboratories during the 1930's. More sensitive equipment, advances in speaker and enclosure designs, vastly improved recording techniques, have made it possible to obtain the optimum in stereo sound reproduction in the home.

Basically, the standard components of high fidelity systems are also used in stereo systems. However, with stereo, a dual sound track is used. It is essential that two individual amplifiers be employed for the sound reproduction and each amplifier feeds its own individual speaker. The two speakers are set apart so that when you are facing the two speakers, the sound from each reaches your ears.

It is often necessary to balance the sound level of the two individual speakers. This is accomplished by a mixer or special unit so that proper sound amplitude is achieved to produce a realistic reproduction of the recording on the turntable, the recording on the magnetic tape played by the recorder, or the broadcast pickup received on the Am-FM tuner.

The diagram below illustrates the simplest form of a stereo set-up. The individual components—tuner, turntable, tape recorder—can be used individually or in any combination. Two amplifiers are necessary; they can be built as a single unit or you can use two independent amplifiers. It is essential to have at least two speakers in proper enclosures for faithful sound reproduction.

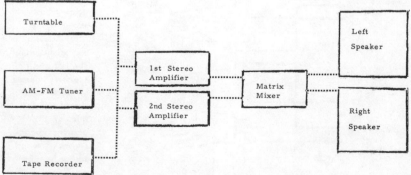

While the stereo system usually employs two speakers, normally set about eight feet apart, there is a trend to add a third or phantom speaker to the system. This third speaker, which is placed between the other two, draws its sound from both channels. This third speaker helps to improve the high level of sound reproduction.

Basic Stereo Terms

The advent of stereo in high fidelity has resulted in the addition of a number of special terms to the audiofile's vocabulary. Among the more frequently used terms are:

Monoral—audio or sound in one channel; for example, the sound received by a single AM or FM tuner using a single speaker.

Binaural—two sound channels are used for sound transmission; frequently, this is achieved by setting up an AM tuner with its own speaker and an FM tuner with its own speaker, both tuned to the same station. The listener hears the music from two different sources.

Stereophonic — two or more sound channels used for reproduc-tion of sound; the phasing is usually different from one sound track to another; that is, there is about 1/20 of a second delay in one sound channel as compared with the other.

Simulcasting—broadcasting of a program over both AM and FM stations at the same time.

Multicasting — broadcasting a stereo program over two FM stations at the same time; it is essential to have two FM tuners to receive this type of a broadcast.

Multiplexing — broadcasting stereo music over a single FM channel with two sound waves; one channel is broadcast in the conventional manner, while the other channel is broadcast as a subcarrier of either 67 kc. or 42 kc. The conventional FM tuner is used to pick up the conventional channel broadcast; a multiplex adaptor is used to pick-up the subcarrier.

Control Balance—this device, a mixer, varies the volume of each speaker relative to the other; at the same time it maintains their combined volume virtually the same. As one speaker increases in volume, the other speaker decreases.

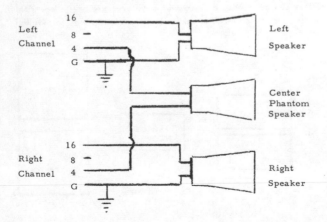

Left Channel — 16, 8, 4, G — Left Speaker

Center Phantom Speaker

Right Channel — 16, 8, 4, G — Right Speaker

Three-speaker stereo system hook-up can be achieved as shown in the accompanying wiring diagram. The left and right speakers operate off their own amplifiers. The third or phantom speaker draws its sound source from both amplifiers.

Recess Your TV Set

If you want to recess your TV instead of building out from the wall to accomodate it, choose a spot against an unused deep space, such as a stairwell, or a closet, utility room or pantry where the small amount of space the set will need can be spared. The opening for the set can then be combined with space for a record player, cabinet or bookcases, depending on what you need and how much space you want to use.

The framing for the wall opening isn't hard to make. If you are making the bookcases, use 1"x12" pine boards for the sidepieces, nailed to the wall. Nailed to these is a front frame made of 1x3 strips,

TV set, viewed from living room at left, protrudes through wall into stairway, saving space. Exposing back also provides good ventilation, easy access.

doweled and glued at the corners, with a crosspiece at the point that divides the lower cabinet from the shelves above. The top and bottom of the bookcase are trimmed with molding to match that in the rest of the room. For details on joints and attaching shelves, see *Furniture*.

Finished off with one coat of flat and two coats of enamel, the result is a fine home entertainment center that takes up little space, yet houses everything needed for hours of leisure enjoyment.

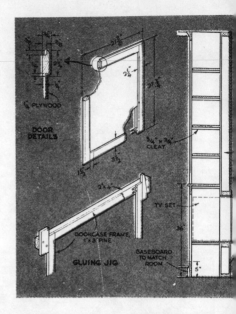

Sides of bookcase (right, above) make use of stock, inexpensive 1"x12" boards, but dimensions can be varied as desired. Jig for gluing front frame can be made with 2x4's and wedges (lower left, above). Doors can be ¼" plywood panels set into grooved frames (top left) or simply plywood panels with decorative molding nailed at edges.

How To Cut and Frame Wall Opening

1. Drill starting hole at corner, insert keyhole saw and cut through stud (you may hit two) and both wall faces at the same time. Ends of cut stud are then trimmed back 1⅝" (the thickness of a 2x4) to take frame.

2. 2x4 spacer is nailed to adjacent stud on one side of opening, and header is shoehorned in to rest on top of spacer. Second spacer is nailed to stud on opposite side of opening to hold other end of header.

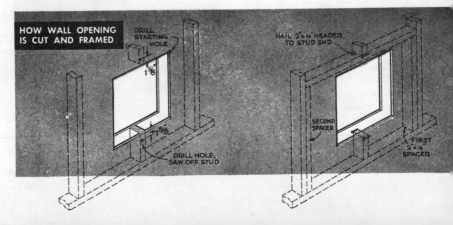

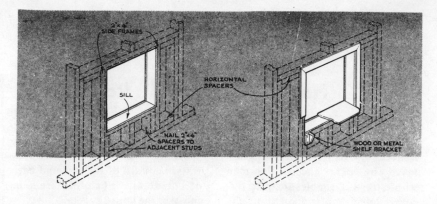

3. Side frames are nailed against horizontal spacers nailed to floor and underside of header on both sides of opening. Two short vertical spacers are then nailed to side frames at bottom and 2x4 sill nailed on top.

4. Opening is trimmed with decorative molding, wide enough to cover saw holes made in wall. Short shelf, deep enough to take set's overhang, is nailed to sill and brackets. Opening on bookcase side is also trimmed.

High Spots

Sketch from "Tool Guide" courtesy of
Stanley Tools

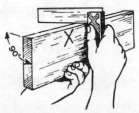

This term is used in machine shop and woodworking shop practice to describe excess areas or surfaces. It designates spots to be taken down by grinding, scraping or planing in order to obtain an absolutely plane or flat surface.

A square is used to test for high spots on a board. A plane is generally used to remove these high spots.

Hinge Nails

These oval-head nails are sometimes used in place of screws to fasten hinges to doors and trim and occasionally used with cabinet door hinges. The light hinge nails are $\frac{3}{16}$″ in diameter, while the heavy type are ¼″ in diameter. Available in sizes from 1½″ to 3″, the heavy type comes up to 4″ long.

A hinge nail has an oval head and is $\frac{3}{16}$″ or ¼″ in diameter.

House—Structural Parts

Residents are often aware of the defects in a house, but sometimes it is necessary to have an inspection made by experienced workmen whose training enables them to discover defects not apparent to the average householder. Some homeowners wish to make their own inspection; the accompanying illustration and list of the essential parts of a house will be helpful when looking over the house in detail.

House—Structural Parts

1. Gable end.
2. Louver.
3. Interior trim.
4. Shingles.
5. Chimney cap.
6. Flue lining.
7. Flashing.
8. Roofing felt.
9. Roof sheathing.
10. Ridge board.
11. Rafters.
12. Roof valley.
13. Dormer window.
14. Interior walls.
15. Studs.
16. Insulation.
17. Diagonal sheathing.
18. Sheathing paper.
19. Window frame and sash.
20. Corner board.
21. Siding.
22. Shutters.
23. Exterior trim.
24. Waterproofing.
25. Foundation wall.
26. Column.
27. Joists.
28. Basement floor.
29. Gravel fill.
30. Heating plant.
31. Footing.
32. Drain tile.
33. Girder.
34. Stairway.
35. Subfloor.
36. Hearth.
37. Building paper.
38. Finish paper.
39. Fireplace.
40. Downspout.
41. Gutter.
42. Bridging.

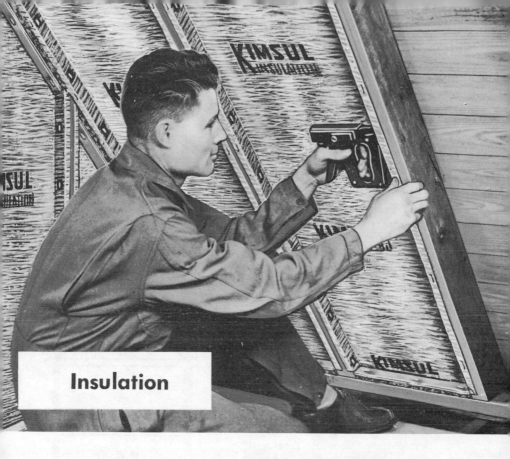

Insulation

Insulating your home has two important advantages. It saves you money on fuel bills and adds to the comfort of your home in both the winter and summer. The reason is simple. Heat always moves toward a colder area. Thus, in hot weather, the sun's heat enters the cooler house, while in the winter much of the heat is wasted because it passes out to the cooler exterior. Materials which block the passage of heat (as the covering on an electrical wire blocks the passage of electricity) are called thermal insulators or, more usually, insulation.

All homes where artificial heat is required or where the heat of the sun is intense should be insulated. Even in a well-constructed house heat will pass through the roof and walls if there is no thermal barrier. With insulation it will take less heat to produce a more comfortably heated house. Insulation should be installed, whenever possible, during the construction of the house, but if your house is uninsulated it can be added.

Where To Insulate

Before you add insulation, make sure there are no cracks or air leaks in walls, floors or ceiling. A lot of heat can get out and cold air can come in even through small cracks. The first step to a well-insulated house is to get your building in good condition.

In the ordinary one-story house, and in many two-story houses, 25% or more of the total heat loss is through the top of the house. So if you can insulate only a part of the house at first, start with the ceiling or roof. It is usually easier to get at and less costly to insulate.

Whether you put the insulation in the ceiling or in the roof will depend on how you plan to use the attic space. The accompanying sketch shows three places where the insulation can be installed. If you expect to use the attic for storage only, you can probably save on cost by insulating between the ceiling joists. This arrangement also gives the greatest summer comfort. But if you plan to heat the attic, then insulate the roof. Always leave an air space between the insulation and the shingles or other roofing material.

If there is no warm basement under the house, you may need insulation in the floor as well. Heat loss through the floor is greater in houses set on piers than in houses with curtain walls between the piers. It is also greater through single than through double floors.

You may need insulation not only in the outside walls of your home but also in walls next to an unheated garage or store room. And you will also need insulation in the floors of second-story rooms over porches.

If you plan to air condition your house, install insulation. It will cut initial costs and operating expenses.

Insulation Terms

When selecting an insulation for your home or when determining the effectiveness of the type you already have in your home, you will come

UNHEATED ATTIC

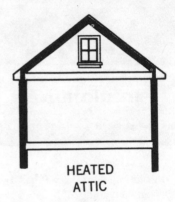

HEATED ATTIC

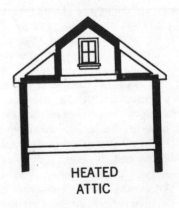

HEATED ATTIC

Insulate ceiling under unheated attic, or roof over heated attic.

across many technical terms in manufacturers' literature. . . . "k" factor, vapor barrier, reflective insulation, to mention but a few. For those of you who are unfamliar with these technical terms of the heating engineer, here, in brief, are some definitions.

Btu—this is a measuring unit of heat—the quantity of heat needed to raise the temperature of one pound of water one degree Fahrenheit.

Batt—a length of flexible insulation, generally not more than 48" long.

Blanket—a length of flexible insulation, usually a roll, ordinarily up to 100' long.

Coefficient of heat transmission —this sometimes is presented as a symbol—"U." It is a measure of the rate at which heat flows in Btu's per hour, per square foot, per degree difference between the temperature on the outside and temperature on the inside. The lower the "U" factor, therefore, the less the heat loss during the winter and the less the heat gain during the summer.

Heat gain—this signifies the temperature increase within the house because of heat entering the house through the roof, walls, doors and windows.

Heat Loss—this is the opposite of heat gain; it is the amount of heat that passes through the roof, walls, doors and windows from the house to the outside.

"k" factor—sometimes referred to as thermal conductivity, this is a measure of heat flow through 1" of a material. It is measured in Btu's

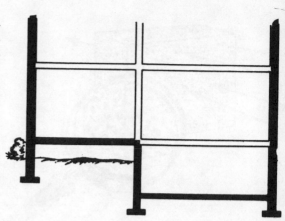

Insulate floor over unheated space.

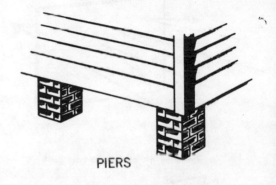

PIERS

Curtain wall saves heat.

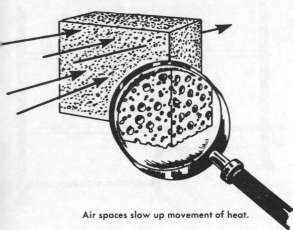

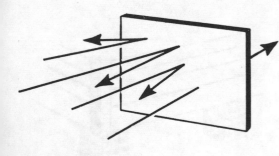

Air spaces slow up movement of heat.

per hour, per square foot of material 1″ thick, per degree difference from one side of the material to the other. It is the common base for comparison of different insulating and building materials.

Radiation—also called *thermal conductance*, it is the rate of heat flow through a material. Sometimes it is indicated by the letter—"C." It is measured in a manner similar to thermal conductivity; that is, in Btu's.

Thermal insulation—this is but a dressed-up name for insulating material, whether it is fill, flexible batts or blankets, reflective material or rigid boards.

Vapor barrier—any material used to keep moisture on the warm side of the insulation from passing through the insulation to the cold side. The vapor barrier used with insulating material is always placed on the side facing the inside of the house.

Reflective insulation turns back heat.

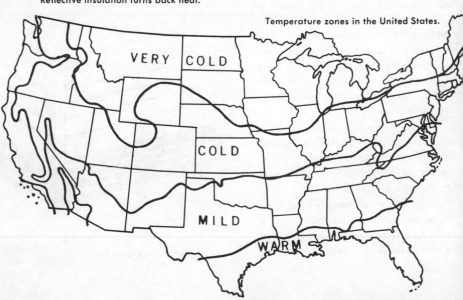

Temperature zones in the United States.

VERY COLD

COLD

MILD

WARM

What Kind of Insulation

The common building materials —wood, brick, and stone—have insulation value. Some are better than others. Wood is a fair insulator. Solid masonry, such as brick or stone, is poor. Hollow masonry, such as cinder block and clay tile, is better than solid masonry because the air spaces in the hollow masonry provide some insulation.

Some of the best insulating materials are mineral wools, including glass wools, mica products, cork. These materials are light in weight and filled with tiny air spaces. Some metal surfaces make good insulators because they slow down heat in another way. They reflect, or turn back, nearly all the heat which is radiated to their surfaces.

Light-weight insulating materials are on the market in four common forms—loose-fill, blanket (or quilt), batt, and board. Reflective insulation comes as metal foil or bright metal sheets. Glossy white paint also deflects some heat.

The form of insulation best suited to your use will depend on:

1. How you intend to use it; that is, whether purely as insulation or as a wall finish.

2. How easy it is to put in, and

3. How much you want to spend.

When you are insulating the walls of an old frame house it is often easier to install loose-fill insulation than blanket or board. If

Various building materials have different insulating values.

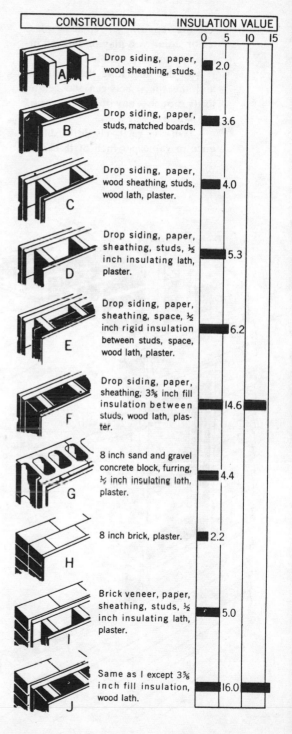

CONSTRUCTION	INSULATION VALUE
A — Drop siding, paper, wood sheathing, studs.	2.0
B — Drop siding, paper, studs, matched boards.	3.6
C — Drop siding, paper, wood sheathing, studs, wood lath, plaster.	4.0
D — Drop siding, paper, sheathing, studs, ½ inch insulating lath, plaster.	5.3
E — Drop siding, paper, sheathing, space, ½ inch rigid insulation between studs, space, wood lath, plaster.	6.2
F — Drop siding, paper, sheathing, 3⅝ inch fill insulation between studs, wood lath, plaster.	14.6
G — 8 inch sand and gravel concrete block, furring, ½ inch insulating lath, plaster.	4.4
H — 8 inch brick, plaster.	2.2
I — Brick veneer, paper, sheathing, studs, ½ inch insulating lath, plaster.	5.0
J — Same as I except 3⅝ inch fill insulation, wood lath.	16.0

you are repairing or replacing plaster or siding you may find board insulation more convenient to install. If you are insulating the ceiling—and the space between the ceiling joists is open—any of these types of insulation can be used.

There is relatively little difference in value per inch of thickness between the various commercial insulating materials except for reflective insulation where value does not depend on thickness. Whatever insulation you buy, make sure that it is resistant to fire, moisture, insects and rodents.

Insulation means fuel savings. Notice that the greatest saving in fuel comes in the first inch of insulation. Increasing the insulation to 2" saves only 3.5% more fuel.

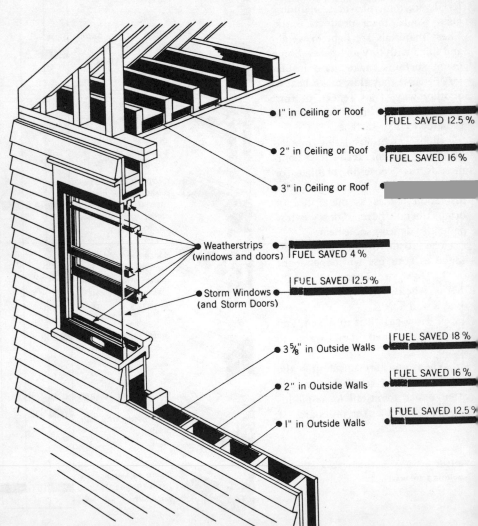

- 1" in Ceiling or Roof — FUEL SAVED 12.5 %
- 2" in Ceiling or Roof — FUEL SAVED 16 %
- 3" in Ceiling or Roof —
- Weatherstrips (windows and doors) — FUEL SAVED 4 %
- FUEL SAVED 12.5 %
- Storm Windows (and Storm Doors) —
- FUEL SAVED 18 %
- $3\frac{5}{8}$" in Outside Walls —
- FUEL SAVED 16 %
- 2" in Outside Walls —
- FUEL SAVED 12.5 %
- 1" in Outside Walls —

Amount of Heat Transmitted

Material	"k" factor or Conductivity	C factor or Conductance (for standard thickness or that noted)
Asbestos shingles		6.0
Asphalt shingles		6.5
Batts or blankets	.27	
Brick, common, 4"	5.00	1.25
Brick, face, 4"		2.30
Brick veneer, 4"		2.27
Clay tile, hollow, 3"		1.28
Clay tile, hollow, 8"		.60
Concrete, sand and gravel	12.00	
Concrete, cinder	4.90	
Concrete, vermiculite	.86	
Concrete block, 4"		1.00
Concrete block, 8"		.60
Corkboard	.30	
Glass	6.00	
Gypsum plaster	3.30	
Gypsum sheathing, ½"		2.82
Gypsum tile, 4" wallboard		.46
Gypsum, ⅜"		3.70
Insulating board	.33	
Insulating fiberboard, 25⁄32"		.42
Metal lath and plaster, ¾"		4.40
Mineral or glass wool	.27	
Plywood, ⅜"		2.12
Plywood sheathing, 5⁄16"		2.56
Slate, ½"	10.00	20.00
Soil	7.00	
Steel	312.00	
Stone, 1"	12.50	
Stucco, 1"	12.50	12.50
Tile or terrazzo	12.00	
Wood shingles		1.28
Wood, fir, 25⁄32"	.80	1.02

LOOSE-FILL INSULATION

Almost all the common insulating materials—the mineral wools, expanded mica, redwood bark, sawdust and planer shavings—are made in this form. Loose-fill is delivered in bags and may be poured in place, or packed by hand into the small places around window frames and

Five types of insulating wool. In the upper right are the enclosed roll blankets. These fit snugly between framing members simply by unrolling. For insulating floors, the blankets can be laid between joists without tacking. In the upper left-hand corner are economy roll blankets, made without perforated breathing paper. Enclosed batts, lower left, are shorter in length than the blankets, making overhead installation easier. Square utility batts in the center are a handy size for reaching hard-to-get-at spots, gaps around doors and windows. The pouring wool, lower right, is used for attic floors and to pack around pipes, in irregular spaces and in small openings.

Photograph courtesy of the Makers of Armstrong's Insulating Wool

chimneys. It is also blown into walls with a special blower but this job is best done by professionals.

BLANKET OR BATT

These types are made of loosely-matted plant fibers, hair, mineral wool, or crinkled paper. They come in widths to fit between wall studs, joists, or rafters, and in thicknesses from ½″ to 3⅝″. The blanket rolls are usually up to 100′ long, while the batts are up to 48″ long. They are covered on one or both sides with paper, and many manufacturers use asphalt-impregnated paper on one side to act as a vapor barrier. While the color of the insulating material may vary from white to dark gray or even brown, there is little difference in the insulating value.

"k" Factor of Flexible Insulation

The thicker the insulating material used, the lower the thermal

A 3″ thickness of vermiculite is being poured between the attic joists to help keep the house comfortable. The only tool needed is the cardboard rake, which is used to level the vermiculite to a uniform depth.

Photograph courtesy of Zonolite Co.

conductivity. There is less heat loss to the outside in cold weather and less heat gain in hot weather.

Here is a guide to the "k" factor for flexible insulation; if the "k" factor of 1″ of the material is .27, then:

$$2'' = .140$$
$$3'' = .090$$
$$4'' = .068$$
$$5'' = .054$$
$$6'' = .044$$

INSULATING BOARDS

You can use this form of insula-tion as a substitute for sheathing or for lath. If you plan to use the insulating material to finish the inside walls or if you need added stiffness in the framework, use board insulation. It is available in a wide range of sizes, from 8″ squares to sheets 4′ wide and 10′ or more long. It varies in thickness from ½″ to 2″. The edges may be cut square, beveled, shiplap or tongue-and-groove. It may be smooth or rough, light-colored or dark according to whether it is to be built into the walls or used as the finished interior wall. For the latter purpose, it may be bought in the form of panels or planks. Some insulating boards are also designed to deaden sound.

Board insulation is relatively soft. It dents and scratches easily.

Photograph courtesy of Owens-Corning Fiberglas Corp.

A recently developed home insulation, these roll blankets are made of Fiberglas and enclosed in aluminum foil. It comes in both roll and batt form in widths of 15", 19" and 23" and thicknesses of 2" and 3".

When you use it to finish inside walls, it is advisable to protect the board to chair height with wainscoting.

REFLECTIVE INSULATION

This form of insulation is usually a metal foil or foil covered surface. Unlike the other types of insulation the number of reflecting surfaces, not the thickness of the material, determines the insulating value. Because it turns back the heat by reflection, the bright surface must be installed so that it does not touch any other surface. If both sides are bright, it is best installed in the center of studs or joists spaces. Sheets of reflective insulation separated by air spaces may be used.

The metal foil can be purchased in flat or accordion-fold form. The latter is less subject to tearing and is easier to install. Since metal foil is an excellent vapor barrier, it is frequently combined with batts or blankets for that purpose. If the metal side faces an air space, it adds to the insulating value as well. There is also an aluminum-foil-surfaced plaster board on the market.

How Much Insulation

There is no set rule on how much insulation to use for best results. The amount needed varies from building to building and from one locality to another. It depends partly on the climate and to some extent on what the house is built of, how well it is built, and how well it has been kept in repair. It also depends on how well it is sheltered from cold winds, or in hot climates, how well it is shaded from the sun.

The thickness of the insulation needed depends in part on the difference between two temperatures —the average low outside temperature and the average temperature you wish to maintain inside the house.

The accompanying illustration shows how the various types of wall construction compare in insulating value. The wall with drop-siding, paper and wood sheathing gives you some idea of how additional thicknesses of wood, air spaces, and insulation increase the insulating value of the wall.

Notice the difference between walls C and E, or between walls C and F. If the entire space in the wall is not filled, the insulation may be placed so that there are two air spaces, as in E. Two small air spaces have a higher insulating value than one large one. Although air spaces add to the insulating value, they are not so effective as good fill insulation.

It is difficult to determine for any one house exactly how much fuel can be saved by insulation. Generally, of the heat lost, beside the amount that goes up the chimney, 25% is through the walls, 25% through the roof, 25% through the windows, 20% through air leakage, and 5% through the floors.

Keep Insulation Dry

If you live in the northern part of the country—any section where the average temperature in January is 35° or less—you may need to install a vapor barrier to protect the insulation from dampness. Dew will not form on the walls or ceiling of a well-ventilated house, but it may condense in the insulation in the walls or on the sheathing or siding. The insulation and wood then become damp. In time this dampness may cause the wood to rot and the paint to peel off.

Vapor barriers come in two forms:

1. *Paint barriers*—Among the best of these is aluminum paint with spar varnish as a vehicle. Paint barriers are used as finishes on inside walls.

2. *Membrane barriers*—Usually a shiny-surfaced, asphalt-treated kraft paper or felt, smooth-surfaced roll roofing, or one of the metal foils.

When it is put in just right, a good membrane vapor barrier will last the life of the house. Since ordinary tar paper and roofing felts are not vaporproof, they will not serve as vapor barriers. Some insulations come with vaporproof paper or foil on them.

Put the paint type of vapor barrier on the inside surface of the wall and the underside of the ceiling. Use asphalt-base paint only where it will not show, because it is difficult to paint over it.

Apply membrane vapor barrier or reflective insulation when used as a vapor barrier to the inside of the studs. Put it underneath the inside of the wall finish. Fasten it carefully around all openings and lap and seal the edges. This will keep vapor from getting through to the insulation.

Ventilation

Insulation is not complete without ventilation. When your house is tightly built, weatherproofed, and insulated, it is more necessary than ever to have good ventilation. You will need controlled ventilation through all parts of the house to carry stale air and excess moisture. You will need ventilation in the kitchen to get rid of grease and cooking fumes as well. Opening doors and windows and using electric ventilating fans to force out the warm air are the usual methods of ventilating homes.

Attic vents help cool the house. The space above an insulated ceiling should be ventilated to allow the removal of any water vapor which may be present. Plan vents of about 4 square feet of clear opening for each 1,000 square feet of attic floor space. In a small house this will be two vents, each at least 24"x28". Even larger vents are desirable. Put vents near the top of the gable. In warm climates many builders use screened vents between rafters under the eaves.

Vents may be placed under eaves.

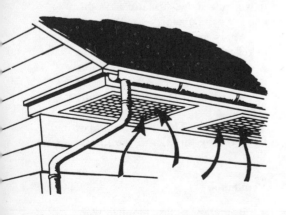

Vents in gable help keep attic cool.

Increased efficiency of attic insulation can be assured by proper installation and sufficient ventilation of space between insulation and roof. Figures 1, 2, and 3 show methods of applying blanket insulation in new and existing homes. Application of insulation directly between entire length of rafters from cornice to roof ridge should be avoided unless unobstructed ventilation can be provided between insulation and roof. In new construction, ends of the insulation should be sealed to plate. In existing homes, where this may be difficult, the blanket should be cut slightly longer than space to be insulated, so it can be tucked in as in Figures 1-A and 2-A. Where attic space is to be used, install insulation as in Figures 2 or 3. Proper construction at intersection of knee wall with floor is indicated in Figure

3-A. Where attic floor has been previously insulated, space between insulation and sub-floor should be insulated as shown in 3-B.

Ventilation of attic space may be accomplished by various methods, but most common is the wall louver jn Figure 4. Inside of louver may be equipped with a hinged door operated by rope and pulley so it may be partially closed in winter —Figure 5. Ventilation of flat roofs is accomplished by a combination of wall louvers and roof ventilator as shown in Figure 6. The attic of a hip roof may be ventilated as shown in Figure 7. Air is admitted through screened openings in projecting eaves and exhausted through special metal roof vents, thereby increasing the efficiency of the insulation.

Also see *Attics*.

An attic fan will carry off summer heat rapidly and help cool the whole house.

Where vents serve chiefly to get rid of summer heat, build them so that they can be closed in winter. Some ventilation, however, is needed under an insulated roof at all times. It keeps dew from forming on the under side of the roof.

Vents are also needed in all foundation and curtain walls.

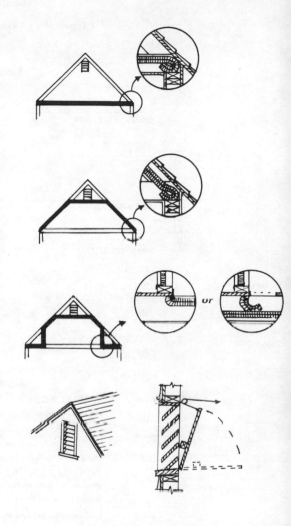

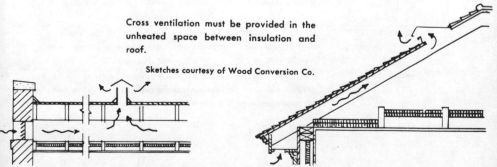

Cross ventilation must be provided in the unheated space between insulation and roof.

Sketches courtesy of Wood Conversion Co.

Insulation
Classified by Types and Uses

Loose Fill

DESCRIPTION	WOOD FIBER comes in bales; expands when opened.
GOOD TYPE FOR . . .	. . . spreading on attic floors; between walls and studs.
ADVANTAGES	Can fill wall space completely, giving extra insulation and fire protection.
DRAWBACKS	Provides no vapor barrier. Not so widely available as some other types.
HOW TO USE IT	Pack between joists or studs. Vapor barrier paper may be added if needed.

Blanket

DESCRIPTION	MINERAL-WOOL blankets may be rock, slag or glass wool.	WOOD-FIBER MATT comes in long rolls completely enclosed in paper.
GOOD TYPE FOR . . .	. . . use where framing is exposed. All blanket types may be used over ceilings, inside rafters, or between studs in side walls. Rolls may be cut to whatever lengths are needed and then installed in continuous lengths without joints, providing an unbroken barrier to heat and moisture.	
ADVANTAGES	Inexpensive, widely available gives continuous vapor barrier.	Efficient, made in variety of widths for different stud spacing.
DRAWBACKS	Must be cut to size. Particles may irritate skin or nose during installation.	Necessity of cutting makes blanket type less convenient for short lengths.
HOW TO USE IT	Staple or tack into place between rafters, studs or joists. For greater efficiency, insulation should bow in enough to form an air space between blanket and wall on each side.	

Insulation

Classified by Types and Uses

MINERAL WOOL (rock, slag, or glass) comes in sacks.	VERMICULITE is expanded mica. It comes in bags.
... pouring onto attic floors where insulation usually is needed most. May be packed into irregular spaces and around pipes. Mineral wool and vermiculite are excellent for insulating walls of existing homes.	
Usually least expensive and widely available. Easy to use.	Very easy to pour. Excellent for filling hollows in masonry walls.
May irritate skin and sinuses when being used. Provides no vapor barrier.	Provides no vapor barrier. May be slightly more costly than some loose fills.
For ceilings, pour insulation between joists. Rake it level with tops of joists or to uniform lesser thickness with home-made cardboard tool.	

COTTON insulation comes as a flame-proofed blanket.	FIBROUS BLANKET is sold as a compressed roll.
. . . use where framing is exposed. All blanket types may be used over ceilings, inside rafters, or between studs in side walls. Rolls may be cut to whatever lengths are needed and then installed in continuous lengths without joints, providing an unbroken barrier to heat and moisture.	
Lighter weight and higher efficiency than most types. Very clean to use.	Compact to carry, non-irritating, easy to cut and handle, may be cut to odd widths.
Somewhat more expensive than most insulations.	Ordinary type may need added vapor barrier in cold climates. (Reflective type has barrier.)
or tack into place between rafters, studs or joists. For greater ncy, insulation should bow in enough to form an air space be- blanket and wall on each side.	First expand by pulling to full length. Then cut and install like other blanket types at left.

Insulation

Classified by Types and Uses

Batt

DESCRIPTION	MINERAL-WOOL batts may be glass, rock or slag.
GOOD TYPE FOR . . .	. . . walls, ceilings and roofs where framing is spaced to fit standard batts.
ADVANTAGES	Widely available, inexpensive, cut to size; vapor barrier usually is built in.
DRAWBACKS	Barrier is not continuous. Types not fully wrapped may shed irritating particles.
HOW TO USE IT	Lay between joists of attic floor. Or nail or staple to studs, using flange attached.

Reflective

DESCRIPTION	ALUMINUM powder (dull) building paper.	ALUMINUM FOIL in rolls (surface is shiny).
GOOD TYPE FOR . . .	. . . walls or under roofs where stout paper with some reflective value is wanted.	. . . insulating ceiling against heat of summer sun.
ADVANTAGES	Excellent vapor barrier and weather seal plus some insulation—at low cost. Tough, easy to use.	Excellent vapor barrier. Moderate cost. Very efficient against heat from above.
DRAWBACKS	Usually not adequate insulation by itself. Gives less sound-proofing than bulk types.	Less efficient at keeping heat in than keeping heat out, especially in ceiling.
HOW TO USE IT	Single-layer foil insulations can be tacked or stapled between studs or joists or over the faces of them. They should be bowed in to form two air spaces. Second layer may be added for more insulation.	

Insulation

Classified by Types and Uses

Rigid	Board
Cellular GLASS or asphalt-impregnated fiberboard.	STRUCTURAL insulation may be board, plank or tile.
. . . use around foundations, under edges of slabs, under built-up roofs.	. . . rooms where wall and some insulation are wanted at modest cost.
Stiffness and moisture resistance permit use where other insulations are not suitable.	Inexpensive, produce a new wall or ceiling in an unfinished room, give some insulation.
Glass type is more expensive. Board type offers less insulating value.	Do not usually have enough insulating value to use alone in cold climates.
Interior: fasten to masonry wall with asphaltic cement. Exterior: place against foundation before backfilling.	Fasten with nails, staples or special clips. Board types call for battens at joints.

Combination

MULTIPLE FOIL in two to four layers comes in rolls.	BLANKET WRAPPED in aluminum foil for double action.
. . . anywhere that framing is accessible. Especially good in hot climate.	. . . anywhere blankets will go. Top choice where temperatures are extreme both summer and winter.
Light and compact to carry, clean to handle. Small bulk lets house cool quickly in summer.	Insulation is fully protected, with vapor barrier. Foil reflects radiant heat, bulk stops conduction.
Cannot be installed after wall is finished. Costs more than many bulk types.	Combination type costs more than most bulk or reflective types alone.
With vapor barrier toward room, along one edge. Staple other edge after pulling to separate layers. Then staple ends.	Staple at sides (and preferably at ends too) between framing members. Method is the same as for plain blankets.

DRAFT STOP

OLD INSULATION

A short piece of the blanket will serve as a draft stop between the kneewall plate and old insulation. The blanket end should be stapled to the kneewall plate to hold it securely in place.

Hints on Installing Blanket or Batt Insulation

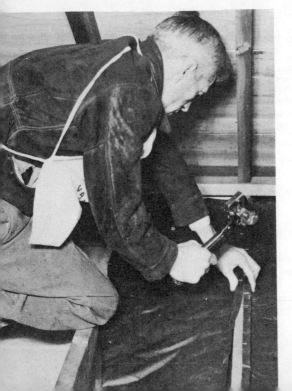

Blanket insulation being stapled to the ceiling joist. When the end is stapled, the blanket is carried up to the top of the joist where it is then stapled across the ceiling joists as shown here.

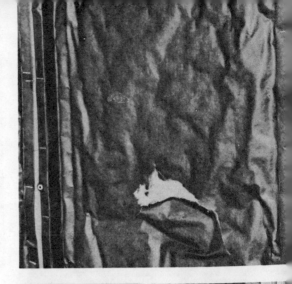

If a tear occurs during application, seal it by brushing the torn area with asphalt and covering with a strip of the blanket liner. The liner can be stapled at the edges in the usual manner. (Asphalt can be obtained from your lumber dealer.)

Small spaces under windows can be insulated last to use short lengths of blanket. The insulating wool fiber removed from the ends of the blanket is being tucked in around the window.

Photographs courtesy of Wood Conversion Co.

This second story interior has been covered with long blankets of insulating wool. The job can be done by one man using a stapling gun or hammer and nails.

1. **Top Attachment**—Fasten blanket at top with ½" staples and fastening strips. (Strips supplied with each roll.)

2. **Bottom Attachment**—Expand blanket downward and fasten at bottom with fastening strips.

How To Insulate a Wall

The blanket insulation being used here consists of many plies of soft, creped cellulose fibers treated for fire resistance to fire, moisture, vermin and fungi. It has a creped aluminum foil cover to reflect radi-ant heat and provide a vapor seal. It is compressed to one-fifth normal size for packaging, so that it can be carried easily. The blanket is stretched to full length during application.

3. **Side Attachment**—Staple fastening flange to side of studs with ½" staples through targets (squares printed at 6" intervals).

4. **Edge Closure**—Fold sealer flange over face of stud. Job is now ready for interior finish.

Photographs courtesy of Kimberly-Clark Corp.

Here is a contemporary compact kitchen for a young couple. A folding screen conceals it when not in use. Plastic-finished wood-grain hardboard is used to cover the cabinets, tongue-and-groove dusty pink planks cover the walls and white interlocking squares are used for the ceiling.

Photograph courtesy of Marsh Wall Products, Inc.

Kitchen

The kitchen is the workshop of the homemaker. In the average household, she spends the equivalent of 3 full months a year—24 hours a day around the clock—in preparing, cooking and serving food, baking cakes and pies, and washing pots and pans.

Modernizing a kitchen to make it more enjoyable to work in, to add extra conveniences and time-savers is the ideal of every homemaker. The kitchen is a room that calls for a large outlay of money, but once it is wisely built, you'll be happy you made the investment.

Until a few years ago, modernizing a kitchen meant purchasing a new refrigerator, range, a combination sink and painting the kitchen in a bright, shiny white. We have come a long way in only a few years. The most striking aspect of the contemporary kitchen is its color. White has been displaced by more sophisticated colors. Counter space has been increased. Storage has been engineered to provide maximum use

The conventional kitchen can be transformed into a bright cheery place in which to work and eat by attractive lighting, colorful decorations and easy-to-clean, matching linoleum counter tops and floor.

Photograph courtesy of Armstrong Cork Co.

The kitchen of tomorrow features new concepts of convenience and comfort for the homemaker. On the walls at the far end of the kitchen are the refrigerator and food freezer in cabinets with horizontal doors.

The cooking center features counter-top range with a dishwasher built into the cabinets. The island sink with adequate work surfaces on either side is built so that the homemaker can sit while working.

Photograph courtesy of Frigidaire Division, General Motor Corp.

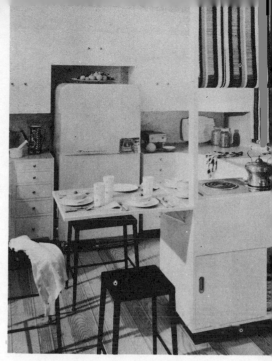

Photographs courtesy of Armstrong Cork Co.

This is a kitchen (left) in a 1923 home. The homemaker was shut off from her family by partitions separating her from the living room and dining area. The kitchen arrangement is jumbled and cramped; it was inefficient, requiring the homemaker to take a lot of unnecessary steps from the refrigerator—to sink—to stove—to work counters. What a change from the old! The kitchen (right) is incorporated into the home's living area, bringing the homemaker in closer contact with her family. Work surfaces have been increased; appliances rearranged to save her steps. Colorful bamboo blinds let in air and make the kitchen area seem bigger. The blinds also hide the clutter when guests arrive.

of all available space. Everything is within easy reach. Today's kitchen blends into the home. It is not a room apart, but a part of the home's living area.

Appliances in the kitchen have gone contemporary! Everything has been redesigned to make life-in-the-kitchen easier and more efficient. Exhaust fans under colorful hoods over the kitchen range remove the grime and dirt as well as unpleasant smoke and cooking odors. In the more modern kitchen, the old range-oven combination has been displaced by counter-top ranges and built-in ovens. Automatic devices practically make the kitchen run itself.

The refrigerator has a new companion in the kitchen. While combination refrigerator-freezers are very popular, many homemakers prefer having an upright freezer in addition to the refrigerator in the kitchen. The white look is passing on. Appliances in attractive colors are gaining in popularity. Models have been introduced where fabric can be added over the appliance door, so that the refrigerator can match the kitchen curtains.

Decorative hoods over the stove put an end to the annoyance of smoke-filled kitchens. They draw off all cooking smoke and vapor, keeping the walls free of grime and dirt. The hoods come in stainless steel, copper or enamel on steel, available in a variety of colors to match any kitchen decor.

Built-in Kitchen Closet

The traditional kitchen has many base and wall cabinets; after the refrigerator, sink and range have been set into place, there is practically no unbroken wall area left. Here is an unusual treatment of a kitchen. This "all-in-one" kitchen closet is one of the best ways of storing kitchen utensils, groceries and cleaning equipment. When it's time to prepare a meal, the doors are opened and everything needed is within easy reach. After the meal, the doors are closed and one end of the room becomes a delightful picture wall. The colorfully decorated doors add a pleasant note to the kitchen area, far different from the pantry entrance found in many older homes.

If you are artistically inclined, you can paint your own attractive door. However, if you feel out of

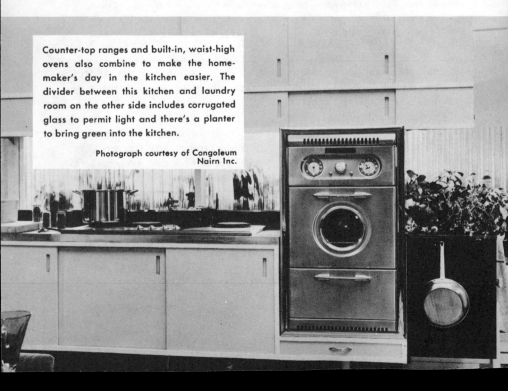

Counter-top ranges and built-in, waist-high ovens also combine to make the homemaker's day in the kitchen easier. The divider between this kitchen and laundry room on the other side includes corrugated glass to permit light and there's a planter to bring green into the kitchen.

place in a painter's smock, you can buy attractive murals in the form of wallpaper and apply these to the door. You can also buy murals in outline form, glue them to the doors, and then paint them yourself following the instructions.

This pantry wall is designed for greatest efficiency. Notice the effective use of hooks to hang utensils and pans. Note, too, the way the lids are stored in the lower part of the door on the right. These are ideas you can borrow and put to use in your existing kitchen.

Even if you don't have space inside of a wall, you can add a wall storage unit to your existing wall. Two doors, made of ¾″ plywood with 1x6 or 1x8 "frame" pieces, can be hinged to a wall. Shelves, perforated hardboard and other kitchen convenience racks can be combined to provide ample additional storage. If you cannot use the entire wall, use only part.

On the following pages you will find many more ideas for getting the most out of existing storage space; you'll find extras for the wall.

Kitchen— Basic Layouts

The efficient kitchen has adequate storage, ample counter space and is arranged to save the homemaker unnecessary steps. While the size and location of the kitchen often determines the layout, you can generally make modifications to produce more efficiency.

A single wall kitchen is a natural choice for a narrow space and one of the four basic arrangements you can follow. The sink, traditionally set below a window, is flanked by cabinets with the refrigerator and range at either end.

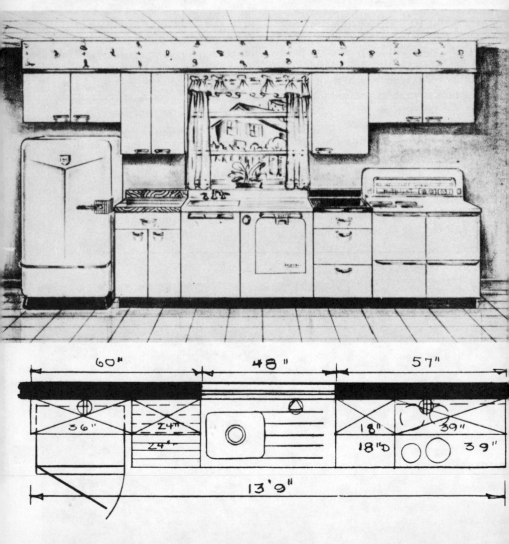

The layout of the kitchen is determined by the arrangement of the appliances and cabinets within the room. All the units can be set against one wall, or two walls or three. Here are four different layouts commonly found in homes:

1. The single wall with the sink in the center and the range and re-

A two-wall kitchen design makes an agreeable solution for some families who must build their kitchens in a room which is narrow but permits a greater choice of work center locations than is possible when a single wall arrangement must be used. Three major pieces of equipment—range, dishwasher-sink, refrigerator—fit into a triangle pattern which leaves adequate counter and work space, yet places them in convenient step-saving positions. The disadvantages of this kitchen design is that the traffic lane to the outside entry passes through the work area.

Sketches courtesy of Hotpoint, Inc.

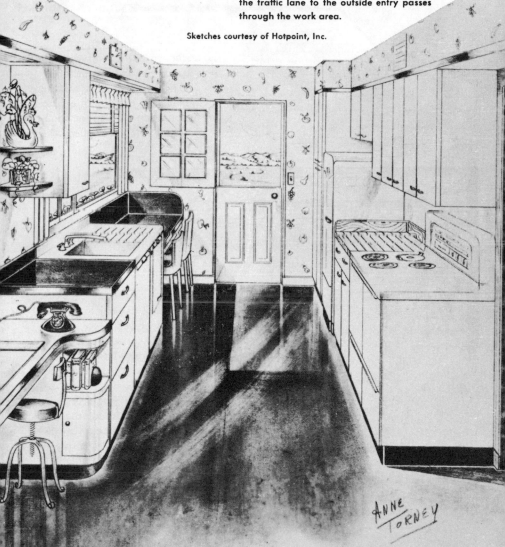

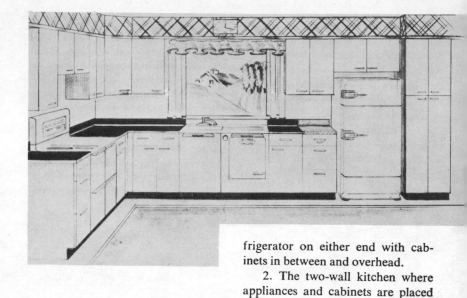

frigerator on either end with cabinets in between and overhead.

2. The two-wall kitchen where appliances and cabinets are placed on two opposite walls in the room.

3. The L-shaped kitchen where

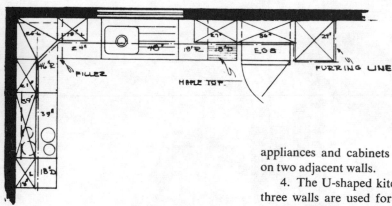

L-shaped kitchens are one of the basic designs which appliance engineers recommend. Correct placement of the appliances, with adequate cabinet and counter space, makes this type of a kitchen a pleasant room in which to work.

appliances and cabinets are placed on two adjacent walls.

4. The U-shaped kitchen where three walls are used for the necessary equipment of the kitchen.

Manufacturers have spent considerable sums and engineers numerous hours in planning the positioning of the different appliances—the range, sink and refrigerator—in the kitchen. You will find many different arrangements within this section. If you need additional help,

The U-shaped kitchen design makes best use of all available space for many families. This basic arrangement is compact, yet provides adequate storage and counter space for "assembly line" food preparation beginning at the refrigerator, progressing to the sink and pushbutton electric range. Center position for sink makes water convenient to both appliances. This is designed for a right-handed woman; if your homemaker is left-handed, better watch those plans.

Sketches courtesy of Hotpoint, Inc.

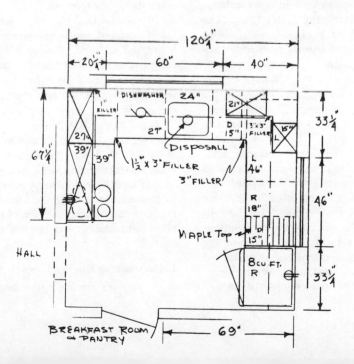

many of the appliance producers have literature designed to assist you in this phase of kitchen planning.

Remember that the kitchen is engineered for work but has to look attractive as well. Combining these two factors is an art, and when you consider that you have to add work counter space and cabinets for storage, you can readily see that planning based on experience is essential. The homemaker, herself, is often a source of many good ideas. After all, she is the one who will have to "live" in the kitchen!

Layout and Open Living

With the contemporary trend toward making the kitchen part of the family living area, modifications are often necessary in the traditional layout of the kitchen. The basic shapes—one-wall, L-shaped, U-shaped, two-wall—still remain. However, the walls in many contemporary kitchens aren't there. The rear of the kitchen cabinets forms the front of storage units in the adjoining room.

Without the floor-to-ceiling walls in the kitchen, where can the cabinets be hung? The basic problem in most kitchens is inadequate cabinet space. What can be done?

If floor space is available, additional base cabinets can be included to compensate for the loss of wall cabinets. On the other hand, these cabinets can be hung from the ceiling and a space between the bottom of the cabinets and the top of the base cabinets can be left open, and used as a work area. Another technique is to open only part of the wall for the "open look."

While the open kitchen is exceedingly popular, there are many homemakers who still prefer privacy for their kitchens. When guests are present, what can be done with kitchen clutter? Nothing looks less inviting than a pile of dirty dishes and pots and pans left about; it certainly is not a pleasant setting for dining. However, you can do something about it.

If the homemaker cleans up and puts things away as she goes along, there is less likelihood of having clutter about. But there is also less likelihood that she will ever get out of the kitchen, let alone get the dinner ready.

Of course, she can use stove-to-table ware to cut down the need for extra pots. This not only removes unnecessary pots and pans but reduces clean-up time later. She can also use some of the attractive tableware that goes from the refrigerator directly to the table.

If you put the lights out, you won't see it! Well, that technique can be used here too! It's not necessary to put out all the lights, but if you dim the kitchen and spotlight the dining area, the clutter will be "hidden" in the dark.

You can also hide the clutter by using a vertical blind on a track attached to the ceiling or a bamboo shade that is lowered when you wish to conceal the state of the kitchen. Drapery can be used in place of the blind but make certain that it's not near the range.

Understanding Kitchen Plans

If you are buying a new house

Allowances for Clearance

Space Needed Around Various Pieces of Equipment and Furniture in Kitchen and Workroom for Safety and Ease of Work

SPACE NEEDED BETWEEN	MINIMUM ALLOWANCE (INCHES)
Sides of range and adjoining base cabinets or wall; or back of range and wall.*	0, 1, 3, 6, 12, 18, 24
Front of range, refrigerator, or sink and front of equipment or cabinets opposite.	48
Front of refrigerator and side of cabinets opposite.	36
Range top and bottom of wall cabinet above that extends 12" from wall:	
With fire-resistant material on bottom of cabinet.	24
Without fire-resistant material on bottom of cabinet.	36
Top of sink and bottom of wall cabinet above that extends 12" from wall.	24
Top of sink and bottom of wall cabinet above that extends 4" to 8" from wall.	14 to 18
Chest-type freezer and wall cabinet above.	Width of freezer lid plus 1
Top of refrigerator and wall cabinet above.	12
Front of base cabinet with drawers and wall, tall equipment, or furniture opposite, to allow:	
For standing space in front of pulled-out drawer.	36
For standing at one side of pulled-out drawer.	30
Front of cabinet and equipment or cabinets:	
If worker need not crouch to remove cabinet contents.	24
If worker must crouch to remove cabinet contents.	36
Dining table and wall or other furniture, to permit a person to push back chair, rise, and pass behind other chairs without disturbing those seated.	30
Dining table and wall or tall furniture, to allow for serving and clear passage.	36 to 40
Set laundry tubs and back or side walls, to permit working at ends or back of tub.	21 to 24
Set tub and nearby obstruction, to store wringer type washer.	30 to 36
Set tub and opposite obstruction, to allow for washer in use, and passage space.	4½ to 5½
Other desirable allowances:	
Length of food-mixing counter—	
Minimum.	36 for 25" width
For greater convenience.	42 for 25" width
Kneehole space for seated person.	18 to 22
Dimensions of seat of work chair.	14 to 16 both ways

*Space to allow varies depending on National Board of Fire Underwriters' specifications for different types and classifications of ranges as related to fire resistance of adjoining material.

or having a contractor do the major and basic modernization of your kitchen, you will undoubtedly be confronted by blueprints. Here are a few of the symbols you will find used in these plans. For additional information, refer to the section *Abbreviations—Building Terms.*

When building a new home or modernizing a kitchen, make provisions for convenient and adequate wiring. There are many kitchen appliances and even if you do not include them all at this time, you might want to add some in the future. Make sure your electrical circuits can take the load.

How Much Space?

How big should your kitchen be? There are many homemakers who prefer large kitchens while others prefer small ones. The table below gives the average size kitchens recommended for different size families. Included in this table is information on the floor size, wall

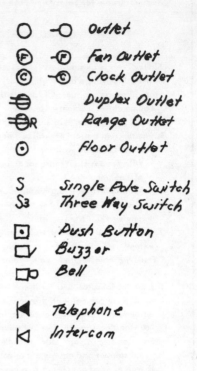

Here are various electrical symbols used in home plans, primarily those used for designation of kitchen wiring.

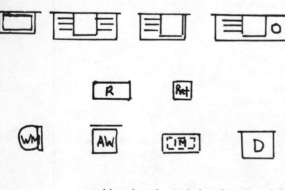

These are the symbols used for kitchen sinks and appliances. Top row (left to right): plain sink, drainboards on both sides of the sink, drainboard on left side only, combination sink and dishwasher, combination sink and laundry tub, single laundry tub and double laundry tub. Center row (left to right): range, refrigerator. Bottom row (left to right): wringer type washer, automatic clothes washer, ironing machine, clothes dryer.

and base cabinet storage and size of refrigerator. Remember, these are only guides for average families. If your homemaker likes lots of elbow room, better use these figures as a minimum.

Later in this section you will find numerous space savers for the kitchen. One way of getting more out of your kitchen is to use the walls. You can also use compact appliances that blend right into the room.

Maybe you like a dining area as part of the kitchen a dinette, for example. How much space you leave for dining depends upon the accommodations you prefer. Some families like to have a snack bar in the kitchen for a light breakfast or meal and have their regular meals in the dining room.

When modernizing your kitchen or planning one in a new home, it is best to recognize that certain clearances must be left unless you want some member of your family or a dinner guest to pop up and down every time someone has to pass by. You should allow for at least 42″ from the front end of the

Perforated hardboard makes an ideal space saver in the kitchen. Saucepans and their covers can be stored conveniently on the wall right next to the range.

chair to the wall behind. This makes it easy to get in and out of the chair and to pass behind the chair while someone is sitting in it.

However, if you have a cabinet behind the chair, you should add the door width to this basic 42″ figure so that the cabinet can be opened

How Much Kitchen Do You Need?

	————SIZE OF THE FAMILY————				
	2	3	4	5	6
Area (Square feet)	80	100	125	150	175
Wall cabinet storage (square feet)	34	40	46	52	58
Base cabinet storage (square feet)	14	17	22	26	30
Counter surface (linear feet)	10	12	14	16	20
Size of refrigerator (cubic feet)	6-8	8-11	10-12	12	14

Here's an all-in one compact unit for the small kitchen. When closed (left), it looks like a TV console fitting into the decor of any room, traditional or modern. The unit —a combination of a range, refrigerator, sink, storage cabinet plus indirect lighting for the counter top—comes in black mahogany or sand color. The unit can be placed in the center or (right) in the corner.

and closed easily. This extra room is not needed if you install sliding door cabinets.

Where there is no chair, at least 24" should be planned for between the end of the table and a wall. This permits the server to pass through conveniently.

On the accompanying page are several suggested room layouts. Examine these to see which fits your needs best and then modify it to meet your exact requirements. These plans apply not only for the kitchen or dinette but for the dining room as well.

The dining area must be provided with proper lighting and convenient electrical outlets. It is best to make provisions for shelves or storage cabinets for the toaster, electric coffee maker, electric frying pan and other modern electrical conveniences for the kitchen.

Dining area lighting should be functional and decorative. Increasingly popular are two forms of lighting for the dining area. One is the retractable reel light fixture which moves up and down above the center of the table. The other is a recessed spotlight above the dining table. Particularly effective is a light-dimmer; this unit controls the brightness of the light. With a unit such as this, you can duplicate theatrical lighting for gracious dining.

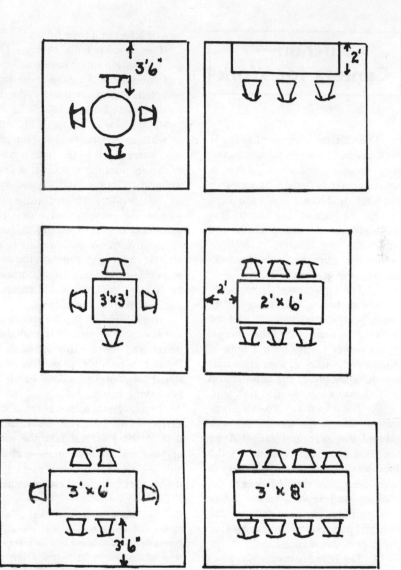

In the sketch above are six plans for dining. Top row-left: circular table must be 3' in diameter to seat 4, 4' diameter for 6 persons and 5'6" in diameter to seat 8. Top row-right: a snack bar should be 18" to 24" deep and there should be 24" of elbow space for each chair. The remaining 4 drawings show seating arrangements at square and rectangular tables. Note the two different arrangements for seating 6 persons at a table (center row-right and bottom row-left). If 3 chairs are set on each side, the table need be only 2' wide, but if you place chairs at each end, the table should be 3' wide. The latter affords more elbow room for everyone.

Kitchen— Centers for Work

The efficient kitchen of today is built around three major work centers. In more and more homes, a fourth center is finding its way into the kitchen. These centers are:

1. The food-mixing center. It is built around the refrigerator, and sometimes the freezer, as well as convenient storage cabinets for baking tins, mixing bowls, etc.

2. The sink center is generally located between the food-mixing center with the refrigerator and the cooking center with the range. Many newer homes have a built-in dishwasher, either as a separate unit which slides under the counter top or built into a combination sink unit.

3. The cooking and serving center or the range center is built around the oven and range. After the food has been prepared at the food-mixing center or washed at the sink center, it normally passes to the cooking and serving center. Here storage must be provided for the pots and pans plus related items (see list later in this section).

4. The laundry center is a newcomer in the kitchen. Gradually the laundry center is being moved out of the basement up into the kitchen to save the homemaker steps.

Work Simplification Principles

Good planning can eliminate much unnecessary work. Six ways to reduce the homemaker's expenditure of effort and time follow:

Use modern labor savers—The use of modern labor-saving utilities and equipment can take some jobs completely off your hands—do the hardest part of other tasks.

Major labor savers available with or without electricity are: Hot and cold water piped to the sink; a power-driven washing machine; a controlled-fuel range; and an automatic refrigerator. To operate water pumps and washing machines, engines may be run by windmills, fuel, or electricity. A gas, gasoline, or electric range may supplant the coal or wood range. The refrigerator may be run by gas, gasoline, kerosene, distillate oil, or electricity

In addition to the foregoing labor savers, if electricity is available, better and more easily maintained lighting is possible, as well as additional large and small pieces of labor-saving equipment.

If you cannot afford every labor-saver you need for your work, think first of the jobs that take the most of your energy and time—and decide which of these you least enjoy doing. Get help for these tasks first.

On the facing page are two unusual kitchens from contemporary plans for homes designed to blend into different sections of the country by Hotpoint. Top: the modern kitchen for a home in the South. It features a built-in oven, counter-top range and pass-through for serving into the dining room. The laundry center has been added at the opposite end of the kitchen. Bottom: the kitchen for the West features convenient arrangement of the basic centers of the kitchen with a laundry center located below large ventilated cabinets with louver doors.

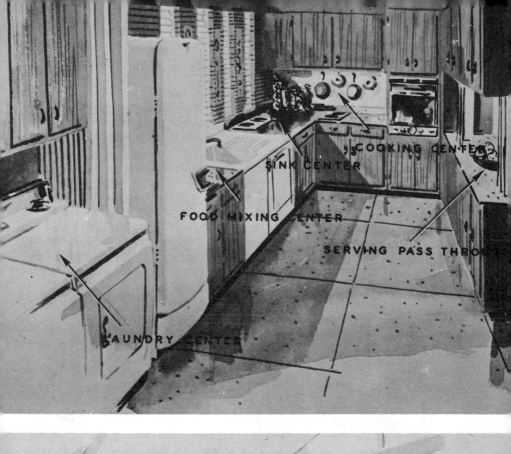

SINK CENTER
COOKING CENTER
FOOD MIXING CENTER
SERVING PASS THROUGH
LAUNDRY CENTER

LAUNDRY CENTER
FOOD MIXING CENTER
SINK CENTER

Before you buy any piece of equipment, consider the work it is to do. Is it a piece of equipment that you want to last as long as the house? Or will you replace it later when the family size changes, when improved models are available, or when you can better afford a more desirable model?

To help you select wisely there are numerous buying guides available in Federal, State, and other publications.

Plan a definite place for each activity. Having a definite place planned to accommodate each activity eliminates much of the confusion that makes work difficult. With good planning some centers can serve more than one activity. How many jobs can be done in one place without confusion depends on the length of time it takes for each one, when and how often each is done, and how work is managed.

Locate activity centers for logical sequence of work. Locate activity areas in relation to each other so that work progresses in a continuous, uninterrupted path—without crisscrossing or backtracking of work paths. This cuts down on walking and the mental and nervous energy expended.

Plan work areas that are adequate but compact. To be adequate, a room must have space enough for the size and kind of equipment wanted and for the number of persons likely to be working in the room. It should also have enough counter space, working space, and storage facilities needed for each task.

You need to know at the beginning of planning the type and size of large pieces of equipment you'll have—and the clearances their use demands.

For compactness, the dimensions of each work area should be kept as small as possible without sacrificing adequacy. When planning for compactness, consider location of doors and windows. These should be located not only for cross ventilation and good lighting on work surfaces, but also so that they won't break up continuity of equipment in work centers.

Planning adequate but compact work areas makes work go more smoothly and quickly with less tax on the worker's nervous energy. It also saves steps and reaches.

Design work centers for easy seeing and picking up of needed supplies and utensils. When you plan arrangement of storage space for each work center let three rules guide you:

First, plan enough storage for supplies and utensils at the center where first used.

Second, locate storage for most-often-used items in the most accessible places—between fingertip and shoulder height. This saves steps, stoops, reaches, and time.

Third, design the storage facilities for the articles to be kept in them.

Select interior millwork and surface materials that are easy to clean and maintain. At best, the kitchen and workroom need a lot of cleaning. Simple design and easy-to-clean, long-lasting materials lighten

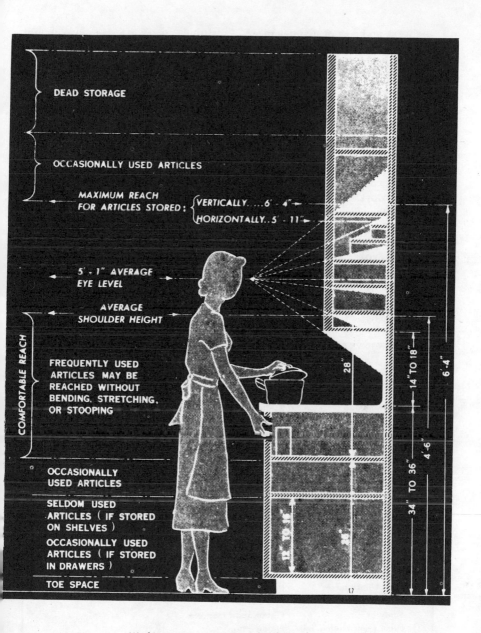

DEAD STORAGE

OCCASIONALLY USED ARTICLES

MAXIMUM REACH
FOR ARTICLES STORED : {VERTICALLY.....6' - 4"
                       {HORIZONTALLY..5' - 11"

5' - 1" AVERAGE
EYE LEVEL

AVERAGE
SHOULDER HEIGHT

COMFORTABLE REACH

FREQUENTLY USED
ARTICLES MAY BE
REACHED WITHOUT
BENDING, STRETCHING,
OR STOOPING

OCCASIONALLY
USED ARTICLES

SELDOM USED
ARTICLES (IF STORED
ON SHELVES)

OCCASIONALLY USED
ARTICLES (IF STORED
IN DRAWERS)

TOE SPACE

28"   14" TO 18"   6'-4"

34" TO 36"   4'-6"

Working at a convenient height makes
work in the kitchen less tiring. Here are
basic standards for cabinets which you can
follow when modernizing your kitchen.

the work and cost of maintenance.

Provide Best Conditions for Necessary Work

Many of the ways of saving labor listed in the preceding section also contribute to better working conditions in kitchen and workroom. However, there are other ways to make a room a better, safer, more pleasant, and more attractive place to work in.

Comfortable work heights— The right heights for work surfaces add much to ease and comfort of work. Provision should be made to enable a worker to sit down instead of stand if she wishes, because changing position while working is restful. Whether she is standing or sitting at work, a homemaker should be able to maintain good posture without muscular strain.

The right height for a work surface depends upon the height, posture, length of arms, girth, and eyesight of the person using the surface. It depends also on the kind of job to be done.

Well-lighted work surfaces— Good lighting helps to prevent fatigue and promotes safety. Work surfaces need enough light for good seeing both day and night. Windows and fixtures should be so located that light never shines directly into the worker's eyes and there are no heavy shadows on the work surface.

The amount of window glass area needed varies with the floor

Guide List For Food-Mixing Center Storage

USED DAILY	USED DURING WEEK	USED OCCASIONALLY
Bowls, mixing	Baking pans—bread,	Apple corer
Bowl scraper	cake, meat loaf, muf-	Custard cups or molds
Cutting board	fin, pie	Extra baking pans
Egg beater	Bottle and can opener	Knife sharpener
Forks, small 3-or 4-tined	Bowl, chopping	Picnic equipment
Fruit reamer and	Bowl, salad	Large pudding pan,
strainer	Casseroles	mold, or casseroles
Knives—case, paring,	Cooky sheet	Tube cake pan
slicing	Cutters—biscuit, cooky,	
Measuring cups	doughnut	
Refrigerator dishes and	Flour sifter	
bags	Food chopper or grinder	
Saucepans	Graters	
School lunch boxes	Pastry blender and	
Shears	brush	
Spatulas	Pint or quart measure	
Spoons—measuring, mix-	Pudding pan	
ing (metal and	Rolling pin	
wooden), tablespoons,		
teaspoons		

area of the room the exposure and with different sections of the country. Considering lighting only, in a region where bright sunshine prevails most of the year, as in the Southwest, the window glass area may be smaller than in other parts of the United States.

For houses in the Northeast section of this country, window glass area in a room should be equal to at least 15% of the floor area. For the Southeast and Northwest, the figure is 12½% and for the Southwest, 10%. These percentages are based on the slant of light, hours of daylight, and climate in the four sections of the country.

Lighting of the work surface is also affected by the amount of light reflected by walls and ceilings and by the amount absorbed by window curtains or lamp globes through which the light must pass. Walls and ceilings of light colors with either a dull or semigloss finish are best for reflecting a maximum of light without glare. Only in a very sunny room

Guide List For Storage at Cooking and Serving Center		
USED DAILY	USED DURING WEEK	USED OCCASIONALLY
Bread box	Cooling racks	Casseroles[2]
Coffee maker	Casseroles[2]	Chicken fryer
Everyday dishes and	Griddle[2]	Deep-fat kettle and
glassware[1]	Ladle[2]	strainer
Forks—long- and short.	Meat-slicing board	Dutch oven
handled	Roaster[2]	Griddle[2]
Fruit reamer and	Tongs	Ladle[2]
strainer[1]		Platters and serving
Fry pans		dishes of good set
Knives—meat-slicing,		Roaster[2]
paring		Steamer
Measuring cup and		
spoons.		
Pancake turner		
Platters, serving dishes		
Pot lids		
Potato masher		
Pressure cooker		
Spatula		
Teakettle		
Spoons (stirring, metal		
and wooden)—table-		
spoons, teaspoons		

[1]May be stored at different center, depending on use.
[2]This item is listed in more than one column. Best storage location depends on family food habits.

LAUNDRY CENTER

FOOD MIXING CENTER

COOKING CENTER

SINK CENTER

Hotpoint's kitchen for the Mid-West is built along two walls with a laundry center next to the sink center. Note the homemaker's corner with a convenient table-desk and chair.

Guide List for Sink Center Storage

USED DAILY	USED DURING WEEK	USED OCCASIONALLY
Coffee maker	Bottle and can opener	Apple corer[2]
Cutting board, for vegetables	Colander	Large coffeepot
Dishcloth and dishtowel racks	Double boiler	for special
Dish-draining rack (and	Funnel	occasions
drain pan)	Kettle, large	
Dishpan	Saucepan[2]	
Dish scraper	Strainer, wire, 6" to 7"	
Drinking cup or glass	Vegetable slicer	
Fruit reamer and strainer[2]		
Garbage container		
Knives—cutting, paring,		
slicing		
Saucepans[2]		
Shears		
Sink strainer		
Wastebasket		

[1] Sink-center storage provides for supplies for food preparation, cleaning, cooking, and serving.

[2] May be stored at different center, depending on use.

SINK CENTER

COOKING CENTER

FOOD MIXING CENTER

Kitchen planning for the East. Here is a U-shaped kitchen **without** the sink on the center wall. Note the unusual effect produced by this arrangement; it provides a free, long counter top for easy work the width of the entire room. Here's an interesting way to store cooking spoons, forks, spatulas and other "tools" of the chef. A perforated hardboard wall panel, decorated in espalier form, is used to hang these cooking accessories, making them easy to reach.

with a large window glass area will the colors that reflect a low percentage of light be satisfactory.

Good temperature and ventilation—For favorable temperature and ventilation, locate the kitchen on the side of the house where it is protected from the coldest winter winds, and where it will get the prevailing breezes in summer. With the house properly located, the prevailing summer winds do not blow toward it from livestock barns or poultry houses.

See that cross ventilation is provided. If good natural ventilation through windows and doors is impossible, a ventilating fan will help. An installed fan needs a duct leading to the outside. This should be kept short to reduce cost of both duct and fan. A long duct requires a more powerful and larger fan.

Safety—As fatigue is one of the chief causes of accidents, a kitchen or workroom that is planned for simplification of work provides for safety to a great extent. Faulty equipment, poor lighting, poor arrangement—all contribute to making a work place unsafe.

Kitchen— Contemporary Appliances

Making things easier for the homemaker and building appliances into the walls is an established trend in contemporary living. Here are a few of the extras for a modern kitchen. They include wall-type refrigerators and freezers, built-in

Built-in oven and refrigerator make this look like anything but a kitchen. Note the wooden cabinet doors without pulls. Special latches, Touch-Locks, work with fingertip pressure to open and close the doors.

Photograph courtesy of Revco, Inc.

Counter-top ranges used in conjunction with built-in ovens make more storage space available in the kitchen. Cabinet below range is used to store pots and pans and other cooking items.

Photograph courtesy of Caloric, Inc.

Here's an unusual contemporary kitchen with a built-in oven and wall-type refrigerator. There's a comfortable table-high surface in the corner for preparing food and a chair to sit in while the homemaker does the job.

Photograph courtesy of Revco, Inc.

ovens, counter-top ranges, work-level dishwashers, to name but a few.

Also in line with contemporary kitchen design is the camouflage of appliances. The wall-type built-ins and fold-away ranges help take away from that old kitchen look. Appliances are being made in high-style, decorator colors.

Custom-made refrigerator doors are possible within minutes. This model has a special molding to hold any fabric the homemaker selects. The job can be done with only a knife and a pair of scissors.

Photograph courtesy of International Harvester Co.

No stoop or bend with this dishwasher! This work-level unit comes in four colors and has storage cabinets below which match wall and base cabinets to achieve a custom-made appearance.

Photograph courtesy of Youngstown Steel Kitchens.

When modernizing your existing kitchen or planning one for your new home, you will find many new model appliances that look as if they belong in the living room rather than the kitchen. Make certain that you select models big enough for your family's use. If space permits, get the larger unit—you'll never know what happened to that "spare" space once you put the appliance to use.

Kitchen— Convenient Storage

About one-fourth to one-third more storage space can be added to the average kitchen without adding any additional wall and base cabinets. Unless your kitchen has been recently built and well-designed chances are that you too can add storage space easily. This does not involve the proverbial room stretcher, but is done by means of specially designed storage units.

There are many small kitchen extras which take advantage of empty door space. These units are attached to the inside face of the cabinet doors. Other units to increase storage space are attached to the underside of cabinet shelves.

Making it easier to reach the inside of cabinets is another way to increase convenient storage space. Special metal guide units can be installed within the cabinet and the shelves can be pulled out so that it's easy to reach any item, whether it is in front or in back on the shelf. Heavy drawers can be suspended on special slides, called phonograph slides; they make it possible to open and close heavy drawers with only a single finger.

Corner cabinets are frequently not used to their maximum because the homemaker finds it almost impossible to get all the way inside. Two choices are available. Either special pivot hinges and hardware can be used to make the entire closet open, thereby making all shelf space available. Or, you can use a "lazy Susan" unit with revolving shelves. These turntables, with as many shelves as you like, help make use of the wasted corners.

If counter space is at a premium, there are a number of kitchen storage extras that can be used. To keep the counter tops free for work, special hinged units can be used to make a mixer disappear into a cabinet. The baking center can be modernized with a flour sifter built into a cabinet plus a storage drawer for flour in place of the cannisters that often clutter up needed counter space.

There is no need to install new cabinets to take advantage of many of these storage extras. They can be installed easily and quickly by the average homeowner. If, however, you are planning an extensive modernization program for your kitchen, you may wish to buy cabinets with these extras already built in or add the extras yourself after the new cabinets are in place.

A truly modern kitchen with many storage conveniences. Note the revolving shelves used in the corner and the pull-out shelves in the cabinet next to it. The heavier drawers are on special slides while convenience extras are used in the wall cabinets.

Photograph courtesy of Washington Steel Products, Inc.

This unusual U-shaped kitchen provides ample space for convenient storage. Note the lid holder used on the door under the range and the bin-type compartments used for vegetable storage below the sink. Baking tins are kept in a file divider unit at the end of the cabinet.

Photograph courtesy of Armstrong Cork Co.

Revolving Corner Shelf Unit

No space in the kitchen is wasted as much as a deep corner cabinet whether it is a wall or a base cabinet. You can make all items stored in such a corner unit easy to reach by installing a unit designed for this purpose. You can buy the necessary hardware plus the metal shelves. All you have to supply are the two doors and, possibly, the existing doors can be cut to the required size.

If you are a somewhat skilled handyman, you can add a light unit inside the closet with a door switch. As soon as either door is opened, the light goes on; when the cabinet is closed, the light goes off.

A corner can be utilized for more convenient storage by the installation of revolving shelves. They are installed in just a few hours with simple hand tools.

Photograph and sketches courtesy of
Washington Steel Products, Inc.

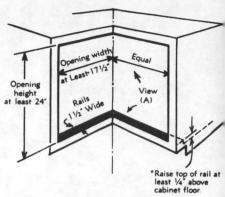

1. To install a base revolving corner shelf unit, make certain that the two cabinets meet at a right angle and that there is at least a 17½" opening for each door. The rail at the base should be 1½" wide. If your existing cabinet does not have a rail of this width, you can add the appropriate thickness of plywood or regular stock lumber, making certain that the top rail is at least ¼" above the lower shelf or cabinet floor.

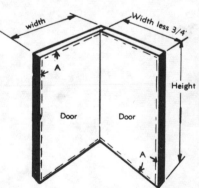

4. The door construction is next. Cut the doors out of ¾" stock, either ¾" plywood or regular 1" lumber. One door is the height and width measured in step 3. The other door is the same height but is ¾" less than the measured width. If you plan to use bullnose edges on the door, cut the edges now, shown as "A" in the sketch, using a plane or shaper. When both doors have been cut and shaped, overlap at one end and nail together.

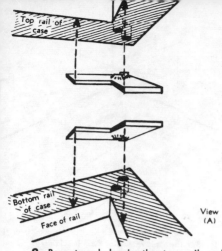

Top rail of case

Bottom rail of case

Face of rail

View (A)

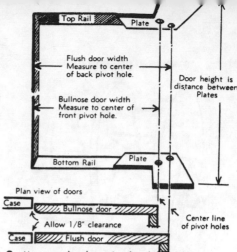

Top Rail Plate

Flush door width Measure to center of back pivot hole.

Bullnose door width Measure to center of front pivot hole.

Door height is distance between Plates

Bottom Rail Plate

Plan view of doors

Case Bullnose door

Allow 1/8" clearance

Case Flush door

Center line of pivot holes

2. Bore two holes in the top rail and then bore two additional holes in the bottom rail for the pivot plate bearings. Use the plates as templates or guides, setting them flush with the cabinet face or outside. Make certain that the plates are aligned; a plumb bob and a piece of string will help you do the job correctly. Attach the plates as shown. If doors are to be flush, use back hole of pivot; for lip-type doors use front hole of plate.

3. Measure the door size by determining the height between the two plates. The width of the door depends upon the type used. For a flush door, measure the distance from the edge of the cabinet to the center of the back pivot hole. For a bullnose door that projects ⅜" in front of the cabinet face, measure the width from the cabinet edge to the center of the front hole in the pivot plate. Allow a ⅛" clearance for the doors to open easily.

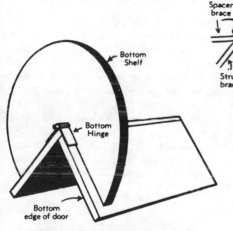

Bottom Shelf

Bottom Hinge

Bottom edge of door

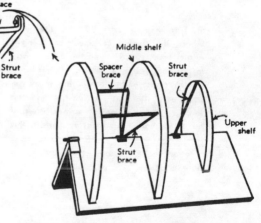

Spacer brace

Strut brace

Middle shelf

Spacer brace

Strut brace

Upper shelf

Strut brace

5. The bottom shelf and bottom hinge are now attached to the two doors which have been nailed together. Attach the hinge first so that it is flush with the bottom edge of the door; screw in place. The bottom shelf is set so that it rests on the bottom hinge. Then attach the shelf to the two doors. Screws are used if you buy the ready-made metal shelf or else nail through the door face into home-cut wooden shelves. Use finishing nails and adhesive for a strong bond.

6. The middle and upper shelves are not attached to the two doors. If you use ready-made metal shelves, use the spacer brace to determine the middle shelf spacing. Spacers, made of metal, are used to support these shelves. If you use wooden shelves, made in your own shop, it is necessary to add wooden braces to keep the shelves steady and to enable them to support a heavy load. Use thin hardboard along the perimeter of the wood shelves to form a lip or an edge.

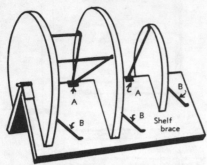

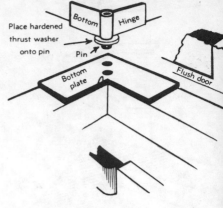

Place hardened thrust washer onto pin

Bottom Hinge

Pin

Bottom plate

Flush door

Shelf brace

7. Using a level or a square, check the alignment of the shelves and fasten the braces in place. With metal shelves, two sets of braces are used; one is used to support the shelf from underneath where the two doors meet and the others are used at the outside edges of the doors to support the shelves from above. The latter is not necessary with home-made wooden shelves if they have been firmly attached with finishing nails and adhesive.

8. Set the unit into place by inserting the bottom pivot hinge in the pivot plate attached to the bottom rail. Remember to use the front hole of the plate if you use a bullnose or lipped type of door. The back hole in the pivot plate is used for flush doors. Hold the top of the unit and see if it moves freely. Do not exert any pressure on the shelves since the door is not fully attached. Also set a washer between the hinge and the plate.

9. Turn the cabinet unit so that the back, where the two doors meet at a right angle, faces you. Holding the door steady in position, you may need a helping hand for this phase of the installation, mark the position of the top pivot hinge and the location of the holes for screws. Pre-drill the screw holes; this helps you attach the top hinge without exerting undue pressure on the entire unit. Now attach the door handles.

10. The same type of a unit can be used when installing a revolving corner shelf unit in a wall cabinet. The cabinet height from bottom to top rail must be at least 24" and the opening for each door should be as least 11½". The technique for installing the plates, measuring and cutting the doors and assembling the unit is the same as for the base cabinet. The installation of the unit in the cabinet, likewise, follows the same procedure as for base.

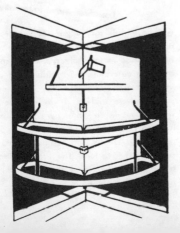

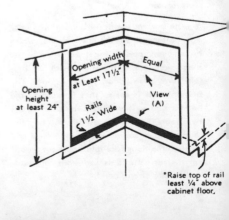

Opening width at Least 17½"

Equal

Opening height at least 24"

Rails 1½" Wide

View (A)

*Raise top of rail least ¼" above cabinet floor.

Lazy Susan Corner

A lazy Susan corner is another way to solve the perplexing storage problem faced in most homes. Here, special hardware is available to be used with conduit, which serves as the center pole. The shelves, cut out of ¾" lumber or plywood, are secured to the conduit pole by special metal brackets. If you feel that you cannot cut perfect circles you may find your lumber yard is willing to do the job at a nominal cost or some woodworking or cabinet shop may do the job for you. It is also possible to use only three-quarters of the circle for the shelves and make a revolving corner cabinet similar to the one shown on the preceeding pages.

Photograph courtesy of Armstrong Cork Co.

A lazy Susan unit makes everything in the corner cabinet easy to reach. Unit shown here has vertical dividers; these can be added or not to the step-by-step instructions which follow, depending upon your own requirements.

Shown are several suggested ways in which you can use lazy Susan revolving hardware in cabinets with doors attached or doors independent.

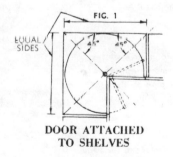

FIG. 1

EQUAL SIDES

45°   45°

DOOR ATTACHED TO SHELVES

FIG. 2

TO FIND DIAMETER OF SHELF, MULTIPLY LENGTH "A" BY 0.8. THIS ALLOWS FOR CLEARANCE. THEN TO FIND LOCATION OF PIVOT, PLACE SHELF IN POSITION IN THE CABINET AND MARK CENTER.

DOOR INDEPENDENT OF SHELVES

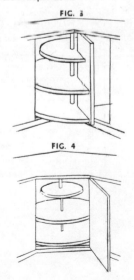

FIG. 3

FIG. 4

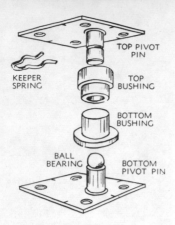

TOP PIVOT PIN

KEEPER SPRING

TOP BUSHING

BOTTOM BUSHING

BALL BEARING

BOTTOM PIVOT PIN

1. Basic hardware for lazy Susan revolving shelves. You can buy this as a kit; all you need to add is the conduit pipe and the wooden shelves cut to size and shape.

2. Fasten top and bottom plates to cabinet, making certain that the centers are plumb. One easy way to do this is by using a plumb bob with a piece of cord.

3. Place ball in grease which is packed inside bottom bushing. For length of conduit, measure from top bushing to tip of upper pivot pin less $\frac{1}{16}$" for clearance.

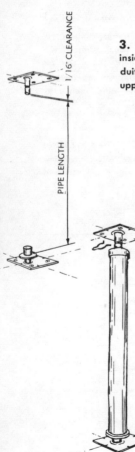

1/16" CLEARANCE

PIPE LENGTH

4. Put bottom bushing in pipe. Hold top bushing and set bottom bushing over bottom pivot pin, tilting pipe up until top bushing drops into the pipe.

5. Put keeper spring into groove of top pivot pin and check for smooth operation. Then remove spring and pipe so that the shelves can be attached to the conduit.

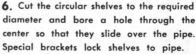

6. Cut the circular shelves to the required diameter and bore a hole through the center so that they slide over the pipe. Special brackets lock shelves to pipe.

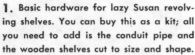

Flour Sifter

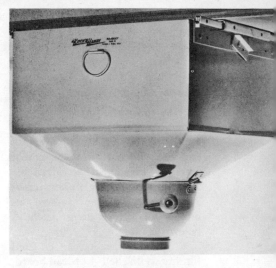

If your family enjoys luscious home-made cakes and pies, here's one kitchen built-in aid you will want. It is a flour sifter, holding up to 14 pounds of flour and ready for instant use. And it takes practically no space at all—it slides on runners fastened to the underside of any kitchen cabinet shelf. There is a companion model which is a sugar dispenser. In place of the sifter handle, the sugar unit has a small lever which regulates the flow of the sugar. Each unit is 12" high, 11" wide and 9½" from front to back. The units can be mounted under any shelf or even under the entire cabinet above the counter top, if that position is more convenient.

Like to bake? Tired of lugging a flour cannister up and down off the shelf? Here is a flour sifter that fastens to the underside of any shelf. It can be used as a sugar dispenser, if you wish. The unit slides out from under the shelf into working position and is ready for instant use. When you're finished sifting flour, merely slide the unit back under the shelf.

It's easy to install the flour sifter unit to the underside of any kitchen shelf. Here's all you have to do:

1. Secure the guides to the underside of the shelf so that the forward end of the guide is about ⅛" back from the front edge of the shelf. The inside edges should be 8⅞" apart. Make sure that the guides are square to the shelf edge and parallel to each other.

2. Slide the runners on the unit into the slides until the unit is completely in cabinet.

3. To remove the container for cleaning, hold the rear ends of both retainers up, and pull the whole unit out of the slides. Otherwise, the retainers prevent the unit from coming all the way out when it's pulled out for sifting flour.

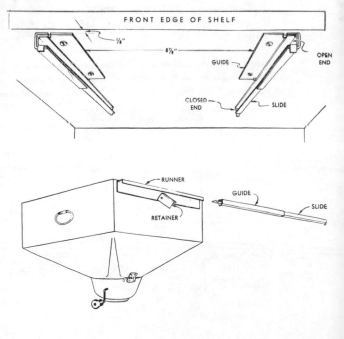

Photograph and sketches courtesy of
Washington Steel Products, Inc.

Disappearing Mixer Shelf

This mixer shelf hardware is designed specifically to swing a small appliance shelf up out of a cabinet and lock it securely at a convenient working height. The adjustable springs can be made to accommodate heavier appliances, such as mixers, or lighter items, such as typewriters.

The two brackets can be used for any width shelf—a bread board, snack bar or mixer shelf. The unit requires only 22½″ from top to bottom; this leaves room for added storage below when a disappearing shelf is added in a base closet in the kitchen. A simple trigger release permits you to close the unit by lowering back into the cabinet. However, the lock mechanism is strong enough to hold the shelf in operating position even when pressure is applied on the shelf so that there's no worry about its giving way under a load.

Here's the handy disappearing mixer shelf ready for use. It requires only 22½″ of vertical space for mounting.

Below are several other uses for the disappearing mixer shelf hardware. The tension springs can be adjusted.

Photograph and sketches courtesy of
Washington Steel Products, Inc.

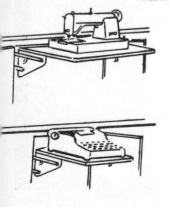

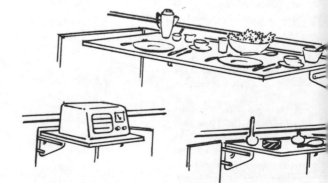

① MINIMUM SPACE REQUIRED

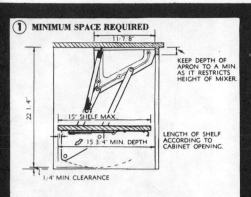

11⅞"

KEEP DEPTH OF
APRON TO A MIN.
AS IT RESTRICTS
HEIGHT OF MIXER.

22 1.4"

15" SHELF MAX.

15 3/4" MIN. DEPTH

LENGTH OF SHELF
ACCORDING TO
CABINET OPENING.

1/4" MIN. CLEARANCE

② CABINET OPENING

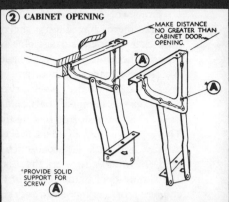

MAKE DISTANCE
NO GREATER THAN
CABINET DOOR
OPENING.

*PROVIDE SOLID
SUPPORT FOR
SCREW Ⓐ

③ LOCATION AND FASTENING

LOCATE PLATES
AGAINST FRONT RAIL
AND UNDERSIDE OF
COUNTER TOP. SEE
FIG. 1 FOR SIDE VIEW.

FASTEN AT
TOP AND SIDE.

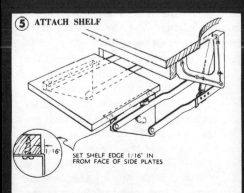

NOTE:
KEEP SIDE PLATES
PARALLEL WITH
EACH OTHER.

④ SHELF SIZE

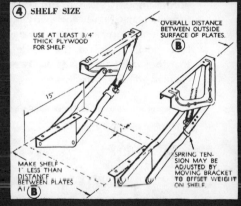

USE AT LEAST 3/4"
THICK PLYWOOD
FOR SHELF

OVERALL DISTANCE
BETWEEN OUTSIDE
SURFACE OF PLATES.
Ⓑ

15"

MAKE SHELF
1" LESS THAN
DISTANCE
BETWEEN PLATES
AT Ⓑ

SPRING TEN-
SION MAY BE
ADJUSTED BY
MOVING BRACKET
TO OFFSET WEIGHT
ON SHELF

⑤ ATTACH SHELF

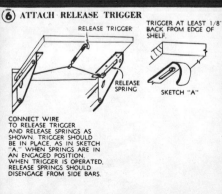

1/16"

SET SHELF EDGE 1/16" IN
FROM FACE OF SIDE PLATES

⑥ ATTACH RELEASE TRIGGER

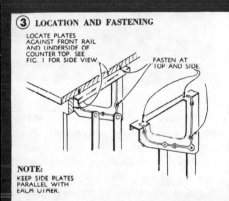

RELEASE TRIGGER

TRIGGER AT LEAST 1/8"
BACK FROM EDGE OF
SHELF.

RELEASE
SPRING

SKETCH "A"

CONNECT WIRE
TO RELEASE TRIGGER
AND RELEASE SPRINGS AS
SHOWN. TRIGGER SHOULD
BE IN PLACE, AS IN SKETCH
"A," WHEN SPRINGS ARE IN
AN ENGAGED POSITION.
WHEN TRIGGER IS OPERATED,
RELEASE SPRINGS SHOULD
DISENGAGE FROM SIDE BARS.

A Bin-Storage Kitchen

Everywhere you turn in this kitchen there are sliding shelves, drop-door cabinets, storage bins and other niches used for storage space. All of these spaces are handy to the housewife. Note the use of drop-doors on the cabinets, particularly the one used for storing baking tins. There are vertical dividers to keep the tins upright and special clips to hold the muffin tins on the door. The sliding shelf in the center of the cabinet provides increased working counter space and is easy to incorporate into any kitchen. Bin storage is particularly handy for many bulk items in the kitchen and you can obtain metal liners for the inside so that they can be removed easily and cleaned whenever necessary.

Photographs courtesy of Armstrong Cork Co.

Pull-Out Panels

Storage space in the base cabinet is exceedingly convenient. By using tambour sliding doors (see *Furniture* for how-to), the closet can be opened and there are no doors to get in the way. Everything is easy to reach as each shelf slides out. Notice the dividers on the left for platters and the pull-out compartment on the right.

The open shelves in place of the conventional wall cabinets are designed so as to make maximum use of every inch of space. In the center section, special racks are used on the top shelf to hold stemware, while on the shelf below, another type of rack is used for bulk storage of cups. Both protect the delicate items and yet permit full use of the limited space to store many items.

Photograph courtesy of American Cabinet Hardware Corp.

More Kitchen Ideas

1. Designed for peninsula or island arrangements in "open" planned homes, these cabinets have double doors on both sides. There is easy access to dishes and other contents from the kitchen or the dining-living areas.

2. Perforated hardboard not only adds a decorative effect to a wall but also provides space for storage. There are many different hooks which can be used with this type of board. This is only one example of what can be done with perforated board over a stove.

3. Adequate lighting is vital in kitchen work areas. There are special light units which fit below wall cabinets to illuminate work counter surfaces. Although only a single unit is used here, you may prefer to use a complete row under all the cabinets.

4. Decorative wood-grain wallboard is used behind the stove because it is easily wiped clean with a damp cloth. A row of six-drawer spice cabinets hold cooking necessities and add a decorative touch above the counter top kitchen range.

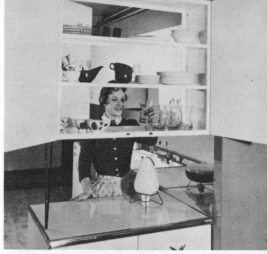

Photograph courtesy of Youngstown Steel Kitchens.

Photograph courtesy of Masonite Corp.

Photograph courtesy of Marsh Wall Products, Inc.

Kitchen—
Extras for Comfort

Adequate ventilation in the kitchen is a must! Kitchen exhaust fans can be installed in a variety of ways. It is no longer necessary to mount the fan directly in the outside wall and have the inside of the fan shown. There are models which fit into a special hood unit mounted over the stove, others that fit into the ceiling while others are mounted above the wall cabinets in the dead space area.

Kitchen ventilating fans are easy to install. Cutting through the exterior wall of the house is not exceptionally difficult except where the wall is masonry. Most homeowners find it difficult to remove the brick because of the lengthy procedure involved when the job is done by hand with a star drill and hammer. Using a masonry bit and an electric drill speeds the work. Most kitchen fans producers have complete step-by-step literature available to help you do this job no matter what type of a wall your home has.

Kitchen ventilating hoods fit almost any cabinet and come in stainless steel or copper finish. Mounted directly above, in the cabinet, is a ventilating fan which removes cooking odors, smoke and heat.

Photograph courtesy of Trade-Wind
Motorfans, Inc.

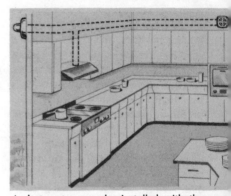

A duct system can be installed with the fan mounted on the outside of the house. This fan does multiple duty—it removes heat and smoke from the built-in oven area and cooking odors from the range.

Photograph courtesy of Stewart Industries, Inc.

Ventilators in the ceiling have been used primarily in the bathroom but they are becoming more popular in the kitchen. Since hot air naturally rises, the kitchen ceiling fan does an effective job.

Photograph courtesy of Pryne and Co., Inc.

Homemaker's Desk

During the course of a busy day, many a homemaker finds it necessary to sit down to make up shopping lists, telephone stores and friends, and she often likes to write a short note to a friend or relative. Providing desk space in the kitchen is a simple task. Here are several ideas which can be incorporated into a kitchen. If you have your own plans and designs, you can find how-to help by referring to the sections on *Built-ins* and *Furniture*.

The handy service desk in the photograph below is built out at the end of the partition that separates the kitchen and laundry areas. The desk adds further convenience in planning menus, arranging household accounts, etc.

The back, sides and front of the desk can be cut out of ½" plywood or 1" lumber stock. Use simple butt joint corners, particularly if you are going to paint the desk. These corners are easy to make and the end-grain of the plywood or lumber can be filled with wood filler before painting.

The bottom of the desk can be fitted into rabbets cut into the back, sides and front. It should be made of at least ⅜" stock, while the desk top should be made of ¾" plywood or lumber. A pair of butt hinges is all that's needed plus a desk lid support to hold the top open when it is necessary to make use of the large storage compartment underneath the desk top.

Photograph courtesy of Armstrong Cork Co.

Simple but Functional

This easy-to-make desk, shown in the photograph on the right, is merely an extension of the counter top of the adjoining cabinet plus a shelf. Note that the desk is conveniently located next to the telephone and the intercom system for the house.

To make this simple desk, you can build the entire unit, cabinet and all, or use a ready-made cabinet. If you use a ready-made cabinet, remove the top and replace it with a long glued-up board or a piece of ¾″ plywood big enough to form the desk top and to cover the cabinet. The outside support for the desk is also made out of a piece of ¾″ plywood and jointed to the top with a simple butt joint. The shelf can be dadoed or fastened in place with adhesive and screws. For a durable, easy-to-clean surface, you can apply a plastic surface over the desk top, such as Formica.

Photograph courtesy of The Formica Company.

Executive Desk

It's possible to use a complete built-in desk in place of base cabinets in the kitchen when there is ample storage space. The desk, shown in the photograph on the left, is built to match the rich wood grain of the cabinets. Note that it is a proper writing height, 29″ to 30″, whereas the corner cabinet counter surface is about 36″ high.

You can make this executive-style desk by following the how-to details in the sections on *Built-ins* and *Furniture*. For step-by-step instructions for the drawers, see that section in this encyclopedia. It is best to make this type of desk out of the same material as the cabinets for it then becomes part of the room and not something extra.

Photograph courtesy of Marsh
Wall Products, Inc.

Kitchen—
Pull-Out Counters

One way of gaining additional space in the kitchen is by having work and snack counters disappear into the cabinets when not in use. These produce a striking effect on guests who are always intrigued by the novelty of such built-ins in the kitchen. While they look complex, they are easy to build.

There are several ways to achieve this disappearing effect. First, the counter can swing in and out of a cabinet. Second, the disappearing counter can slide in and out, and, third, the counter can be hinged to fold over the existing counter top. The latter is particularly useful in smaller kitchens where deep counter space is not possible because of limited space.

The swing-out snack counter pictured on this page can be built by cutting two surfaces to match the shape of the cabinet counter top. Both are finished, in this case, with linoleum tops and metal side edging. The snack counter is pivoted to the cabinet tops with a countersunk bolt. The new top is set over it and secured only at the ends where it will not interfere with the movement of the swing-out snack counter.

The fold-away counter, also featured on this page, is made by building an extra top for the cabinets and finishing it on both top and bottom. It is hinged to the regular cabinet top with simple butt hinges. To support the hinged top, pull-outs are added below. These are simple 1x2's which slide into the cabinet between counter top and drawers below.

Photographs courtesy of Armstrong Cork Co.

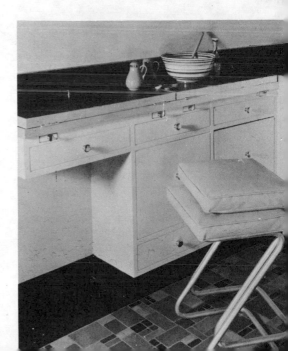

This unusual kitchen not only features hinged shelves but a novel arrangement of cabinets. A U-shaped work center is the answer to a kitchen with not enough wall space. Extra storage is gained by turning the ends of the work center into the room. Note the two hinged shelves at the end of each counter. The lower ones serve as a table for the younger set, while the upper ones increase counter work space.

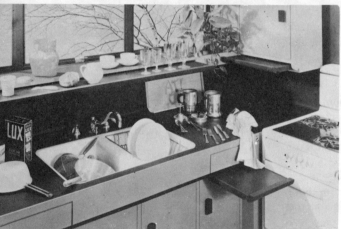

If the sink center does not have sufficient counter space alongside, you can add this space with pull-out shelves. In this kitchen, there is a pull-out shelf on each side of the sink which can be used to hold glasses, cups and other items before or after they are washed and dried. The shelf can be secured in any number of ways, just as a drawer. See section on **Drawers** for techniques of making the shelf slide.

Kitchen— Space Savers

There are many products available on the market today which can help you get more out of your existing kitchen. A screwdriver is frequently the only tool needed, although a drill and bit to drill the pilot holes for the screws is helpful.

On this and the following pages are but a few of the items which you can obtain for your kitchen. In every case, unused space is put to work or kitchen items are stored in more compact and more convenient fashion. If you browse through the stores or catalogs, you will undoubtedly find many more. In fact, if you look through your kitchen and decide upon what you'd like, chances are that you'll find a product to do the job.

Many of these items, although designed for the kitchen, can be used successfully in other parts of the house. Some can be adapted for use in the laundry room, bathroom, workshop; others can be used in built-ins. The sliding pan storage rack, for example, has been used by handymen to hang a set of open-end or Stilson wrenches, while an amateur photographer has used the disappearing towel rack to hang negatives on to dry. Just look them over and you're bound to come up with many other uses for these space savers.

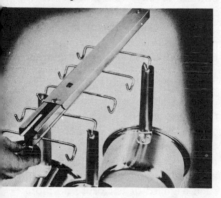

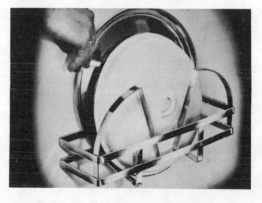

This disappearing pot holder can be attached to the underside of any shelf or the counter top of a base cabinet. It holds 10 pans but takes only 5¾" in the width and 18" in the length.

Do all the pot lids come tumbling out when you reach for one? This lid holder can be fastened to the back of any cabinet door. It's 12" wide and can hold lids of any pot, no matter how big.

Photographs courtesy of Washington Steel Products, Inc.

Many homemakers like to keep wet and soiled dish towels out of sight. Here's the item to do just that—it's a disappearing towel dryer, 19" long with three telescoping rods.

Step-on garbage cans and cabinet sinks with hinged doors just don't mix. You have to raise the lid by hand. But here is a pop-up can that mounts on the door. As you open the door, the lid opens; shut the door and the lid closes by itself.

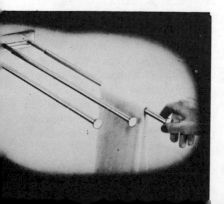

Kitchen— Safety Checklist

Thought given to providing for safety in a kitchen and workroom, when these rooms are planned, can do much to prevent such accidents as falls, cuts, fires, burns, collisions, electric shock, and asphyxiation. The following are main points to check.

General Room Planning

1. Rooms planned for work simplification.

2. Adjoining rooms on same level, if possible; no raised thresholds. If rooms must be on different levels, a minimum of three steps between levels, with steps well lighted.

3. Play space for children within sight of mother while she works —but outside work and traffic areas.

4. Doors—Located to provide unobstructed, quick exit from room and house in case of fire.

Located to keep traffic out of work areas, to swing back against walls or side of equipment (or use sliding doors), and so they do not interfere with each other. Screened.

5. Windows—Of sufficient size and located to provide for good visibility at all work centers.

Located to provide for cross ventilation. Will open enough to supply needed ventilation and comfortable temperatures. Screened.

6. Floors—Even, level, nonslippery surfaces that will not splinter, crack, or become uneven.

Equipment Selection

1. Smooth, even surfaces, not likely to splinter or develop jagged edges.

2. Rounded corners on exposed edges of cabinets and other large equipment.

3. Fire-resistant material on bottom of any wall cabinet closer than 36" above range top.

4. All electrical equipment, appliances, cords, and plugs approved by the Underwriters' Laboratories, Inc.

5. All gas appliances and accessories approved by the American Gas Association.

6. Driving parts of mechanical equipment so guarded that user is not exposed to accidental contact with moving parts. Any opening in such a guard or enclosure no more than ⅜" wide.

7. Any equipment involving feeding of food or clothes into machine, and any cutting or slicing mechanism on any food-preparation equipment, so designed or guarded that operator's fingers need not be endangered.

8. Doors on wall cabinets narrow, sliding, or folding—so they do not project beyond counter edge. Safety locks on revolving shelf cabinets—for children's protection.

9. Ranges, electric or gas— With well-insulated, temperature-controlled oven. Surface heating units far enough apart for use of a large utensil without displacement of an adjoining utensil.

Control switches or gas cocks so located that a person can operate them without reaching across sur-

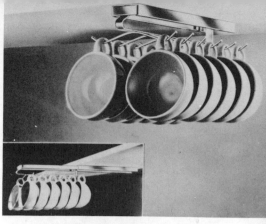

face-heating units on the range.

Safety cock on every burner of gas range. Automatic ignition for gas range surface burners.

10. Clothes washers, automatic—Inlet waterpipe high enough above water level in the machine to insure that wash water is not siphoned back into water supply system.

Safety lock on cover of top-opening washers if design of spinner basket is such that it might be thrown out when the machine is operating and the top is opened. Safety lock on door of front-opening washers to keep children from opening them.

11. Clothes washers, nonautomatic—Safety release device on wringer, that is readily accessible in any wringer position, that is easily operated, and that will work when wringer is under a heavy load.

12. Ironer—With a dependable and easily operated release mechanism for separating ironing and heating surfaces and provision for separating surfaces when current fails. With ends of shoe heated separately and thermostatic controls on all heating units. With indicating light to show when current is on.

13. Iron, electric—With automatic heat control. For iron without safety heel or side, a stand of metal or asbestos should be provided.

Handy storage of paper towels and waxed paper is a must in any well-run kitchen. This functional unit can be fastened to the back of any door or even to the wall.

Kitchen Space Savers

Storing cups in a kitchen cabinet invariably becomes a problem—you just waste the space above each stack. Well, this sliding unit can be fastened to the underside of a shelf and it holds 12 cups.

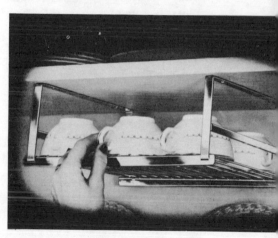

Here's another way to store cups. This open-wire shelf is secured to the underside of any closet shelf and the cups fit on it. The unit is 10" from front to back, 12" wide and 4½" deep.

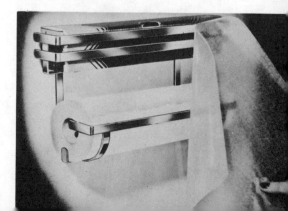

14. Step stool—Of firm construction, with nonslippery step surfaces.

15. Fire extinguisher—Easy to handle, with a chemical whose fumes are not noxious in close quarters.

Equipment Location

1. Ranges—Located and installed to conform with Code of National Board of Fire Underwriters. Surface heating units at least 2′ away from any curtained window unless bottom of curtains is held on rod.

Table top on each side of range surface-heating units to aid in keeping handles out of reach of children, and out of way of passersby or swinging door.

Coal or wood range near chimney, with short, direct stovepipe connection to chimney—never across a doorway.

2. Refrigerator—Placed so that door opens on side adjoining counter, and can be opened wide.

3. Storage facilities—A place for pot holders, burn remedies, and salt and soda to put out flames of burning grease—within easy reach of range.

Places to put supplies or utensils that may be dangerous to small children out of their reach. These include: Special drawer section or rack for sharp knives; place for poisons and matches; place for immediate disposal of burned-out light bulbs, broken glass, and tin cans.

4. Fire extinguisher—In easily accessible location.

Provision for Safe Use of Gas

1. Gas installation to meet approval requirements of National Board of Fire Underwriters.

2. Equipment supplied with automatic shut-off that operates when the flame goes off.

3. Liquid gas or natural gas supplied with a warning odor, in case of leaking gas.

4. Portable electric fan that can be used at floor level in case of leaking liquid-gas fumes, to force expulsion of accumulated heavier than-air fumes that may asphyxiate children playing on the floor or may explode.

Provision for Safe Use of Electricity

1. Enough circuits and outlets for future as well as present needs to prevent overloading.

2. Wiring done so that it conforms with Code of National Board of Fire Underwriters.

3. Each circuit—including main circuit to house—protected with fuses or circuit breakers of rating to agree with carrying capacity of wire —to prevent overloading of wires.

4. Proper fuses—never substitutes.

5. Plug-in outlets with ground connections for grounding all major electric appliances, with 3-prong plugs that fit outlets.

6. Light switches near room entrances.

7. Flush plates of outlets of nonconducting material.

8. Outlets installed high enough to keep cords off floor, close enough to where used to make long cords unnecessary.

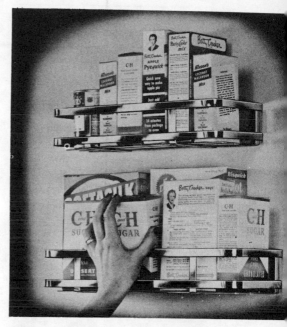

Utility shelves are always useful in a kitchen. Add another shelf and the homemaker will put it to use. Here's one to hold the cleaners on the inside of the under-the-sink door.

9. Outlets far enough from water taps so that both cannot be touched at the same time.

10. Insulation link in all pull-chain switches.

11. Wall sockets with covers or of type into which children cannot poke their fingers or metal objects.

12. Rubber-covered cords where equipment cords may be wet.

Package shelves are very similar in design to the utility shelves—only they're bigger. These shelves come in many different sizes and certainly put the inside of the doors to work.

Kitchen Space Savers

Spices can be stored on utility shelves on doors or on special open-wire shelves suspended from the underside of any cabinet shelf. These shelves can also be used to hold small packages.

Photographs courtesy of Washington Steel Products, Inc.

Kitchen—
Special Projects

The decorative motif of this charming Early American styled kitchen was inspired by the needlework samplers, which, at one time, were part of the training of almost every little girl. The theme is set by the colorful panel over the stove painted in needlework technique, and is easy to do. The design is laid out in small squares and each square is filled in with color. The sampler

cross-stitch is also adapted to the trim around the work counters, cupboards and windows in this kitchen.

An important feature of every kitchen is adequate space—both in the cupboards and on work counters. Notice the stepped-back construction at the base of the cabinets which provides a series of small drawers under the cabinets for the convenient storage of the most needed cooking ingredients. Beneath the counter, the stepped-back arrangement provides extra knee space, so that it is possible to sit comfortably while working.

The work counter, shown as a snack bar and again as a baking center in the accompanying photographs, is a modern version of the old kitchen table. In addition to providing extra work surface, it offers handy storage for cooking utensils and converts into a spacious dining table for four. A convenient lazy Susan arrangement at the end keeps cooking equipment within easy reach. The counter is mounted on casters and can be rolled to wherever it will be most useful. It can even be moved to the dining room as an extra service table. When not in use, the table is placed in a recess to form a continuous counter along the wall opposite the window.

The moving work table is 22" wide and 45" long. With the two leaves that slide under the top fully extended, the table is 54" wide. Note that these leaves are 18" wide and fit one over the other when set into the table (see detailed plans).

The lazy Susan at the end is made out of two pieces of lumber or

Photographs courtesy of Armstrong Cork Co.

plywood. One is 16″ wide and the other is 8″ less the thickness of the lumber used. This unit swings on two special pins, or you can use the pivot hinges shown earlier in this kitchen section.

The other end of the moving table is completely closed as is one of the sides. The other sidee, however, has two doors so that items stored within the table can be reached easily.

If your kitchen is conveniently located next to your outdoor dining area, it is possible to roll this table outdoors. All the items needed for cooking and dining can be set inside the table. In fact, you can make this unit as an outdoor dining piece. Instead of the linoleum top, a varnished exterior-grade plywood top should be used.

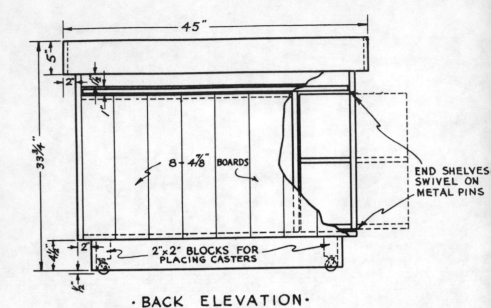

45"

5"

2"   ½

1"

33¾"

8 - 4⅞" BOARDS

END SHELVES
SWIVEL ON
METAL PINS

4½"   2"

2"x2" BLOCKS FOR
PLACING CASTERS

½"

· BACK ELEVATION ·

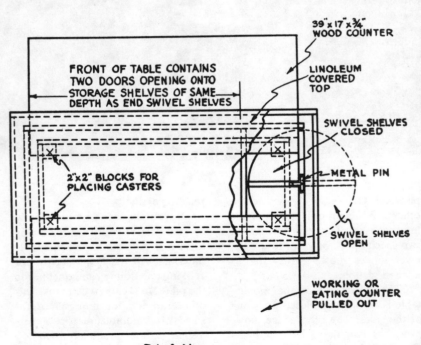

39" x 17" x ¾"
WOOD COUNTER

FRONT OF TABLE CONTAINS
TWO DOORS OPENING ONTO
STORAGE SHELVES OF SAME
DEPTH AS END SWIVEL SHELVES

LINOLEUM
COVERED
TOP

SWIVEL SHELVES
CLOSED

METAL PIN

2"x2" BLOCKS FOR
PLACING CASTERS

SWIVEL SHELVES
OPEN

WORKING OR
EATING COUNTER
PULLED OUT

· PLAN ·

Working plans for the moving work counter which can also be used as a dining table for four. The counter top, doors, apron, sliding counters and the lazy Susan end are made of ¾" plywood. The closed end and side are made of 1x5 stock. Note that 2x2's are used as blocks for the mounting of swivel casters. The use of casters makes it simple to roll the unit wherever it is needed. The top of the counter and shelves is covered with linoleum to match the floor linoleum and other counter tops.

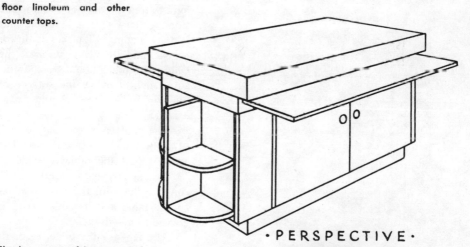

· SIDE ELEVATION ·

· PERSPECTIVE ·

SHOWING END WITH
SWIVEL SHELVES &
FRONT WITH TWO
DOORS OPENING ON-
TO STORAGE SHELVES

Sketches courtesy of Armstrong Cork. Co.

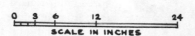

SCALE IN INCHES

Breakfast Nook

Here's an idea on how to provide a breakfast nook in your kitchen that's both attractive and practical. The table is portable—it can be stored when not in use for the legs fold up under the table top. It's ideally suited for a corner of a kitchen which is normally used as a traffic aisle. The roomy benches are easily cut from plywood and fit flush with the walls so that they take up a minimum of space in the kitchen.

MAKING THE BENCHES

The benches should be cut out of ¾" plywood or you can use 1" stock by gluing the boards as necessary.

The two end pieces can be cut in any pattern you desire. Certain re-

strictions are necessary in order to produce the proper balance.

• The height of the side should be no more than 40" above the floor.

• The width of the side at the base should be a minimum of 14".

• The width at the seat level should be at least 15" in order to hold the seat securely.

Cut the sides to shape with a coping, jig or band saw and then sand the edges smooth. If you plan to use a natural finish, you might want to apply a special plywood tape. This is made of thin strips of matching wood and is glued to the plywood edge by applying light heat to the already-glued tape.

The seat and back are cut to fit between the two sides. You can, if you're handy with tools and have the equipment, use a stopped dado joint to join the back and seat to the sides. Otherwise, use a simple butt joint, fastening all pieces with adhesive and flathead screws, the heads of which should be countersunk slightly below the surface of the wood. The seat should be at least 15" deep.

The table is made out of ¾" plywood cut into a quarter arc. The apron under the table is made of ½" stock. Two pieces are joined to run parallel with the square edges of the table and the other strip is curved to match the arc.

The legs for the table, made of 2x2's or bought ready-made, are attached to the underside with special hinges used for folding table legs. It is, therefore, possible to fold the legs and put the table away when not in use.

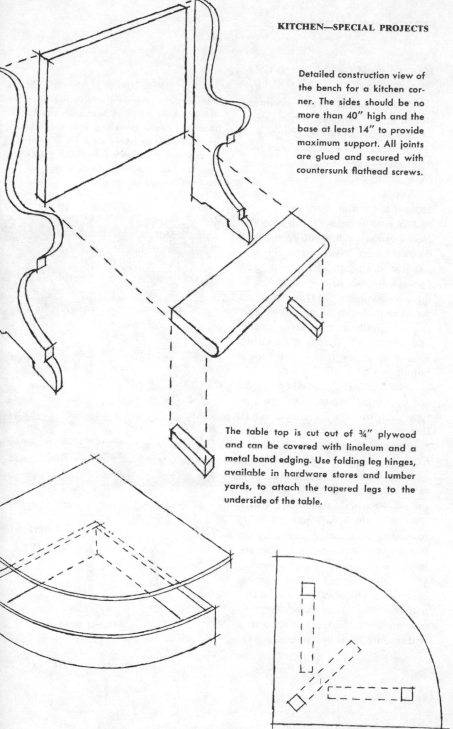

Detailed construction view of the bench for a kitchen corner. The sides should be no more than 40" high and the base at least 14" to provide maximum support. All joints are glued and secured with countersunk flathead screws.

The table top is cut out of ¾" plywood and can be covered with linoleum and a metal band edging. Use folding leg hinges, available in hardware stores and lumber yards, to attach the tapered legs to the underside of the table.

How To Build Good Kitchen Cabinets

The cabinets and counters shown here are based on modern kitchen studies. They're designed to speed work by working smoothly themselves—and to keep working for years to come.

Supply areas are grouped around the major work centers, so that an entire operation can be completed at each point before moving on to the next, saving steps. Shelves are just deep enough to hold one pan or one dish, so there's no reaching over something in front to get at something else in back. Doors and drawers, built to take abuse, open and close at a touch, eliminating jams that jar even the best cook's humor.

The cabinets are designed as self-contained units. The frame-type construction for the counters insures lasting strength, and the notched joints can be easily cut by hand.

For the upper cupboards, use rabbeted and dadoed joints as shown. Plywood, a bit more costly than solid stock, will pay off in its resistance to splitting and warping in an area where heat and moisture levels are always high. Whether you're building new cabinets or re-organizing old ones, you can adapt many of the ideas shown here to custom-tailor the kitchen shop to a real smooth-flowing production line.

Pans are stored individually in two deep cabinets over range so that each can be reached without grappling with a whole stack. Skillets are held on back of door in rattleproof brackets (see sketch). Rack for lids has sloped-top dividers that roll lid knobs snugly toward rear.

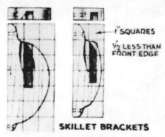

' SQUARES
½ LESS THAN FRONT EDGE

SKILLET BRACKETS

HEIGHT TO SUIT LID SIZE

4"

45°

1 x 7 x 12"

LID RACK

Counters and Canned-Food Racks Expand a Range Into a Complete Cooking Center

Shallow shelves above range are one-can deep so entire supply can be seen at a glance. Cupboards (see sketch) are held at top by cleats screwed to ceiling and at bottom by metal angles on wall. If you can't find studs, fasten cleats and angles with toggle bolts.

Range is flanked by twin counter-and-drawer units that increase work space and storage. Frames (see sketch) are made from stock 1x2 surfaced lumber, notched as shown, and glued and nailed. Use ¼" hardboard on inner sides, ¾" plywood on outer ones.

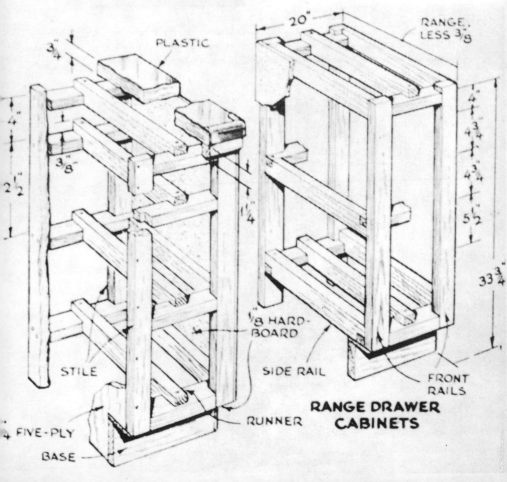

PLASTIC

20"

RANGE, LESS ⅜"

STILE

⅛ HARD-BOARD

SIDE RAIL

FRONT RAILS

RUNNER

FIVE-PLY

BASE

RANGE DRAWER CABINETS

Mixing Center Speeds Flow of Food
Between Refrigerator and Sink

Mixing center provides everything needed for whipping up cakes, tossing salads and preparing other foods. Placed between refrigerator and sink, it permits the housewife to reach stored vegetables on one side and wash them on the other without moving more than a step. Adjustable top on counter unit (see sketch) can be raised or lowered to comfortable working height, then locked tight by wing nuts riding in slots.

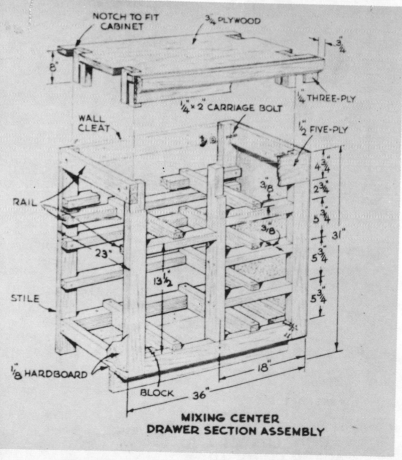

NOTCH TO FIT CABINET

¾ PLYWOOD

8"

¾

¼ THREE-PLY

¼ × 2 CARRIAGE BOLT

WALL CLEAT

½ FIVE-PLY

RAIL

4¾"

2¾"

3/8

5¾"

31"

3/8

5¾"

23"

13½

5¾"

STILE

⅛ HARDBOARD

BLOCK   36"

18"

MIXING CENTER
DRAWER SECTION ASSEMBLY

Upper cabinets hide electric mixer, plugged in for use, and other bulky appliances. Shelves, just big enough for each item, save space and clutter. Rack at left keeps clattering cake tins in neat order on top shelf. Swing-out spice rack at right duplicates some seasonings used at range, but saves many steps.

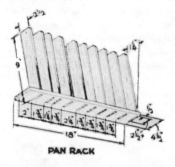

PAN RACK

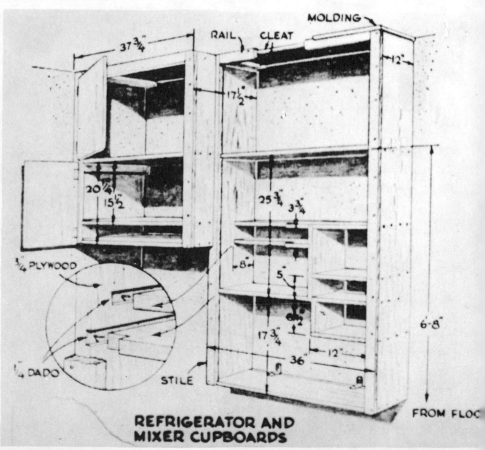

REFRIGERATOR AND MIXER CUPBOARDS

Under-sink clutter can be quickly put to rights with a couple of these easily built shelf-tables. They can be made any shape or height to sneak around plumbing pipes, slide quickly out for cleaning.

UNDER-SINK SHELVES

SPICE RACK

ANGEL FOOD PAN PEG

Use dado head on circular saw to groove sides of cabinets for shelves. On "blind" dadoes that don't run all the way across, clamp a wood block to the saw table to stop the board just short of the dado end. Then finish the dado with a chisel. To hang doors, first make a gage block (see sketch) to mark hinges. Round the door edges on a shaper or molding head, or by hand with plane.

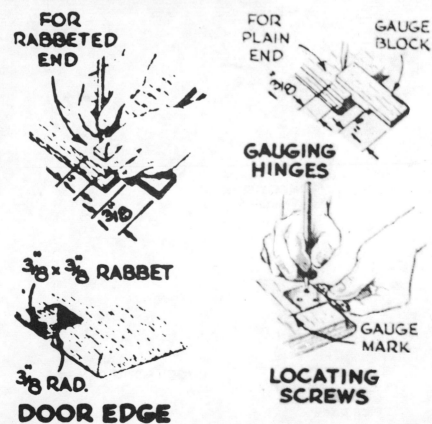

FOR RABBETED END

$3/8$

$3/8 \times 3/8$ RABBET

$3/8$ RAD.

DOOR EDGE

FOR PLAIN END

GAUGE BLOCK

$3/8$

GAUGING HINGES

GAUGE MARK

LOCATING SCREWS

Closely Spaced Shelves Cram Stacks of Cups and Plates Into One Compact Wall Cabinet

Dish and glassware cupboard can be placed anywhere you have wall space, but go best near door to dining room or over a breakfast table, which makes a good place for stacking dried dishes before putting them away. Cabinet above has recessed shelves for sliding doors, which are easier to handle than large hinged doors that swing out into the room. Rollers, riding in metal tracks, are mortised into lower edges of doors by drilling a series of holes, then cleaning out waste with a chisel. Narrow wood strips guide doors at top edge.

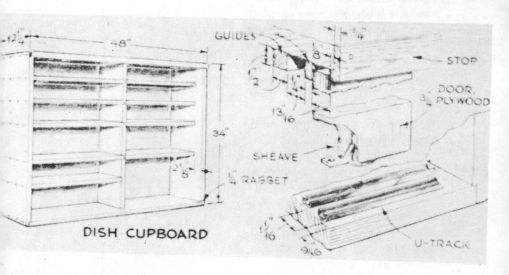

DISH CUPBOARD

GUIDES

STOP

DOOR, ¾ PLYWOOD

SHEAVE

¼ RABBET

U-TRACK

Greenhouse Snack Bar

Snack bars are built in many parts of the kitchen but few are more attractive than this one built along the window edge with a greenhouse built onto the house. It provides a cheery spot for a quick breakfast in the morning or a light snack in the afternoon.

The counter is built out of the wall at table-top height. A piece of ¾″ plywood will do as the base. It should be covered with a washable material, like linoleum or laminated plastic, such as Formica, Micarta, Conolite or Consoweld. The counter top is supported by a cleat attached to the underside next to the wall and through which screws are set into the studs.

It's easy to make this greenhouse out of any window. All you need do is to remove the window sash and trim around the opening with attractive wood, if you prefer a natural finish, or regular stock, if it is going to be painted. A large and deep window box is fastened on the outside of the house. The sloping windows can be bought ready-made in lumber yards or you can make your own with power tools.

While it is possible to make these windows so that they are hinged at the top and open out and up for ventilation, it is better to anchor them so that they cannot be moved. This eliminates a considerable amount of work and also reduces the possibility of leaks when it rains or drafts in blowy weather.

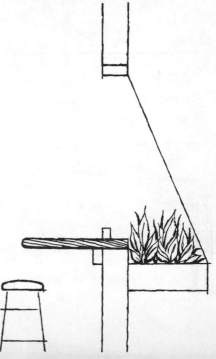

Photograph courtesy of Hotpoint, Inc.

Ceramic Tile Counter Tops

Started along the Pacific coast and moving eastward rapidly, are ceramic tile counter tops in kitchens. These are making some inroads into the linoleum and plastic tops, but often ceramic tiles are used in conjunction with the other materials.

You may consider applying your own ceramic tops to the counters. Tiles are easy to work with once you get the knack of cutting them. However, tiles are available in many different sizes and shapes so that you can select a pattern or tile size that virtually eliminates any need for cutting. For how-to see *Tiles*.

In many homes, not only are the counter tops done in tile but the backsplash—the wall surface just above the counter top—is also tile. Matching or complementary tiles can be used on the kitchen floor to complete the room's decor in tile.

The island or peninsula (see photograph to the left, below) is likewise becoming increasing popular. Many of these units have doors on both sides, thus eliminating the need for walking around to get something out. Some peninsulas are made extra wide—equal to the width of almost two cabinets. These provide massive work surfaces and contain two sets of base cabinets placed back to back.

Decorative Dinette

In some homes the dinette is completely separated from the kitchen work areas, while in others there is no set line of demarcation. If you wish to create a separate feeling for the dinette, it can be accomplished by unusual decorating.

Simplest way to do the job is to use a different colored paint or wallpaper in the dinette area as contrasted with the kitchen. Here is one technique, shown in the photograph below, which brings a touch of the outdoors inside the house.

Louvered shutters are hung with hinges on the kitchen windows. They are used in place of Venetian blinds or window shades. A wallpaper with a brick pattern is used inside the dinette while another type of paper is used for the kitchen proper.

The attractive dinette light fixture plus the scalloped valance complete the optical illusion of a separate dinette. The valance is made out of ½ x6 lumber and cut to shape with a coping or jig saw. A 1x1 cleat is used to fasten the ½ x6 valance to the ceiling.

Here's all you do:

1. Cut the valance to size and shape.

2. Attach it to the 1x1 cleat with #9 flathead screws 1″ long.

3. Attach the cleats to the ceiling with the appropriate anchors depending upon whether the ceiling is made of plaster or board.

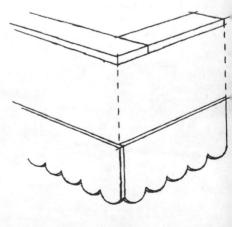

Select any pattern you wish and trace it on the 12x6 valance and cut to shape with a coping or jig saw. You will find many patterns in literature available at your local lumber yard.

Distinctive Drawers

If you haven't the necessary power tools or you're just not handy enough to make a number of drawers for a kitchen cabinet, you will find that ready-made drawers will save you time and effort. There is available a number of molded drawers made of Bakelite phenolic resin, designed for use in cabinets, chests, kitchen work counters—in fact, almost anywhere you would like to have a drawer.

These light-weight drawers have a smooth, splinter-free surface which requires no finishing or painting—if you wish to keep their original black color. They are unaffected by weather changes, heat and most chemicals. If you wish to match the drawers and change their color, you can do so in several different ways.

1. You can apply a plastic surface to the face with a contact cement.

2. You can add a false face made of wood; see section on *Drawers*.

Photograph and sketches courtesy of Bakelite Company, Division of Union Carbide and Carbon Corp.

3. You can apply a coat of paint, matching the cabinet, wall or trim finish.

Of particular interest to the homemaker is the interior shape of the drawers. They have molded rounded corners—an end to dust collectors.

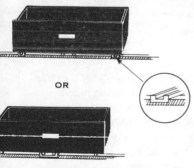

OR

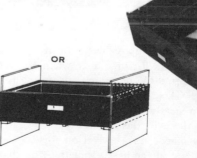

OR

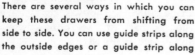

There are several ways in which you can keep these drawers from shifting from side to side. You can use guide strips along the outside edges or a guide strip along the center. It is also possible to use a narrow molding strip along the side of the drawer to act as a track. See section on **Drawers**.

Television Kitchen

Sketch courtesy of The Kitchen Maid Corp.

It is often impossible to bring the youngsters in for dinner when their favorite TV programs are on the air. This kitchen solves that problem neatly. Since the kitchen adjoins the activities room, the TV set was placed on a swivel on the counter top of the base cabinets. A snack bar on the other side of the range makes an ideal eating place while watching the television set.

There are three other "extras" in this kitchen. Note the hide-a-rack for hanging freshly ironed clothing that fits into the wall cabinet. There is also a pull-out ironing board that fits below the base cabinet counter top. Thirdly, there is a convenient hamper with a bin-type front, which can be rolled to the washer, which becomes part of the room's base cabinets when stored.

Nautical Kitchen

If you love sailing, you'll feel right at home in this exciting kitchen. A U-shaped work area is built into the kitchen with a snack bar as a peninsula. All counter surfaces are covered in easily-washed, durable plastic.

Those attractive chairs with life-preserver backs make an ideal project for the handyman over a rainy week-end. You can alter the appearance of any chair easily by removing the back framework, leaving only the two outside uprights. The life preservers are fitted over these uprights and secured with adhesive.

If you'd like to try your hand at painting, you too can make an attractive wall. However, you can make a large blow-up of a favorite photograph and fasten it to the wall with wallpaper adhesive. The use of fish net draperies completes the striking decor.

Photograph courtesy of General Electric Co.

Corner Breakfast Nook

For the homeowner too busy to build his own breakfast nook, here is a ready-made unit that is easily attached by nailing two cleats to each wall. The upholstered backs and seats come complete with the cleats and are upholstered in washable plastic. The upholstered units can be snapped in and out for cleaning.

Different sized units are made to fit different kitchens. The units can be used with any conventional table. If these two seats do not provide sufficient seating for the family, chairs can be used on the other sides of the table.

Photograph courtesy of The Dormalux Co.

Kitchen— Storage Cabinets

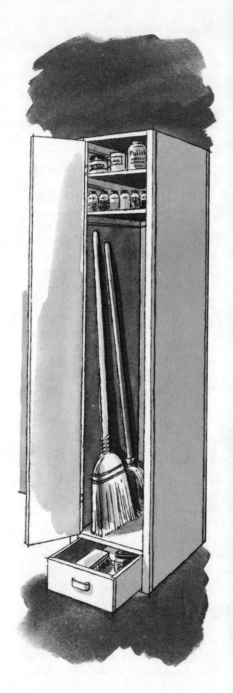

While there are many types of kitchen cabinets available which can be purchased ready-made with space-saving extras already installed, there are some handymen who prefer to make their own cabinets. In some cases, this is necessary because of the unusual size or shape of the cabinet.

Construction techniques can be made as simple or complex as you feel necessary and are capable of. It is recommended that you read through the sections on *Built-ins, Furniture* and *Wood Joints,* before you start to build. In those sections you will find the basic essentials for making different types of units. The section on *Drawers* will guide you in their construction.

On the following pages you will find detailed plans, showing dimensions for each piece, for two units often used in the home. While they can be used in the kitchen or pantry, they can also be used in the laundry room or recreation room. The first is a utility cabinet—an 18"x24" storage unit 88" high. The other is a wall cabinet, 24" wide, 12" deep and 36" high. Here you will find the details for making dividers, useful for storing baking tins and muffin pans as well as pot lids.

Utility Cabinet

This 21 cubic foot storage cabi-

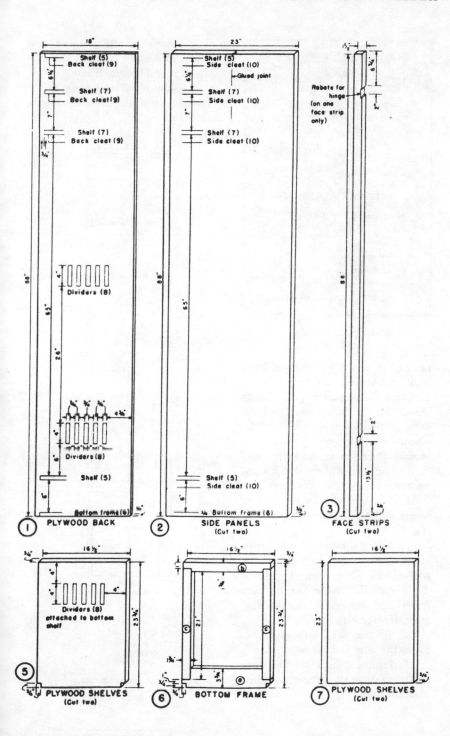

① PLYWOOD BACK

② SIDE PANELS
(Cut two)

③ FACE STRIPS
(Cut two)

⑤ PLYWOOD SHELVES
(Cut two)

⑥ BOTTOM FRAME

⑦ PLYWOOD SHELVES
(Cut two)

MATERIALS NEEDED:

5 pieces of 1x12—8" long
1 piece of 1x8—4' long
1 piece of 1x4—8' long
4 pieces of 1x2—8' long
1 piece of 1x2—10' long
1 piece of ½x8—6' long
¾" plywood—3'x4'
¼" plywood—3'x8'

HARDWARE NEEDED:

2 hinges, 1½"x2"
1 door pull
1 drawer pull
2 friction catches
13 small hooks
4d and 6d finishing nails
3 dozen #8 screws, 1¼" long

6. Assemble the drawer and slide it into place between the bottom shelf and bottom frame.

7. Now fill all end grain of the plywood, sand all surfaces smooth, and paint.

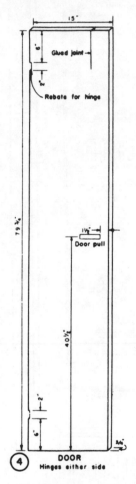

net can be made with simple hand tools, but you can do the job faster and easier with power tools. Study the detailed parts drawing and cut each section as shown. After the pieces have been cut, you can assemble them using adhesive and nails or screws. Follow this assembly procedure:

1. Join the sides to the bottom frame and one of the two plywood shelves.

2. Add the cleats for the three other shelves and then insert the shelves and secure them in position.

3. Add the dividers to the back panel and bottom shelf, holding them in place with glue.

4. Set the back into place between the sides and fasten.

5. Fit the hinges on the door and one side of the cabinet and then hang the door.

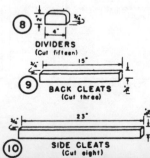

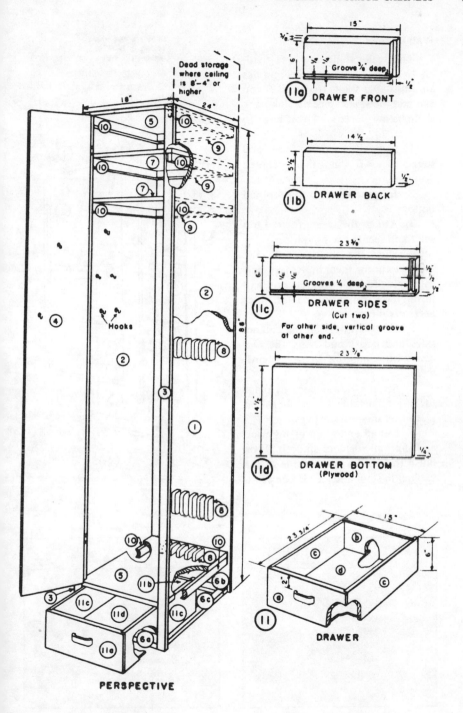

DRAWER FRONT

DRAWER BACK

DRAWER SIDES
(Cut two)
For other side, vertical groove
at other end.

DRAWER BOTTOM
(Plywood)

DRAWER

Dead storage
where ceiling
is 8'—4" or
higher

Hooks

PERSPECTIVE

Wall Cabinet

This wall cabinet features dividers to hold platters and tins and has an adjustable shelf. If you like, you can add the small spice or nick-nack shelf below. Here's all you have to do:

1. Cut all parts to size and shape shown in the detailed sketches.

2. Join the sides to the top and bottom.

3. Attach the cleats for the top shelf and secure shelf in place.

4. Slide the dividers into the grooves cut for them in the top shelf using glue to hold the base and nail through the top to hold each divider perfectly plumb.

5. Set the hinges on the cabinet sides and doors and hang the two doors, attaching the necessary hardware.

6. Set the dowel pegs in place for the adjustable lower shelf and place that shelf on the pegs.

7. Fill all end grain of plywood and sand all surfaces smooth. Then finish the insides and outside of the cabinet in stain and varnish or paint.

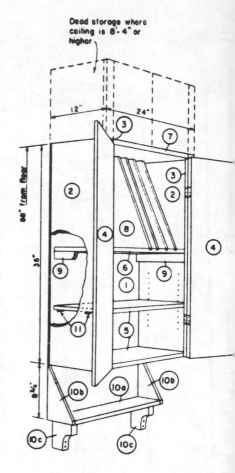

MATERIALS NEEDED:
1x12—12′ long
1x12—8′ long
1x6—3′ long
1x2—8′long
2x6—1′ long
¼″ plywood—3′x4′

HARDWARE NEEDED:
2 pairs of hinges, 1½″x½″
4d and 6d finishing nails
2 dozen #8 screws, 1¼″ long
6 toggle bolts, ⅛″x3″
2 door pulls
2 friction catches

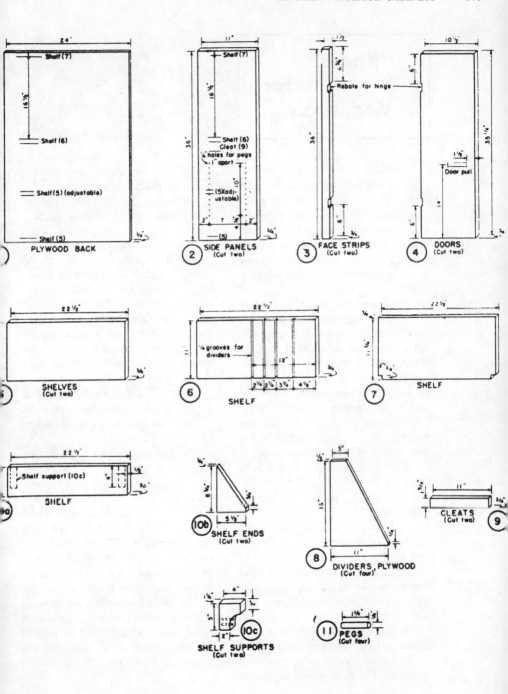

PLYWOOD BACK

② SIDE PANELS (Cut two)

③ FACE STRIPS (Cut two)

④ DOORS (Cut two)

SHELVES (Cut two)

⑥ SHELF

⑦ SHELF

SHELF

⑩b SHELF ENDS (Cut two)

⑧ DIVIDERS, PLYWOOD (Cut four)

⑨ CLEATS (Cut two)

⑩c SHELF SUPPORTS (Cut two)

⑪ PEGS (Cut four)

Kitchen— Timetable for Modernizing

Improving your existing kitchen is not a job that can be done overnight. It is best to make detailed plans after studying the different space savers and extras you can add in your kitchen. Then make a scale drawing of the floor area and see how the individual items fit together in the room.

Whether you make your own cabinets or buy them ready-made, you should count on getting the most out of all available space. In the preceding pages, there were numerous ideas and projects—enough to keep the homeowner busy for weeks. Of course, all the innovations cannot be added to any one kitchen. You should select those best suited to your requirements.

Here is a timetable and checklist to help you in planning—do the first jobs first to produce the best results.

1. Does the plumbing and heating have to be altered to fit into the new kitchen plan? See *Plumbing*.

2. Are there sufficient electrical outlets, handy at all the work centers and with heavy enough wires to carry the load?

3. Does your kitchen have adequate lighting? Is it necessary to add wall switches, extra ceiling or wall fixtures? Do you want semi-concealed lighting above the counter tops? See *Electrical Wiring*.

4. How's the kitchen window? Will a new type of window, such as an awning window, make your kitchen more attractive and airier?

5. What are you going to do with the walls? Want to paint them? Or do you prefer washable wallpaper or plastic-surface hardboard panels or simulated brick? See *Painting, Walls* and *Wallpapering*.

6. How's the ceiling? Is it the type that will quiet the clatter of dishes? See *Ceiling Tiles*.

7. Do the doors to the kitchen get in the way of cabinets? You can replace swinging doors with folding doors.

8. Are the counter tops durable and easy-to-clean? If you wish replace them or just the area around the sink.

9. Don't forget the built-ins and space savers in the kitchen. You can get much more space and produce a striking effect in the kitchen with proper planning and designed built-ins. See section on *Built-Ins*.

10. The floors get a lot of wear and tear in the kitchen. A new floor often makes a surprising change in the appearance of a room. See the section on *Floor Tiles*.

Modernizing Ideas for the Kitchen

Simulated brick made of polystyrene plastic comes in sheets and is applied with adhesive like wallpaper. It produces a marked three-dimensional effect and makes a striking accent wall in any kitchen.

Photograph courtesy of National Vacuum Molding Co.

Washable three-dimensional wallpaper comes in many attractive patterns and can be applied over any wall surface.

Photograph courtesy of Wall Trends, Inc.

If you prefer a tile pattern, here's a tempered hardboard with a plastic finish that can be applied over any wall or ceiling. It comes 4' wide in lengths up to 12'.

Photograph courtesy of Armstrong Cork Co.

Tempered hardboard with a plastic finish is also available in 16" planks and squares. The planks are attached over an old wall with special clips so that there's no visible fastening.

Photograph courtesy of Marsh Wall Products, Inc.

Photograph courtesy of Rubber Manufacturers Association.

Spruce up your kitchen floors with tiles. While many dramatic effects can be produced with linoleum, many homeowners find tiles easire to handle. You have a wide selection of types and colors.

Photograph courtesy of The Hough Shade Corp.

If you want to close off your kitchen from the dining-living area, you will find a folding door is just the answer. You can have open-living planning with a touch of privacy when you need it.

Acoustical ceiling tiles in a kitchen are both decorative and functional. Not only do they make the room quieter but add to the overall appearance, giving a note of quality.

Durable, easily-washable counter tops can be yours in just a few hours. Decorative laminate surfaces can be adhered with contact cements after the wood surface has been prepared.

Photographs courtesy of Armstrong Cork Co.

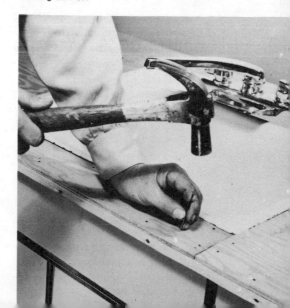

Lighting and Color

Modern lighting fixtures can do much to enhance the appearance of any room. Which type of light you use depends upon the fixtures but certain types of light highlight some colors more than others. Therefore, for a dramatic effect in your home, select the right light for the colors you wish to emphasize in the room's decoration.

Numerous studies made by lighting companies have revealed many interesting results of highlight lighting. They have been made primarily for retail stores but the homeowner can borrow a leaf from their book to "put on his own show." In a study made by Sylvania Electric Products, it was found that:

1. Pure incandescent lighting enriches dark reds and the brightness of yellow. It has, however, a darkening effect on most other colors.

2. Warmtone fluorescent lamps brighten reds and yellow too. But they add warmth and clearness to most of the other colors.

3. Standard white fluorescent lamps brighten yellow, greens and some of the tans. They, however, gray the blues.

4. Soft, white fluorescent lamps brighten and increase the clearness of the reds, pinks, pinkish tans and blues. On the other hand, they dull the yellows and gray the greens.

5. The 4500° white illuminating lamps seem to show colors at their best without any severe distortions. This illumination does, how-ever, tend to gray most colors.

6. The daylight fluorescent lamps cool and pale all colors except blue and green. This light helps to emphasize wood finishes.

Color Terms

Whether working with lighting fixtures and bulbs or with paint, you will come across several terms used to explain fine differences in color. Here are five color phrases that often confuse the layman and sometimes confuse the expert:

1. *Primary colors* are green-blue, magenta-red and yellow—although it is perfectly all right to say blue, red and yellow.

2. *Hues* are the primary colors and their mixtures—for example, when you combine a blue and red and obtain a violet, that color is a hue.

3. *Tints* are obtained by mixing hues with white.

4. *Shades* are obtained by adding black to a hue.

5. *Tones* are hues plus both black and white.

You can readily see that by combining the primary colors in varying proportions, you can obtain an infinite number of hues. By adding black, white or both to any of the hues, you can obtain an infinite number of shades, tints and tones.

Because so many factors go into the making of a color, it is therefore obvious that the reaction of the light fixture or the sun on the painted surface can be critical. The rays of the light bulb or the sun may pick up part of the color and emphasize it so that the color will appear different in natural light, in artificial light and in a cloudy, sunless day.

Lighting Fixtures

All lighting can be divided roughly into three classes:
• direct light
• indirect light
• semi-indirect light.
Some fixtures are designed to provide a combination of these three types of light.

Direct light is provided by flood lights, spot lights, recessed lights, accent lights and others in which the source of light entirely or largely directs the light. This type of lighting often creates a varying density of shadow and contrast. It is used to highlight some specific area with dramatic results.

Indirect light is provided by concealed sources of light such as cove lighting or some of the ceiling-suspended fixtures that direct the light upward to reflect off the ceiling, or dome reflectors which are part of the fixtures themselves. This type of light is used to provide a level of general lighting and because it is solely reflected light, it is softer and more glare-free than other types of light.

Semi-indirect lighting is provided by fixtures which direct the greater part of their light upward, but which also produce some downward light. Bent-glass bowl fixtures are in this category. Semi-indirect lighting is used for general lighting.

Types of Fixtures

There are many different types

Direct light is harsh and produces sharp shadows and contrasts.

Indirect light is reflected either from the ceiling (as shown) or from the walls.

(c)
Semi-indirect light combines both but the major portion of the light is reflected off the ceiling.

of fixtures but here in graphic presentation are some of the more commonly used fixtures together with what they are used for.

See section on *Lighting for Your Home.*

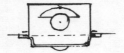

Recessed lights are incandescent or fluorescent fixtures set into the ceiling (sometimes the wall) so that the fixture is flush with the surface. They are used for general illumination or accent lighting.

Ceiling mounted fixtures are installed close to the ceiling and are fastened directly to the outlet box. Those with glass shades provide both indirect and semi-indirect light. This type of fixture is used primarily for general illumination.

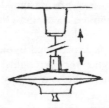

Stem or chain fixtures are suspended from the outlet box in the ceiling. Depending upon the fixture, they provide direct, indirect or semi-indirect lighting or a combination of these. These lights are used for general illumination; when hung low, provide downlight for localized lighting.

Reel fixtures are similar in appearance and use to stem-hung fixtures, but are suspended from the ceiling on an enclosed reel that permits the fixture to be raised or lowered. Some reel fixtures have the reel attached part of the way down from the ceiling.

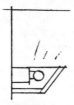

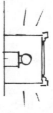

Cove lighting is indirect light produced by lamps concealed in a molding of wood, metal, plaster or glass, fastened to the upper wall or an actual part of the wall itself. They are open at the top so that the light is directed to and reflected from the ceiling. Strip light fixtures are generally used for this type of lighting.

Wall lights are equipped with fluorescent lamps and while primarily used for general illumination, they are often installed as window valances as well as bed lamps, over-the-sink lights and desk lights.

Sketches courtesy of Thomas Industries, Inc.
—Moe Light Division.

Wall brackets are fixtures that mount on the wall. They can provide any of the three types of light or a combination thereof. They are used for localized lighting, decorative lighting or to add to the general background illumination.

Accent lights are adjustable lights that can be mounted on the walls or ceiling. They direct their light onto a specific object or area. They provide direct light and are used for creating effect and dramatic interest.

Lighting for Your Home

Lighting in the home serves a dual purpose—it is both functional and decorative. While it is best to plan for your wiring needs before actual construction or remodeling begins, it is impossible to anticipate all your lighting needs. You may have to make modifications as you change the layout of the furniture in a room.

For complete how-to, see *Electrical Wiring*.

Lighting Terms

Over and over again, you will read or hear interior decorators and architects using lighting terms that need some explanation. Here are some of the more commonly used terms:

General illumination refers to over-all illumination. This involves raising the light level of the room to a point where shadows are at a minimum.

Localized lighting refers to lighting for a specific area such as reading, sewing, etc.

Decorative light is used to identify a fixture which is important in the lighting plans because of its appearance. The lighting fixture itself adds to the room's decorative scheme as well as illuminating the room as a whole or a specific area.

Accent lighting refers to the achievement of an unusual or dramatic effect by means of light without drawing attention to the light fixture itself. It is used to highlight a planter, a painting, sculpture, etc.

Wall lighting is often *valance lighting* when the fixture is used over a window or it can be used to describe any fixture attached to the wall for general illumination or accent lighting.

Lighting the Living Room

Before you can decide upon lighting, from a decorative viewpoint, you must decide upon the location of the furniture and furnishings. Ordinarily the center of family

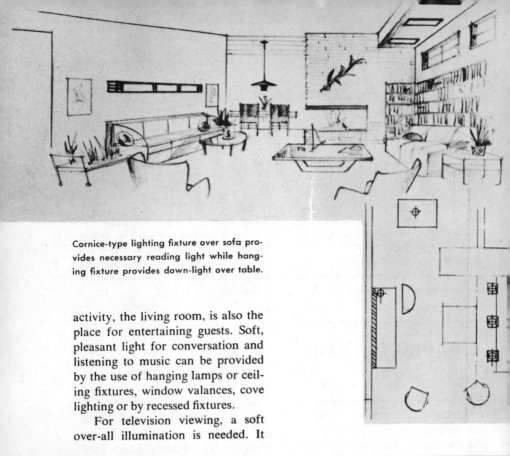

Cornice-type lighting fixture over sofa provides necessary reading light while hanging fixture provides down-light over table.

activity, the living room, is also the place for entertaining guests. Soft, pleasant light for conversation and listening to music can be provided by the use of hanging lamps or ceiling fixtures, window valances, cove lighting or by recessed fixtures.

For television viewing, a soft over-all illumination is needed. It

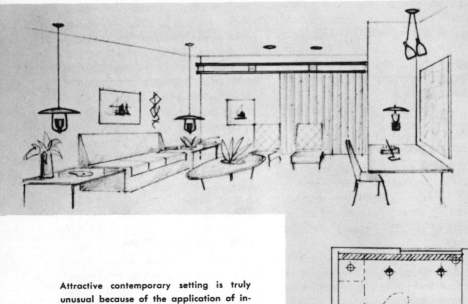

Attractive contemporary setting is truly unusual because of the application of inspirational lighting.

This room is rich with the tradition and luxury of a period setting. Fixtures over end tables blend with styling.

reduces the sharp contrast between the lighted screen and the darkness of the room, which causes discomfort and eyestrain. Wall or valance lighting is particularly effective so long as it does not reflect in the television screen.

Light for reading may be provided by hanging reel-type lamps,

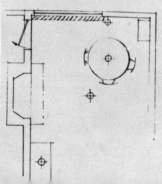

Distinctive blending of contemporary with traditional styling is noted in this living room.

Sketches courtesy of Thomas Industries Inc.—Moe Light Division

End wall of this living room is strikingly interesting because of the accent lights on the paintings.

Like an illuminated frame for a lovely picture, this cornice light unit over the window draws attention to the outside view.

The attractive wall-cornice light serves to light dramatically the bookcase and provide light for reading.

Another application of a window valance light fixture over a picture window to highlight the decorative effect of the furnishings.

accent lights or wall lights. Make provision for accent lighting of unusual pieces in the living room, such as a piano, a distinctive table, chair or the fireplace.

Valance Lighting

Wall and window valance lighting fixtures usually utilize lengths of fluorescent tubes (24"—20 watts, 33"—25 watts, 48"—40 watts) and provide an abundance of softly-diffused light over the walls, draperies and ceilings. In so doing, they create the illusion of spaciousness, thus making the room appear larger and airier.

Most modern homes have fairly low ceilings (approximately 8'). In these rooms, wall lights should be installed approximately 5' to 5½' from the floor. Custom-made window valances and coves give maximum reflection from the ceiling when they are installed with approximately 10" between the top of the valance and the ceiling, and the lamp 4" from the wall.

In many older homes, ceilings run rather high, 10' to 12' or more. The height at which the window valance light is installed depends upon the height of the window. The illusion of lowering the ceiling in these rooms can be effected by installing window valance and wall lights slightly lower than recommended for modern homes with 8' ceilings, and by painting the portion of the upper part of each wall, above the valance height, to match the ceiling.

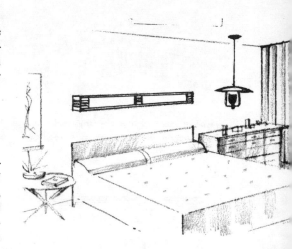

Wall lighting is used for reading in bed; there's plenty of natural light. The hanging fixture is for general illumination.

Sketches courtesy of Thomas Industries, Inc. —Moe Light Division.

This buffet is made more attractive by a wall light placed above it. The unit serves as a shelf to hold small knick-knacks.

Insporational lighting for the bedroom; this hanging fixture serves as a reading lamp for both beds.

Localized lighting at the dressing table is essential to good grooming. It supplements the general room lighting.

In a child's room, the wall-cornice light fixture not only provides needed illumination but adds a decorative touch.

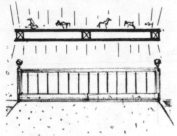

An adjustable hanging light fixture is ideal for reading; it can be lowered to the best height for reading.

Lighting for the Bedroom

Because bedrooms of today are used for many activities—study, sewing, writing, reading, etc.—carefully planned lighting is essential.

The general illumination requirements of the bedroom can be answered by a ceiling-mounted fixture. If it is the proper size, it will provide sufficient general illumination for dressing, for seeing into drawers and for cleaning the room.

Most people select bedroom fixtures that are too small. A good rule of thumb in picking the correctly proportioned fixture, according to the Moe Light Co., is to use the formula:

> Length plus width divided by two, times one and one-half equals the fixture diameter.

For example, if your bedroom is 12′ by 16′, you'd use the formula as follows:

12 plus 16, divided by 2 equals 14. Now multiply that figure by 1½ and you get 21. Therefore, 27″ is the proper diameter for a lighting fixture for that

Wall valance lighting is available as portable units; it can be moved from the bedroom to the desk in the study whenever needed.

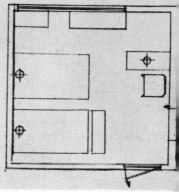

Here's a well-lighted bedroom with individual bed lamps and a hanging fixture for general illumination.

room. This diameter can vary one or two inches either way with satisfying results.

You will also want to provide accent lighting for the dressing table, localized lighting for reading in bed and, if you have a cozy corner, you will want a decorative light for illumination.

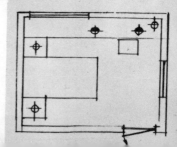

Sleekly modern, the clean, straight lines of the furnishings are set off by contemporary-styled lighting by Moe Light.

Sketches courtesy of Thomas Industries Inc.—Moe Light Division.

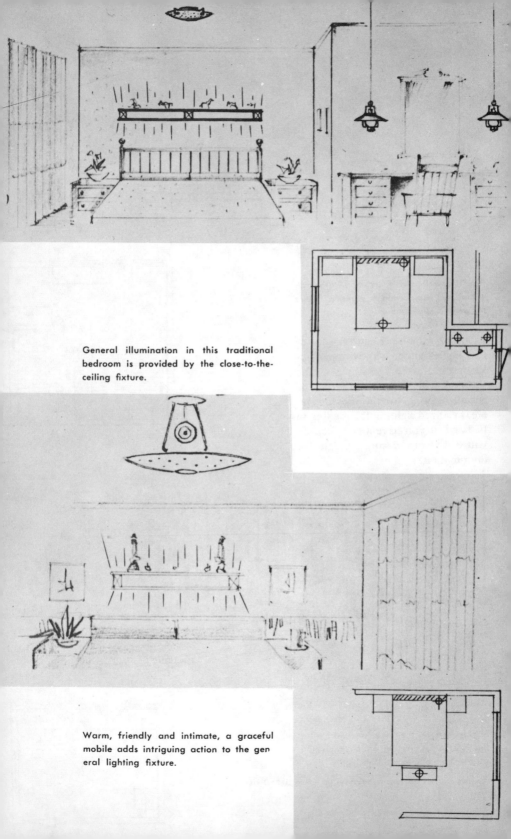

General illumination in this traditional bedroom is provided by the close-to-the-ceiling fixture.

Warm, friendly and intimate, a graceful mobile adds intriguing action to the general lighting fixture.

Lighting Hallways and Stairs

Entrance halls vary from mere suggestions of halls—a planter box or a divider closet, setting off the entry hall from the room—to elaborate foyers. The lighting possibilities for these areas are extremely varied and should conform to the space, decoration and architecture.

Planters downlighted by contemporary accent lights or recessed boxes placed directly above them have a special night-time beauty. In the traditional setting, lantern type fixtures will add a soft welcoming light and decorative charm.

Indoor hallways and stairs are among the most important places in the home for proper lighting. A poorly lighted stairway is a source of accidents. It is only good sense to place a light at the head of the stairs and another at the foot of the landing. If any fixtures are needed along the stairs, they should either be recessed in the ceiling or wall or attached to the wall with a shield so as not to blind anyone walking on the stairs.

Have more than one light in a hallway if it's long. Space them at a ratio of one fixture every 10' of hall length. These fixtures should have a minimum of a 100-watt bulb.

Sketches courtesy of Thomas Industries
—Moe Light Division

A flush-mounted wall unit helps to illuminate the stairs and a recessed unit illuminates the entry of this home.

Traditional lighting of an entrance hall can be obtained by using the proper size fixture.

Period in design, this hall fixture provides all-around illumination for the entire area.

Hallways require adequate lighting and here it is provided by two spotlights attached to the wall.

Sketches courtesy of Thomas Industries
—Moe Light Division

Not only is this entrance well lighted but the ceiling fixtures spotlight the attractive planter at the base of the stairs.

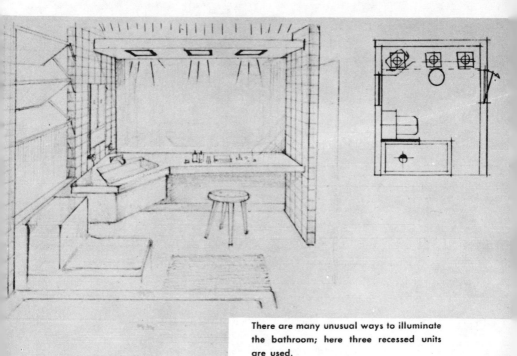

There are many unusual ways to illuminate the bathroom; here three recessed units are used.

A recessed light over the tub and two brackets on each side of the mirror provide light in this bathroom.

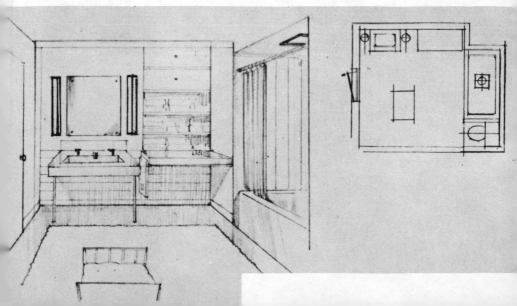

Round recessed lights in the ceiling are an unusual way to accent the decorative effect of lighting fixtures.

Traditionally styled bathroom is lighted by the close-to-ceiling fixture plus wall brackets.

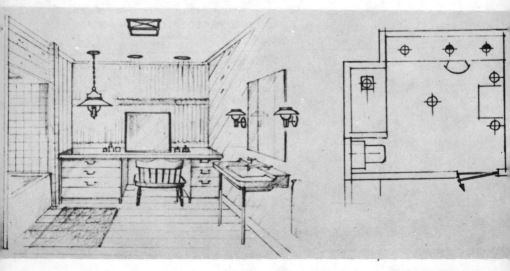

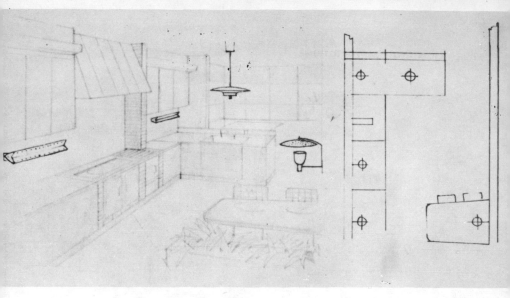

Kitchen lighting can be both dramatic and functional. Here is one example of how this can be done.

Lighting in the Kitchen

Not only do you need general illumination in the kitchen but you need localized lighting for the different work centers. Lighting in the kitchen should be planned as thoroughly as that of an office.

If you have a long narrow kitchen, use two separate fixtures for general illumination. These should be spaced one-half the room length apart, each located one-fourth the room length from a wall.

Strip lighting can be used effectively over the counters. Use a 20-watt bulb for each 30″ to 36″ of counter space. These fixtures should be placed under the wall cabinets so that your eyes are shielded from the light when you are working at the counters.

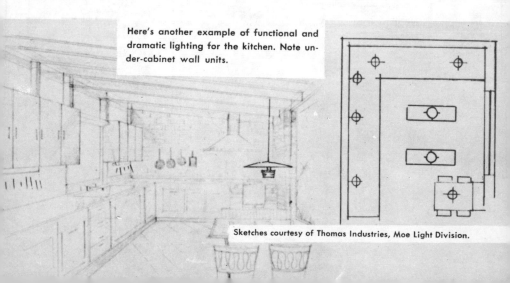

Here's another example of functional and dramatic lighting for the kitchen. Note under-cabinet wall units.

Sketches courtesy of Thomas Industries, Moe Light Division.

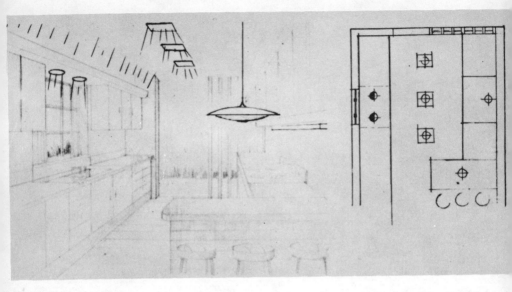

Recessed lights produce an unusual effect in the kitchen and are exceedingly practical above the kitchen sink area. Over the breakfast nook, you will find localized lighting most striking. A reel type fixture is not only decorative but very functional in this setting.

General illumination is provided by recessed light units and spots help to illuminate the sink area.

Sketches courtesy of Thomas Industries
—Moe Light Division.

A Moe Light reel type fixture helps to highlight the attractive breakfast nook in this kitchen.

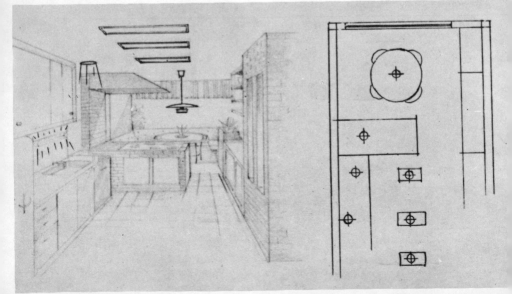

LIGHTING IDEAS FOR THE KITCHEN

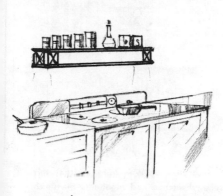

Ideal and attractive—a wall light above the kitchen range in a fixture that also serves as a convenient shelf.

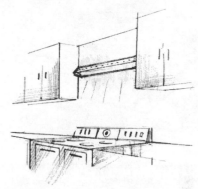

A perforated metal shield over a wall light above the range provides glare-free illumination.

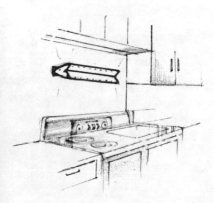

Recessed lights set into the soffit illuminate the top of the sink, provide sufficient light for the work center and dispel head shadows.

For shadow-free lighting, use a twin wall valance lighting fixture.

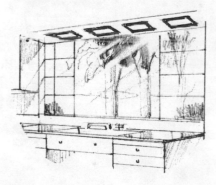

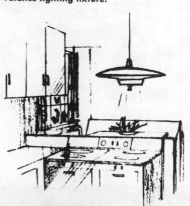

This range set into an island in the kitchen between the work and dining areas is provided with localized lighting by a reel type fixture.

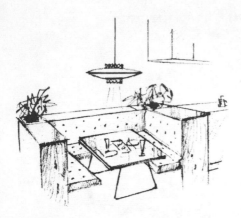

A reel-type fixture makes this breakfast nook bright and cheery.

A decorative hanging light enriches this Colonial kitchen and highlights the finish of the knotty pine and birch snack bar.

Also see *Outdoor Lighting*.

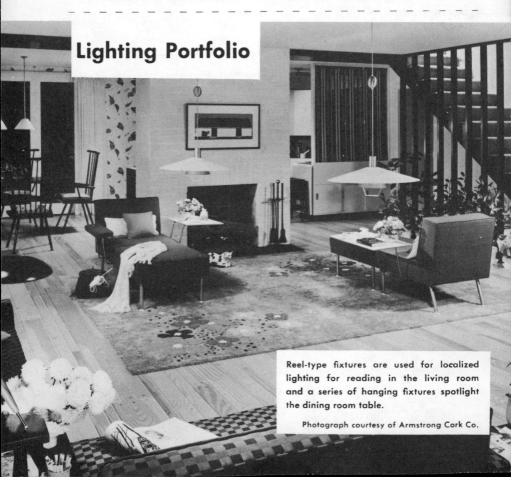

Lighting Portfolio

Reel-type fixtures are used for localized lighting for reading in the living room and a series of hanging fixtures spotlight the dining room table.

Photograph courtesy of Armstrong Cork Co.

Wall fixtures for direct and indirect lighting add a decorative touch to this living room setting. These lights are also used for television viewing.

Here are additional lighting ideas for the home. Some fixtures are easily installed in place of your existing light fixtures. For some, it may be necessary to add additional outlets. For how-to, see *Electrical Wiring*. For lighting displays built into walls and furniture, see *Built-ins* and *Furniture* for techniques of construction.

...sual reel light not only moves up and ...wn but also rides in a track attached ...he ceiling. The fixture can be moved ...rever it is needed most.

Striking lighting of bookshelves. Strip fluorescent lighting is mounted to the underside of each shelf to produce a dramatic effect.

Cove lighting is used for general illumination in this attractive room. Note that the wall above the lighting unit is painted to match the ceiling. Strip lighting is recessed into the sides of the open display shelves on each side of the window.

Photograph courtesy of Sylvania Electric Corp.

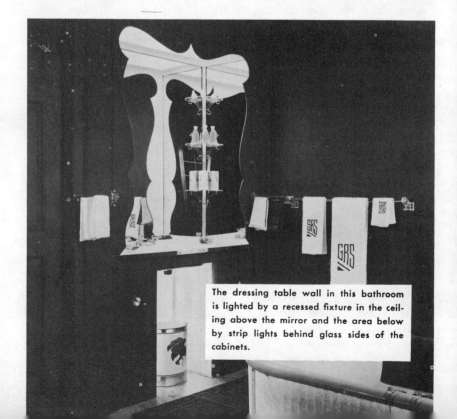

The dressing table wall in this bathroom is lighted by a recessed fixture in the ceiling above the mirror and the area below by strip lights behind glass sides of the cabinets.

Here's a bright, cheerful room—the Luxtrol unit is in the full on position.

It's getting dark inside as the dimmer is put into operation; subdued lighting produces a striking effect.

The dimmer is installed in place of the conventional light switch to control the lights in the room.

Decorate with Light

Light, properly used, can enhance the beauty of your surroundings. By varying the intensity of the light, the color tones and textures in fabrics of draperies, furniture and carpets are accentuated or subdued, thereby altering the character and spirit of your surroundings. It is possible to vary the intensity of the light in any room with a Luxtrol Dimmer.

The special electrical unit, a powerful rheostat to work on regular household current, is simple to install. It goes between the power supply from the fuse box and the light fixture. It incorporates an on-off switch as well as a control to set the lights from very dim to full brightness. It can be used in any room of the house and is particularly effective in the television-recreation room.

Minimum light, controlled by the wall unit, makes it possible to view TV with ease and comfort.

Photographs courtesy of The Superior Electric Co.

How-To Ladder Guide

1. Never stand on the top of a stepladder. You may lose your balance and fall or you may topple the ladder sideways.

2. Don't go higher than the second step from the top of a stepladder. If you select the proper height stepladder you will avoid difficulties of this kind.

3. If working in front of a door, either lock it or leave it wide open for safety. It is also a good idea to put up a warning sign if the door is closed, to caution anyone about opening the door.

4. Use the pailholder of a stepladder for your working equipment. Don't use the top of the ladder; things fall off too easily.

5. As you work, don't reach out too far on either side as the uneven distribution of weight may cause an accident. Ladders should be placed so that the working space can be reached easily. Don't overreach under any circumstances! Move the ladder.

6. For roof work, an extension ladder should always be at least 2' higher than the point at which the ladder rests so that you can walk off of the ladder onto a roof. It makes stepping off a ladder safer. Never climb over the top of an erected ladder.

7. If you need safe footing on the roof, there are three ways to secure an extension ladder to the roof. There are steel brackets that can be hooked over the ridge of the roof, a rope can be run down the other side of the roof and fastened securely, to a tree for example, or you can use skid-proof rests which can be attached to certain types of ladders.

8. For any prolonged work on a ladder, use a step rest. It is easily hooked on the rungs and can be moved quickly. The step rest helps to relieve the strain of standing on the rungs.

9. Always face the ladder when working. Always hold on with one hand.

10. If it is necessary to use both hands, you can brace yourself by hooking one leg around a rung for greater security.

11. If the work on the roof is away from the ladder, be sure that the ladder is secured so that the wind doesn't blow it over. Lash the ladder fast through a window to secure it.

12. Do not overload a ladder.

13. Do not test-load wooden ladders for you may injure the side rails.

Lumber

A general understanding of tree classification and wood structure helps the woodworker make the best use of his materials.

Classification of Trees

Nearly all trees are included in the most important of the four major plant groups, the Spermatophyta. This group is divided into Gymnosperms and Angiosperms.

• The Gymnosperms include the conifers, known in the lumber industry as softwoods.

• The Angiosperms include the monocotyledons (palms, yuccas, bamboos) and the dicotyledons. The latter are much more important. They include all hardwood trees.

• The terms hardwood and softwood should be used only in considering a group as a whole. Actually, the wood of certain softwood trees is harder than that of certain hardwood trees.

Tree Structure

A tree is a complex structure of roots, trunk, limbs, and leaves. Only the larger portion of the trunk or bole is used for lumber. This portion is first crosscut into logs.

Tissue zones—A cross section of a tree trunk shows the following well-defined tissue zones in succession from the outside to the center: bark, wood, and pitch, a small spot at the center, usually darker in color than the wood.

Heartwood and Sapwood—In most species, wood at the center of the trunk (heartwood) is darker than wood in the outer part (sap-

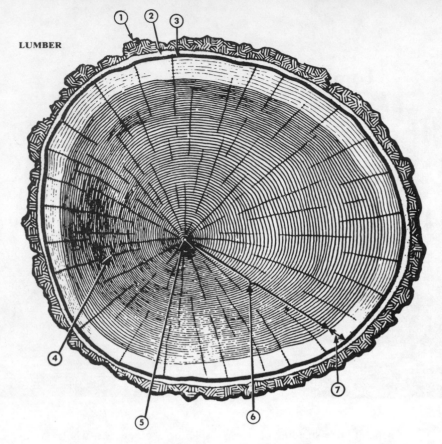

① Outer bark. ③ Cambium layer. ⑤ Pith. ⑦ Sapwood.
② Inner bark. ④ Wood rays. ⑥ Heartwood.

wood) and varies from it slightly in physical properties. The relative proportions of heartwood and sapwood in a tree vary with species and environment. Sapwood normally can be seasoned more easily than heartwood. It is more susceptible to fungus and insect attacks, but is more easily impregnated with wood preservatives. There is no difference in strength.

Strength

Strength of wood depends on the species, growth rate, specific gravity, and moisture content. Ex-

tremely slow growth produces a weaker wood. Softwoods (conifers) also are weakened by extremely rapid growth. Wood with low specific gravity or high moisture content is generally weaker. Defects such as grain deviation caused by spiral growth, knots, and burls, also result in weaker wood.

Appearance

Structural defects frequently enhance the appearance of wood. Spiral growth results in a winding stripe on turnings. Butt wood shows the assembly of root branches and crotch wood has a merging or diverging pattern. A burl produces attractive boards showing tissue distortion. The bird's-eye figures resulting from the elliptical arrangement of wood fibers around a series of central spots do not weaken maplewood appreciably. Some quarter-sawed woods show pronounced whitish flakes where the wood rays are exposed. This forms an interesting pattern, especially in oak and sycamore.

Lumber

Ways of Cutting—Lumber is sawed from a log in two distinct ways, with the plane of the cut either radial or tangential to the annual rings.

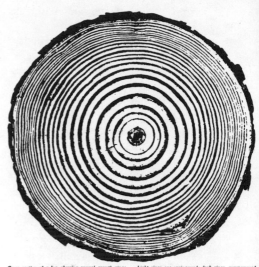

Cross section of a log, showing annual growth rings.   Light rings are springwood; dark rings, summerwood.

1. When the cut is tangent to the annual rings, the lumber is known as plain-sawed (hardwoods) or flat-grain lumber (softwoods).

2. When the cut is in a radial plane (parallel to the wood rays) the lumber is known as quarter-sawed lumber (hardwoods), or edge or vertical grain lumber (softwoods).

3. It is commercial practice to call lumber with annual rings at angles from 45° to 90° with the board surface "quarter-sawed," while lumber with rings at angles from 0° to 45° with the surface is called "plain-sawed." Unless the logs are very large, the average sawmill output consists mainly of plain-sawed lumber.

The relative advantages of plain-sawed lumber are:

• Usually cheaper than quarter-sawed lumber because it can be cut

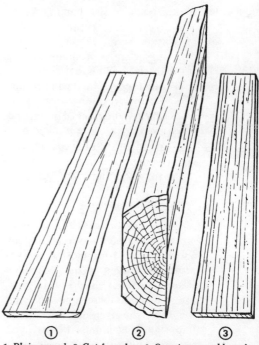

1. Plain-sawed. 2. Cut from log. 3. Quarter-sawed boards.

from the log faster and with less waste.

• Is less likely to collapse in drying.

• Shakes and pitch pockets extend through fewer boards.

• Round or oval knots affect surface appearance and strength less than the spike knots in quarter-sawed boards.

• Figures formed by annual rings and other grain deviations are more conspicuous.

Advantages of quarter-sawed lumber are:

• Shrinks and swells less in width than plain-sawed lumber.

• Cups and twists less.

• Does not surface-check or split as badly in seasoning and use.

• Wears more evenly.

• Raised grain caused by the annual rings is not as pronounced.

• Is less pervious to liquids.

• Most species hold paint better.

• Figures resulting from pronounced rays, interlocked grain, and wavy grain are more conspicuous.

• Width of the sapwood appearing in a board is no greater than that of the sapwood ring in the log.

Seasoning Lumber

As it comes from the sawmill, lumber has a high moisture content and is unsuited for most shop use. Moisture content is the weight of water contained in the wood, expressed as a percentage of the weight of the oven-dry wood. It is important that lumber be seasoned until the moisture content is in equilibrium with the conditions under which the wood will be in service. When a condition of equilibrium in moisture content is reached, the lumber has no tendency to shrink, expand, or warp. Because of normal changes in atmospheric moisture, this condition never holds constant. It is desirable, however, that an approximate equilibrium in moisture content be reached.

As the moisture content of a piece of wood decreases, the wood shrinks. Shrinkage begins when the moisture content drops below the fiber-saturation point. In most woods this is about 30%, the moisture content at which all free water disappears from the cell cavity, while the cell walls are still saturated. Normal air-seasoning practices reduce the moisture content of lumber to between 12% and 15%. If this wood is made into an article which is subjected to further drying action, shrinkage continues. Conversely, if the moisture content of a piece of wood is increased, the piece swells.

Wood expands or shrinks only 0.01% to 0.02% along the grain in length, but can change considerably across grain in width and thickness. Limits vary by species between 4% and 14% for tangential shrinkage and between 2% and 8% for radial shrinkage. The variation in expansion is about the same. Even when painted, wood continues to absorb and lose moisture according to long-time changes in atmospheric humidity. Therefore, it is always good policy to keep a small stock of lumber in the room in which it is going to be worked.

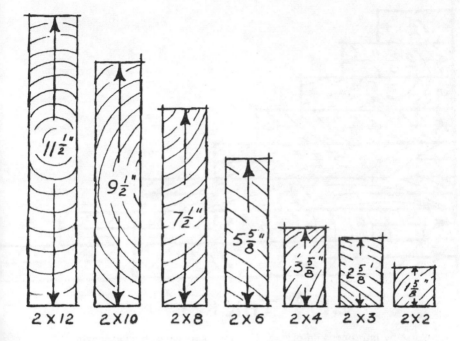

2 X 12   2 X 10   2 X 8   2 X 6   2 X 4   2 X 3   2 X 2

Lumber can be seasoned by natural air-drying, by kiln-drying, or by various chemicals (common salt, urea, and so on) in combination with the first two methods. The time available for drying, the species of wood, and the ultimate use of the wood are important factors in determining the method of seasoning.

(1) *Time*—If the lumber must be dried and ready for use in a limited time, it is seasoned by kiln-drying. Depending on species and size of stock, kiln-drying requires at least 3 days, while air-seasoning normally requires at least 2 months.

(2) *Species*—Some species need special treatment to prevent checking and warping. For example, black and tupelo gum boards can be kiln-dried slowly with excellent re-sults, but usually warp badly when air-dried if the lumber is not properly piled.

(3) *Ultimate use*—The moisture content of cabinet woods must be within a range of 5% to 7%. Since this percentage cannot be reached with normal air-seasoning, such wood must be kiln-dried.

Kiln-Drying

Kiln-drying is the common commercial practice. The modern compartment kiln has positive control over temperature, relative humidity, and air movement. Progressive type kilns are satisfactory for some kinds of lumber but are not so readily controlled as compartment kilns.

Seasoning defects are made

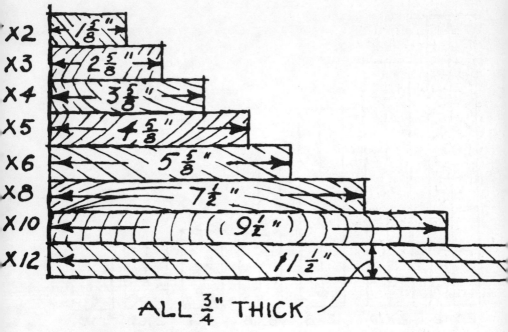

X2 $\frac{5}{8}$"

X3 $2\frac{5}{8}$"

X4 $3\frac{5}{8}$"

X5 $4\frac{5}{8}$"

X6 $5\frac{5}{8}$"

X8 $7\frac{1}{2}$"

X10   ($9\frac{1}{2}$")

X12 $11\frac{1}{2}$"

ALL $\frac{3}{4}$" THICK

worse by improper kiln-drying. The most common seasoning defects caused by faulty kilns or poor operation are:

(a) Casehardening, a condition in which such stresses are developed in a board that the outside is in compression and the inside is in tension even when both are equally dry. A flat casehardened board cups when sawed.

(b) Honeycombing (interior checking).

(c) Collapse of cell structure, manifested by an irregular cross section and surface corrugations.

(d) Warping in any or all of four forms:

1. Crook—edge of board convex or concave along its length.

2. Bow—face of board convex or concave along its length.

3. Cup—face of board convex or concave across its width.

4. Twist—the turning or winding of the edge of a board so that the four corners of any face are no longer in the same plane.

(e) Brashness, a condition characterized by low resistance to shock; caused in part by exposure to excessive heat.

(f) Surface and end checking (longitudinal radial cracks or separations formed to relieve drying stresses).

Chemical Seasoning

Chemical seasoning in combination with air- or kiln-drying is used by certain lumber companies for seasoning high-quality lumber.

Green lumber is taken directly from the grading table and treated with one of several chemicals. Urea has proved particularly effective in kiln-drying Douglas fir timbers.

There should be a fairly high concentration of the chemical in the surface of the lumber. The zone of chemical concentration has a lower vapor pressure than water, so the surface layer is water-hungry and pulls the moisture from the interior of the board to the surface. Theoretically, the surface zone remains moist at the expense of the interior. This is a reversal of the usual method of seasoning, in which the surface dries first. It sometimes makes possible seasoning of large timbers without the serious surface checking formerly accepted as inevitable.

Defects in Lumber

Most lumber has some defects. The most common defects are:

a. *Warp*—

b. *Grain Deviation*—Grain deviation is a condition in which the grain does not run parallel to the plain of the board. It may be due to natural or artificial causes. Spiral, wavy, curly, or bird's-eye figures and distortions caused by an injury or knot are natural grain deviations. Artificial deviations result when the plane of the saw cut is not parallel to the outside surface of the log. Grain deviation weakens a board; so, if strength is an important consideration, lumber with grain deviations must not be used, particularly if the grain slope exceeds 1 in 15.

c. *Knots*—Knots are portions of what once were limbs. As the tree grows, they become embedded in the trunk. If the limb is alive when the tree is cut, the knot is sound and tight. If the limb is dead, the knot is usually loose, at least in the part of the trunk that grew after the limb died. The grain deviation around a knot, rather than the knot itself, weakens lumber. Knots are round, oval, or spiked-shaped, depending on whether the log is plain- or quarter-sawed.

d. *Compression Wood*—Compression wood is frequently found in conifers on the underside of branches and leaning trunks. It is often characterized by an eccentric pattern of annual rings with an excess of opaque summerwood. The higher specific gravity of compression wood does not mean that this wood is stronger than normal wood. On the contrary, it is weaker and shrinks more in length.

e. *Injuries From Handling*—If a log is dropped across a rock, or a falling tree strikes a stump, the fibers are likely to be crushed and much of their tensile strength is lost. This defect, known as compression failure, appears on a board as a fine irregular line across the grain.

f. *Shakes*—A shake is a separation of wood along the annual ring. All causes of this defect are not known.

g. *Checks*—

h. *Molds, Stains, Wood Rots*—Wood is subject to the destructive action of a large number of fungi. These are microscopic saprophytic plants growths. Molds attack only the surface of the wood, and do little more damage than a layer of dirt.

Properties and Uses of Common Furniture Woods

Wood	Tree Range	Color of Heartwood	Color of Sapwood	
Alder, red (Alnus rubra)	Pacific coast	Light pinkish brown to white	Same	
Ash, green, black, white (Fraxinus)	Eastern United States	Light grayish brown	White	
Beech (Fagus grandifolia)	Eastern United States	White to slightly reddish	Same	
Birch, yellow and black (Betula)	Eastern United States	Light to dark reddish brown	White	
Cherry, black (Prunus serotina)	Eastern United States	Light to dark reddish brown	White	
Chestnut (Castanea dentata)	Eastern United States (now practically all blight-killed)	Grayish brown	White	
Elm, American and rock (Ulmus)	Eastern United States	Light grayish brown often tinted with red	White	
Gum, red (Liquidambar styraciflua)	Eastern United States, Mexico and Guatemala	Reddish brown	Pinkish white	
Gum, tupelo (Nyssa aquatica)	Southeastern United States	Pale brownish gray	White	

Propertiees and Uses of Common Furniture Woods

Pattern Figure	Warpage	Strength	Uses
Obscure	Minor	Medium	Panel cores, table tops, sides, drawer fronts, exposed parts of kitchen furniture. Stains readily in imitation of mahogany or walnut.
Pronounced	Minor	High in-bending	Solid tables, dressers, wardrobes; wooden refrigerators.
Obscure	Pronounced	High	Chairs and exterior parts of painted furniture. Bends easily and is well adapted for curved parts such as chair backs. Also used for sides, guides, and backs of drawers, and for other substantial interior parts.
Varying from a stripe to curly	Minor	High	Solid and veneered furniture. Same uses as hard maple.
Obscure	Minor	Medium	Solid furniture. Relative scarcity causes it to be quite expensive.
Conspicuous	Minor	Medium	Cores of tables and dresser tops, drawer fronts, and other veneered panels. Used with oak in solid furniture.
Conspicuous	Pronounced	High	Used to some extent for exposed parts of high-grade upholstered furniture. Easily bent to curved shapes such as chair backs.
Obscure to figured	Minor	Medium	Gum furniture may be stained to resemble walnut or mahogany. Also used in combination with these woods.
Obscured to striped	Pronounced	Medium	Cores of veneered panels, interior parts, framework of upholstered articles.

Propertiees and Uses of Common Furniture Woods

Wood	Tree Range	Color of Heartwood	Color of Sapwood	
Mahogany (Swietenia, Khaya)	Mexico, Central America, West Indies, Africa	Pale to deep reddish brown	White to light brown	
Maple, hard (Acer saccharum)	Eastern United States	Light reddish brown	White	
Oak, red and white (Quercus)	Eastern United States	Grayish brown	White	
Pine, ponderosa (Pinus ponderosa)	Western United States	Light reddish	White	
Poplar, yellow (Liriodendron tulipifera)	Eastern and Southern United States	Light yellow to dark olive	White	
Rosewood (Dalbergia nigra)	Eastern Brazil	Dark reddish brown with black streaks	White	
Sycamore (Platanus occidentalis)	Eastern United States	Reddish brown	Pale reddish brown	
Tanquile (Shorea)	Philippine Islands	Pale to dark reddish brown	Pale grayish to reddish brown	
Walnut, black (Juglans nigra)	Eastern United States	Light to dark chocolate brown	Pale brown	

Propertiees and Uses of Common Furniture Woods

Pattern Figure	Warpage	Strength	Uses
Ribbon or stripe	Minor	Medium	All solid and veneered high-grade furniture, boat construction, and cabinet work.
Obscure to figured	Minor	High	Bedroom, kitchen, dining, and living room solid furniture. Some veneer (highly figured) is used. Most furniture is given a natural finish.
Conspicuous	Minor	High	Solid and veneered furniture of all types. Quartered-oak furniture compares favorably with walnut and mahogany pieces and is often preferred in offices.
Obscure	Minor	Medium	Painted kitchen furniture.
Obscure	Slight	Medium	Cross banding of veneers, inexpensive painted furniture, interior portions of more expensive furniture, frames of upholstered articles.
Obscure streaked	Slight	High	Piano cases, musical instruments, handles, and so on.
Obscure to flake	Pronounced	High	Drawer sides, interior parts, framework of upholstered articles.
Ribbon or stripe	Slight	Medium	Similar to true mahogany.
Varying from a stripe to a wave	Minor	High	All types of solid and veneered furniture.

Since penetration is slight, molds often may be dressed off lumber. Stain fungi discolor wood but do not destroy much of the structure. Wood-rotting fungi break down the wood structure and in time reduce the wood to dust. Warmth, moisture, and air are necessary for fungus growth.

i. *Insect Damage*—Insect damage to seasoned or even partially seasoned lumber is usually slight. Certain woods are susceptible to Lyctus (powder-post) beetles. If a powdery substance is noticed coming from small holes, these beetles have attacked the wood.

Preservation

This term usually refers to the treatment of wood to make it resistant to fungi and insects. The most common method is to treat the wood with a substance poisonous to the destructive organism. The so-called "Penta" preservatives, creosote, salts such as zinc chloride, and organic compounds such as beta naphthol are effective.

Furniture Woods

The following characteristics are desirable in wood used to make or repair furniture:

a. Stability, or ability to keep its shape without shrinking, swelling, or warping.

b. Ease of fabricating, surfacing, and finishing.

c. Pleasing appearance.

d. Suitable strength and grain characteristics.

e. Availability.

Properties and uses of common furniture woods are listed on the accompanying table.

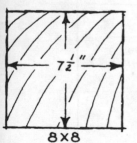

8 X 8

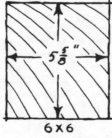

6 X 6

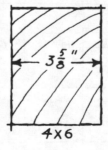

4 X 6

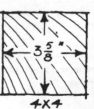

4 X 4

3 X

Lumber—How to Buy

All the miracles of modern synthetics haven't ousted wood from its spot as our number-one building material. It is easy to work, plentiful, durable and versatile. You can pick it for toughness, flexibility, beauty, hardness or softness. In the form of plywood, it comes in almost any size you need.

But the handyman who goes to the lumberyard with a gleam in his eye may come out with a glazed look and a thin wallet. Confusion about grades, dimensions, and prices may needlessly skyrocket a materials bill.

Actually, there is no mystery about lumber grades, sizes and charges. But the man at the stacks hasn't time to explain them. In the following pages you will find basic facts and money saving tips about structural lumber, boards, plywood, millwork and craft woods. These will help you decide what you need, and when to accept or reject substitute material. If you want the dealer's assistance, try to go to the yard on a weekday. Saturday is his busy day and he may not have the time to be helpful.

WOOD FOR THE HOME CARPENTER

There are three ways to buy wood for the project you're planning. All cost money, but a couple can be downright extravagant. One is to tell the yard man you want "some ¾" stuff about so big and that long" and hope for the best.

Another is to tell him what's building and let him try to outguess you as to construction, finish, and how much money the job is worth to you. He may play safe and sell you top-grade stuff, charging you accordingly.

The third is to know how lumber is sold and figure out what you want before stepping out of the house. This can save you time at the yard, keep the dealer your friend and earn you cash saving. To buy like this, you need only know some basic facts about the trade.

Hardwood or Softwood?

Whether the wood is easy or hard to dent or drive a nail into is

Picking out your own may pay even if the dealer charges for restacking afterward. You can pick straight 2x4's for door or window frames, clear joists where strength is critical. You are free to reject cupped or twisted stock you might get in a delivery.

Sorting cull lumber is one way to save money. Short lengths of the proper width, for instance, may serve for fire stops, bridging between joists, and braces. But usually you will have to square both ends of cull stock, which means one extra cut per member.

not what decides its type. Some hardwoods are fairly soft, and vice versa. Hardness will vary, too, with the part of the tree the piece comes from, and its moisture content. There is no sharp dividing line.

Woods are properly classified as hard or soft solely by the two groups of trees they come from. Those from broad-leaved deciduous trees (which shed their leaves each year) are hardwoods. Those from coniferous trees or evergreens, which have needles or scalelike leaves, are softwoods. Most of the wood in the ordinary lumberyard belongs to this class.

How Dry Is It?

If you're putting cupboards in a heated house, the wood had better be well seasoned or you'll wind up with cracks where the joints used to be. For exterior work it can be less dry, and for framing a house even poorly seasoned lumber will do in a pinch. Such wood is easy to nail, can be straightened if crooked, and will be fairly dried out, if the weather stays good, by the time you get around to enclosing it.

Green wood may be so wet it spouts water when a nail is driven in. You can sometimes buy unseasoned wood so much cheaper that it may pay to "stack and stick it" yourself for air drying. Or you may be able to put it up green in such a way that the opening of joints won't show. One way is to nail battens along the joints to one board only, and nail them to the other only after shrinkage has occurred. The wood is, of course, left unpainted. Remember that wood shrinks least lengthwise, and most across the grain. In a long board, however, even lengthwise shrinkage can open a corner joint half an inch.

If you want to test wood for moisture content and shrinkage, saw off a piece 1" long and exactly 6" across the grain. Weigh it carefully. Bake in the oven at 212° for at least four hours. Then measure it or compare it to an undried piece of the same stock. If you want moisture content, find the difference between wet and dry weight, and divide the difference by the dry weight. Example: a piece weighing 12 oz. originally and 8 oz. after drying (difference 4 oz.); dividing 4 by 8 gives $\frac{1}{2}$, or 50% moisture content.

For interior applications such as trim and cabinets, lumber should be kiln-dried. Such stock may have from 6% to 12% moisture content.

WOOD... HOW WOOD IS CUT

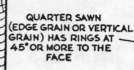

QUARTER SAWN (EDGE GRAIN OR VERTICAL GRAIN) HAS RINGS AT 45° OR MORE TO THE FACE

PLAIN SAWN (FLAT SAWN OR SLASH GRAIN) HAS ANNUAL RINGS AT LESS THAN 45° TO THE FACE

HOW YOU ARE CHARGED

YARD LUMBER IS PRICED BY BOARD MEASURE

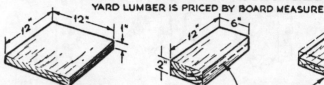

A BOARD FOOT IS 1"×12"×12" OR ITS EQUIVALENT

CUT APART, THIS WOULD MAKE A PIECE 1"×12×12"

A 12-FT. TWO-BY-FOUR CONTAINS EIGHT BOARD FEET

THIS ONE-BY-EIGHT BOARD CONTAINS EIGHT BOARD FEET

THIS FOUR-BY-FOUR CONTAINS EIGHT BOARD FEET

TO GET BOARD FEET, MULTIPLY THICKNESS IN INCHES BY WIDTH IN INCHES BY LENGTH IN FEET AND DIVIDE BY 12

$$\frac{T'' \times W'' \times L'}{12} = BD. FT.$$

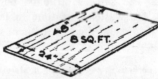
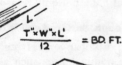

THIN LUMBER, PLYWOOD AND SIDING GO BY THE SQ. FT.

STANDARD 4 FT. × 8 FT. PANEL CONTAINS 32 SQ. FT.

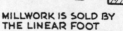

MILLWORK IS SOLD BY THE LINEAR FOOT

SHINGLES ARE SOLD BY THE SQUARE, ENOUGH TO COVER 100 SQ. FT.

LATH IS SOLD BY THE THOUSAND BUT PACKED IN BUNDLES OF FIFTY

You pay for the amount of wood in a piece before surfacing. For example, stock dressed to 1¾₆" is called 1" stock and priced accordingly. A surfaced 2x4 is considered 2" thick and 4" wide although it measures ⅜" less each way. A board 1¹⁄₁₆" thick will be charged for as 1¼". Wood thinner than ¾₆" involves extra labor and more waste, so it is sold by the square foot, which is the same as a 1" thickness.

HOW A TWO-BY-FOUR DWINDLES

| ROUGH LUMBER IS NOMINAL SIZE | SURFACING ONE EDGE REDUCES WIDTH | SURFACING ONE SIDE ALSO CUTS THICKNESS | SURFACING ALL AROUND LEAVES IT THIS SIZE |

Why it measures less than the size you buy. Shrinkage accounts for some of the difference, surfacing for the rest. Standard 1″ boards dress to between ¾″ and ¾₆″ thickness, lose ⅜″ to ½″ in width.

Framing lumber may be either kiln- or air-dried and have up to 20% moisture. Anything with more than that is usually considered green lumber. Beware of painting such wet wood; chances are the paint will not hold, but only retard seasoning.

Rough, Surfaced and Worked

Lumber comes from the saw cut to nominal sizes such as 2x4, 2x6, 4x4, and so forth. In this form it is classified as "rough." Run through a planer, it is known as "surfaced," and decreases in size by the amount of wood removed. A nominal 2x4 surfaced on four sides (S4S) thus shrinks to 1⅝″x3⅝″ in cross section, a 1x6 board to 2⁵⁄₃₂″x5⅝″. A "five quarter" board, nominally 1¼″ thick, comes to 1¹⁄₁₆″ when dressed.

Some lumber can be bought surfaced two sides (S2S) or one side and one edge, and so forth. Rough lumber, if available, is a good choice for some jobs, although

hard on the hands. Rough rafters may be good, for example, while rough studs may cause trouble, since difference in width would make the walls irregular. Dressed or surfaced lumber, on the other hand, is uniform. Planing straightens the pieces and makes the sides and edges parallel. Uniform width or thickness is important when pieces are to form an even surface for further construction. Studs in a wall, for instance, are placed on edge and therefore should be sized across the width on one or both edges. The same is true of floor joists. It's wasteful of time to lay odd widths and then dress them to match.

Pitch pockets, open seams containing liquid or dried resin, spoil a board as far as they reach when as big as this one. Small pitch pockets are harmless except for their sticky drippings. Decay spots weaken the piece as much as knots the same size.

FRAMING GRADES

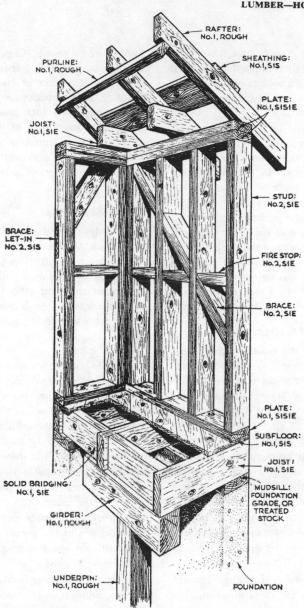

RAFTER:
No.1, ROUGH

SHEATHING:
No.1, S1S

PURLINE:
No.1, ROUGH

PLATE:
No.1, S1S1E

JOIST:
No.1, S1E

STUD:
No.2, S1E

BRACE:
LET-IN
No.2, S1S

FIRE STOP:
No.2, S1E

BRACE:
No.2, S1E

PLATE:
No.1, S1S1E

SUBFLOOR:
No.1, S1S

JOIST:
No.1, S1E

SOLID BRIDGING:
No.1, S1E

MUDSILL:
FOUNDATION
GRADE, OR
TREATED
STOCK

GIRDER:
No.1, ROUGH

UNDERPIN:
No.1, ROUGH

FOUNDATION

Typical uses of No. 1 and No. 2 common framing lumber are shown above. In general, members used in a horizontal position are under greater stress and should be No. 1 grade. For vertical members such as studs, No. 2 is adequate. Initials in above drawing refer to dressed members: S1S meaning surfaced one side; S1E, surfaced one edge; S1S1E, surfaced one side and one edge. Accurate sizing assured by surfacing is important where pieces form a base for a flush surface.

A third classification, "worked" lumber, refers to stock that has been run through a molder or similar machine and made into siding, casing, bead or molding.

Surfaced, or sized, lumber is grouped in three categories: Yard lumber includes boards and dimension lumber up to 5" thick. Structural timber are 5" or more. Both groups are graded as to quality with the use of the entire piece in mind, therefore a bad defect downgrades the piece. Factory and shop lumber, on the other hand, is meant to be cut up and permits defects between usable sections. This grouping has special interest for the craftsman.

How Wood Is Graded

All but the most expensive lumber has defects. Grading regulates the size and number of these. You should know enough about grading to buy the cheapest lumber suitable for your purposes and also to recognize inferior grades if they are sent to you by mistake. The safety and durability of a garage or house addition may depend upon your caution. Where building inspectors check on construction, you may have to rebuild anything in which less than required grades have been used.

In grading framing lumber, strength is the chief criterion. For this reason not only the size of the defects and whether they're sound or loose, but also their location is taken into account. A knot near the end of a 2x4 impairs its strength less seriously than one in the middle or near the edge. Therefore larger end

knots are allowed. Checks (end cracks) may be only one-fourth the thickness of a piece of No. 1 common; or, if two checks are opposite each other, their total must be no more than one-fourth of the thickness. In No. 2 common this tolerance goes up to one-third. An accompanying diagram shows these grading principles.

Money-Saving Tips

Besides using the lowest serviceable grade for the job in hand, you can sometimes trade time for a cash saving by picking over cull lumber. Plenty of split and otherwise damaged stock is usable. But it may require extra sawing to square off the ends, and only you can decide whether it pays.

Milling defects sometimes put lumber on the bargain counter. Hit-and-miss surfacing, in which the knives missed low sections, still leaves boards suitable for sheathing and subfloors, for instance. Some price arithmetic will show whether such lumber is worth buying.

Large beams, like those over wide garage doors, can be bought as timbers, but inside defects may be hidden and the pieces are hard to handle. A good alternative is to spike two pieces of 2" stock together side to side. Another lumber-saving device, building regulations permitting, is to use 2x4 ceiling joists over halls and for spans of 10' or less.

Weaknesses in rafters and joists that show up after they are in can be corrected by nailing "scabs" of 1" stock on each side of the piece. They should extend about 2' each

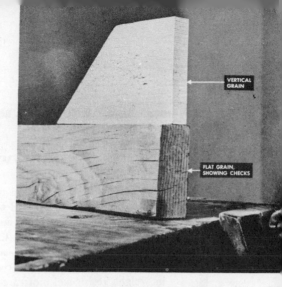

way beyond the defect. Studs bowed edgewise can be straightened by making a saw cut in the concave edge and expanding it with a wedge, afterward reinforcing the spot with scabs.

It's a good idea to clamp the member against a stiff, straight piece before you nail on the scabs.

Clear stock for porch columns comes high. A stained or natural finish can be satisfactory even if there are a considerable number of firm knots. For a painted finish you can use even rough or knotty pieces. Chisel back the knots, plug the holes with wood held in with waterproof glue, and fill rough spots with a good surfacing putty or fine sawdust mixed with waterproof glue. Sand well all over when the glue has set.

It's good practice to set door and window jambs before plastering, letting them take the place of plaster grounds. If you want the best finish in the least time, use kiln-dried grade B and better, vertical grain. This grade allows only two or three pitch pockets in a 12' length of 8" board, no knots or skips on the face, and no cupping.

If you can pick your own jamb stock and are sure of getting straight pieces, buy as near finished width as possible. For delivery, sight unseen, better get it wider so that edges can be jointed straight without making the material too narrow. This also applies to "pulley stile," jambs for double-hung windows already grooved for the parting bead. If this material is bowed edgewise, jointing the edges will still leave the groove curved.

Plain and quarter-sawn. Top piece was quarter-sawn, cut across the annual rings. Lower one was plain or flat-sawn, cut tangent to the rings. Plain sawing is less wasteful, produces wider boards. Quarter-sawn stock has attractive grain, shrinks and splits less.

Unless you are certain of getting worked stock that is straight, you'd better buy plain boards and groove it yourself after jointing to width.

Grain appearance is a clue to how well the wood will hold paint. Flat-sawn lumber with wide slashes of hard grain may flake paint off the hard parts. If hard grain appears as threads, it should hold paint well, but the broad hard grain of summer wood makes a board a poor prospect for painting.

When You Want Boards

By boards the lumberman means stock less than 2" thick and usually over 6" wide (narrower boards may be classified as strips). Pricewise, such stock adds up fast. Therefore it's important to buy sizes that will cut with a minimum of waste, and to get the cheapest grade adequate to the job.

What Wood Will You Use?

Coast to coast, our forests offer a variety of useful building lumber. Your dealer will ordinarily stock the kind that grows nearest and therefore costs least to haul to his stacks. It will usually cost you less, too.

Douglas Fir (also known as Oregon Pine) is neither fir nor pine but a species in its own right. It is very strong for its weight, resists soil moisture and decay, takes a good finish, and is made into plywood, doors and trim as well as framing stock.

White Pine (also known as Northern, Eastern and Canadian White Pine) grows from the East Coast to Minnesota and as far south as Georgia. It is much used for millwork as well as framing, is easy to work and less resinous than other pines.

Idaho White Pine (Western White Pine) has characteristically colored small tight knots. Better grades are used for the same purposes as Northern White Pine, while the lower grades are used for construction lumber and knotty-pine paneling.

Ponderosa Pine (California White Pine or Western Yellow Pine) has a number of regional names but is not truly a white pine. It is much used for millwork. If it will be exposed to weather, it should be treated to resist moisture.

Southern Pine (Southern Yellow Pine) takes in loblolly, pond, slash and other pines growing from Virginia to Texas. Some are known commercially as North Carolina Pine. Uses run from structural timber to molding.

Eastern Hemlock is found as far west as Wisconsin. West Coast Hemlock is often intermixed with Douglas Fir, and can be had in wide sizes of vertical-grain boards.

Redwood is also a West Coast wood, valuable for purposes ranging from ceiling to sheathing. Free from resin, it takes paint well and is resistant to weather and decay.

Cedar and Cypress are useful for sheathing, exterior trim, and siding.

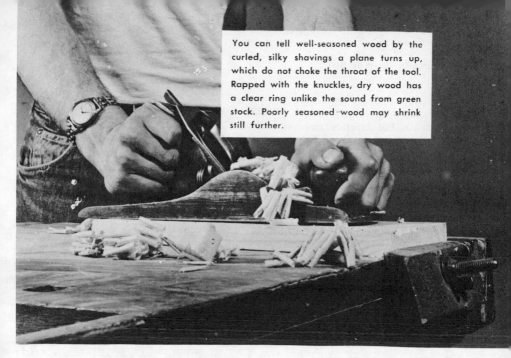

You can tell well-seasoned wood by the curled, silky shavings a plane turns up, which do not choke the throat of the tool. Rapped with the knuckles, dry wood has a clear ring unlike the sound from green stock. Poorly seasoned wood may shrink still further.

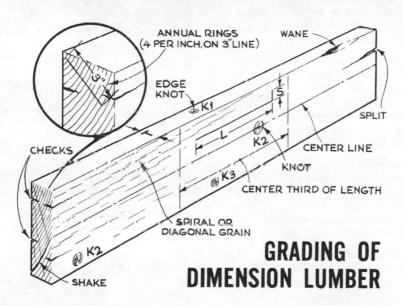

ANNUAL RINGS (4 PER INCH, ON 3" LINE)
WANE
EDGE KNOT
K1
S
SPLIT
T
L
K2
CENTER LINE
CHECKS
K3
KNOT
CENTER THIRD OF LENGTH
SPIRAL OR DIAGONAL GRAIN
K2
SHAKE

GRADING OF DIMENSION LUMBER

How it's graded: in framing lumber, the size of permissible defects is a fraction of the width or thickness (W or T). Where they may appear is shown above. Example: in No. 1 common, K3 may be W/4; that is, face knots near one edge in the center third of the length may be one-fourth the width in diameter. On the center line or at end (K2) knots may be a third the width in size. Edge knots (K1) may be T/3. Spiral or diagonal grain is measured in center of piece as slope (S) in a given length (L)—1 in 10 for No. 1 common, 1 in 8 for No. 2.

Grading is not an exact science, but depends upon the judgment and experience of the grader. The American Lumber Standards permit a 5% below-grade variation between graders. For this reason, and also because no two pieces of wood are identical any more than two thumbprints, even photos of typical grades can give only a rough idea of what may be expected. The better face of a board governs its grading. Within limits, the back may be poorer.

Here are the six commonest pine-board gradings. The sketches suggest typical projects for which each grade might be used.

B and better (also called 1 and 2 clear) is top quality, almost free from blemishes, and practically perfect even on the back. It's a luxury unless intended for the finest natural finish.

C select may have more defects, but all are minor ones such as small tight knots and small to medium pitch pockets, It will take a nice natural finish and is a fair substitute for B and better.

D select is the lowest grade of finish lumber, with medium or loose knots and other faults. The back may have more serious ones. But face defects can usually all be hidden by paint.

No. 1 common may have many small, smooth knots, all sound, none larger than about 2", and rarely on edges. Surfacing around knots is smooth. Paint hides most but not all its defects.

No. 2 common, an all-around utility grade, has the same defects as No. 1 to a greater degree. Knots may be up to 3½", though the average is much less. Even paint won't hide all its faults.

No. 3 common allows bigger, coarser knots, loose knots and knotholes, as well as some shake splits and pitch. Often a single large flaw will downgrade a No. 2 to No. 3.

SHOPPING FOR PLYWOOD

No craftsman should pass up the great advantages of plywood. It's the ideal material for all sorts of projects ranging from outdoor playhouses to furniture.

You can choose plywood for weather resistance, beautiful grain, plain toughness, flexibility or a combination of these. Often it will save you an enormous amount of work by eliminating framing.

The trick of gluing together layers of wood goes back to the ancient Egyptians, who left some nice examples. Yet until recent years veneered furniture carried a stigma because of a tendency to come unstuck or peel in time.

Plastic-resin and other modern adhesives and modern plywood presses have laid that ghost. Today's plywood is more resistant to splitting, warping and shrinking than natural wood. Pound for pound, it is stronger than steel.

Core Construction

If you look at plywood edges, you'll find two main kinds. Some plywood has a comparatively thick middle layer of solid wood, with a ¼₆″ layer on each side and the very thin face veneer (⅟₂₈″ thick) outside. This is lumber-core plywood. It is just the thing for projects like furniture, which call for doweled, splined or dovetail joints.

Fir, pine and some hardwood-veneer plywoods may show three to seven layers of similar thickness on the edge, with the grain of adjacent plies at right angles. This is veneer-core plywood. It is cheaper but not

Standard panels are 4′ by 8′, but many yards have a stockpile of smaller sizes. Type and grade are marked on panel edges. When you cut one up, mark pieces for identification.

Pregrooved plywood combined with louvered doors, wire grilles and scrollwork make this unusual dividing wall, the grooved panels simulate planking, but are easier to install.

as desirable where edge joints must be made or where edges will be exposed.

Will It Stand Weather?

Plywood is manufactured with different kinds of adhesives for various kinds of service. All three types are clearly identified on the panel edges.

The Face Woods

Veneers for plywood are cut three different ways. For common fir plywood, it is usually rotary cut —sliced off the logs as an apple is peeled. This gives it a wild zigzag grain that is hard to hide or sand smooth. Other veneers are quarter-sliced or flat-sliced. Each method produces its own characteristic grain. By the last two methods, slices can be pieced together for matched-grain effects.

Hardwood-veneer plywood makes beautiful kitchen cabinets. Doors are self-supporting without framing. Clear lacquer finish leaves the grain fully visible.

Fir plywood, the most economical, comes in a number of grades differing in surface quality and price. The best buy for general utility and for projects in which grain appearance does not matter, it comes in thicknesses from $\frac{1}{4}''$ to $1\frac{3}{16}''$. The standard panel is 4' by 8', but many yards have a stockpile of smaller random sizes.

Ponderosa-pine plywood is widely used for interior paneling and cabinet and furniture making. Its clear white color makes it ideal for natural or color-stain finishes. You can also buy it prefinished.

Hardwood-veneer plywood is available in over 30 woods. The veneers are variously cut to obtain the most beautiful grain possible, and panels with matching grain can be had. Face woods include birch, walnut, butternut, bubinga, cherry, elm, gum, hardwood, mahogany, oak, teak and many others.

In addition to plain panels, some hardwood veneer plywoods come in checkerboard panels, in prefinished, edge-grooved wall panels, and random-grooved panels.

Plywood Grades

All fir-plywood panels are clearly edge-marked with their type and grade. By careful buying you can stretch your shopping dollar. Why cut a cabinet back from the best grade at 20 cents a foot if 12-cent wallboard grade will do?

The quality of the two faces of a panel determines its grade. A "good" face consists of a single sheet of smooth, clear veneer. A "sound" face may consist of two pieces of veneer per panel, perfectly

joined but with small imperfections such as patches, stains or sapwood. A "utility" face may have knots, pitch pockets, knotholes and splits (up to $\frac{1}{16}''$ wide) that impair the looks but not the strength of the panel.

Obviously the best grade has two good sides (designated as G2S). This grade is called for when both sides will show and are to have a finish revealing grain. Where only one side will show, a "good-one-side" panel (G1S) will save you about five cents a square foot. The other side is sound.

For projects that are going to be painted, the sound-two-sides (S2S) grade or even (when only one side will show in the finished job) sound-one-side (S1S) will do. Wallboard grade (WB) has a sound face and utility back. Sheathing (SH) has two utility faces and comes unsanded, in $\frac{5}{16}''$ to $\frac{5}{8}''$ thickness. A special grade for concrete forms, made with highly water-resistant glue, can be used again and again. The edges of this $\frac{3}{4}''$-thick panel are sealed with paint, and the faces are oiled.

Another marking system designates faces as A, B, C and D. Therefore an A-A panel would have two good faces, one marked A-C a good face and utility back, while sheathing might be marked C-D or D-D.

Occasionally your yard may have reject panels, at savings of two to three cents per square foot. Some will be sanded, others not, and the defects for which they are rejected will vary greatly. Unless you can pick them out yourself, they may not be a good buy. The accompany-

Texture treatments either emphasize face grain or disguise it. Weldtex (top) is fir plywood, machine-grooved to produce a striated panel. Malarkey Shadowood (center) is available in both clear and knotty redwood with the soft grain wirebrushed down. Wedge-Wood (bottom) has a rotary-cut hemlock face treated to give a sculptured effect.

ing photos show how, with some extra work, you can save money by using the lower-grade panels.

Special Surfaces

Striking effects are achieved by texturing the surfaces of plywood panels. A series of machine-cut grooves all over the face, for example, produces a novel striated effect. Besides concealing the wild grain fir, this also disguises butt joints between panels so that no molding is required over them. Striated plywood is popular for interior wall paneling, and cheaper than hardwood veneers. It can be finished natural, stained, or painted.

Striated plywood is also made for siding. This is a three-ply exterior type ⅜" thick, precut 15 ⅞" long and 48" wide. It is somewhat cheaper than standard siding and faster to install.

Another surface treatment is produced by wire-brushing, which cuts down the soft parts of the grain faster than the hard, leaving these in relief. This kind comes in regular 4′ by 8′ panels and also in panels grooved to stimulate planking.

Finishing Plywood

Rotary-cut fir plywood is notorious for its wild grain. A good sealer such as Rez or Firzite will make finishing easier. Lacquer or wax may be used for a quick, durable one-treatment finish. Color stains produce striking modern effects. Striated and wire-brushed surfaces respond well to two-color treatment.

MORE PLYWOOD FOR LESS MONEY

If the going rate for standard "sound-two-sides" or "good-one-side" plywood panels has you stopped, consider what you can do with muscle instead of money. The cheaper grades of fir plywood are not sold for interior finish, but you can use them by putting in some extra work.

Occasionally a lumberyard will have a stock of "reject" panels. These may have excessive splits, open knotholes, or patches. Again they may be almost indistinguishable from better grades. Sometimes they are sanded, sometimes not.

Even if your yard has no rejects, it certainly carries sheathing grade. This comes in three-ply panels 5/16" and ⅜" thick, and in five-ply panels ½" and ⅝" thick. Neither face is sanded, but it costs little more than half the price of the top grade.

Examine the panels carefully to make sure you're putting their best faces forward. Then use one of the tricks shown in these photos to suit your plans and pocketbook.

FOUR WAYS TO LICK THE ROUGH GRAIN OF CHEAP PLYWOOD

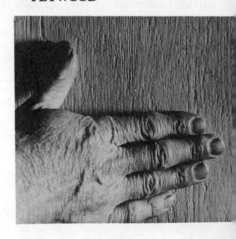

Pleasing finish is obtained on pieces without serious surface defects by just applying paint. Brush on two coats; sand lightly between.

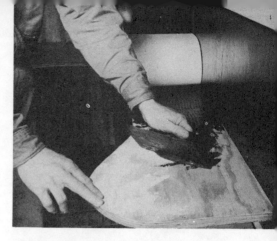

Wire-brushing emphasizes the grain nicely, but is feasible only on small areas. Use a flexible cable or electric drill. Brush with the grain.

Linoleum is a good covering for rough plywood used as a desk or counter top. Fill and sand big cracks before spreading linoleum paste.

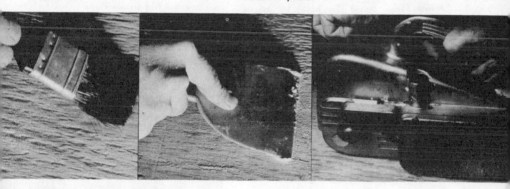

Wood-putty type of water-mixed filler will level off plywood surface and make a good paint job possible. First wet the wood with a brush (left above). Make a thick mix of the filler; spread it with a wide putty knife (center). Smooth with power sander.

The difference between a sound and a reject panel may be as great as that shown here. Note patch in sound face above. Defects at right are worst you'll find. For painting, they can be puttied or plastered.

PATCH

SOUND-ONE-SIDE PANEL

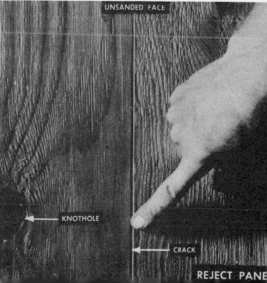

UNSANDED FACE

KNOTHOLE

CRACK

REJECT PANE

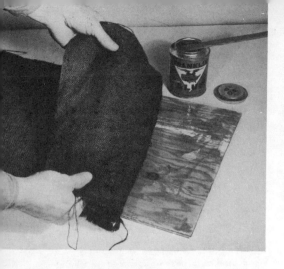

Burlap facing can transform cheap plywood into good-looking doors. Fill worst cracks; then spread glue, apply burlap.

Turn over and drop burlap-covered panel into rabbeted frame as above. Nail burlap in place and trim excess cloth.

Finished door is light, non-warping and attractive. Other cloths and patterned material might be used. Glue should be non-staining kind.

Plaster-base crack filler such as spackle can be used to get a smooth painting surface. First give the panel a priming coat of paint (left). Smooth on the filler with a putty knife as evenly as possible (center). After it has set, sand the surface smooth.

LOW-COST WOOD FOR CRAFT-WORK

Woodworking hobbyists waste thousands of dollars every year cutting up expensive lumber into little pieces. Nine times out of ten the fellow who turns bowls or lamps, carves plaques, or builds nick-nack shelves will bring home clear stock of finish grade—the most expensive he can buy. Yet he could get wood just as good for his purpose at about half the price.

Shop Grade

The secret of saving money is to buy factory- and shop-grade lumber. If the nearest yard doesn't carry this, it will pay to find one that does.

Shop-grade lumber is none too pretty at first glance. It has plenty of knots, many of them along the edges, and some holes where loose knots fell out. Your first reaction may be to wonder how you can use it.

But this material is a gold mine to the craftsman, especially if he has a power saw. By cutting around

Apple-box wood was raw material for the projects directly above. Saw out the knots from the shop-grade lumber (below) and the pieces left will be clear grade, at half price.

Cash and carry will save you money at most lumberyards. A car-top carrier makes it easy to take your purchase home. Shopping in person also gives you your pick of the stacks.

Mill ends, manufacturing scraps, lumberyard shorts and even waste from building jobs can yield valuable material. This trailer load could keep a craftsman happy for months.

the defects, he winds up with a lot of pieces just as good as the finish grades that coast so much when bought as boards. For many projects—lamps, book ends, corner shelves and candlesticks, only small pieces are needed.

Shop-grade lumber is a good bet, too, for the man who does weekend carpentering around the house. He will need more ingenuity to use the odd-sized pieces for shelves, racks, vegetable bins and so forth, but the saving makes it worthwhile.

Use Those Boxes

Don't overlook the lowly apple box and packing crate as wood sources. The ends are often ¾″ thick soft pine, which is suitable for many small projects. Crates are sometimes made of hardwood in the poorer grades, but between the splits and knots you may find short pieces of usable craft wood.

The thin sides of fruit boxes are ideal for such small items as birdhouses, spice shelves, spoon holders and other colonial reproductions.

When You Want Hardwood

You may find wonderful hardwood in your own or a neighbor's attic. Old pieces of furniture—bed headboards, chests, and especially old extension-table leaves—are good sources.

The only drawback to using such material is the old finish, which usually has to be removed. Don't make the mistake of trying to sand it off on your disk or belt-sander—it will clog the abrasive cloth rapidly.

There's good wood in fruit crates and boxes. The rough sides can be sanded to yield ³⁄₁₆″ to ⁵⁄₁₆″ stock. To avoid splits, hammer against piece of wood as shown below.

Coarse, open-grained paper of the kind used on floor sanders is better. But the safest way to strip the wood is with paint remover and a scraper.

Try Your Lumber Yard, But . . .

Scraps of new hardwood are sometimes obtainable as mill ends. Look for a lumberyard that does millwork. Sometimes you may need stock of less than standard thickness, which is hard to come by as a regular thing. The mill may have leftovers, of ³⁄₈″ or ½″ thickness from large milling orders.

But the chances are that your local lumberyard will carry chiefly the softwoods commonly used for construction work. That means that if you're bound to use hardwoods you may have to forget about a low-cost job. The lumber dealer may be able to order any special hardwoods you want. Or you can order them yourself from one of the mail-order houses specializing in craft woods.

Among these wood specialists are Albert Constantine and Son, Inc., 2050 Eastchester Rd., New York 61, N.Y.; Craftsman Wood Service Co., 2727 S. Mary St., Chicago 8, Ill.; and Frank Paxton Lumber Co., First and Kansas Ave., Kansas City 3, Kansas.

Wood from such sources will be perfect, every piece selected and usable to its full size. Naturally, it also costs more.

HOW TO IDENTIFY WOODS

When you order birch or maple from a craft-woods dealer, you get what you ask for. But there's a trick to it: the dealer keeps each kind in a separate stack. Once let them get mixed, and even the experts couldn't put them all back just right.

Nature never quite duplicates anything and, wood being a natural product, no two pieces are ever exactly alike. Although one may unmistakably be maple, you can look farther and find a piece of maple anybody might take for birch. Furthermore, there are varieties even within a kind—nine, for example, of white oak. So don't underrate yourself if you aren't sure which is which.

The photos below show typical examples of eight common woods, and the captions give clues to help you tell one from another. But grain, color and even hardness may vary widely. If you keep a mixed stack, the surest way to tell the kinds apart is to mark each piece the day you get it.

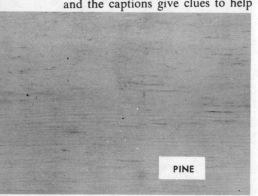

PINE

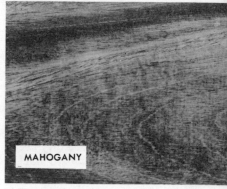

MAHOGANY

Light in color and weight, most pines range from off-white to light tan, sometimes with an orange cast, and weight less than 2½ lb. a board foot (kiln-dried). Southern pine is brownish yellow.

Don't be fooled by the color. Mahogany is a medium reddish brown, similar to finished mahogany furniture. It has open pores, moderate hardness, and is fairly heavy.

CHERRY

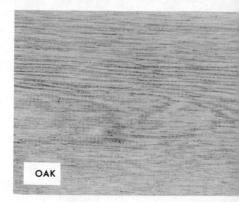

OAK

Cherry furniture is often deep red, but the wood is actually a light reddish brown—about as dark as white oak—with perhaps a green cast. It is close-grained, fairly hard and heavy.

The open grain is the best tip-off to the oaks. White oak ranges from light tan to light brown in color; red oak is reddish or light reddish brown. Wood from the oak trees is extremely hard and heavy.

BIRCH

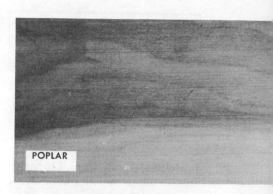

POPLAR

Fairly light in color, birch has a yellowish white sapwood with a reddish brown heartwood. It is a close-grained wood, hard and reasonably heavy, weighing approximately 3½ lb. per board foot when kiln-dried.

Poplar, often called whitewood, has the lightest color of the eight woods shown here. The sapwood is almost white, but the heartwood is pale olive to yellow brown. It is moderately soft and lightweight.

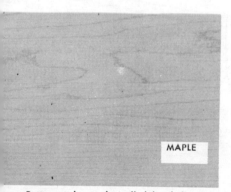

MAPLE

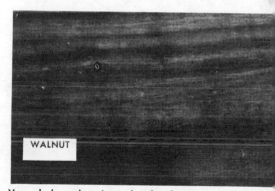

WALNUT

Better-grade maple, called hard, lives up to its name—it is hard and heavy. The color is a light tan, lighter than pine but darker than poplar. It has very fine texture and grain, weighs about 3½ lb. per board foot.

Very dark, walnut is a chocolate-brown color, often with a purplish cast. It has open pores and is moderately dense and hard. The texture is fine and even. The kiln-dried wood weighs about 3½ lb. per board foot.

Magnetic Circuit Breaker

This is an electromagnetic device which opens the circuit if there is a short or an overload.

See *Circuit Breaker* and *Electrical Wiring*.

Marking Gage

Woodworking layouts are usually marked off with a chisel-pointed pencil. Extremely accurate layouts, for cutting special joints, are made with a sharp knife-point. Lines parallel to edges and ends are quickly marked with the marking gage. Keep the spur point of this gage sharply pointed so you will get a clean, fine line.

This gage marks best when it is pushed with just enough pressure to make a distinct line. Keep the face of the gage head pressed snugly against the edge of the board, or the marked line will be wobbly and inaccurate.

Before you mark with the gage, check the measurement from the spur point to the head with a rule—the scale on the gage beam may possibly be inaccurate.

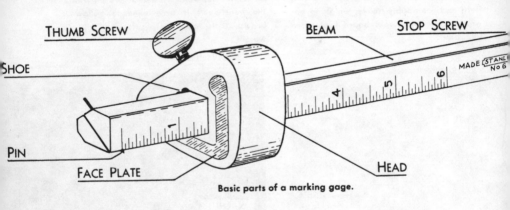

Basic parts of a marking gage.

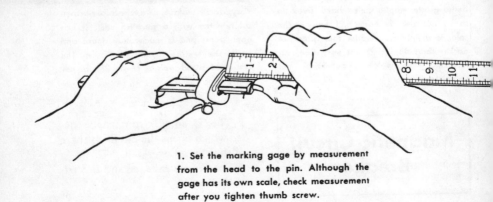

1. Set the marking gage by measurement from the head to the pin. Although the gage has its own scale, check measurement after you tighten thumb screw.

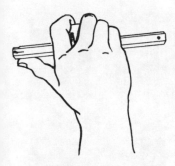

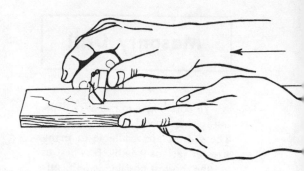

2. Hold the gage as you would a ball. Advance your thumb toward the pin so as to distribute the pressure evenly between the pin and the head.

3. Lay the beam flat on the wood so that the pin drags naturally as the marking gage is pushed away from you. Do not roll the gage; the pin and the line should always be visible as you mark.

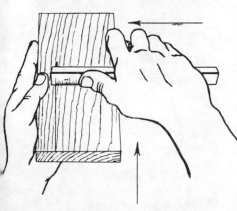

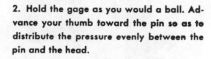

4. To make the gage line, push the unit forward with the head held tight against the work edge of the wood. The pressure should always be applied away from you and toward the edge of the board, in the directions shown by the arrows in the sketch.

Sketches from "Tool Guide" courtesy of Stanley Tools.

Masonry Anchors

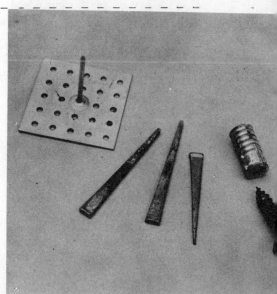

Various types of fastening devices can be used to attach wood and other items to masonry surfaces, such as brick, concrete and stone. For full details, see section on *Anchors for Concrete*.

Here are several types of masonry anchors (left to right): special adhesive nail, steel cut nails, lag screw and lead shield.

Masonry Drill

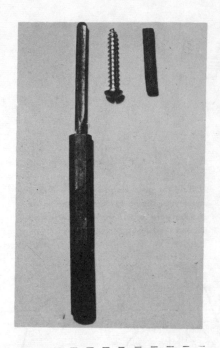

To bore a hole in masonry without power tools, use a star drill. These drills are available in many sizes in various lengths. It is best to use the shortest possible length, sufficient to go through the thickness of the masonry when making an opening, because this insures accuracy and makes swinging the hammer less tiring.

This is a star drill together with a fiber plug and the screw used to attach any item to a masonry wall.

Oilstone

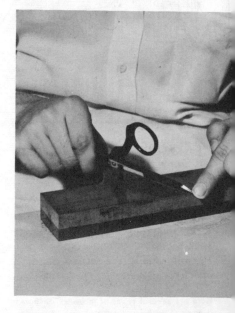

This is used for honing edged tools, and to remove any "wire-edge" left by the grinder. Some oilstones are made of a combination of materials, but others are of natural stone. The natural stones have exceptionally fine grains and are unsurpassed for putting razor edges on fine cutting tools.

Oilstones come in many sizes and shapes—square, triangular, rectangular, round, round edge slip, and tapered concave-convex gouge slip.

MAINTENANCE

• Soak new oilstone in engine or machine oil before using unless

Oilstones are used for sharpening edge tools, such as knives, scissors, chisels and planes, as well as removing "wire-edge" left by a grinder. See Files and Sharpening.

OILSTONES

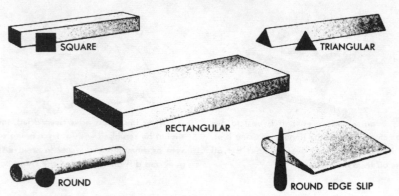

SQUARE

TRIANGULAR

RECTANGULAR

ROUND

ROUND EDGE SLIP

Oilstones come in various shapes and sizes depending upon use.

To keep a stone in "working" order, it should be serviced regularly. Before using an unfilled stone, soak it in oil (left) for several hours. Each time you use the stone, apply a light coat of oil (center). After you have finished using the oilstone, wipe it clean with a cloth or cotton.

An oilstone requires periodic dressing to remove any ridges or grooves. Do this by rubbing the stone over abrasive paper.

DRESSING OILSTONE

HOW TO MEND A BROKEN OILSTONE

1. If an oilstone breaks, it is best to dry the stone. This can be done by placing it on a hot plate or in an oven to drive out all the oil from the inside.

2. After the pieces have been dried, they should be scrubbed with a drycleaning solvent or ammonia and water to remove the gum and dirt on the face of the stone.

3. To join the two pieces together, it is necessary to sprinkle ground or flake orange shellac thickly on the broken edge of both pieces, into all the cracks and openings along the edges.

4. Reheat both pieces of the stone in order to melt the shellac. Remove the stones with tongs and set the pieces together with clamps to join while cooling.

WRONG

RIGHT

An oilstone should never be used dry. Always lubricate the surface before sharpening any tool. Otherwise, the surface will glaze and become clogged.

Don't keep an oilstone in the sun or where it is hot. The heat will cause the oil to become gummy. Store the oilstone in a cool, moist place in the workshop.

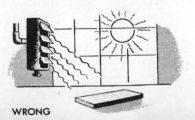

WRONG

RIGHT

stone has been oil filled by manufacturer.

- Prevent glazing by application of light oil during use of stone.
- Wipe stone clean with wiping cloth or cotton waste after each use.

CLEANING

Wash glazed or "gummed up" stone with dry-cleaning solvent (such as carbon tetrachloride) or ammonia water. If this treatment fails to completely clean the stone, scour it with aluminum oxide abrasive cloth or flint paper attached to a flat block.

DRESSING

True uneven surfaces on coarse, medium, or fine oilstones by rubbing on the side of an old grinding wheel or a grindstone. Or you can cover a smooth cast iron block with waterproof abrasive paper. Then rub the stone on the abrasive paper, using water as a lubricant, until the surface is true.

Special shape stones can be formed by making a groove of mating shape in a cast-iron block. Use waterproof abrasive paper and water and draw stone through groove.

COMMON MISUSES

Do not use stone dry. This causes glazing and clogging. Apply light engine oil or a half-in-half mixture of machine oil and kerosene (or even water in an emergency) before using stone.

Do not store stone in a hot place. Heat will cause oil to form a gummy residue on stone. Store in a cool, moist place.

Do not attempt to do a honing job with the wrong stone. Such procedure wastes time and energy and causes unnecessary stone wear. Use stones as follows:

Coarse—To sharpen large and very dull or nicked tools.

Medium—To sharpen ordinary mechanics' tools not requiring a fine finished edge such as tools for working soft wood, cloth, leather, and rubber.

Fine—To sharpen tools requiring a very fine edge such as used by machinists, engravers, instrument workers, and cabinet makers.

One-Evening Projects

While maintaining and improving a house often may appear to be a full-time job, you will frequently find a spare evening or two to tinker in the workshop. In just a few hours, you can complete an entire project and produce a useful and attractive addition to the home.

These one-evening projects are designed both for the amateur and the experienced craftsman. Often, it is possible to bring the lady of the house into these projects and have her lend a helping hand.

On the following pages are 30 of these one-evening projects—enough to keep the handyman busy every night of the month. Of course, few handymen, even the most ardent craftsmen, can find the opportunity

to tinker in the workshop every night. If you're the average handyman, here are enough projects to keep you busy for the year. If you want additional ones, just pick up and thumb through the pages of magazines that feature craftwork such as "Popular Science Monthly."

Wrought Iron Lamp

Coat-hanger wire and quarter-inch hail screening form the "wrought ironwork" for this attractive modern lamp. First, solder a lamp socket to a washer. Then remove the paint from several straightened coat hangers with sandpaper. Cut and bend the three legs and solder them securely to the washer.

Make two 4"-diameter rings, filing slots where the ends of the wire meet, and floating in solder for strong joints. Cut a 2½"-wide strip of hail screening, bend it into a cylinder, and solder the ends of the cylinder to the inner surfaces of the rings. Position the resulting shade cage on the tops of the three legs and

solder the legs to the ring at 120° intervals.

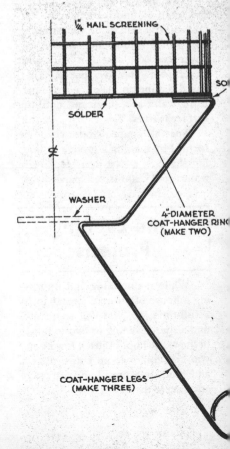

Scrub with detergent to remove soldering paste; then apply flat black paint. Set a 2½″ cylindrical shade in the wire-mesh cage.

TV Lamp

A porcelain vase makes a restful TV viewing lamp. Drill one ⅜″ hole through the bottom of the vase and another through one of its sides, using kerosene on the bit to ease it into the porcelain. Pass a ⅜″ bolt through the hole in the base from below and thread it into the back of a light socket. Use the other hole as an outlet for a lamp cord with a feed-through switch cut into it at a point several inches from the vase.

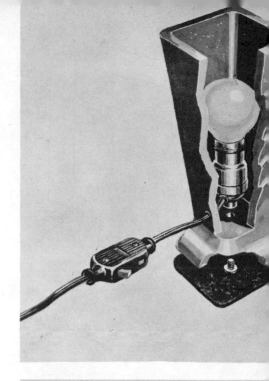

Water-Well Lamp

A wood-turning lathe with a faceplate will help you give this "old-oaken-bucket" lamp a whirl. Turn the base, well-body and bucket from maple or beech, and the windlass from ½″ doweling. Make the windlass frame from ¾″-square strips of the same wood. Drill a hole in the center of the cross member for a light-socket bushing and nut; then carve a groove in its undersurface to carry the lamp cord to one of the uprights. Drill a ¼″ hole through the upright and the section of the base beneath it. A quarter of the base circumference away, drill a ⅜″ hole into the edge of the wood for another cord bushing. Connect the two holes with an L-shaped channel carved or routed in the underside of the base.

Before bradding and gluing the parts together, attach the lamp socket and thread the cord through

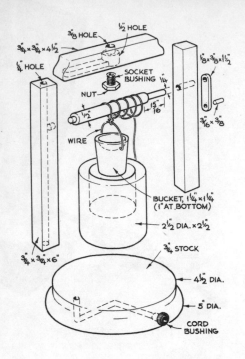

the holes and channels. Also insert the windlass in the bearing holes before attaching the upright on the crank handle from doweling. Drill holes in the bucket for a wire bail and tie a piece of cord a foot or more in length to the bail for a bucket rope.

Give all wood parts but the well-body a natural finish (two coats of shellac or varnish). Paint the well-body brick red and apply gray mortar strips with a brush or striping tool. Finally, wind the bucket rope around the windlass and, with bucket at height indicated, secure it with several drops of cement.

Dowel-Wire Magazine Rack

Your favorite magazines are neatly held in a rack of oak or other hardwood and No. 9-gage steel wire. Trim and true the base. Mark 1⅜" holes 2" from two corners joined by a diagonal, and bore at a 100° angle.

The arch is of 1⅜" dowels mitered 40° for the joints. A guide block helps start the crosspiece cuts at the same point on the circumference. Using a block jig, drill for ⅜"

doweling, and glue in place. Glue in the uprights, drill through the ends of the base, glue in anchor dowels, trim flush, and clamp until the glue sets.

Hammer sharp right-angle bends in the wires, and glue them into No. 9-gage holes drilled ½" into the uprights.

Sand, stain, and finish with clear varnish. Enamel the wires dull black.

Perforated Steel Magazine Rack

This informal magazine rack, useful in a small den or playroom, has two sloping sides of ¾" stock nailed to a ¾"x3"x12" bottom piece and a back of ½" plywood. The front is perforated sheet metal held in place by a three-sided rabbeted-and-mitered frame. Screw it to the back of a door to save that much-needed space.

Junior Clothes Pole

This junior clothes rod that grows with the child has one-by-two pine or fir end racks bored to take a length of 1″ dowel or broom handle and fitting snugly the closet depth. Assemble, bracing with narrow strips of scrap 1″ lumber, and install by nailing the top ends. Saw at top and renail to raise the height as needed.

Muffin-Tin Drawers

These handy drawers are a convenience, almost a necessity, in both the workshop and sewing room. With the flanges running in cleats attached to the underside of a table or shelf, the compartments hold nails, screws, bolts, cotter pins and washers, or buttons, hooks-and-eyes, snap fasteners, pins and the like.

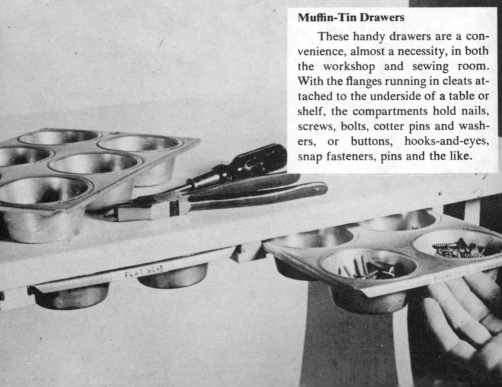

Brass Ash Tray

No butts about this ash tray. Rubber-cement the old goat's paper likeness on sheet brass. Cut the outline with a jeweler's saw and smooth all edges with a fine file. Solder the round head of a No. 6–32 bolt in the notch in the bottom and pass it through a hole drilled in the center of a metal tray or china saucer, where it's secured with a thin nut. For china, drill hole with a ⅛" brass rod, rotated in a little pool of No. 150 silicon carbide grains mixed with turpentine.

ACTUAL-SIZE PATTERN

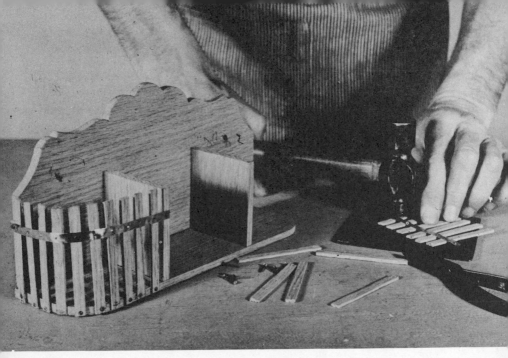

Garden Clock

Old hardwood boards, some ⅟₁₆x ¼ " strips of the same material, and a couple of sheet-metal bands are needed to make this flower-flanked clock shelf. Glasses holding water for the cut blooms are set behind the miniature picket fence, formed by riveting the metal bands to the upright strips. A drawer for house keys provides a raised base for the clock.

TV Lamp

The colorful shade of this lamp comes ready-made as a 12"x18" bamboo place mat. From ¾" wood, cut a 4"x5" block, around which the mat just fits snugly. Drill a corner hole for the lamp cord and another opposite for the switch leads. Fasten a flush-mounting socket in the center. Drill two holes in each leg piece for ⅝" wood screws. Then screw on the legs and complete the wiring.

Cut 2" from the width of the mat. Glue it around the base, bend a strip of light aluminum molding or linoleum binding around over it, and secure it with escutcheon pins. Tie the ends of the mat together with a strong thread midway and at the top. Then shape a second piece of molding like the first. Cement it around the top of the shade. Use only small bulbs that cannot touch the shade.

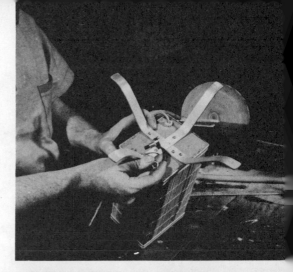

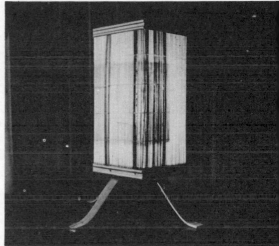

Copper Jewel Box

A short piece of copper stack pipe of 3⅛" diameter, left over from a plumbing job, provided the inspiration and center section for this project. You can quickly fashion the square mahogany base and octagonal lid which convert it into a handsome jewel box. Rout shallow recesses in each of the hardwood members to receive the pipe, and glue suede or felt in them to serve as cushioning. Mount a knob on the lid.

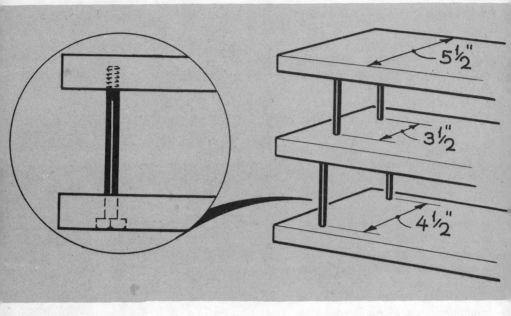

Plant Shelves

Pots of ivy look fine on this triple shelf. It is made of three pieces of ¾″ oak, 5 ½″ wide, arranged in step fashion. Eight ¼″ bolts 6″ long hold the shelves together. The holes were all bored slightly less than ¼″ so that the bolts would be a tight fit. The holes were countersunk under the two longer shelves to take the bolt heads. Make the shelves any length.

Trivet

A decorative tile resting on this small stand serves as a hot plate for a tea party. It consists of a wood base sawed to the size of the tile, and four ¼″ by 6″ bolts screwed into each of the four corners at a 60° angle. Use a drill a little less in diameter than the bolt to insure a tight fit. A drill press will simplify such angle drilling. If you must use a brace or hand drill, first make a guide hole at the proper angle in a block of wood and use this block as a jig by clamping it on the wood to be drilled. Screw all bolts into the holes the same distance to level the tile.

Small Magazine Rack

For digest-size publications, use ¼″ by 6″ bolts placed at 70° angles along two sides of a piece of hardwood. This makes a table rack; for a floor rack for large magazines, use ½″ by 16″ or even larger bolts in a base about 1⁵⁄₁₆″ thick. Be careful to drill all holes at the same angle; a simple jig will make sure they are right.

Attractive Book Rack

A simple book rack that you can complete in a short time is shown here. Drill three ¼″ holes ½″ in from each end of a piece of hardwood ¾″x5½″x12″, spacing them evenly between the sides. Turn three ¼″ by 6″ bolts into the holes at one end. Turn three ¼″ by 1½″ bolts into the holes at the other end—from the opposite side of the board —to serve as legs for the rack. That's it.

Candle Holder

The materials necessary for making the holder are a 5″ disk of ¾″ stock and three 1½″ disks of ¼″ stock, plus three ¼″ by 3″ machine bolts. Scribe a 3″ circle in the center of the large disk. At three equidistant points along its circumference drill three ¼″ holes at angles of 60°. Counterbore the holes underneath the disk to take the bolt heads. Run the bolts through and turn them into holes drilled in the small disks. Two screws anchor each candle.

TV Seat

A light seat next to the TV set makes it more comfortable to adjust the controls. Here it is—a 12″ equilateral triangle cut from 1″ stock with angled legs of ½″ by 16″ carriage bolts. Screw the legs into holes drilled at 60° angles into the two thicknesses of wood at the corners. Glue the corner blocks into place under the top.

Modern Apple Basket

Take a 6″ disk sawed from ¾″ stock, bore a dozen ¼″ holes around the edge at an outward angle of 70°, turn in a dozen ¼″ by 6″ bolts, and you've got it.

Attractive Footstool

Making this handsome footstool is pretty simple. Fir plywood scarp will do for the top, and almost any ¾ " solid stock can be used for the rest.

Make a cardboard template for the ends so that they will be exactly alike. The scroll on the bottom will have to be done on the jigsaw. To saw out the mortises for the stretcher, drill starting holes, then tilt the jigsaw 83°. Drill holes for the pegs, squaring them with a chisel. Cut and attach the ½ " cross strips with glue and screws. Two coats of orange shellac, each rubbed down with fine steel wool, will give a natural finish.

Cover the top with a 13"x21" piece of leatherette over a 1½ " layer of upholsterer's cotton. Tack the plastic to the underside with carpet tacks, then add decorator's tacks around the edge.

Aluminum Light Switch Plates

Here's an easy way to liven up plain-looking light switches and help keep them clean to boot. These decorative wall plates, snipped from aluminum sheet, not only add a novel touch to any room, but their projecting edges channel smudgy fingers toward the switch itself, keeping them off the wall. They're also a helpful guide in the dark.

The miniature serving tray spells food on the way in the kitchen or dining areas. The plainer picture-frame type fits nicely in other spots. For a hammered finish, as shown on the tray, tap all over with a ball-peen hammer.

The patterns shown are for single-toggle switches. For multiple types or outlet boxes, use the existing plates as guides for cutting the openings.

Make cardboard pattern, as shown, to be sure that corners fit neatly and toggle opening lines up with screw holes. Then lay pattern on 1/16″ aluminum sheet and trace around it with scriber. To cut handle slots, drill 1/8″ holes and saw out waste between.

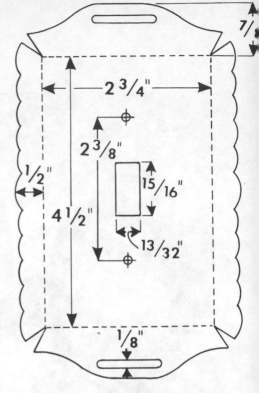

Cut out aluminum with jeweler's saw, as shown, or fine-tooth coping saw. Drill starting hole for toggle opening. Bend up sides, solder corners, and file edges smooth.

Picture-frame plate has simple lines that suit any room. Outer edges project farther than center, letting plate hug wall where boxes protrude.

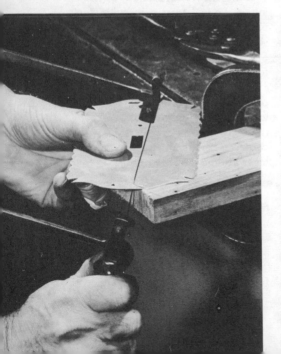

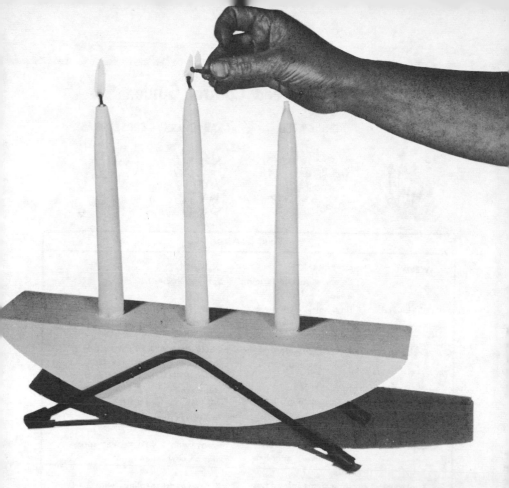

Three-Light Candelabra

Candles go modern in these up-dated holders. Saw the long one from 3″ stock 14″ long, making the curve of 14″ radius and 3″ deep. Bore ¾″ holes 1″ deep for the candles. Bend 14″ lengths of ¼″ rod to 120° and attach with small screws, making certain all four feet touch.

Lay out the triangular holder on 2x6 stock, rounding the sides to a 12″ radius as in the drawing. Use a string tacked to a block if you haven't a compass big enough. Legs are 16″ lengths bent 90°. Holder shown is charcoal gray, spattered with yellow.

How-To Weed Control Guide

BUCK HORN	CHICKWEED	CRAB GRASS	GOOSE GRASS

Weed Control

WEED	APPEARANCE	CONTROL
Buckhorn	Common, rosette-forming weed.	Spray with 2,4-D.
Chickweed	Tiny, hairy, dark green leaves; small white flowers.	Spray repeatedly with potassium cyanate (PC) or 2,4-D.
Crabgrass	Annual, wiry, hard to mow; creeping stems.	Apply PMA or Crag Herbicide in the seedling stage three times at directed intervals. For mature stage use PC.
Goose grass (Poa Annua)	Variation of annual grasses.	Try PMA, PC and 2,4-D but chemicals are seldom effective. Weed by hand.
Ground Ivy	Rounded leaves, tiny blue flowers, mint-like odor.	Spray with 2,4-D. Repeat sprayings on new seedlings.
Knotweed	Long stems spread flat; blue-green leaves; green-white flowers.	Spray young seedlings with 2,4-D or PC. Use 2 more applications at 3-week intervals.
Quack grass	Tough perennial, forms an open sod. Coarse, resembling crabgrass.	Neither chemicals nor hand weeding are effective, since it sends out underground shoots. Good lawn care is the cure.
Self-Heal (Penny Wort)	Mat-forming weeds.	Sodium arsenate; 6 oz. to 1,000 sq. ft. of lawn.
Sorrel	Creeping rootstocks. Light green leaves, arrow-shaped at base.	Spray with 2,4-D.

GROUND IVY	KNOTWEED	SPEEDWELL	SELF HEAL	SORREL

Packaging Efficiency

For purposes of storing or sending parcels, here are a few good ideas to assist you:

Labeling for Storage—Put a label on every package which you put away in the attic or cedar closet or basement, to indicate what is inside that box or package. Then, when you open up the package, you will save time and energy by identifying the contents at once.

Labeling for Mailing—If you make a package to be sent by mail or messenger, and want to be sure that the address you wrote will not become blurred through handling or bad weather, put a strip of transparent cellophane tape over your writing. Or, if you don't have such cellophane tape, you can take a white candle and rub the bottom of it over your writing; this acts as a protective coating.

Tying a Package—Tying with a damp cord is a unique way to make a strong package. Wet the cord or twine (but not excessively so it will soak through the wrapping) before you use it to tie the package. The cord shrinks as it dries on the package, and this, of course, makes the knot much tighter.

Packing

Special impregnated cord is used to prevent leaking at valve joints in plumbing lines; this cord is referred to as packing. See *Faucet* and *Valves*.

Handle Screw
Handle
Cap Nut
Cone Bonnet Packing
Top Bibb Washer
Stem

Paint Remover

To remove paint from any surface, you have a choice of four different methods; you can use:

1. sandpaper, either by hand or with a powered sander
2. heat, with a blowtorch or an electric paint remover
3. special scrapers designed to "plane" the layers of paint off the surfaces
4. a chemical paint remover.

Using Chemical Removers

There are many different chemical paint removers available. Some come in powdered form and have to be mixed, others come in pres-

Chemical paint removers should be laid on wtih the flat side of the brush. Unlike paint, it should not be "worked out" or spread over the surface. Furthermore, do not go over an area once the remover has been applied, unless another coat is needed.

Once the chemical remover has loosened the paint film, use a putty knife or scraper to peel off the old paint layers down to the bare wood.

A blowtorch can be used to remove old paint from any type of a surface. Keep the torch far enough away from the surface so as not to cause the paint to burn but close enough to soften it. Once it is softened, use a putty knife to scrape off the old paint.

Photograph courtesy of Prepo Corp.

Hand sanding is another way of removing paint from a surface. However, a surface with many layers of paint on it would require an extensive amount of sandpaper and a great deal of time to clean to the bare wood. Sanding is often necessary after the paint has been removed by other methods to make the surface smooth.

Photograph courtesy of Monsanto Chemical Co.

surized aerosol cans and others come in liquid form, ready-mixed, under various trade names such as Wonder-Paste.

To use the liquid chemical removers, you need a full-haired brush, a 2" scraping knife, a bucket for the remover, steel wool, dropcloths, wire brush, cloths, alcohol for washing the surface after the paint has been scraped off.

The paint remover is applied with a brush, laying it on with the flat side of the brush, in one direction only (as shown in the accompanying photograph). Give it a good full coat for you should not go back and brush over it again. Con-

tinue to apply the remover over the remainder of the area, covering as much as you can in twenty minutes.

Once the twenty minutes are up, go back to where you started with a scraping knife. Test to see if the film has softened all the way down to the wood. If it has, go ahead and scrape off the paint layer. If the film has not softened all the way down to the wood, recoat the area again in the same manner as you did before.

Unless the finish is very old, two coats and one hour of time will be sufficient to soften the whole paint

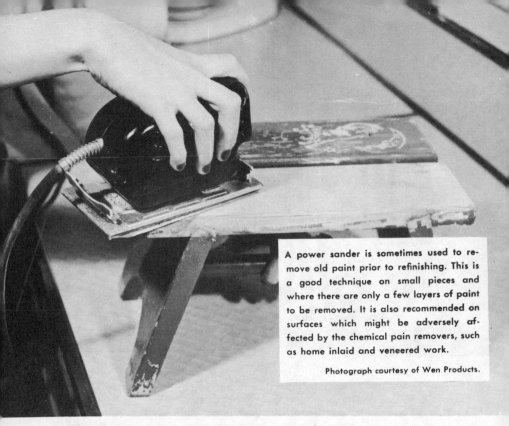

A power sander is sometimes used to remove old paint prior to refinishing. This is a good technique on small pieces and where there are only a few layers of paint to be removed. It is also recommended on surfaces which might be adversely affected by the chemical pain removers, such as home inlaid and veneered work.

Photograph courtesy of Wen Products.

film. Don't rush the remover. Let it do all the hard work! If more time is needed, allow it! On extremely heavily coated surfaces, a third coat of the remover may be necessary.

After you have scraped the paint from the surface, wash with cloths saturated with alcohol. When using removers, it generally will not be necessary to sand the surface since the remover does not raise the grain. However, check the grain by hand; if it's raised, then sand with fine sandpaper until smooth.

Using a Blowtorch

Extreme care is necessary when working with a blowtorch to remove paint to make certain that you do not violate safety rules concerning fire. Do not work near open windows and flying curtains; make certain that there is nothing inflammable about. When removing paint from around a window, keep the torch moving and avoid playing the flame on the glass—it's likely to crack it.

It is best to keep the torch in motion all the time you are playing the flame on the painted surface. If the paint starts to burn, you are holding the torch too close. Hold the blowtorch close enough to heat the paint film, but not to start a fire.

Furthermore, by continually moving the torch, you will avoid the possibility of scorching the wood. If you are removing paint from metal, make certain not to touch any part, even where the torch did not heat it. The metal conducts heat and the entire piece may cause a burn or even start a fire if you are not careful.

Using Sanders and Scrapers

There are many different types of scrapers that can be used to remove paint. Some are flat surfaces while others are made irregular in order to reach into grooves around moldings or trim.

Sanding requires care, especially when working with a powered sander. In using the latter, keep the sander moving at all times so that you do not "eat" into the wood and cause an uneven surface.

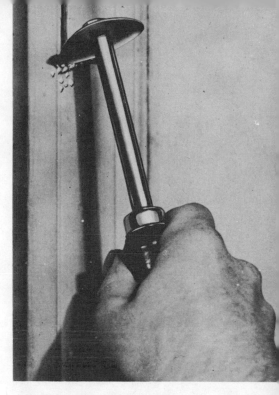

Scrapers come in many shapes, depending upon the job for which they are designed to do. This "Ogee" or "Half-Ogee" hand scraper is made to remove old paint from crevices and recesses, which cannot be reached with flat scrapers or putty knives.

Photograph courtesy of Red Devil Tools.

Painting

Amateur house painters never had as much help as today. Scores of new paints and equipment placed on the market in the last few years make it possible for the weekend handyman to paint his own house almost as easily as a professional. From one-coat paints to disposable blowtorches, everything has been designed to make the job go faster, look better and cost less.

With the new outside rollers, you can paint an average-size house in a couple of days. Add an extension handle and you can roll a terrace without stooping down, reach a roof without leaving the ground.

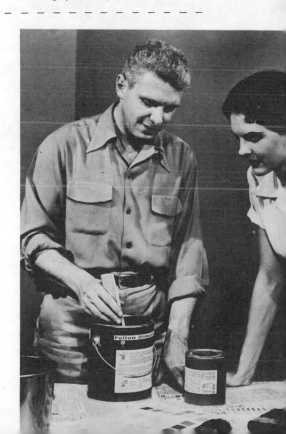

Paintbrush on a pole spreads paint on the high spots without special ladders or scaffolds, is one of many new tools that help amateurs do a professional job. Holder shown takes either brush or roller, fits on mop or broom handle and can be set at any angle to get in corners, crevices and under overhangs.

Painting Hard Spots

Badly rusted metal can be covered over with this new paint, saving work of cleaning metal first. Paint stops rust chemically, comes in several colors and can be used as finish coat or as undercoat for regular paint.

Specialized aids with built-in know-how tackle the hard spots for you.

Better still, you don't have to spend hours getting ready and hours cleaning up afterward. Premixed paints, electric-drill attachments and self-dispensing calking guns make short work of preparation. Cleaning up is a soap-and-water job for the rubber paints, or a quick dip in special cleaners for the oils. Disposable dropcloths and paper paint pails are used once and thrown away.

In this section are some tips on techniques and tools that make it easier to paint your house than ever before—not the way the "pro" does, perhaps, but with much the same results.

The term paint is used to include paints, varnishes, enamels, shellacs, lacquers, and stains.

• Paints are composed of mineral pigments, organic vehicles, and

Spray cans get in where brushes won't reach, provide easy way to paint screens, shutters, iron grillwork. Screens stacked this way can be sprayed three or four at a time to save paint. Spray screens from both sides.

a variety of thinners all combined.

• Varnishes are resins dissolved in organic thinners.

• Enamels are pigmented var--nishes.

• Shellac is lac gum dissolved in alcohol.

• Lacquers may be both pigmented or clear—the liquid portion usually is treated nitrocellulose dissolve in thinners.

• Stains may be pigmented oil or a penetrating type.

Many of these materials, such as paints, varnishes, and lacquers, are formulated for specific purposes:

• Outside house paints and exterior varnishes are intended to give good service when exposed to weathering

• Interior wall paints are formulated to give excellent coverage and good washability.

• Floor enamels are made to withstand abrasion.

• Lacquers are formulated for rapid drying.

• There are also formulas which provide extra self-cleaning, fume-resisting, waterproofing, hardening, flexibility, mildew-resisting, resistance to fading, and breathing qualities.

Interior paints are used to obtain pleasing decorative effects, improve sanitary conditions, and insure better lighting. These paints may be divided into four types: wall primers; one-coat flats; flat, semigloss, and gloss; and water paints.

Wall primers or primer-sealers are intended to be applied directly to bare plaster, wallboard, and similar porous surfaces to provide a uniform, sealed surface for subsequent coats of paint. A typical wall primer may be made from varnish or bodied-oil vehicle and hiding pigments. It is intended to penetrate only slightly into porous surfaces.

Rubber-base masonry paint lets you put a quick coat on brick, stucco or cement without mixing up powders or using special undercoats. It comes ready to use, is waterproof, can also be used on asbestos shingles.

You can roll paint on a concrete porch or outdoor terrace with an extension handle and this rubber-base enamel. Enamel is tough, wears better than ordinary concrete paints, is not affected by moisture in exposed slabs.

The primers are best applied with a wide wall brush.

One-coat flat paints are organic-solvent-thinned paints intended to accomplish priming, sealing, and finish coating in one operation. They are often sold in thin paste form so that additional inexpensive thinner may be added and mixed before application to increase the volume of

WHICH PAINT TO USE . . . AND WHERE

Exterior Surfaces

Surface	HOUSE PAINT	WATER REPELLANT	CEMENT BASE PAINT	RUBBER-BASE PAINT	EMULSION PAINT (NOT LATEX)	PENETRATING PAINT (INCLUDING LATEX)	ALUMINUM PAINT	WOOD STAIN	TRIM-AND-TRELLIS PAINT	AWNING PAINT	SPAR VARNISH	PORCH-AND-DECK PAINT	PRIMER OR UNDERCOATER	METAL PRIMER
WOOD SIDING (Painted)	✓•												✓	
WOOD SIDING (Natural)						✓		✓			✓			
BRICK	✓•	✓	✓	✓	✓								✓	
CEMENT & CINDER BLOCK	✓•	✓	✓	✓	✓								✓	
ASBESTOS CEMENT	✓•		✓	✓									✓	
STUCCO	✓•	✓	✓	✓	✓								✓	
STONE	✓•	✓	✓	✓	✓								✓	
ASPHALT SHINGLE SIDING	✓•			✓		✓								
METAL SIDING	✓•								✓•					✓
WOOD FRAME WINDOWS	✓•								✓•		✓			
STEEL WINDOWS	✓•								✓•					✓
ALUMINUM WINDOWS	✓•								✓•					✓
SHUTTERS & OTHER TRIM									✓•		✓			
CLOTH AWNINGS										✓				
WOOD SHINGLE ROOF								✓						
WOOD PORCH FLOOR												✓		
CEMENT PORCH FLOOR				✓								✓		
COPPER SURFACES											✓			
GALVANIZED SURFACES	✓•						✓•		✓•		✓			✓
IRON SURFACES	✓•						✓•		✓•					✓

Black dot indicates that a primer or sealer may be necessary before the finishing coat (unless surface has been previously finished.)

paint by one-fourth or more.

Flat, semigloss, and gloss interior paints and enamels vary in degree of gloss, hiding power, and other properties. Paints giving the best hiding power are normally paints of lowest gloss, although some modern high-gloss enamels also have good hiding power.

Water-thinned interior paints are calcimine, casein, resin-emulsion, and gloss water paints. Calcimine consists of powdered whiting and clay mixed with an animal-glue binder and a preservative. It cannot be recoated, but can be easily washed off before redecorating.

It is not necessary to remove casein before recoating but, if desired, it can be softened by washing with hot solutions of trisodium phosphate. Resin-emulsion paints, marketed in paste form, are to be thinned with water and, when properly made and applied, adhere well to plaster and provide a good decorative medium. They need not be removed before redecorating, provided the film is in sound condition. This is also true of gloss water paints.

New Paints Give You Pro's Skill

Painting your house will be easier than ever—if you get the right paint. But it's going to be harder than ever to pick it.

Years ago, paint was paint. One kind looked, smelled, was applied and eventually dried much like an-

Getting Ready

Rough spots on old paint are quickly smoothed down with sanding wheel in electric drill. Same treatment with wire-brush wheel (in foreground) takes rust and scale off metalwork. Cracked and peeling paint can be removed with several types of hand scrapers.

Disposable blowtorch takes off heavily built-up or alligatored paint, needs no pumping or priming, is simply fitted with new tank when old one runs dry. Wide-mouth burner tip spreads flame over large area. Long-handled scraper keeps fingers out of way.

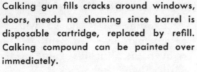

Calking gun fills cracks around windows, doors, needs no cleaning since barrel is disposable cartridge, replaced by refill. Calking compound can be painted over immediately.

V-shaped putty knife spreads smooth, professional bead of putty along window sash. Loose old putty should be removed and window primed before new putty is applied.

other. Things are different now. Besides oil paints, you can choose from a new set of paints. It'll pay you to know about them.

• There are water paints you can use outside. (You clean your brushes under the faucet and use the garden hose to get spatters off the shrubbery.)

• There are finishes so tough they withstand even attacks from the neighbors' children.

• There are paints that dry so fast you start the second coat as soon as you finish putting on the first.

• There are colors in glittering confusion.

No single product can do all these things. There are several types, all available under a variety of trade names. The trade names are, to put it kindly, confusing. For example, two brands of the new paints use "rubber" in their trade names, yet neither is a rubber-latex paint and

each is actually an entirely different type of paint from the other. To get the right paint you have to read the fine print on the label and find out what is actually inside the can.

Vinyl is a cousin to the tough plastic used for upholstery and floor tiles, but it comes thinned with water ready for you to brush, roll or spray on. The label on the can may say vinyl, vinyl emulsion, polyvinyl acetate or PVA.

You can use vinyl on almost any exterior except previously painted wood. It works fine on wood shingles and shakes, asbestos shingles, brick, stucco, concrete and masonry blocks. One manufacturer says you can even put it on wood clapboard if the clapboard is new and unprimed.

The major advantage of vinyl is the thinner—water. You get all the advantages of easy cleanup that have made interior water paints so popular.

Extension ring fits top of paint can, making it easy to mix paint and add thinner without spilling. Ring has its own lid so it can be left on and paint kept covered. Ring can be used again with other paint.

Suppose it rains while you're working? Vinyl paint dries fast—as quickly as 10 to 30 minutes—and will withstand a shower after that time. It takes another 12 hours to "cure," by then forming an exceptionally tough, long-lasting film that stands up well against weather, sun, salt air and factory smoke.

One precaution: You can't paint with it in cold weather. The chemical reaction that transforms the water solution into a durable finish will not take place if the temperature is below 50°. (Conventional oil paints don't stick well in cold weather, either.)

Some manufacturers recommend their vinyl paints for interior as well as exterior use; others say no, not so good. There are vinyls made specifically for interiors.

Definitely good inside the house is a new vinyl primer-sealer to be used as a base coat under any paint. It dries in as little as 30 minutes.

You can put it around a room and probably follow immediately with the finish coat. It can be applied with brush or roller.

Acrylic is the second new name for magic in paints. This is also a plastic-in-water. Solid acrylic you know as the beautiful, glasslike Plexiglas and Lucite.

Inside the house is where acrylic shines. It dries faster than other types, and it keeps its color better, without yellowing. One disadvantage: It costs more.

Some acrylics are also recommended for exteriors (over the same kinds of materials as vinyl paints). Here it has a big advantage—you don't have to pick your painting weather so carefully. It can be applied on humid days and in cold seasons, so long as the temperature is a few degrees above freezing.

Alkyd is an old interior paint made newly popular by a change in solvent—a super-refined petroleum chemical that has almost no odor. It is not a water paint. You thin it and clean brushes with mineral spirits or turpentine, or, if you want to retain the odorless feature, with the new odorless solvent. (Ask the paint-store man for just that, odorless solvent.)

Alkyd has solid advantages overriding the slight cleanup inconvenience. It is exceptionally tough and very resistant to scrubbing. It stands up well in the trouble spots—trim, bathroom, kitchen. And it is easy to apply, producing a smooth, even finish free of streaks and brush marks.

The alkyds have little odor, but don't forget that the solvent is a petroleum product and its vapor is there even if you can't smell it. It can make you sick and it burns very easily, like the vapor of older paint solvents. So play safe: Keep windows open and keep flames away.

The old reliables are not to be overlooked either. Conventional *oil paints* can now be had in deodorized version, made with the same odorless solvent used in the alkyds. And oil paint has much in its favor. It is sold everywhere; its virtues and faults are well established through centuries of use; it makes a tough film on almost any surface; it offers the greatest color range; and it is often cheaper.

Water-thinned *rubber-latex* paint is already an old reliable,

WHICH PAINT TO USE . . . AND WHERE
Interior Surfaces

Surface	FLAT PAINT	SEMI-GLOSS PAINT	ENAMEL	RUBBER BASE PAINT	EMULSION PAINT (INCLUDING LATEX)	CASEIN PAINT (MOST LATEX)	INTERIOR VARNISH	SHELLAC	WAX (LIQUID OR PASTE)	WAX (EMULSION)	STAIN	WOOD SEALER	FLOOR SEALER	FLOOR VARNISH	CEMENT PAINT OR ENAMEL	ALUMINUM PAINT	SEALER OR UNDERCOATER	METAL PRIMER
PLASTER WALLS & CEILING	✓•	✓•		✓	✓	✓											✓	
WALL BOARD	✓•	✓•		✓	✓	✓											✓	
WOOD PANELING	✓•	✓•		✓	✓•		✓	✓	✓		✓	✓					✓	
KITCHEN & BATHROOM WALLS		✓•	✓•	✓	✓												✓	
WOOD FLOORS							✓	✓	✓•	✓	✓	✓•	✓•	✓•				
CONCRETE FLOORS										✓•	✓•	✓			✓			
VINYL & RUBBER TILE FLOORS									✓	✓								
ASPHALT TILE FLOORS										✓								
LINOLEUM									✓	✓	✓		✓	✓				
STAIR TREADS								✓			✓	✓	✓	✓				
STAIR RISERS	✓•	✓•	✓•	✓			✓	✓			✓	✓						
WOOD TRIM	✓•	✓•	✓•	✓	✓•		✓	✓	✓		✓					✓		
STEEL WINDOWS	✓•	✓•	✓•	✓												✓		✓
ALUMINUM WINDOWS	✓•	✓•	✓•	✓												✓		✓
WINDOW SILLS			✓•				✓											
STEEL CABINETS	✓•	✓•	✓•	✓														✓
HEATING DUCTS	✓•	✓•	✓•	✓												✓		✓
RADIATORS & HEATING PIPES	✓•	✓•	✓•	✓												✓		✓
OLD MASONRY	✓	✓	✓	✓	✓	✓									✓	✓	✓	
NEW MASONRY	✓•	✓•	✓•	✓	✓										✓		✓	

✓• Black dot indicates that a primer or sealer may be necessary before the finishing coat (unless surface has been previously finished.)

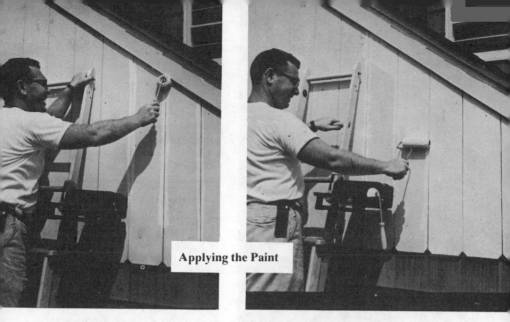

Applying the Paint

Exterior rollers now let you paint outside with the same ease as inside. Small doughnut-shaped roller (left) gets in corners, under edges of clapboards and between joints in vertical siding. Then large roller is used to fill in broad areas (right). Special long-nap roller also puts paint on brick, stucco and other rough-surface masonry. Paint tray clamps to side of ladder, can be adjusted to any angle.

Miniature roller lays narrow ribbon of paint on window sash without getting paint on glass. Roller comes with its own tiny paint tray, has metal tip that rides against glass to keep paint from smearing. Another type of sash painter (on window sill) has plush pad set in plastic handle. Pad is saturated with paint, then wiped along sash with plastic edge held against window to keep paint off glass.

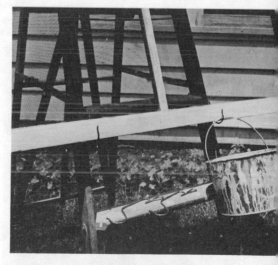

Easel for painting screens and storm windows is made by clipping special wire hooks to stepladder rung. Hooks also serve as paintcan holders for working atop ladders.

You can stand on ground and still reach first-floor roof overhangs with roller on extension handle like this. You paint as fast as you walk, don't have to keep moving ladder. Same extension will reach second-floor overhangs from stepladder.

though it is only about 10 years old. It accounts for a big percentage of all paint sold and is still the most widely available of the easy-to-use finishes. One new type is a combination vinyl-rubber paint that is said to do a better job on interiors than either vinyl or rubber alone because it dries faster, lasts longer and has less sheen.

Trick ladder does several jobs in one. As stepladder, it stands 7', lets you reach well above first-floor line. By locking one half to other, it converts into 13' extension ladder, for reaching high spots. Halves can also be used separately as short ladders so two persons can paint at once.

Here's the Score on the New Paint	Emulsion Finishes				Solvent Finishes	
	RUBBER	VINYL	RUBBER-VINYL	ACRYLIC	ALKYD	OIL
Exterior	No*	Most	No	Some	No	Most
Interior	Yes	Some	Yes	Most	Yes	Some
Thin With	Water	Water (Unless can label specifies special reducer)	Water	Water	Mineral spirits, turpentine or odorless solvent if paint is odorless type	Mineral spirits, turpentine or odorless solvent if paint is odorless type
Clean Up With	Water	Water	Water	Water	Mineral spirits, turpentine or odorless solvent	Mineral spirits, turpentine or odorless solvent
Drying Time (Time between coats)	3–4 Hours	2 Hours	2 Hours	1–2 Hours	Overnight	Exterior: 2–3 Days Interior: 8 hours

*Generally not recommended for exterior use, but some special types are available for outdoor use.

Paint Selection

Most paints are purchased ready-mixed but, in their selection, consideration should be given to the fact that surfaces vary in their adaptability to paint and atmospheric or other conditions having an adverse effect on paint performance. In addition to the normal weathering action of sun and rain, outside house paints are sometimes exposed to other atacking elements, such as corrosive fumes from factories or excessive amounts of wind-driven dust.

For localities where such conditions exist, self-cleaning paints should be selected. These paints are usually so designated on the label. Concrete, plaster, and metal surfaces each present special problems in painting. For instance, paint for use on masonry or new plaster must be resistant to dampness and alkalies, and paints used on steel must have rust-inhibitive properties.

Color—The paint makers are out to sell the lady of the house and color is their come-on. They are tempting her with a kaleidoscope's variety; one firm offers more than 6,000 different shades.

Practically every manufacturer has a "color system," a fat book of color chips with instructions for duplicating each chip. This is accomplished by intermixing cans of colored paint, by adding a concentraed color to a can of white or colored paint, or by adding concentrated color or colors to a can of neutral "base" paint. And for those who don't want any guesswork there's the Color Carousel that mixes the paints right in the store. Whatever the method, the result is a range of colors such as no amateur painter has seen.

Mixing

Paste paints, such as aluminum, resin-emulsion, and lead-in-oil, should be stirred with a stiff paddle and reduced to painting consistency with the liquids recommended on the manufacturer's labels.

Paints in powdered form require the addition of a liquid to prepare them for use. The manufacturer's directions as to the amount of oil, varnish, water, or other vehicle required should be followed.

"Boxing" is a good method of mixing paints. Since paint is a mixture of solids and liquids, it is important that it be mixed thoroughly before using. To do this, the greater portion of the liquid contents of the can should be poured in a clean bucket somewhat larger than the paint can. Then, with a stiff paddle, the settled pigment in the original

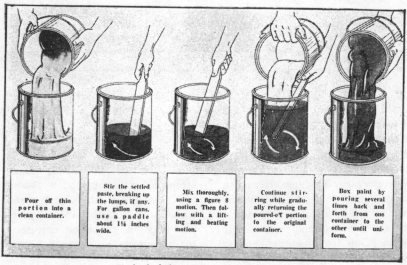

Pour off thin portion into a clean container.

Stir the settled paste, breaking up the lumps, if any. For gallon cans, use a paddle about 1½ inches wide.

Mix thoroughly, using a figure 8 motion. Then follow with a lifting and beating motion.

Continue stirring while gradually returning the poured-off portion to the original container.

Box paint by pouring several times back and forth from one container to the other until uniform.

Method of "boxing" or mixing paints.

Disposable dropcloths keep paint off shrubs and walks. Made of paper, they're cheap, light, won't damage bushes and flowers, can be used several times.

Rollers are quickly cleaned in tank of special fluid. Roller is simply dropped in and tank shaken like cocktail for one minute. New ring-shaped scraper is then slid along roller to squeeze out the excess cleaner.

Cleaning Up

Paper paint pails save buying and cleaning more expensive metal ones, are handy for mixing. Costing only a few cents, they're used once, then thrown away.

Waterless hand cleaner takes off both oil- and rubber-paint, will not irritate skin as solvents may. Paste is simply wiped on hands, then wiped off, taking paint with it.

container should be loosened and any lumps broken up. After this, mix the material in the container thoroughly, using a figure 8 motion, and follow with a lifting and beating motion. Continue stirring the mixture vigorously while slowly adding the liquid that was previously poured off the top. Complete the mixing by pouring the paint back and forth from one container to the other several times until the entire amount is of uniform consistency.

Paste and powder paints should be mixed in quantities sufficient for immediate use only, as these materials often become unfit for application if allowed to stand for three or more hours.

If paints have been allowed to stand and hard lumps or skin have formed, the skin or scum should be removed, after which the paint can be stirred and strained through screen wire or through one or two thicknesses of cheesecloth.

If a desired shade is not obtainable in custom- or ready-mixed paints, white paints may be tinted with colors-in-oil. To do this, mix the color-in-oil with a small amount of turpentine or mineral spirits and stir this into the white paint, a little at a time. If a blended color is desired, more than one color may be added, such as a chrome green and chrome yellow pigments to produce a lettuce green shade.

Painting—Basic Preparation of Surfaces

A satisfactory paint job requires cleaning, scraping, sanding, and puttying the surface prior to application of the paint. Do not try to cover chipped or cracked paint on woodwork. If dirt and rough spots are painted over, the new coating may peel, crack, blister, or wrinkle.

To prepare a surface for repainting, all loose paint should be removed with a putty knife or wire brush, rough spots sanded, and bare spots given a priming coat after the edges of the old paint film have been "feathered" or tapered off with sandpaper or steel wool. Nail holes should be filled with putty after the

priming coat is applied and, where a surface has been patched, the new surface should be primed before succeeding coats are put on.

To clean a painted surface that is cracked, checked, or "alligatored," paint remover should be applied with an all-hair brush and allowed to stand until the paint loses its adhesion. It can then be scraped off with a putty knife or paint scraper and wiped off with turpentine or mineral spirits. (See *Paint Remover*.) The spot can then be repainted.

New Interior Wood Surfaces

New interior wood surfaces generally can be cleaned simply by wiping with a rag soaked in solvent such as mineral spirits or turpentine. This will remove dust, greasy film and grimy dirt. If oil or wax has been spilled on the surface, re-

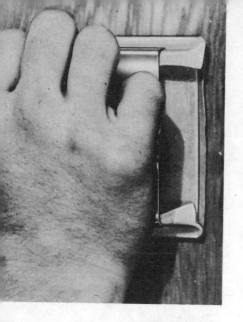

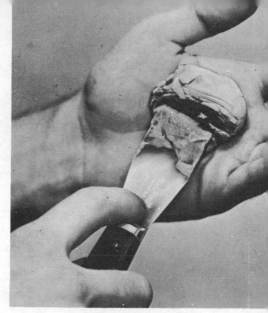

Sanding new wood surfaces smooth can be done effectively with a hand sanding block. Remember to sand with the grain finishing the job with #00 or finer paper. See **Abrasives**.

Any holes or cracks in the wood surfaces should be filled with wood putty, forced into the openings with a putty knife.

move by repeated solvent washings followed by immediate wipings with a clean, dry rag.

If the surface is to be varnished, shellacked, or finished in natural wood, sand to a smooth surface. Sand with the grain using #2 paper for rough and #00 or finer for finish sanding. Dust with a moist rag after sanding.

On open-grain woods such as oak, ash, hickory, mahogany and chestnut, apply one coat of clean or stained wood filler following manufacturer's directions. Close-grained woods such as maple, pine, cherry, or birch should be stained without filler. After the application of filler or stain and one coat of finish, putty-up nail holes and imperfections. Tint putty by mixing with small amount of stain and press into nail hole with thumb. Cut off with forward stroke of putty knife and smooth with a backstroke.

The reason that the filler or stain and one coat of finish are applied prior to puttying is to prevent the wood from absorbing the vehicle from the putty and becoming discolored. The absorption would also make the putty hard and brittle, eventually causing it to chip out.

If the surface is to be painted, sand as in the case of varnish, shellac or natural finish, wipe with moist cloth, apply one coat of wood primer, putty the imperfections, and follow with coat of enamel undercoat. Surface is then ready for any desired paint or enamel.

Painted Interior Wood Surfaces

Previously painted wood surfaces should be cleaned by wiping with a rag wet with a solvent such as mineral spirits or turpentine and immediately wiped dry with a clean rag. This should be done while the surface is wet, otherwise evaporation of the solvent will simply re-deposit the oils, grease, and dirt. If the surfaces are not waxed they may be cleaned with a solution of household kitchen detergent followed by thorough rinsing with clear water.

If the old paint or varnish is badly cracked, crazed, or wrinkled, it should be removed to the bare wood before repainting. This can be done with a chemical paint remover and 1½" or 2½" wood scraper. (See *Paint Remover*.)

Dirt should be cleaned from crevices and recesses using an "ogee" or "half ogee" scraper. If it is desired to remove moldings use a molding remover. It is good practice to scuff the surface of the old paint lightly with fine sandpaper, in the interests of better adhesion of the new paint.

On restaining work, particularly if the color of stain is to be changed, it is necessary to remove all old finishes down to the bare wood.

Where a stain color change is involved, try bleaching with a commercial wood bleach to lighten the stain that has penetrated into the wood. The surface should then be refinished as outlined above for new wood.

Plaster Walls

For new plaster walls, go over walls thoroughly to see that they are smooth, knocking off any mortar or plaster splotches with a 1¼" putty knife. Remove all dust from walls with a vacuum cleaner. Allow

Sometimes it is necessary to remove old painted moldings. For example, if you wish to remove the paint and bleach the wood for a light natural finish. In such cases, use a molding chisel, shown here.

Old paint can be removed from wood by applying a chemical paint remover or heating the surface with a blowtorch and then scraping the painted film off with a putty knife.

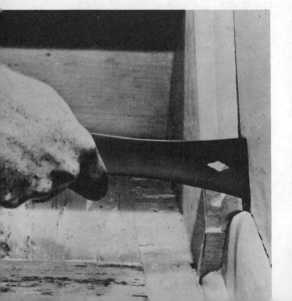

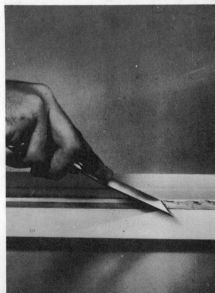

walls to season for 3 to 6 months before painting, or paint them with an alkali-resistant finish as the first coat.

Painted plaster walls should be cleaned, and cracks and broken areas repaired before repainting.

Peeling paint should be removed with a wall scraper.

To patch larger-than-hairline cracks (hairline cracks can be covered with sealer), first form a keyway for new plaster. Do not shape crack into a "V" because patched plaster later may fall out. Wide deep cracks should be filled with oakum or similar material to within ⅛" of the surface. Moisten crack before plastering. Spray water into the cracks, do not brush in. Brushing may sweep dirt into the base plaster and new plaster won't stick. Water can be sprayed into cracks by flicking from the end of a small brush. Apply plaster to cracks with a putty knife, the 1¼" size being recommended. Paint patched cracks color of walls or ceiling to prevent showing through when repainted.

To repair small cracks and broken areas, apply spackling (also spelled "spachtling"), which is somewhat like patching plaster, with a 5" spackling knife. For larger areas use patching plaster. Such patched areas should be sanded smooth the next day.

One coat of paint usually is sufficient although two sometimes are required. Two may be needed when going from a dark shade to a light shade or if the original paint is in very bad condition. Brush or roller may be used.

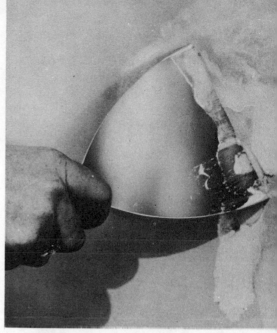

Photographs courtesy of Red Devil Tools.

Plaster walls should be prepared carefully and all holes and cracks filled. Spackling is best applied with a special 5" spackling knife, shown here, which resembles a putty knife but is much wider.

Preparation of Papered Walls for Painting

There are several ways to remove wallpaper, when required, before painting the wall (see later section on *Painting—Interior*).

Many people still use plain water, which will work after a fashion, but it is a slow and laborsome job. The warm water is applied with a sponge, brush or cloth. After the surface has been soaking for about 10 to 15 minutes, use a scraper to peel the paper off. Start at the top, keeping the blade against the wall. If the scraper is lifted at each stroke, it may nick the plaster or plasterboard each time it is reapplied and these nicks will have to be patched.

Removing old paint with a chemical paint remover is one way to insure a good painting job. This badly damaged exterior wood wall has had its paint removed with a chemical remover; once the paint film has softened, it's simple to remove it with a scraper or putty knife.

Removal of wallpaper is quick and easy with chemical wallpaper removers. Mix the concentrated solution with warm water and apply to the paper. Then scrape it loose without fear of damaging the surface of the wall proper.

Many wallpapers made and sold in recent years have been "washable." This means that they resist water and permit washing. Therefore, plain water is not very effective when removing this type of wallpaper.

Wallpaper steamers (available on a rental basis from many hardware stores) have been in use for many years. They will do a good job of loosening the paper from the wall surface, but in the process they will saturate the entire room. Furthermore, if you have drywall construction, the steamer may loosen the protective top coat of the wall surfacing material itself.

Chemical wallpaper removers have gained in popularity because they are easier to use. Many of them are sold in concentrated form and are diluted in warm water. The solution can be applied with a brush, sponge or even a paint roller. After the paper has been saturated, it will peel off quickly and easily.

Outdoor Wood

The first step in preparing new outdoor wood surfaces for painting is to seal all knots with shellac or with the newer vinyl resin-type knot sealers. Next, apply a prime coat of paint and then putty up all cracks and nail holes. Calk all joints and openings and proceed with final painting.

For painted outdoor wood surfaces, nail down all loose boards, preferably with aluminum nails, Countersink nails and fill nail holes with putty. Scrape off all loose or scaling paint. If old paint is peeling, checked or blistered, remove with tungsten carbide scraper; by burning with a torch and scraping with long handled putty knife or scraper; or by using a wax-free paint and varnish remover and scraper.

In repainting sash, scrape away loose putty, and prepaint the sash and that portion of the glass which will be covered by putty. Apply new putty when paint drys. Allow a few days for putty to harden.

Metal Surfaces

Remove peeling paint with carbide scraper and remove rust with emery cloth. Touch-up exposed areas with rust inhibitor, let dry and apply new paint. Allow new downspouts and gutters to stand a year before painting. They will oxidize and absorb paint better. If it is desired to paint immediately, age with strong vinegar or diluted acetic acid, wash clean and apply prime coat.

Masonry Walls

Peeling paint can be removed from smooth cement with a carbide scraper, or a wire brush may do the job on rough cement. If not, virtually nothing short of sand or steam blasting will do the job. Repaint when surface is clean and dry. (If there is a moisture or leakage problem, this must be corrected before painting.)

- -

Painting—Brushes and Rollers

You have a choice of three different "tools" with which to paint.

• You can use the oldest and most common tool—the paint brush,

• or you can use the paint roller, which has advanced considerably in design since it was introduced about 1945,

• or there is the paint sprayer.

Which tool you use depends upon the job to be done and your skill. Here are some facts about each:

Brushes—Good quality brushes are not cheap, but a good brush, properly cared for, can last many years in the hands of a homeowner. Most handymen possess sufficient skill to use a brush but many do not know the fine techniques necessary for a professional-looking job. See section on *Brushes*.

Rollers—It is possible for the average homeowner to do a better paint job with a roller than with a brush. It is easy to develop the right skills and before you know it, you can work like a professional.

Sprayers—Considerable practice is needed in order to do a topnotch job with a sprayer. A poor sprayer in inexperienced hands will

BRUSH NOTES

Photographs courtesy of Pittsburgh Plate
Glass Co.

1. Select a quality brush for the job it is designed to do. Here (left to right) are: 1½" sash brush, 2" trim brush, 3½" and 4" wall brushes.

result in a poor job; so will a good sprayer in inexperienced hands. However, once you acquire the few simple skills, it is possible to do an outstanding job with a sprayer.

Covers for Rollers

The first practical paint-roller cover material, developed about 1945, was wool. However, after a great number of covers were used, it was found that wool did not provide a practical all-purpose cover. Sheep coming from different climates have different types of coats. The most desirable skin for a wool paint roller was a heavy, dense but medium-fine wool that was straight. Production methods were slow, because each skin had to be measured and only the select covers could be cut out. The remainder was scrapped. All of this was done with hand labor.

Wool covers are fine for oil flat paints. They are useless in the new water and rubber base paints. Because wool absorbs roughly 14%, it soaks to the core, and the fibrous, resilient, paint-holding structure of the wool is lost, thereby making it worthless.

As a result, new fabric coverings were developed.

Dynel has the all-purpose characteristics needed to make a fine paint roller. It absorbs less than ½% water; therefore, it is excellent for water base paints. In oil base paints it works as well as wool. Because it is man-made, the denier and density of the cover are controlled to meet exact specifications.

2. When using a paint brush, dip it about half the length of the bristles into the can of paint. You should never get the ferrule (metal band) wet with paint.

3. Lightly wipe the excess paint off the brush by pressing it against the side of the can. Note that pressure is exerted just above the ends of the bristles.

4. Lay the paint on with short, slightly curved strokes, lifting the brush gradually at the end of the stroke. Note the correct way to hold the brush.

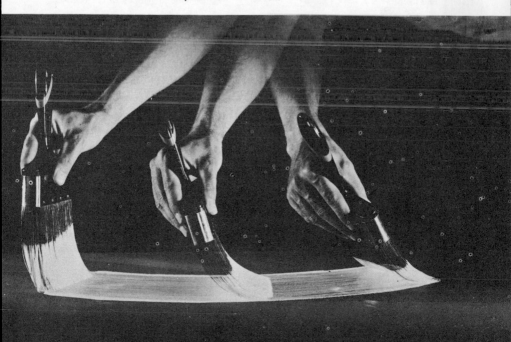

5. After you have finished painting, clean the brush thoroughly by submerging it and working the solvent well into the bristles. Use the right solvent for the paint.

6. Squeeze the bristles between the thumb and your fingers to work the paint out of the heel of the brush. It is essential not to leave any paint on the bristles.

7. After all the paint has been removed and the solvent squeezed out of the bristles, comb the brush. This will reset the bristles and keep them in working order.

8. When storing a brush, one that will be used again shortly, do not set it on its bristles! Instead, suspend it in a container or jar with solvent up to the ferrule.

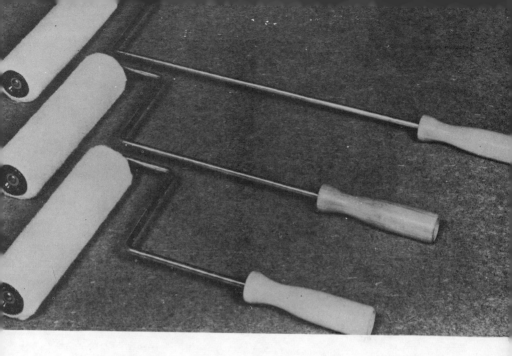

Dip-type rollers are made in a variety of sizes with different types of coverings designed for special surfaces. Here are three rollers, 14", 18" and 24" long; the length of the handle varies in order to enable you to reach out-of-the-way places.

Lonel is one of the finest of all synthetic paint roller fabrics on the market, and the most versatile. It is a fabric that will work in practically any kind of oil or water base paint, be it interior or exterior, gloss or flat.

The following paragraphs describe the specialized fabrics which have been developed to do specific jobs with special types of paint.

1. *Mohair*—Mohair rollers are short-nap rollers, less than ¼" in depth. This is a woven material that is specially designed to do a good job of applying heavy bodied enamels without showing a stipple.

2. *Dacron*—Dacron is the latest find in a roller material that is exceedingly fine in denier. It is woven into a cover that is especially designed to apply heavy-bodied exterior paints without showing an undue

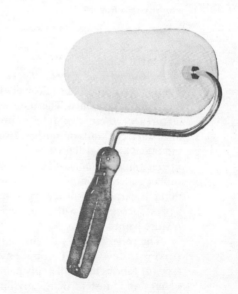

Fountain type rollers are often used by home handymen. Instead of dipping the roller into the tray to pick up the paint, the paint is poured into the cylinder.

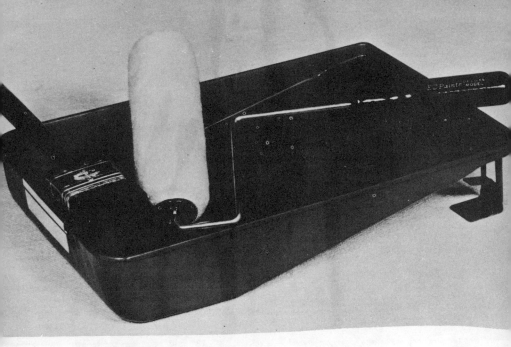

Dip-type rollers come with paint trays. This tray is used for interior painting and conveniently fits onto any step ladder. A special rest is available in order to hold a brush on the tray.

Photographs courtesy of E Z Paintr Corp.

amount of stipple.

3. *Carpet and Fleecy Types*—These covers are used exclusively to apply oil-base paints. The different textures of these two fabrics produce different kinds of finishes, from sand float to Spanish textures.

4. *Sponge Rubber*—The sponge rubber roller accomplishes the same thing as carpet and fleecy types, but works successfully with water base texture paints.

The roller industry is constantly striving to develop and produce new types of fabrics that will apply paints better and faster than anything known before. Fabrics that are in test and have been used are: long cotton staples, Orlon, nylon, Acrilan, acrylics, etc.

Types of Rollers

Dip Roller—The most popular rollers developed are of the dip type. They range in size from 1″ to 13½″.

They work for such highly specialized uses as painting the underside of clapboard with the beveled 1″ roller (to be finished off with a 5½″ roller).

Corner rollers that are used to trace around ceilings, corners, and moldings prepare the way for 7″ or 9″ rollers which are used to finish the large surface of the wall.

There are 9″ to 13½″ rollers that are used for industrial purposes to cover large areas rapidly with the use of extension handles.

Floor to ceiling may be reached with 48″ handles, and greater distances may be reached with an aluminum, telescopic extension handle.

Short and long nap rollers made of the previously discussed fabrics are designed to paint almost any

For exterior use, a specially designed tray is used. It comes with a handy swivel hook which grips onto an outside ladder. Note the two different rollers; one is a "doughnut" shape used to paint inside of corners or edges of clapboard trim. The other is a 5½" dip-type roller for narrow surfaces, such as the face of clapboards.

type of surface, including smooth clapboard walls on the exterior of a house, shingles and stucco or masonry blocks.

Interior rollers can paint any type of wall construction. A roller applies the paint in an even paint film, applying only the proper amount of paint. Too little or too much paint cannot be applied with the roller, which works very much like a roller on a printing press. If a surplus of paint is applied to the wall, the roller will pick up the excess and apply it to a dry surface. When exactly the right amount of paint has been applied to a surface, the roller cannot pick this up and spread it out too thinly. In other words, a roller can apply just so much paint and no more. The amount put on is the correct amount.

Fountain Model Rollers—These are very practical to apply either flats or enamels to a wall. The advantage of a fountain model roller is that it eliminates dipping. Up to a pint of paint can be poured into a fountain roller, which is the reservoir for the excess paint. The cover is constructed to permit the paint to ooze through the fabric and be rolled onto the surface.

The first fountain rollers developed were constructed of metal, which made them heavy. Modern fountain rollers are constructed with nylon parts that are long-wearing, strong, and light. The inside fabric, which acts as the resilient part of the roller, is lonel, woven into a cushion, and is covered with a sleeve of nylon which creates a thin, even, smooth surface with any kind of paint.

Pressure Rollers—These are designed wholly for professional use. Such rollers are ideally used in large buildings such as schools, hospitals warehouses, etc., where there are large surfaces, hallways, or rooms in which a single color is used. A pressure roller consists of a three-gallon material tank, from which an air-pressure pump ejects paint through a 15′ hose and into the base of a 7″ paint roller. The amount of paint that is allowed to flow into the roller is adjusted by a button in the handle. A pressure roller paints in a fraction of the time required by conventional methods, since it is basically designed for regulated, constant use.

Roller Cores

Construction of the various roller cover fabrics and their uses have already been discussed. However, there are three basic constructions of cores about which the covers are constructed:

1. *Wire* is superior to all other cores because of its plated, rust-proof characteristics. It can be re-used many times and formed into a perfect round shape when it is placed over the roller's adjustable drum. Wire is not affected by heat, cold, water, or oil.

2. *Plastic* cores constitute the middle quality of roller core construction. Plastic is practical. Because of its smooth inside diameter, it slips on and off roller handles quickly and easily. It is solvent-proof and durable.

3. *Fiber* cores are impregnated with waterproof and oilproof compounds to make them stand up in either water or oil base paints. They are lower in price than those of the two other cores. Because of its cheapness, fiber may be used once in a given color, then disposed of, rather than having to clean it for re-use. Fiber is serviceable and durable.

Roller Technique

As more and more Americans join the ranks of home decorators, the paint roller has become an important part of everyday life. Rollers now make it possible to paint expertly, with greater ease and with almost no mess. As with any job, a few rules of advance know-how can greatly lighten the task.

There is scarcely anything which the roller cannot paint easily and swiftly. Paint may be rolled right over wallpaper, plaster, wallboard, brick, clapboard, concrete, and other surfaces. Even wire fences can be painted by a long-nap roller.

Oil, rubber base, and water base paints can be used with equal success with rollers. These include flats, gloss and semi-gloss, enamels, sizing, varnish, aluminum paint, and shellac. Most of these can be used just as they come from the can. Ordinary instructions should be followed if thinning is needed.

The surface to be painted should be prepared as for any brush or spray painting: clean and free from oil, dust, or foreign matter. If the surface is new, a primer coat may be essential, but follow instructions on

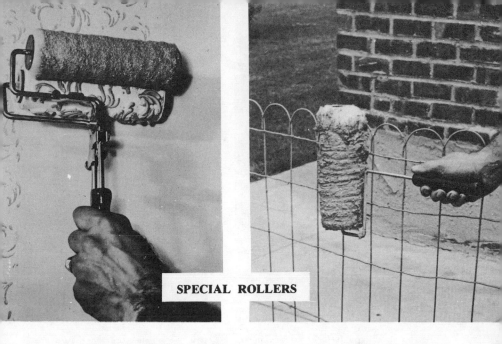

SPECIAL ROLLERS

You can paint your own patterns on the wall with a design roller. There are many different patterns available from which to choose. It works like an ordinary dip-type roller; the roller is soaked in paint and transfers the paint to the design roller, which in turn transfers the paint to the wall.

Wire fences are easy to paint in almost a single stroke. Extra long-nap rollers are used and, as they are rolled across the face of the wire fence, the paint is applied to the front and sides of the wires.

the label of the finishing material to be used.

To begin painting, the roller tray, which can be placed conveniently on the floor or table, or attached to the ladder top or rung, should be filled to the "shore line," about half way up its slanted surface. Lining the tray with heavy paper or foil will save cleaning and permit quick changes of color.

Before actually painting the main surface area, a trim roller, a brush or one of several special devices which will be mentioned should be used progressively along the edges of the ceiling, floor, and woodwork. Do not trim the edges of more than one wall at a time, how-

ever. This will prevent shading.

The large roller should be loaded by rolling into the "shore line" of the paint, then back and forth on the ribbed surface of the tray to remove excess. Paint is applied to the surface with an easy back and forth rolling motion in any direction. Some "pros" recommend a crisscross starting stroke. Be sure to keep the roller on the wall without spinning at the end of the stroke, and progress slowly and carefully into the previously trimmed edge, to within 1½" of windows, corners, and edges.

"Roller" Aids

There are several devices which

If you have large surfaces to be painted, such as a patio floor or a basement floor, special rollers with handles are available for the job. The long nap of the rollers gets the paint into all the crevices.

More like a miniature blackboard eraser, this "roller" is designed for painting window sash trim. It's almost impossible to get paint on the glass.

provide the home decorator with invaluable supplementary tools to meet the problems of painting in corners and other hard-to-get-at areas. One of these is a 3"x5" wool surface padding which gives a finish of roller rather than brush consistency. A protective blade permits it to be used against ceiling, moldings, etc., without smearing. An extension handle facilitates painting behind radiators, pipes, and similar awkward spots.

Another device is a small felt surface mounted on a plastic handle. This can be drawn over window sash and other edges without allowing paint to run over. A guard blade prevents smearing. With such helpful gadgets as these, the need for masking tape is eliminated.

Painting ceilings, one of the messiest painting problems, is effortless with the long-handle roller. For greater than usual heights, there has recently been introduced a lightweight aluminum telescopic extension handle, to which a regular roller may be attached for reaching up to 14'.

There are three important tips for success in ceiling painting:

1. The roller should be worked easily back and forth across the narrowest dimension.

2. Care should be taken not to lift the roller from the surface nor to spin it.

3. Work should not be stopped until the entire ceiling is completed (this will prevent lapping).

There is no more bending, stooping, or tedious kneeling to floor painting with a long-handled roller or regular roller attached to an extension handle. Floors of concrete, wood, or linoleum can be covered with equal success.

Exterior Rollers

The exterior roller is versatile. Barns, silos, storage tanks, wagons, pens, picket fences, brick walls, boats, garden furniture, porches, and children's playthings are only some of the myriad things on which the exterior roller set can do a first-rate job.

Exterior paint rollers are similar to interior rollers, and may be cared for in the same way. Exterior rollers are generally larger, and the fabric is of a different type, to prevent the heavier bodied paints from stippling.

Here are a few precautions which, together with directions ordinarily found on paint cans, will produce really professional results in exterior painting.

New, unpainted wood surfaces should be allowed to dry thoroughly before painting. Knots and resin streaks should be sealed with a modern knot sealer or shellac to prevent bleeding or discoloration of paint film. Before painting old surfaces, loose paint should be removed with a scraper. Necessary repairs should be made: loose boards nailed down; projecting nail heads secured; cracks and nailhead pits filled in with putty. Finally, the area should be sanded smooth.

When preparing concrete surfaces it is important to remember that no paint will adhere to a loose, crumbly surface, so all loose part-

icles, dirt, etc., should be removed before painting. It is necessary to be sure that loose joints are routed out and "tuck pointed"; that cracks and crevices are filled; and that broken corners are replaced.

On clapboard walls the underedges should first be painted, one section at a time, with the small lap roller. Start at the top and work down. Follow with a 5½″ roller on flat surfaces. Be sure that the roller contains no excess paint, and roll easily on the surface without spinning the end of the stroke.

If the surface of cement block or stucco is extremely rough, a long-nap roller is required. The long-nap roller is also effective on siding and shingles with deep crevices, as well as in such special work as painting wire fences.

Modern exterior roller trays have the gradually slanted surface of ordinary trays, but with a protective covering over the deeper end. Exterior trays may be attached to the sides of extension ladders, and fixed so that moving the ladder will not spill paint out of the tray. Still attached to the ladder, the tray may be moved to a vertical position and used as a pail for mixing paint. Another ladder lock permits the tray to be fastened to the top surface of a step ladder. This same ladder lock can be transposed into a carrying handle for the full tray when it is once again in vertical position.

Cleaning rollers has ceased to be a difficult problem. After the use of oil paint, the excess should first be squeezed out of the removable roller cover. This may be done without messiness by using a handy squeegee especially made for this purpose. Another tip: place the cover inside of a plastic or heavy paper bag and squeeze by hand.

Next, the roller cover should be saturated with a specially prepared roller cleaner, or turpentine, fuel oil, kerosene, or mineral spirits. The cover should be agitated in the solution, squeezed dry, then the process repeated. After painting with latex or water paint, the cover is similarly cleansed, but with soap in lukewarm water followed by a very thorough rinsing.

Before storing, remember to wipe the roller dry. Storing in a plastic container keeps covers fresh and clean for an indefinite period of time.

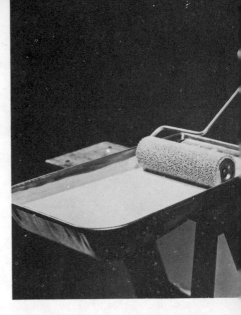

1. When using a roller, revolve it several times in the paint at the deep end of the tray. Then, get the surplus paint off the roller by squeezing it against the ramp of the tray.

HANDLING A ROLLER

2. Start the roller off with several criss-cross strokes on the area to be painted, then continue to work up and down to spread out the paint over the area.

Photographs courtesy of Pittsburgh Plate Glass.

3. After you have finished painting with a roller, clean it in the proper solvent. Agitate, squeeze out excess liquid and wipe the roller with a cloth. Then set cover aside to dry.

Painting—Common Failures and Their Cure

While it's true that no paint lasts forever, you have probably had some paints "fail" you. Within a matter of weeks or months, or even a year, there are imperfections, blisters; layers are peeling off. The term generally applied in such cases is "paint failure."

However, the chances are that it's not the paint's fault. Unless you have used an inferior paint, the cause of failure is either in your failure to prepare the surface properly to receive the paint or in your failure to apply the paint properly.

Of course, anyone who has wielded a paint brush immediately considers himself an experienced painter. Why, there's nothing to it—just put the paint on the brush and lay it on the surface. But painting is not that simple.

In the following parts of this section, there are detailed instructions on how to apply paint. For the present, however, let us concern ourselves with the "paint failures" and what we can do about them. Understanding why the paint failed is half the battle.

In the accompanying photographs, you will see some of the common types of paint failure. There is also information about possible causes together with information about cures.

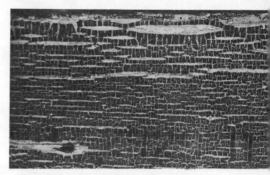

Alligatoring is an advanced form of checking, causing the paint film to take on the appearance of alligator skin, hence the name. It is usually caused by an improperly built-up paint film. Possibly, incompatible paints were used; perhaps the undercoat was not given sufficient time to dry; maybe the surface was never cleaned and the paint was applied over grease.

Blistering is a defect frequently caused by the construction of the house and not by the paint. It may be due to excessive moisture present behind the paint film. Maybe the wood was not dry when painted; maybe water seeped in behind the wood after it was painted and there is no way out but through the surface.

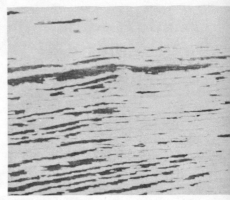

Checking is a minor paint failure; unless it is extensive, it can be ignored. It may be due to poor workmanship or the use of improperly formulated materials; maybe the undercoat was not dry when the final coat was applied. You can prevent checking by allowing sufficient drying time between coats. While some manufacturers say 24 hours are enough, it's better to wait 3 to 7 days between coats.

Cracking is sometimes caused by improperly made paints which dry too hard for the conditions of the particular job. The use of undercoats and finish coats of equal elasticity, possessing equal ability to expand and contract, will safeguard against this condition. Therefore, use the undercoat recommended by the manufacturer or one identical to it.

Staining is used to cover a variety of blemishes for which there are many causes. Water drips from metal (copper or iron pipe and gutters) can cause unsightly streaks. You can prevent this by painting the metal gutters and downspouts. Storm spots come from exposure to continuous rains and electrical storms. Usually weathering takes care of this damage and soon restores the original color to the paint film. When damp wood is painted, the water finds its way into the paint film carrying with it substances that cause brown stains. You can prevent this type of stain by making certain that the wood is seasoned and dry before painting. Structural defects must be watched for and eliminated; seal all knots to prevent the resin from seeping through and staining the paint film.

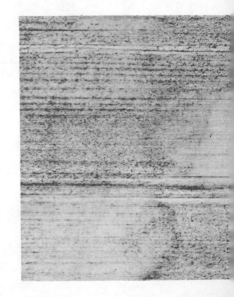

Spotting is caused by unequal oil absorption. A poor paint will soon show its weakness by extensive spotting. Adequate sealing of the surface is the secret of a good paint job. There is no economy in insisting on a low price paint or doing a shoddy job.

Wrinkling is a leather-like surface on a paint film. It can be caused by too heavy a coat of paint, improper brushing or it may be due to an improper combination of oil and pigment in the finish coat.

Photographs courtesy of Pittsburgh Plate Glass Co.

Paint Failure and Wood Rot

Sometimes paint failures are due to the improper preparation of the wood itself. Where wood is exposed to excessive moisture, more than paint is needed to keep it sound. It is best to treat the wood surfaces chemically to prevent wood rot and then paint over the treated wood.

Painting—Exterior Surfaces

For exterior wood and metal surfaces, painting should be done only in clear dry weather and generally the temperature should not be below 50° F. When the weather is cold, work should be stopped early enough in the afternoon to allow the paint to set before a sudden drop in temperature occurs. Woodwork should be thoroughly dry and seasoned before paint is applied. Temperature conditions should be the same for painting exterior masonry as for wood and metal. Masonry surfaces must be dry if oil base paints are to be used, while other masonry paints such as cement-water and resin-emulsion may be applied to damp surfaces.

Sufficient time should be allowed between coats so that the paint film will dry hard before more paint is applied. Oil paints on exterior wood should dry at least 24 hours, several days' drying time being preferable.

USE THE RIGHT PAINT

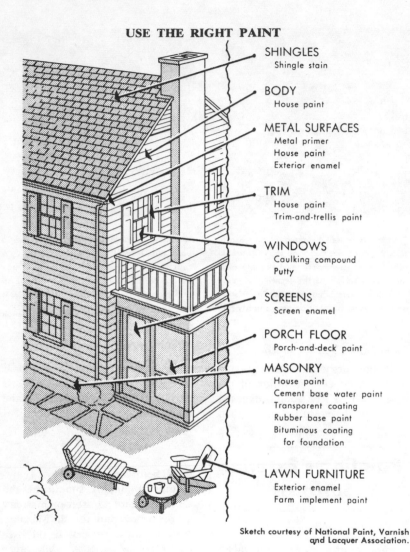

SHINGLES
Shingle stain

BODY
House paint

METAL SURFACES
Metal primer
House paint
Exterior enamel

TRIM
House paint
Trim-and-trellis paint

WINDOWS
Caulking compound
Putty

SCREENS
Screen enamel

PORCH FLOOR
Porch-and-deck paint

MASONRY
House paint
Cement base water paint
Transparent coating
Rubber base paint
Bituminous coating
for foundation

LAWN FURNITURE
Exterior enamel
Farm implement paint

Sketch courtesy of National Paint, Varnish
and Lacquer Association.

Two-Coat Paint System

A minimum of three coats was formerly the accepted practice for initial painting on exterior wood, and this practice is still largely followed. However, by using special primers, two-coat paint systems for wood have been developed that are durable and satisfactory. The prin-ciple of the two-coat paint system is that as much paint is applied in two coats as normally would be applied in the three-coat method of painting. On smoothly planed wood, the usual spreading rate for three-coat painting is about 550 to 600 sq. ft. per gallon for the first or priming-coat paint and about 600 to 650 sq. ft. per gallon for each of the next two coats. In the two-coat paint system, the primer is spread at the rate of about 450 sq. ft. per gallon and the finish coat about 550 sq. ft. per gallon. Rough surfaces and weather-beaten wood require much more paint than is indicated for smoothly planed wood.

Three-Coat Paint System

Mixed-pigment prepared paints are available for three-coat work, in addition to linseed-oil white-lead paints which may be mixed on the job or purchased ready-mixed. The manufacturer's directions should be followed in thinning the first and second coats. It is sometimes advisable in moist atmospheres, particularly at the seashore, to add a small amount (1 pint to a gallon) of good exterior varnish to the top coat of paint. The varnish should first be tried in a small amount of paint to make sure that the two are compatible and that the varnish will not cause the paint to thicken.

Shingle Stains

Shingle stains are pigmented oil stains, similar to very fluid paints, which can be applied by dipping, brushing, or spraying. They are intended for application to comparatively rough exterior wood surfaces where it is not necessary to bring out the grain and texture of the wood to which they are applied, and they dry to a matt or semi-transparent finish. Durable pigments, such as iron oxides, are used for the colors red through brown; chromium oxide, for green; and zinc oxide

Make certain that you cover all edges and spaces between boards when painting exterior wood.

Photograph courtesy of Valspar Corp.

or white lead tinted with lampblack, for gray.

Shingle stains should not cake or change color in the container and when stirred should settle very slowly. With the exception of some dark brown stains, which are simply refined coal-tar creosote with volatile thinners, shingle stains are usually made from very finely ground pigments, drying oils, and volatile thinners. Many commercial shingle stains contain some creosote oil from coal tar or water-gas tar which is intended to act as a wood preservative. While pressure treatment with creosote is one of the most effective methods of preventing wood from rotting, the small amount that penetrates the wood from a single dip or brush treatment probably has very little effect.

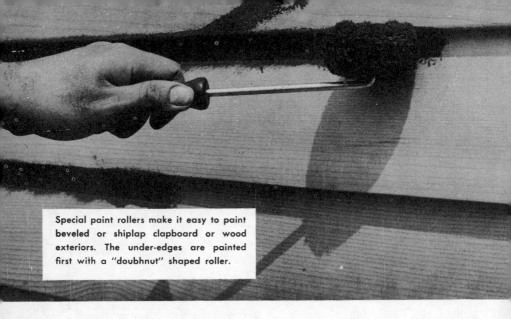

Special paint rollers make it easy to paint beveled or shiplap clapboard or wood exteriors. The under-edges are painted first with a "doubhnut" shaped roller.

Paint applied over creosote stain is likely to be ruined by the creosote bleeding through. If there is any possibility that the shingles may be painted at some future time, pigment oil shingle stains without creosote should be used.

Masonry Surfaces

Paints for masonry wall surfaces may be divided into four types: Cement water paint, resin-emulsion paint, oil paint, and paint containing rubber in the vehicle. These paints are also suitable for use on such masonry surfaces as foundations, gate posts, and fence or enclosure walls, but they should not be used on floors which are subject to abrasion. For such surfaces, a very hard-drying paint with good water resistance and gloss retention is recommended.

Cement-water paints are water-dilutable paints in which Portland cement is the binder. They are particularly suitable for application on

Photographs courtesy of E Z Paintr Corp.

The wider sections of the board are then given the finishing touches with a special 5½" roller. In this way, all surfaces and edges are protected with paint.

damp, new, or open-textured masonry surfaces. These surfaces include those walls that are damp at the time of painting, or that may become damp after painting as a result of structural defects or other causes; new structures (less than 6 months old) which normally contain water-soluble alkaline salts; and open-textured surfaces such as cinder, concrete, and lightweight aggregate block. These paints are not recommended for stopping leakage through porous walls that are exposed to water pressure, particularly if the paint is applied to the inside of the wall. For such conditions, a coating of hot bituminous material applied to the outside of the wall is preferable.

Close-textured surfaces which are relatively dry, such as cast concrete, asbestos-cement siding, and tile, may be painted with resin-emulsion paint or paints containing rubber in the vehicle. Walls which are dry at the time of painting, and are so constructed as to remain dry after painting, may be decorated satisfactorily with oil paints.

CEMENT-WATER PAINT

Cement-water paints are water-dilutable paints, packaged in powder form. They are composed chiefly of Portland cement or Portland cement and lime and possess good decorating qualities or hiding power and color. However, when wetted, as by rain, they become somewhat translucent and darker in color. When again dry, the film returns to its original opaqueness and color.

To clean a surface for the application of cement-water paint, thoroughly remove all dust, dirt, and efflorescence, old coatings of whitewash, and flaking or scaling cement-water paint by brushing vigorously with a wire brush. Firmly adhering coatings of cement-water paint or cement-water paints which are "chalking" or "dusting" need not be removed, but should be brushed with a stiff bristle brush to make the surface uniform.

Before applying the paint, whether initially or on a previously painted surface, the masonry should be thoroughly wetted, preferably with a garden hose adjusted to produce a fine spray. A superficial dampening with a brush dipped in water is not adequate for exterior walls but may be satisfactory for cool basement walls. Usually, wetting the walls in one operation not more than an hour before painting is sufficient. The water should be applied so that each part is sprayed three or four times for about 10 seconds each, time being allowed between applications for the water to soak into the surface. If the surface dries rapidly, as it may in hot weather, it should be redampened slightly just before painting. The wall surface should be moist, not dripping wet when paint is applied.

Cement-water paint powder should be mixed with water in accordance with the manufacturer's directions. Paints may be tinted by adding suitable amounts of coloring pigments but, due to the difficulty of producing uniform colors by hand mixing, it is suggested that commercial brands of tinted paints be purchased which have been mill ground in the factory.

Paint rollers can be used to cover brick. It is best to use a long nap roller so that the paint covers the brick surfaces and the mortar joints as well.

look well at first but will generally lose their opacity and protective value much sooner than thicker films. The proper spreading rate is difficult to estimate for Portland cement paint because of the difference in the texture of the masonry to be covered. However, on smooth masonry, 1 gallon of mixed paint should be sufficient to cover 100 sq. ft. with two coats; and, for rough masonry, 1 gallon should be sufficient to apply two coats to 50 sq. ft. of surface.

After painting, it is desirable to sprinkle the freshly painted surface two or three times a day with a fog spray, such as is used for dampening walls prior to painting, and it is recommended that this be done between coats and for 2 days after the final coat, starting as soon as the paint has set, usually 6 to 12 hours after application.

RESIN-EMULSION PAINT

Resin-emulsion paints are water-thinned materials whose dry-film properties closely resemble those of a flat oil paint. They may be used on most porous masonry surfaces, including asbestos-cement siding, which has not been previously coated with a waterproofing compound. They should not be used on magnesite stucco.

To prepare the surface for resin-emulsion paints, remove by brushing or washing all dust, dirt, efflorescence, and loose particles from the surface; and also remove any flaking or scaling paint by scraping or wire brushing. Glossy areas should be dulled by sanding; oil, grease, and

Cement-water paint should be applied in two coats. Preferably not less than 24 hours' drying time should be allowed between coats. The first coat should be slightly moistened with water before applying the second.

Most Portland cement paints cannot be satisfactorily applied with the ordinary hair-bristle paint brush. Proper application requires a brush with relatively short, stiff, fiber bristles such as fender brushes, ordinary scrub brushes, or roofers' brushes.

While thick films are to be avoided, there is a tendency to use too much water in cement-water paint and to brush it out too thin. Coatings applied in this manner may

wax should be removed by scrubbing with mineral spirits. Then wash with water containing trisodium phosphate (about 2 ounces to the gallon), and rinse thoroughly with clean water.

Resin-emulsion paints are packaged in paste form and need to be thinned with water before being applied. They should be mixed in clean metal containers (not wood) in accordance with the directions given on the manufacturer's label and not allowed to stand after mixing for more than a week.

Resin-emulsion paint should be applied in two coats and the air temperature when painting should be above 50° F. A sizing or priming coat is not generally required except on open-textured masonry. For that, a cement-water paint containing sand should be used to fill the voids in the wall surface. On very warm days, it may be advisable to moisten the surface to be painted with water, prior to applying the paint. Resin-emulsion paint will dry in 1 to 4 hours, and may be recoated in 6 to 8 hours; the film becomes hard overnight. One gallon of the paste paint will cover approximately 200 to 450 sq. ft., depending upon the surface and the application. Brushes and spray guns should be washed with warm soapy water immediately after using.

OIL PAINTS

Oil paints intended for use on masonry are usually ready-mixed paints containing weather-resistant opaque pigments suspended in drying oils, resins, and thinners. They should be formulated so that the first coat seals the surface sufficiently to prevent spots or flashes of the second coat. Two coats are necessary for good hiding and durability.

Moisture back of the paint film will seriously impair the life of a coating of oil-base paint, therefore the application of oil paint to new masonry should be deferred until the walls have had time to dry. This may require 3 months to a year, depending upon the thickness and porosity of the wall and the weather conditions. Because of the importance of preventing water from entering the walls after painting, repairs of structural defects, such as leaks around flashing, doors, and windows, should be made before applying oil-base paint.

Dust and dirt should be washed off and efflorescence should be brushed off with a stiff fiber or wire brush. All traces of oil should be removed with steel brushes, abrasive stones, or a lye solution. However, if the surface is badly stained, it should be lightly sandblasted.

Caution:—When using lye (caustic soda, sodium hydroxide), avoid splashing the eyes, skin, and clothing because it may cause burns.

Old coatings of organic paint or cement-base water paint in sound condition need not be removed. Whitewash or peeling, scaling, or flaking paints should be completely removed.

Oil paints should not be applied during damp or humid weather or when the temperature is below 50° F. At least 1 week of clear dry weather should precede the application of the first coat. As masonry surfaces tend to chill and collect

It's easy to paint rough concrete with a roller. This is a job that would take a long time and ruin a paint brush. But with a roller, you can apply the paint just as easily as if you were painting a flat interior wall.

Photograph courtesy of E Z Paintr Corp.

condensed moisture, painting early in the morning and late afternoon should be avoided except in dry climates.

A minimum of 90 days' drying time should elapse before applying oil paint over a cement-water base or over mortar-filled joints and cracks. When it is not practicable to wait this long before painting, a calking compound rather than cement mortar should be used as a crack filler.

RUBBER-BASE PAINTS

There are two types of rubber-base paints, the rubber-solution and rubber-emulsion types.

Rubber-solution paints are available at most paint stores and usually sell for slightly more than oil-base masonry paints. They may be applied by brush, spray or roller to dry or slightly damp walls. They are suitable for painting asbestos-cement siding and shingles. These paints are also useful for "sealing in" stains on old masonry, and as protective primers under finishing coats of resin-emulsion or oil-base paints.

The same procedure outlined for preparing the surface for oil-base paints should be followed for rubber-base paints in removing dust, dirt, loose mortar, form oil, and efflorescence on dense surfaces.

Oil paint coatings must be removed before applying rubber-solution paints because the thinners used in these paints act as solvents for the oil paints. This is not necessary when applying rubber-emulsion paints over oil paints that are in good condition since they do not contain solvents that will soften the oil paints.

Rubber-base paints may be applied to dry or damp walls. It is usually necessary to thin the paint for the first coat, using the thinner recommended by the manufacturer, as some paint thinners are incompatible with rubber-base paints. The paint dries to the touch within three hours but, at least 18 hours' drying time should be allowed between coats, otherwise the succeeding coat will "lift" or soften the undercoat.

The brushing technique for rubber-base paints is the same as for applying enamels. "Back-brushing" or "working" the paint will cause it to roll and pull under the brush. As the paint tends to "set" rather quickly, it is advisable to work in shade rather than sunlight.

Brushes and spray guns should be cleaned with paint thinner immediately after they are used, because dry paint is difficult to redissolve once it has hardened.

Iron and Steel Surfaces

The chief reason for applying paint to exterior metalwork, particularly iron and steel, is to control and prevent corrosion. For best results two coats of priming paint followed by two coats of top or finishing paint are recommended on new work. For repainting, a spot coat followed by a full priming coat, and then one or two finish coats are recommended. The usual recommended spreading rate of each coat of paint is about 600 sq. ft. per gallon. It should be stressed that the preparation of the surface, particularly steel, prior to painting is important, for unless the surface is properly cleaned so that the priming paint comes in direct contact with the metal, early failure of the paint film will probably occur.

Cleaning is the most important step in preparing metalwork for painting. It can be divided into two phases; the removal of oil and grease, and the removal of rust, dirt, scale, old paint, and moisture. All oil and grease should be removed before using mechanical methods of cleaning. The usual method is to wipe the surface with clean cloths and mineral spirits or carbon tetrachloride. The liquid as well as the cloths should be kept clean by frequent renewals to avoid leaving a thin, greasy film on the surface. When the oil and grease have been disposed of rust, scale, and old paint may be cleaned from the surface with wire brushes, steel wool, or motor-driven rotary brushes.

The paint should be applied in bright, warm weather to metal surfaces which are clean and dry. Painting should not be done early in the morning when the surface to be painted is damp from dew. Ample time should be allowed for each coat of paint to dry before applying the next coat.

Since the main function of a priming coat is to protect metal from corrosion, it should contain rust-inhibitive pigments. It can be applied by either brush or spray but particular care should be taken to cover the surface completely with the proper thickness of paint. Two coats of primer are recommended for new work. The second coat may be tinted to a slightly different color to make sure of adequate surface coverage. Ample time should be allowed for drying before application of succeeding coats.

Two practical coatings for steel surfaces are red-lead and iron oxide paints, red lead being used as a primer and iron oxide as a finishing material. Dull red and brown iron-oxide paints are economical for painting terne-plate roofs and structural metal. They are durable and are frequently referred to as roof and barn paint.

Red lead is available in three types: Type I, red-lead linseed oil paint which should be allowed to dry for a week between coats; type II, semi-quick-drying red-lead paint

Photographs courtesy of E Z Paintr Corp.

which is an easy brushing material suitable for general use and dries in 24 hours; and type III, red-lead paint in a varnish vehicle which dries within 8 hours and may be used for touch-up work on clean smooth steel.

Zinc-dust primers have good rust-inhibitive properties and are particularly effective for galvanized iron and sheet zinc. While the primary function of these paints is to provide adequate adherence on galvanized metal, they are also satisfactory as finish paints and may be used in one or more coats.

Quick-drying metal primers for home workshop machinery and automobiles are iron-oxide primers in which the vehicle is a thin varnish. They dry to a smooth velvety, flat eggshell finish, and give excellent foundations for decorative coats.

As finish coats on iron or steel, black and dark-colored paints are more durable than light-tinted paints. Red-lead paint should not be used as a final coat, since it does not retain its color. One of the best finish coats for metal is aluminum

It just isn't possible, nor is it safe, to try to hold a paint tray in one hand and paint with the other when standing on a ladder. However, special trays are made for outdoor use; they attach conveniently and easily on the ladder.

paint made by mixing about 2 lbs. of aluminum powder or paste with 1 gallon of spar varnish.

Copper

Copper gutters and flashings, as well as copper or bronze screening, may cause yellowish-green stains on light- or white-painted houses. One way to avoid this is to paint or varnish the copper or bronze. The surface of the metal should be cleaned by washing with gasoline or turpentine, and a priming coat composed of 1½ to 2 lbs. of aluminum powder to 1 gallon of aluminum mixing varnish applied, followed by the desired color coat. Weathered copper or bronze fly-screening should be dusted and then given two coats of thin black enamel. Zinc dust-zinc oxide paints may also be used on copper and bronze if a gray color is acceptable.

Planning to paint the outside of your house?
Here are some color suggestions for you.

If your house has shutters, paint the trim the same color as body of house—or white. If not, use these suggested colors for trim.

If the roof of your house is	You can paint the body	...and the trim or shutters and doors															
		Pink	Bright red	Red-orange	Tile red	Cream	Bright yellow	Light green	Dark green	Gray-green	Blue-green	Light blue	Dark blue	Blue-gray	Violet	Brown	White
GRAY	White	X	X	X	X	X	X	X	X	X	X	X	X	X	X		
	Gray	X	X	X	X			X	X	X	X	X	X	X	X		X
	Cream-yellow		X		X		X		X	X							X
	Pale green				X		X		X	X							X
	Dark green	X				X	X	X									X
	Putty			X	X				X	X			X	X		X	
	Dull red	X				X		X						X			X
GREEN	White	X	X	X	X	X	X	X	X	X	X	X	X	X	X	X	
	Gray		X			X	X	X									X
	Cream-yellow		X		X			X	X	X						X	X
	Pale green			X	X		X		X								X
	Dark green	X		X		X	X	X									X
	Beige					X			X	X	X		X	X			
	Brown	X				X	X	X									X
	Dull red					X		X		X							X
RED	White		X		X			X		X		X					
	Light gray		X		X			X									X
	Cream-yellow		X		X					X		X	X				
	Pale green		X		X												X
	Dull red					X		X		X	X						X
BROWN	White			X	X		X	X	X	X			X	X	X	X	
	Buff				X				X	X	X					X	
	Pink-beige				X				X	X						X	X
	Cream-yellow				X				X	X	X					X	
	Pale green								X	X						X	
	Brown			X		X	X										X
BLUE	White			X	X		X					X	X				
	Gray			X		X						X	X				X
	Cream-yellow			X	X								X	X			
	Blue			X		X	X					X					X

To paint clapboards, first run your brush along the edge where one strip of siding overlaps the next. Then "spot-paint" a strip of the siding by striking your newly-filled brush to the wood at intervals. Join the spots with smooth brush action that spreads the paint evenly, making sure that you cover the entire board.

Paint the trim before painting the siding on upper sections of a house where you need to use a ladder. This eliminates the danger of marring newly painted surfaces with the top of the ladder. On lower sections of a house, the siding can be painted before the trim.

At right, the man of the household works on the trim, while the shutter receives feminine attention.

Before the finish coat is applied, all surfaces must be carefully prepared. Rough spots should be sanded smooth; all rust removed. Cracks should be filled. Any spots of bare wood or metal must be primed.

How to Paint a Clapboard House

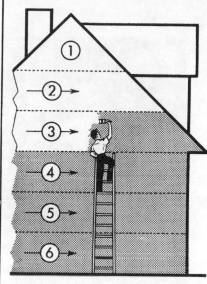

When painting the side of a house, start at the highest point and apply paint in horizontal strips about 3 feet wide, working from left to right. When possible, paint above the top of the ladder. This enables you to reach a wider area. Never stop in the middle of a strip for any great length of time. For safety and working ease, the distance between the house and the base of your ladder should be about 1/4 to 1/3 of the ladder's length.

1. Load your brush, then apply two or three dabs of paint along the joint of the siding. This helps to distribute the paint quickly and easily.

2. Next, brush the paint out well, being sure to coat the clapboard under-edge.

3. "Feather" the ends of your brush strokes so the coat will be smooth where one section joins another.

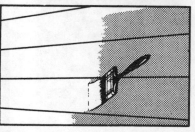

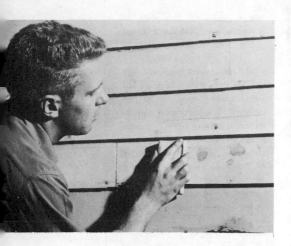

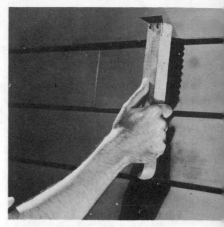

Check exterior wood siding and wood trim for loose paint. You can remove small areas with sandpaper and sanding block.

A wire brush comes in handy to remove any grime and surface dirt before applying the paint.

10 Steps to Successful Outdoor Painting

Where necessary, calk joints around windows, doors and chimneys. You can do this with a putty knife and calking compound or it's easier and quicker to do a better job with a calking gun.

Check around the window panes for loose putty. If any is missing or loose, replace it with sound putty. See **Glazing**.

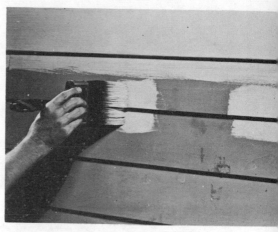

Start painting on the outside at the highest part of the house. Make certain that the ladder is secure before you climb it.

Lay brushload of paint on in two or three places and then brush out well. Note that you never soak the entire brush in paint; do not get ferrule wet.

Photographs courtesy of Pittsburgh Plate Glass Co.

When painting clapboard or beveled or shiplap siding, always paint the edges first, using the brush on its flat side, never its edge. You can do the same job with special rollers.

After brushing out the paint, finish with tips of the brush to a thin feather-edge. Now continue to lay on brushloads of paint, working from the wet edge outward.

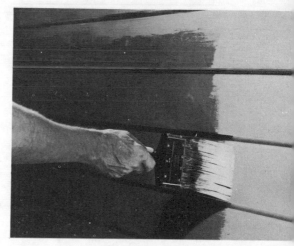

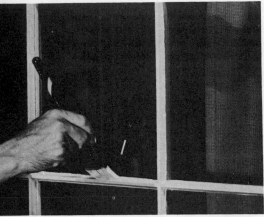

Photographs courtesy of Pittsburgh Plate Glass Co.

When painting around window sash outside the house, keep the sash brush well loaded for full-bodied stroke. In this way, you will be able to do a better job with less smearing of paint on the glass.

If the surface coat of gutters and downspouts is still good, you can apply the final coat immediately. Otherwise, it is essential that a prime coat be applied before the final coat.

Painting—Interior

Interior painting requires as careful preparation of surfaces as does exterior painting. The advent of odorless paints now makes it possible to paint any time of the year. Formerly, most interior painting in the home was done in the fall or spring, when it was possible to leave the windows open to ventilate the room. But open windows brought dust into the room to mar the finished painted surface.

A good interior paint job is often 50% preparation and 50% painting. Do not rush in preparing the surfaces in your eagerness to get at the brush or roller. If you do not prepare the surfaces properly, you'll be back with the paint brush or roller in a few months.

It is recommended that you re-read the section on *Painting—Basic Preparation of the Surfaces*. Then, in this section you will find the necessary information on the application of different types of paints on various interior wall, ceiling and floor materials.

Plaster

New dry plaster in good condition, which is to be finished with a paint other than water paint, should be given a coat of primer-sealer and allowed to dry thoroughly before being inspected for uniformity of appearance. Variations in gloss and color differences in the case of tinted primers indicate whether or not the whole surface has been completely sealed. If not, a second coat of primer-sealer should be applied. If only a few "suction spots" are apparent, a second coat over these areas may be sufficient.

A flat, semigloss, or high-gloss finish may be applied to the primed surface. For a flat finish, two coats of flat wall paint should follow the priming coat. For a semi-gloss finish, one coat of flat wall paint and one coat of semi-gloss paint should be applied to the primed surface. For a high-gloss finish, one coat of semi-gloss paint and one coat of high-gloss enamel should be used over the priming coat.

Before applying water paints of the calcimine type to new plastered walls they should be sized, using either a glue-water size or, if the plaster is dry, a thin varnish or primer-sealer. Cold water paints of the casein type may be applied either directly to a plastered surface, or the surface may be first given a coat of primer-sealer to equalize uneven suction effects. The same is true of resin-emulsion paints, with the recommendations of the manufacturer of the product being given preference in case of doubt. Since resin-emulsion paints usually contain some oil in the binder, they should ordinarily be applied only to plaster which has dried thoroughly.

Texture wall paints may also be used on plaster surfaces. The ad-

PAINTING POINTERS

Avoid a ring of paint where you put down can by keeping a paper plate under it. Daub a little paint on the bottom of can, press the plate against it and the plate will stick.

Unpainted furniture should first be sealed by brushing a very thin wash coat of shellac on the raw wood. When dry, smooth lightly with sandpaper. Apply undercoat, brush out thoroughly, let dry at least 24 hours and sand again. Apply finish coat with smooth, light brush strokes, using just the tip of the bristles.

Fit a disk of window screening inside can after mixing paint well. As the screen sinks, it will carry lumpy paint particles to bottom.

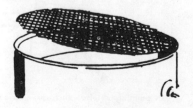

FINGERING   FISHTAILING   CURLING   SWELLING

These paintbrush defects all result from misuse of the brush: Painting with side of brush is a major cause of "fingering." If you use a wide brush to paint pipes and similar surfaces it will take a fishtail shape. Swelling may occur if you dip the brush too deeply. If paint hardens in the heel, it will swell the ferrule. Avoid curling by hanging the brush up.

PAINTING POINTERS

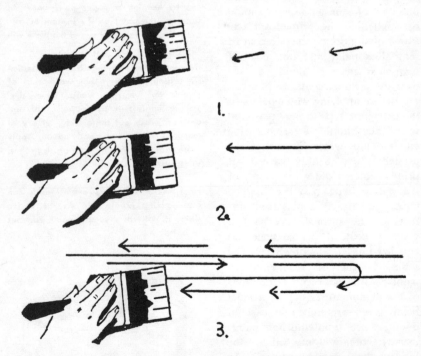

1.

2.

3.

In painting exterior surfaces, you can get a smoother and more uniform job by daubing paint on in spots (1) before stroking. Then use long, leveling brush strokes (2) to spread the paint smoothly. Finish the brush stroke (3) in a zigzag path and you'll have a good-looking job.

Keep bugs out of wet paint applied outdoors by adding insect repellent to each batch that you mix.

Remove knobs or handles and other hardware. You'll find it easier to brush paint smoothly on drawer fronts and cabinet doors. Attach knobs to cardboard as shown above and paint them with a small brush.

Save priming time by using the widest brush you can for each job. A 4" brush is the most popular width for large, flat surfaces. Use a trim or sash brush, available in 1" to 3" widths, for woodwork, paneling and trim. For narrow table legs and chair rungs, use the narrowest sash brush. A sash brush may be flat or oval.

Keep bristles pointed downward, or at least tilted at an angle below the horizontal, while you work. Tilt a brush upward only for ceiling work. Pointing the bristles down helps keep paint from running into the heel. If the paint hardens in the heel it will swell the ferrule and perhaps ruin the brush. For the same reason, dip a brush no more than halfway into paint each time you charge it.

Blend each stroke toward the wet paint area, not away from it, to avoid ridges and lap marks.

PAINTING POINTERS

Angle your brush into corners; never paint with its sides. Angling in protects the bristles and gives you a smoother, more even finish.

• • •

You can lengthen the life of a fine, pure bristle brush by using it only to apply finish coats. Keep brushes with synthetic or mixed bristles handy for priming and for use on rough surfaces that wear down bristles fast.

• • •

Use masking tape where two shades are to meet. Paint on one color, let it dry, apply tape at the dividing line and then brush on the second color. The result will be a neater job and you'll save time.

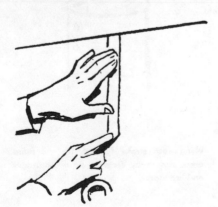

vantages of this type of paint are that one coat economically produces a textured decoration and relieves the monotony of smooth flat paint. It also covers cracks or patches in the plaster more completely than ordinary wall paint. The disadvantages of texture wall paint are that they collect dust and are difficult to restore to a smooth finish. These materials are available as water- or oil-base paints, are thicker than ordinary wall paints, and may be applied to wallboard as well as plaster to produce textured effects such as random, Spanish, mission, and multicolored.

For more information, see the section on *Plaster*.

Composition Wallboard

Composition wallboard usually presents no particular painting difficulties if the ordinary precautions are observed, such as making certain that the surface is dry and free from grease and oil. The painting procedure for wallboard is the same as for plaster; it requires a priming and sealing coat followed by whatever finish coats are desired, or may be given one-coat flat or resin-emulsion type paint.

Wallpaper

Water-thinned paint may be applied to wallpaper that is well-bonded to the wall and does not contain dyes which may bleed into the paint. One thickness of wallpaper is preferable for paint application. Paints other than those of the water-thinned type may also be applied to wallpaper by following the directions given for painting plaster. However, wallpaper coated with such a paint is difficult to remove without injury to the plaster.

Wood Walls and Trim

New interior walls and wood trim should be smoothed with sandpaper and dusted before painting or varnishing. To preserve the grain of the wood, the surface may be rubbed with linseed oil, varnished or shellacked, and waxed. If an opaque finish is desired, semi-gloss paint thinned with 1 pint of turpentine per gallon of paint or the primer-sealer previously described for walls may be used as a priming coat on wood. One or two coats of semi-gloss paint should then be applied over the thoroughly dry prime coat, or if a full-gloss finish is desired, the last coat should be a high-gloss enamel.

Wood Floor Finishes

For information on varnishing wood floors, refer to the section on *Floors, Wood—Finishing.*

Masonry Walls and Ceilings

Interior masonry walls and ceilings above grade may, in general, be painted in much the same manner as plaster surfaces. Here again,

PAINTING POINTERS

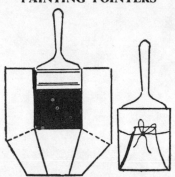

Wrap brush for storage, using heavy paper, oilcloth or aluminum foil. Be sure that the bristles lie straight and that end of brush is not compressed by the wrapping. Suspend the brush with the bristles down. If it's a fine-quality brush used in oil paints, saturate the brush with linseed oil before wrapping it.

Brush storage rack can be made by driving short nails part way into ¾" plywood so brushes can rest on handles. Mount board on door or shop wall. Wrap brushes before storage.

Store brushes in solvent overnight, suspending them in the container by one of the methods illustrated here. In method at far right, the handle is tied to thin stick extending beyond bristles. Brush can then stand upright without resting on bristles.   Sketches courtesy of Baker Brush Co.

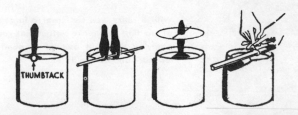

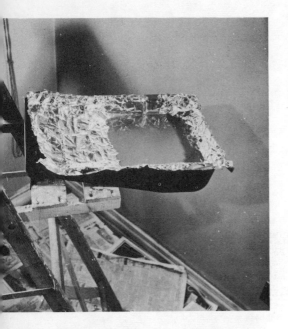

Easy way to avoid cleaning the tray afterwards is to line it with aluminum foil before you pour the paint into it. Use a fairly thick piece of foil or several sheets of the household type.

With a roller, you can cover a large area at one time and make certain that you are applying the right amount of paint—not too much and not too little.

it is necessary to allow adequate time for the masonry to dry before applying paint and, in addition, attention should be given to the preparation of the surface. When decorating a wall containing Portland cement (concrete, for example), it is essential to take precautions against the attack of alkali. For this purpose, alkali-resistant primers such as rubber-base paints may be used when oil paints are to follow.

Cement-water paints are best suited for application to basement walls which are damp as a result of leakage or condensation. To apply these paints, the same procedure should be followed as is described here for painting exterior masonry walls.

Concrete Floors

Two general types of paints for concrete floors are varnish and rubber-base paint. Each has its limitations and the finish cannot be patched without the patched area showing through. Floor and deck enamel of the varnish type gives good service on concrete floors above grade where there is no moisture present.

Rubber-base paints, which dry to a hard semi-gloss finish, may be used on concrete floors below grade, providing the floor is not continually damp from seepage and condensation.

Paint should not be applied to a concrete basement floor until the concrete has aged for at least a year. The floor should be dry when painted, the best time for application being during the winter or early spring (assuming there is some heating apparatus in the basement), when the humidity in the basement is low. In general, three coats of paint are required on an unpainted floor, and the first coat should be thin to secure good penetration. After the paint is dry, it should be protected with a coat of floor wax.

In repainting concrete floors, where the existing paint has been waxed and is in good condition except for some worn areas, the surface should be scrubbed with cloths saturated with turpentine or petroleum spirits and rubbed with steel

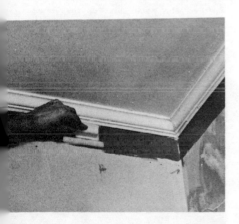

Special rollers make two-color painting easy. This is a blackboard type of roller with a plastic shield along one edge. In this way, it is easy to apply one color paint to the wall and another to the trim and still get perfectly straight line between them without intermixing the colors.

No more standing on a plank in the air or climbing up and down a ladder to paint a ceiling. A convenient extension handle is attached to the ordinary roller. It makes it easy to reach the ceiling while standing on the floor.

Photographs courtesy of E Z Paintr Corp.

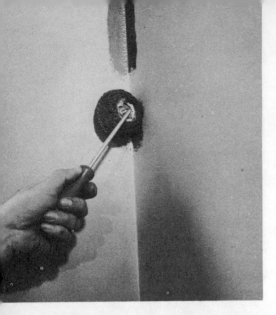

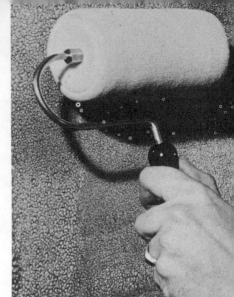

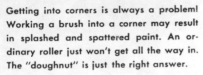

Getting into corners is always a problem! Working a brush into a corner may result in splashed and spattered paint. An ordinary roller just won't get all the way in. The "doughnut" is just the right answer.

For a stippled effect, you can use a roller with a special cover that will produce the stipple effect with enamel paint. Here, a stipple coat is being applied over glass.

Photographs courtesy of E Z Paintr Corp.

Two-tone painting is simple with a roller on textured plywood. The base or first coat is applied with a long nap roller, making certain that you work the paint into all the crevices.

The top or second coat is applied with a short-nap roller that just skims over the surfaces. The paint stays on the raised portions of the textured plywood while the base or bottom coat remains untouched.

wool while wet, to remove all wax before repainting. If this is not done, the paint will not adhere and dry satisfactorily. If the old paint is badly worn, it should be removed by treating with a solution of 2 lbs. of caustic soda (household lye) to 1 gallon of hot water. This may be mopped on the surface and allowed to remain for 30 minutes after which the floor can be washed with hot water and scraped with a wide steel scraper. Another method of application is to spread a thin layer of sawdust, which has been soaked in caustic solution over the floor and allow it to stand overnight. The following morning, the floor can be washed with hot water and the paint scraped off. The surface should then be rinsed thoroughly with clean water.

If you're looking for a place to rest that brush, here's a handy clamp that fits onto the can or even a tray for a roller.

Photograph courtesy of W. I. Sims

If rubber-base paint has been used, the caustic soda treatment may not be effective and it may be necessary to use an organic solvent type of paint remover.

Caution:—When using caustic soda or lye, avoid splashing eyes, skin, and clothing.

Interior Metal

Interior metal, such as heating grilles, radiators, and exposed water pipes, should be painted to prevent rust and to make them as inconspicuous as possible. New metal should be cleaned of grease and dirt by washing with mineral spirits, and any rust should be removed by sanding, after which a metal primer should be applied. The finish coat may be either a flat wall paint or a semi-gloss enamel.

If you are not sure of the primer to use on metal, the paint dealer or manufacturer will give you this

There are many gadgets besides a steady painting hand to avoid getting paint on glass when you paint the windows. An old but still reliable technique is to coat the glass with a soap-and-water "paste." When the job is over, just wash the windows and the paint smears come right off with soap. But wait until the paint is dry before you wash the soap off.

If you have tileboard made of hardboard in your home and you want "mortar" lines, you can paint them in. An easy way to do this is with a striping tool; it comes with various wheels, depending upon the width of line you wish to paint.

Photograph courtesy of Masonite Corp.

information, dependent on the type of metal to be painted.

Usually on exposed air ducts of galvanized metal a primer coat of zinc dust-zinc oxide paint is used, before the finish coat is applied.

The paints may be applied by brush or spray; the small spray attachment for vacuum cleaners is very convenient, especially for painting radiators.

Brass lighting fixtures and andirons may be polished and kept bright by coating with metal lacquers. The lacquers, held in cans under pressure, may be sprayed directly from the container. Old-fashioned or unattractive lighting fixtures may be painted with ceiling or wall paint to harmonize with the surrounding surfaces.

Special Surfaces
WHITEWASH

Whitewashes and lime paints must be thin when applied. In fact, best results will be obtained if the application is so thin that the surface to which it is applied may easily be seen through the film while it is wet. The coating will dry opaque, but two thin coats will give better results than one thick coat.

A large whitewash brush is best for applying the wash. One should not attempt to brush out the coating, as in applying oil paint, but simply spread the whitewash on as evenly and quickly as possible.

The principal ingredient in whitewash is lime paste. A satisfactory paste can be made with hydrated lime, but better results are obtained by using quicklime paste that has been slaked with enough water to make it moderately stiff. The lime paste should be kept in a loosely covered container for at least several days. Eight gallons of stiff lime paste can be made by slaking 25 lbs. of quicklime in 10 gallons of water, or by soaking 50 lbs. of hydrated lime in 6 gallons of water. After soaking, the paste should be strained through a fine screen to remove lumps or foreign matter.

Whitewash can be made from various combinations of lime paste and other ingredients. The following two formulas are satisfactory.

Formula No. 1

Casein .... 5 lbs.
Trisodium phosphate   3 lbs.
Lime paste .... 8 gals.

Before applying any paint—either under-coat or final coat—to a wall surface, wash it thoroughly to remove all dust and grease. Otherwise, you are bound to wind up with a "paint failure."

When painting an entire room, start your painting job with the ceiling. When painting a ceiling always work across the narrow dimension.

Cracks in plaster walls should be filled before starting to paint. See **Plaster** section for detailed how-to.

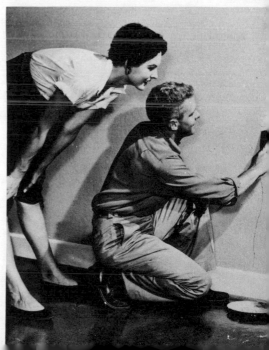

When painting a wall, keep painting strips on wall narrow so that you are always working with a wet edge. Otherwise, you may see the "joints" where new brush strokes are laid on.

Photograph courtesy of Pittsburgh Plate Glass.

Paint shields are helpful in keeping paint off the glass when painting the window sash.

The casein, which serves as the glue binder, should be soaked in 2 gallons of hot water until thoroughly softened, which should be approximately 2 hours. After dissolving the trisodium phosphate in 1 gallon of water it should be added to the casein, stirring the mixture until the casein dissolves. This solution should be mixed with the lime paste and 3 gallons of water.

Formula No. 2

Common salt	12 lbs.
Powdered alum	6 lbs.
Molasses	1 qt.
Lime paste	8 gals.

The salt and alum should be dissolved in 4 gallons of hot water, after which the molasses may be added to the mixture. The resulting clear solution is then added to the lime paste, stirred vigorously, and thinned with water to the desired consistency. This whitewash has a yellow tinge when first applied, but the color disappears in a few days leaving a white film.

Another satisfactory whitewash can be made by diluting a moderately heavy cold lime paste (about 33 lbs. of hydrated lime and 8 gallons of water) with 5 gallons of skim-milk.

The area covered by a gallon of whitewash depends upon the nature of the surface, but ordinarily a gallon will cover about 225 sq. ft. on wood, about 180 sq. ft. on brick, and about 270 sq. ft. on plaster. The formulas mentioned will make from 10 to 14 gallons of whitewash. If a smaller quantity is desired, the amount of each ingredient should be reduced proportionately.

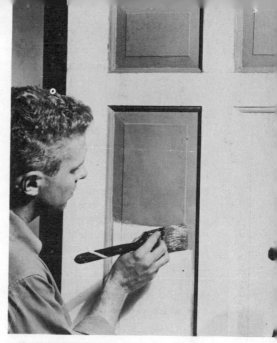

A paint shield also comes in handy when painting the baseboard molding or the bottom of a door. It protects the floor from splashes.

If painting the panels with enamel, smooth the surface with light, upward strokes, using a brush that is almost dry.

When painting a panel door, always paint the insides of the panels first with horizontal strokes.

STIPPLING

Whether you desire the effect of stippling (tiny paint dots) as a decorative effect, or if you have a wall which has an uneven surface and you feel you can hide the defect by stippling it, you may accomplish this result very simply.

For stippling you need a special brush; get one that is flat, and has short, stiff bristles.

The first step is to cover the surface with a coat of paint, using your regular paint brush, or spray, or roller. Then, while the surface is still wet, take the dry stipple brush and energetically with short strokes drive the ends or the bristles into the wet paint. Be sure not to brush across. The result will be clusters of dots. Every few minutes wipe the brush with a cloth, to keep the bristle ends clean and dry.

STENCILING

You may want designs on the walls, or perhaps even on floors and ceilings, in some of the rooms or hallway. You may buy or make your own stencils, which should be on heavy paper, stencil board, plastic, or metal. Avoid stencils made of lightweight paper which will get soaked when touched by wet paint. Your paint dealer will suggest the best paint for you to use, as it will depend a great deal on the surface over which you want to put the sten-cilled designs. Generally a heavy paint is used, so that it will not spread under the stencil while you are applying it.

The stencil must be held very firmly against the surface with one hand, and the stencil brush worked over it quickly with the other hand. Or, if you have an assistant, it is best for one person to keep the stencil steady, while the other does the painting. In removing the stencil, make sure you pick it up without smudging.

Painting—Miscellaneous Surfaces

Awnings and Deck Chairs

Faded or discolored awnings where the canvas is in good condition may be freshened by coating with awning paints which are available at most paint and hardware stores in a variety of nonfading colors. These materials are easily applied with a brush, are nonpenetrating, and dry to a smooth flat flexible finish. They may also be used to renew the color of old canvas on deck chairs, lawn umbrellas, or glider cushions.

Porch Decks

Exposed canvas porch decks are difficult to maintain, but may be painted with porch and deck enamel or aluminum paint. The coating should be renewed annually if the deck is to remain leakproof. Porch and deck enamel produces a glossy finish; and aluminum paint a silvery metallic finish.

Doors

In painting a door, the type of wood, the severity of exposure, the finish and color desired, and the type of paint should all be taken into consideration. When applying each coat of paint, finish the panels first, the center rail next, then the top and bottom rails, next the vertical stiles, and finally the edges. If the surface is kept smooth by rubbing with sandpaper between each coat, the door should present a smooth velvetlike appearance when finished.

Windows

Before painting a window sash, be sure to scrape off all the old, loose putty and coat the wood recesses with linseed oil before applying the new putty. A shield cut from a piece of tin will speed the work of painting by protecting the glass from "run overs" while still permitting enough

How to Glaze and Paint Wood Sash

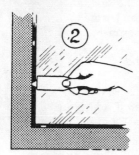

After removal of cracked glass and old putty, coat rabbet (groove) with boiled linseed oil. Let dry.

Place ribbon of putty in rabbet. Bed glass firmly against putty. Then fasten with glazing points.

Next, apply ribbon of putty to glass; smooth with putty knife. Let it set for a few weeks before painting.

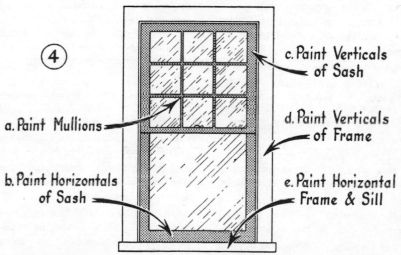

④

a. Paint Mullions

b. Paint Horizontals of Sash

c. Paint Verticals of Sash

d. Paint Verticals of Frame

e. Paint Horizontal Frame & Sill

Painting window sash is not at all difficult. Apply the paint with a small varnish brush or a flat or oval sash tool. Start with the mullions and continue as the arrows indicate. If there are paint spatters on the glass when you have finished, remove them with a razor blade soon after the paint dries.

paint to flow on to the muntins or sash bars to give a good seal between the wood and glass. The muntins or sash bars should be painted first, then the stiles and rails of the sash, next the window frames and trim and, finally, the sill and apron below.

Screens

Door and window screens will last longer and look better if kept well painted. For this, special screen paints are best, but they should be thinned to avoid clogging the mesh. A coat of thinned white paint applied to the screen wire makes the interior of the house less visible from the outside.

The necessary tools and materials are a screen paint applicator and bristle brush; special screen paint, spar varnish, or enamel in desired color and small amount of boiled linseed oil or turpentine for thinning.

A cheap grade of screen wire will probably require painting every year, while galvanized wire may show signs of rust only after long use and may then require only a light coat of paint. Copper or bronze screen wire will not deteriorate if not painted, but the corrosion products resulting from weathering make it advisable either to paint or varnish copper or bronze screens to avoid staining the trim and outside walls of a house. If it is desirable to retain the original copper or bronze color of the screens, a high-grade spar varnish should be applied in two coats to both sides of the screen cloth. Inasmuch as this will not last as long as the enamel, the screens

A life-saver for worn and scuffed articles made of leather or leatherette is a special flexible paint. It is brushed on like lacquer and dries in a few minutes to form a durable, non-bleeding film as flexible and natural-looking as the leather itself. It comes in a variety of colors for use on upholstery, luggage, convertible tops, awnings and boat decks.

Photograph courtesy of Wayne Products Co.

will need to be coated with spar varnish at least every other season. If a dark color is not objectionable, a coat of black enamel should last several seasons.

Paint may be applied evenly and economically to screens with a special screen applicator. Most paint dealers carry these applicators but, if not available, they are not difficult to make. A block of wood 1"x3"x8" may be covered with thick felt or carpet attached to the face side of the block with the nap outward. A cleat of wood for a handle should be nailed along the center of the opposite side of the block. The carpet may be fastened by glue or tacks but if tacks or brads are used, the heads should be well embedded so that they will not catch on the wire mesh while the paint is being applied.

The screen should be placed on a level surface like a table top, and cleaned of all dust, soot, and loose rust with a bristle brush. If more thorough cleaning is necessary, the screen may be washed with soap and warm water applied with a brush, rinsed with clear water, and dried with a cloth. After the screen has been cleaned on both sides and dried thoroughly, paint may be applied by brushing the face of the applicator with a moderate amount of paint and spreading the paint over the screen with the applicator. In this way, the screen may be painted quite rapidly and easily with a thin even coating without clogging the mesh.

The frames should not require painting oftener than once in every 3 to 5 years. If the screening is cleaned and painted once a year as described, its life will be prolonged and the screens will present a neat appearance.

Swimming Pools

Vitreous tile is the preferred coating for swimming pool wall and floor surfaces, but there are three general types of paint which may be used as decorative finishes: Cement-water paints, enamel paints with water-resisting varnish vehicle, and waterproof enamel paints. These paints are available in appropriate light blue and light green colors.

The advantages of cement-water paints are their ease of application and low cost; their disadvantages are their tendency to absorb body oils and grease and to accumulate algae when it exists. One season is the maximum period that wall and floor surfaces of a much-used pool coated with cement-water paints can be kept in good condition without repainting.

Enamel paints must be applied only to clean surfaces and no water should be put into the pool for several days after the application of each coat. Enamel paints give a smooth attractive surface that may last for a season, but may develop blisters and peel during that time.

A deep luster can be obtained and the color of the wood preserved by applying a protective surface coat over either interior or exterior wood furniture. This final coat can be brushed on or, if you have the equipment, sprayed on.

Photograph courtesy of Monsanto Chemical Co.

Waterproof enamel paints will probably give the least trouble since they dry to a smooth hard-gloss finish and are chemically resistant to moisture and water-purifying agents.

Wood Furniture

For information on various finishes—refer to the section on *Furniture Finishing*.

Baby Furniture

Furniture with which the baby comes into contact must be finished with a non-poisonous paint, especially if the child has a tendency to lick, taste, and chew everything within reach. Buy special baby enamel, which comes in pretty colors and is washable. This applies to painted toys, too.

Fiber Rug

This may be painted with canvas or awning paint.

Painting— Technique of Spraying

Applying paint with a sprayer is faster than with either a brush or a roller, but you'll need more experience in handling this "tool" than either the brush or roller to produce a satisfactory job.

Spray painting can be done in a variety of ways:

1. You can use the simple spray attachment that usually comes with a vacuum cleaner, particularly the tank type cleaner. However, the air pressure is low and this type of sprayer works best on thin liquids. This sprayer has an elementary control and is not suitable for fine lacquer or precision spraying.

2. You can purchase pressurized-aerosol cans with different types of paints in a variety of colors. This technique works fine for touch-

Guns having internal-mix nozzles generally have three interchangeable nozzles to produce different types of patterns. The 45° nozzle is very useful for spraying floors or ceilings, since you can paint at an angle without tipping the gun.

The overshot type of external-mix nozzles produce a round pattern, while the other external-mix nozzles produce a fan-shaped pattern. The higher-priced guns of this type usually are made with a built-in spray-pattern adjustment to vary the pattern from round to fan-shaped—the one nozzle serves all purposes.

up painting, especially on appliances. However, because of the limited amount of paint held by the pressurized can, this is a costly method for painting large areas.

3. Inexpensive vibrator-type sprayer guns are available and they are considerably better than the attachments made for vacuum cleaners. However, they vary in the quality of performance and some can-

not be used for really efficient spray painting. Others, however, are satisfactory and work well with most types of paints.

4. Sprayers of the diaphragm type or working off a compressor are the more professional tools to use for spraying. These are more expensive than the vibrator type and, on the average, perform more efficiently than the vibrator type.

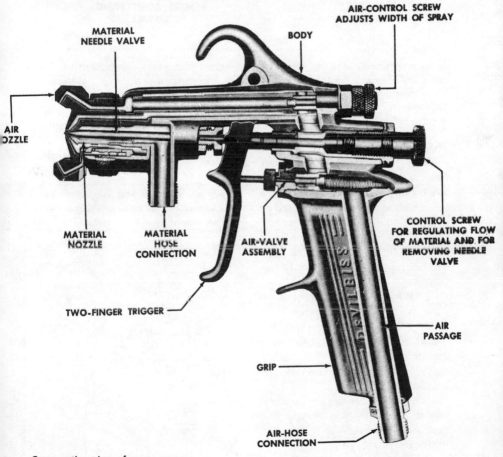

Cross-section view of spray gun.

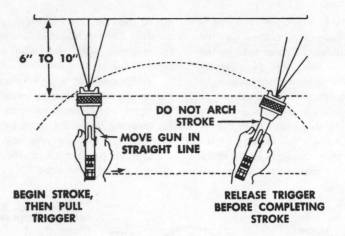

6" TO 10"

DO NOT ARCH
STROKE

MOVE GUN IN
STRAIGHT LINE

**BEGIN STROKE,
THEN PULL
TRIGGER**

**RELEASE TRIGGER
BEFORE COMPLETING
STROKE**

Proper way to spray a surface—begin the stroke and then pull the trigger, continuing to move your hand in a straight line. Release pressure on the trigger and stop spraying before you complete the stroke.

Selecting the Sprayer

You can paint about four to six times faster with a sprayer than with any other painting tool. When you select a paint sprayer, you should be guided by the following factors:

1. Capacity—how much will the sprayer hold? Can it be used with all types of paints or only certain ones?

2. What is its speed—how much paint can it deliver per minute?

3. What are its design qualities —is it convenient to handle? Is it easy to operate? Can you clean it easily? Does it have interchangeable nozzles?

While these are the primary factors to consider, you should also examine three other points governing the use of sprayers:

1. Type of air supply

• Bleeder-type guns are de-

signed for direct connection of the gun to the compressor so that the air is blowing through the sprayer at all times. The trigger action is used only to control the flow of the paint through the gun.

• Non-bleeder guns operate

Spray gun should be held perpendicular to the surface. If held at an angle, there will be an uneven deposit of paint.

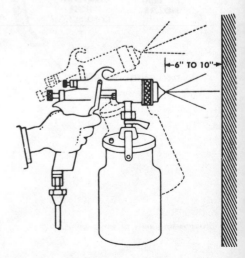

|◄—6" TO 10"—►|

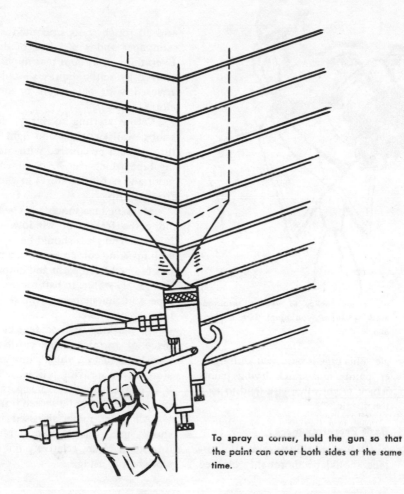

To spray a corner, hold the gun so that the paint can cover both sides at the same time.

with the trigger shutting off both the air supply and the paint. They cannot be used with continually-running compressors since shutting off the air flow at the gun would result in the bursting of the air supply line or blowing the safety valve on the compressor.

2. Paint feed to the nozzle

• Pressure-fed guns have an airtight cup to hold the paint. Air pressure on the top of the paint forces it up to the gun nozzle.

• Syphon guns depends upon suction to lift the paint from the cup or container into the air stream at the outlet of the nozzle.

3. How the paint is atomized for spraying

• Internal-mix nozzles atomize the paint in a mixing chamber inside the nozzle. This provides for a better mixing of the heavier paints used with a spray gun.

• External-mix nozzles atomize the paint in air jets outside the noz-

It's a wise policy to wear a respirator mask whenever you paint with a spray gun.

and all rough spots smoothed with sandpaper and wiped free of dust. Everything in a room that might be marred by settling spray should be covered with old sheets or drop-cloths.

Before starting to spray, door knobs, wall switches, and light fixtures should be covered with masking tape which can be obtained in paint and hardware stores in widths from ½″ up.

Masking tape should also be laid along the frames of windows and mirrors. The glass should be coated with masking compound which may be obtained from paint and automotive supply stores. In bathrooms, use tape and newspapers to mask tub, lavatory and toilet.

If masking is not feasible, a piece of metal or stiff cardboard may be used as a shield, moving it along as the spraying proceeds. This is a convenient way to separately spray screen wire and screen frames.

All paint materials used in a spray gun should be strained through a clean, relatively lint-free cloth before using.

zle. This type is best used with lighter paints and quick-drying paints which might otherwise tend to clog the nozzle.

Basic Preparation

Before starting to spray, the surface should be thoroughly cleaned

TYPE OF MATERIAL	TYPE OF FEED REQUIRED			TYPE OF NOZZLE REQUIRED		
	Pressure	Syphon	Either	Internal Mix	External Mix	Either
Enamel			x			x
Lacquer			x		x	
Shellac	x				x	
Stain			x			x
Undercoat	x			x		
Water Paint			x			x
Oil Paint	x			x		
Synethetic Paint			x			x

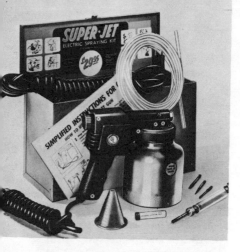

Spray guns come in various shapes and sizes. This model with an adjustable nozzle can be used with paint in the large aluminum can or with a special plastic hose to draw the liquid out of a large drum so that there is no stopping for refilling.

Photograph courtesy of Champion Sprayer.

Spraying With a Gun

When spraying paint, always wear a respirator. It gives valuable protection against paint poisoning and should be worn even for outdoor work with a cap to keep drift

Touch-up painting is easy with a pressurized spray can. Here, lacquer is used to refinish a lamppost outside the home.

Photograph courtesy of Plasti-Kote, Inc.

spray out of the hair. Do not smoke while spraying. (If the respirator is worn, this will be impossible.) Also make sure that ventilation is adequate for health as well as fire safety. Never spray near an open flame. or where there is a possibility of sparks flying, as spraying mixes paint and air to an explosive proportion. When painting indoors, always have the windows open wide; never spray in a closed room unless an exhaust fan is in operation that will change the air every 3 minutes.

Before actual painting operations are started, adjust the gun and practice spraying on scrap material to obtain the proper flow of paint. Hold the gun in one hand and with the other keep the hose clear of the surface that is being sprayed. The spray tip should be held 6" to 10" from the surface to which the paint is being applied.

If a large panel or wall is being sprayed, begin at the upper corner and work from right to left. Move down as each swath is laid on. Since the center half of the last sprayed

Enamel can also be sprayed out of a pressurized spray can to touch up rusted metal work outside the home.

Even the baby buggy can be put into trim shape with "canned" paint. The spray is fine enough to cover only a limited area so that no masking is required. Pressurized spray cans make it easy to reach out-of-the-way places.

Photographs courtesy of Plasti-Kote, Inc.

strip gets the thickest coat, lap the upper fourth of each new stroke over the lower fourth of the preceding stroke.

On each stroke, begin swinging the gun from a point to one side of where the spray is to begin. When the starting point is reached, press the trigger and hold it until the other edge of the panel sweep is reached.

Always sweep the spray stroke so that the tip of the gun stays the same distance from the surface and so that the spray will strike at right angles. The pace of the stroke should not change. Any hesitation or halt without releasing the trigger will let too much paint pile up, and a sag or run will result.

Holding the gun too close to the work will also produce a sag or run, and holding it too far away will fog the finish and produce a dull effect. Meeting points of the surfaces, such as corners and sharp edges, are spots

that tend to catch too much paint and are sprayed best with short successive spurts, aiming the gun so that each spurt is at right angles to the nearest surface. This technique applies to any finish.

A few specific suggestions follow:

1. In spraying paint, varnish, and enamel, the material should first be thinned in accordance with the manufacturers' instructions.

2. The first coat should then be "fogged" on, holding the gun a little further from the surface than the suggested 6" to 10".

3. One coat of primer and one coat of finish may cover a surface, but two finish coats are better.

4. Allow the paint to dry thoroughly between coats, and on small objects a better finish is obtained if the surface is lightly sanded between coats.

Lacquers are rather thin materials which dry very rapidly. They should be applied in three to five coats, using the thinner recommended by the manufacturer. Lacquer cannot as a rule be successsfully applied over paints, varnish, or enamel.

Among the common faults in spray finishes are sags (finish laid on so thick that it flows downward in drapes); runs (longer drops streaking down, usually from sags); holidays (spots left bare); orange peeling (bumpy finish); and fogging (dull, pebbled finish usually resulting from the gun being held too far from the surface).

Parallel Circuit

A circuit is said to be in parallel when there is a common feed and a common return between two or more fixtures or outlets, and each receives a separate portion of the current flow from the common feed. See *Electrical Wiring*.

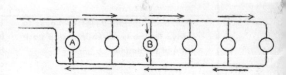

Lights and outlets in parallel.

Lawn Mower Motor Guide

Trouble-Shooting Checklist	
SYMPTOM	CURE
Motor will not run unless the choke is pulled all the way out.	Take a screwdriver and turn the needle valve counter-clockwise one full turn. The fuel mixture was too lean and you have to increase it.
Motor smokes excessively while running at any speed.	Take a screwdriver and turn the needle valve clockwise one-half turn. The fuel mixture was too rich. It may be necessary to make another half-turn if the smoking continues.
Motor misfires and sputters while operating.	First, check the spark plug. Make certain that the contacts on the top are clean; use sandpaper if necessary. If engine still misses, remove the spark plug and have the gap checked. If the spark plug is working, the condenser is faulty and should be replaced by a repairman.
Motor misses—it doesn't run smoothly.	Here again, it may be spark plug trouble. Follow the same technique as if the engine misfired. Otherwise, the fault may be with the magneto; it should be repaired or replaced by a serviceman.
Run-away motor—motor continues to drive the mower even in a stop position of the handle.	The idle speed bar may be stuck or bent so that the motor is continually fed gasoline. If the bar is in working order, reset the idle speed adjustment screw. Turn this screw clockwise one-half turn and try the motor again. If it is still running away, try another half turn and then another until the difficulty is corrected.

Plumbing

Since plumbing covers a wide area, and the subject is discussed in its various phases throughout these volumes, refer to the sections named in the following classifications for the additional information you need for your plumbing chores:

Bathroom Planning—This section discusses the general plumbing, the location of waste pipes, traps and vent pipe, and fixture installations.

Drainage System—Here you will find detailed information on traps, how to prevent and cure any stoppage; the use of the plumber's friend, chemical cleaners, and other methods to clean out the clogged trap; repair and care of the water closet, flush tank and flush valve.

Faucets—Description of the compression, Fuller ball, and ground-key faucets, and the way to install and repair them, is given in this section. How to eliminate noise in faucet is also explained.

Frozen Pipes—The way to prevent freezing through pipe insulation is included in this section, as well as how to lay underground pipes, and thaw out frozen pipes and drains.

Heating Systems—The operation, maintenance, and repair of the different types of heating systems are explained in these sections. Also included is the way to insulate the pipes, boilers, and ducts in heating systems, as well as the insulation of hot-water tanks. The different heating fuels and methods are explained: coal, oil, gas, etc.

Plastic Pipe—Extruded poly-

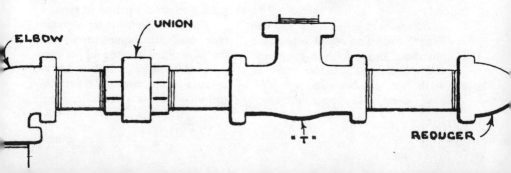

ELBOW   UNION   "T"   REDUCER

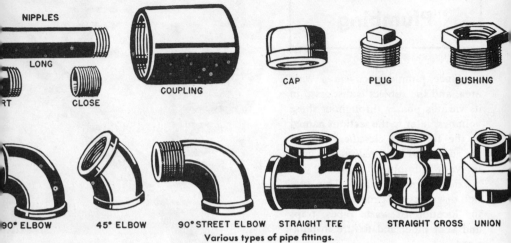

Various types of pipe fittings.

ethylene and vinyl pipe is available for the home handyman. This pipe is easy to work with and all you need to join the pieces together is a screwdriver and adhesive. Plastic pipe is particularly adaptable for exterior use for its does not have to be drained because of the danger of freezing during cold weather.

Pipe Fittings—To connect different sections of pipes, to make iron pipes turn corners and to join two pipes of different diameters, it is necessary to use a pipe fitting.

Valves—Whereas faucets control the flow of water at the end of a pipe, a valve controls the flow of water between pipes. See this section for details about the different types of valves.

Water, Shutting Off—For information on the shut-off methods to control or stop the flow of water to the house, see this section.

Plumbing— Basic Data

In this section, you will find the basic information about pipes and plumbing. In the following sections you will find the details on how to work, first, with brass and iron pipe and, second, with copper tubing.

Types of Pipe

Black iron pipe is not suitable to carry water in either the supply or drainage systems for it rusts too quickly and will cause stoppages in a relatively short period of time.

Galvanized pipe is the standard type used for home supply and drainage lines because of its comparatively low price and its fair resistance to corrosion. It resists corrosion better than black iron pipe but rates poorly when compared with brass or copper.

Cast iron pipe, normally large diameter pipe, is used primarily for drainage systems.

Brass pipe offers the advantages of iron pipe plus the fact that it does not rust. Furthermore, because of its smoother interior wall section, it offers less resistance to the flow of water. It has, therefore, replaced galvanized iron pipe in many homes equipped with "better" plumbing.

Tools To Do the Job

While it is impractical to buy all the tools needed for every type of home improvement and repair, there are certain specialized tools which the homeowner should add to his tool collection. Some of the other, more expensive and specialized tools, can be rented from hardware stores. However, if you do extensive plumbing—either repairs or improvements—it may be wise to purchase some of the equipment you might normally rent.

1. A vise for holding the pipe while it is being cut is absolutely necessary when working with brass or iron pipe. It is unimportant if you use copper tubing. You can get a pipe vise or use pipe jaws in a regular vise.

2. Pipe cutters make it easier to cut pipe; they are faster than a hacksaw and produce a better job—the end of the pipe is cut perfectly flush. This square cut is particularly important when it is necessary to thread brass or iron pipe or flare copper tubing for solderless connectors.

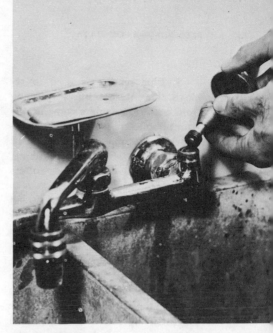

A bibb seat dresser is used to smooth the worn surface of a faucet seat to prevent the chewed-up metal from eating away the washer.

Pipe jaws in a machinist's vise holds the pipe with head stock and a die cutter is used to thread the iron or brass pipe.

3. Pipe reamer is used to remove the internal burrs resulting from cutting. Reamers come in different diameters, adjustable for several sizes of pipe. They are used with a brace. For copper tubing, however, the better pipe cutters have a reamer attached.

4. Pipe dies are used to thread the end of brass or iron pipe. They come in sets, normally, together with a handle.

5. Pipe taps are used to make internal threads. The size of the tap is normally marked on the shank. In using the accompanying table the suggested tap size is recommended for the nominal diameter of the pipe and not its actual diameter.

Here is a table of American National Pipe Threads containing nominal pipe size, threads per inch and specific tap size required.

A hacksaw can be used to cut brass or iron pipe as well as copper tubing.

This is one type of a flaring tool. The nut end of the fitting is placed over the pipe and the flaring tool inserted into the open tubing. A few taps with the hammer will flare the end of the tubing.

Nominal size of the pipe	Threads per inch	Tap Size
⅛"	27	$^{11}\!\!/_{32}$"
¼"	18	$^{7}\!\!/_{16}$"
⅜"	18	$^{37}\!\!/_{64}$"
½"	14	$^{23}\!\!/_{32}$"
¾"	14	$^{59}\!\!/_{64}$"
1 "	11½	1 $^{5}\!\!/_{32}$"
1¼"	11½	1 ½ "
1½"	11½	1$^{47}\!\!/_{64}$"
2 "	11½	2 $^{7}\!\!/_{32}$"

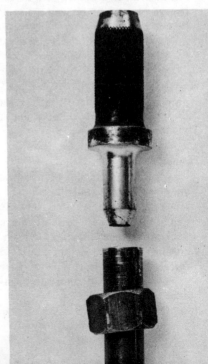

6. Pipe wrenches vary depending upon their purpose. Wrenches used with pipe must have jaws that will grip the round exterior surface securely. Normally, Stillson wrenches are used for the job, but it is also possible to use a strap wrench (a belt is used in place of the jaws) or a pipe tongs (a link chain is used in place of the jaws).

The hexagonal fittings of solderless connectors, tops of valves and faucets, and other non-round surfaces require the use of other types of wrenches. A monkey or open-end wrench is best for these uses. A parrot-head pliers can be used if the surface is protected by tape to prevent the plier's teeth from "chewing" into the metal.

For additional details about which size wrench to use, see the table under "Pipe Fittings" in the section: *Plumbing—Working with Brass and Iron Pipe.*

7. Hacksaw can be used for cutting pipe or tubing. Set the blade in the frame so that the teeth point forward because the cutting is done only on the forward stroke.

• For iron and brass pipe, use a saw blade with 24 teeth per inch.

• For conduit and thin tubing, use a blade with 32 teeth per inch.

8. A blow torch is necessary when working with cast iron pipe as well as soldered fittings with copper tubing. This can be the gasoline pump type or the pressurized-fuel, disposable can type.

9. Tube benders are used with soft copper tubing. With the tube bender or bending spring, the tube can then be bent to any angle without collapsing the walls of the tube. Tube benders usually come in kits but individual sizes can be purchased.

10. Flaring tool is used with solderless connectors and copper tubing. There are two types available. One is a tapered unit which is inserted into the tubing and the outside end hit with a hammer to flare the pipe. The other is a yoke unit

This is another type of flaring tool. The tubing is set into the proper opening and clamped in place. It is then flared by turning the handle which depresses the flaring end of the yoke unit.

Taps are used to cut internal threads in pipe.

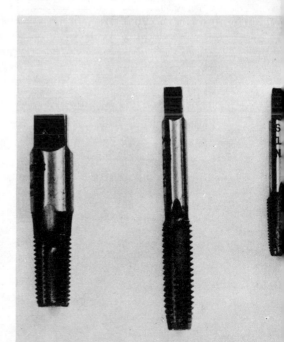

which is adjustable for copper tubing of varying diameters.

11. A standard plunger or any of the special types of plungers is used to remove obstructions in the pipe by air pressure.

12. Closet auger or "snake" is used to remove obstructions within a pipe by physical means. The metal spring steel or coiled wire is pushed through the pipe to clean it out.

13. Bibb seat dresser is used to resurface the seat of a faucet or compression valve.

Pipe Measurements

When making a new installation or a repair, it is necessary to measure the pipe accurately. This is important whether you order the pipe and have it cut to size and threaded by a professional or you cut and thread the pipe yourself.

The easiest way to measure pipe, if a professional will cut and thread it, is to draw the exact pipe diagram and then mark the measurements. The professional can figure out the exact size of each piece.

The accompanying tables and diagrams should help you make an exact dimension drawing or determine the sizes yourself.

PIPE FITTING DISTANCE	
Size of Pipe	Distance Pipe is Screwed into Fitting (A in Sketch)
$\frac{1}{8}''$	$\frac{1}{4}''$
$\frac{1}{4}''$	$\frac{3}{8}''$
$\frac{3}{8}''$	$\frac{3}{8}''$
$\frac{1}{2}''$	$\frac{1}{2}''$
$\frac{3}{4}''$	$\frac{1}{2}''$
1 $''$	$\frac{9}{16}''$
$1\frac{1}{4}''$	$\frac{5}{8}''$
$1\frac{1}{2}''$	$\frac{5}{8}''$
2 $''$	$\frac{11}{16}''$

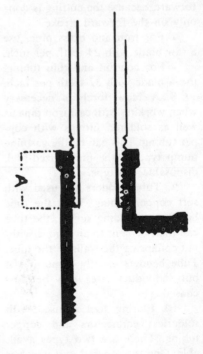

Fitting distance, that is, the distance that a pipe will screw into a fitting, valve or faucet, depends upon the diameter of the pipe. See the accompanying table for exact details.

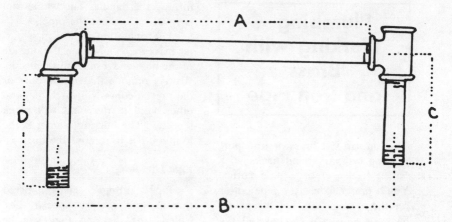

Methods of measuring pipe—A is a face-to-face measurement but it does not take into account the additional piece of the pipe that goes into the fitting; use the fitting table to obtain the exact size of the pipe; B is a center-to-center measurement; C is a center-to-end measurement; D is an end-to-face measurement; add the part that fits into the fitting and you have the exact length of the pipe.

Pipes have to be measured and cut exactly to prevent leaks in the system. It is important to determine the distance from the end of a pipe to the center of the fitting; that is, distance X in the sketch. This varies depending upon the diameter of the pipe as noted in the accompanying table.

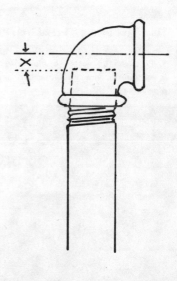

DISTANCE FROM END OF PIPE TO CENTER OF FITTING	
Size of Pipe	Dimension X*
½"	⅝"
¾"	$13/16$"
1 "	⅞"
1¼"	1⅛"
1½"	$1 5/16$"
2 "	$1 9/16$"

* This applies to 90° elbow, Street L and T's.

Plumbing—Working with Brass and Iron Pipe

You can cut brass or iron pipe with an ordinary hand hacksaw, a power hacksaw, or a pipe cutter. You'll prefer to use the pipe cutter for the average job, but the power hacksaw is faster if you have a large number of pieces to cut or if the pipe has a thick wall. The pipe cutter has a special alloy steel cutting wheel and two pressure rollers. These are adjusted and tightened by turning the handle. The whole tool is revolved around the pipe.

The operation of the pipe cutter leaves a shoulder on the outside of the pipe and a burr on the inside. Always remove that inside burr or the ragged edges will catch dirt and other solid matter, and will block the flow. The burring reamer is the tool you use to remove the burr.

Pipe Threading

Pipe fittings have tapered threads and require special dies, called pipe dies, so they can be turned up tight and leakproof. A stock is used to turn the dies, and the same stock can be used for threading several sizes of pipe. Most pipe dies can be adjusted to cut

How To Cut and Thread Iron Pipe

1. Pipe can be cut in a pipe vise or in a machinist's vise equipped with special pipe jaws.

2. After a piece of pipe has been cut to the required size, any inside burrs are removed with a reamer. The outside burr can be removed with a file.

slightly different depths of thread so that a longer or shorter thread on the end of the pipe can be obtained as desired. To cut the threads, secure the work and hold the stock; then proceed as when using any other die; keep the work well oiled. It is a good idea to test the thread with a standard pipe fitting when the operation is finished.

Pipe Assembly

Threaded water pipe joints are usually made up with red lead as a seal. Steam pipe threads are sealed with graphite paint. Put the sealing compound on the pipe threads only —so it won't get inside the pipe and form a dangerous obstruction. Make sure the threads are clean before you apply the sealing compound.

Threaded joints should be screwed together by hand and tightened with a pipe wrench—commonly called a "Stillson." The pipe should be held in a pipe vise during assembly, but if it's impossible to use a vise the pipe may be held with another pipe wrench.

How tight should you tighten a joint? Experience is the best teacher. Usually you will have two or three unused threads on a properly cut pipe thread. If all the threads are used, the wedging action of the tapered thread may cause the fitting to split.

Pipe wrenches are made in a number of sizes (lengths). Use the following table as a guide for selecting the best size to use:

Wrench Size	for (in inches)	Pipe Size
6		¼
10		⅜ and ½
14		¾
18		1 and 1¼
24		1½ and 2

Size of Brass and Iron Pipe		
Nominal Size	Inside Diameter	Outside Diameter
⅛	¼	⅜
¼	⅜	$17\!/\!32$
⅜	½	$11\!/\!16$
½	⅝	$13\!/\!16$
¾	$13\!/\!10$	1
1	$1\frac{1}{16}$	$1\frac{5}{16}$
1¼	1⅜	1⅝
1½	1⅝	1⅞
2	$2\frac{1}{16}$	2⅜
2½	$2\frac{9}{16}$	2⅞
3	$3\frac{1}{16}$	3½
3½	$3\frac{9}{16}$	4
4	4	4½

3. You can thread your own pipe or have the hardware dealer do the job for you. Thread-cutting die equipment can be rented for a nominal amount if you wish to do the job yourself. All you have to do is set the die stock in place and start turning it on the pipe. While threading the pipe, apply liberal doses of pipe cutting oil. This makes the job easier and results in less wear-and-tear on the die head.

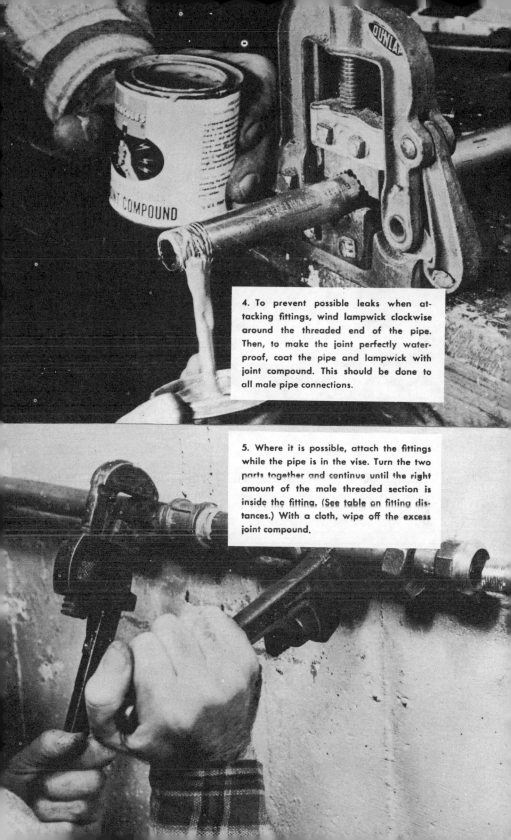

4. To prevent possible leaks when attacking fittings, wind lampwick clockwise around the threaded end of the pipe. Then, to make the joint perfectly waterproof, coat the pipe and lampwick with joint compound. This should be done to all male pipe connections.

5. Where it is possible, attach the fittings while the pipe is in the vise. Turn the two parts together and continue until the right amount of the male threaded section is inside the fitting. (See table on fitting distances.) With a cloth, wipe off the excess joint compound.

6. If the pieces have to be put together without the aid of a vise, then two wrenches are needed for the job. One wrench is used to hold the installed pipe steadily in place and the other is used to turn on the fitting. Remember, you turn clockwise to tighten, counter-clockwise to loosen the pipes.

Plumbing— Working with Copper Tubing

Adding plumbing for a new bathroom, piping a cellar tub or darkroom sink, or running underground lines to outdoor pools or sprinkling systems are weekend projects, requiring only a hacksaw to make a few cuts and a small torch to solder connections together.

There's no need for the Stillsons, threading dies, or pipe vises that you need for galvanized-steel plumbing. In many cases, you can use simple screw-together fittings that eliminate even the job of soldering.

Types of Tubing

Enormous presses cold-extrude seamless copper tubing from solid billets of the pure metal. The tubing comes from the die work-hardened, and some of it is then annealed to soften it.

You can snake this easily bent, soft-tempered tubing down through

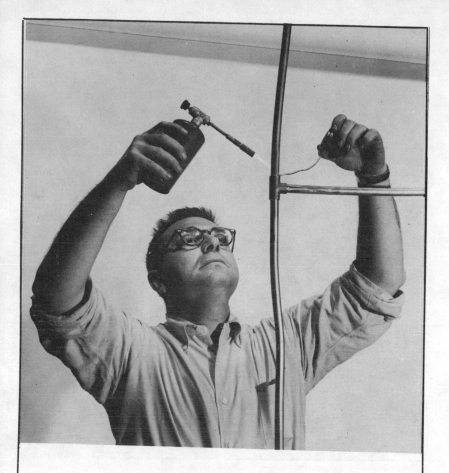

10 Ways to Improve Your Home Plumbing
with Copper Tubing

1. Extend a branch water line to supply an added-on bathroom.

2. Replace old radiators with modern baseboard or radiant wall units.

3. Run an underground water line to a garage or other outbuildings.

4. Replace rusted and lime-clogged water lines where pressure has dropped.

5. Install a sink in a basement darkroom or playroom bar.

6. Run a fuel line from an outdoor oil tank (but not gas without an expert).

7. Install a permanent sprinkling system for your lawn.

8. Mount a shower head over a bathtub that doesn't already have one.

9. Put in extra sill cocks around your foundation for garden hoses.

10. Pipe underground water to a garden pool, fountain, or bird bath.

Thread it through—You can easily string soft-tempered, flexible tubing through holes in floor joists or wall studs. Straight hard-temper sections can be notched into edges of beams if code permits, or nailed to face with small pipe straps. Make bends gentle to ease water flow, avoid strain at sharp corners. Soaping outside of pipe first helps you slide it through holes.

walls and through holes bored in studs and joists just like electrical wiring. When you come to a corner, you simply bend it where you want it to go, saving the installation of an angle fitting. Because it comes in lengths up to 100', you can make long, unbroken runs that virtually eliminate all connections except at the ends.

Outdoors, the flexible soft tubing withstands an occasional accidental freeze without bursting. When run underground, it "gives" as the earth settles and heaves, minimizing breakage. It also is less subject to damage from expansion and contraction, which in hotwater lines is as much as 1¼" per 100'.

Hard-temper tubing, not annealed, comes in standard 20' lengths. Use this rigid tube if you're a stickler for neatness and also in places where exposed lines may be kicked, knocked or otherwise damaged.

Hard tubing can be bent, but only in a leverage-type tube bender. If one isn't available, it's best to

Cut off the end—In tight spots where you can't saw tubing, use this roller-type cutter that's simply clamped to pipe, then twisted around it. Cutter leaves heavy burr on inside edge that must be reamed out before attaching fittings.

Saw it to length—Simple miter box made of wood scraps insures square cuts. Space sides of box apart same width as tubing (¾" spacer for ½" pipe; 1" for ¾" pipe) to hold it snugly during sawing. Use 32-tooth hacksaw blade.

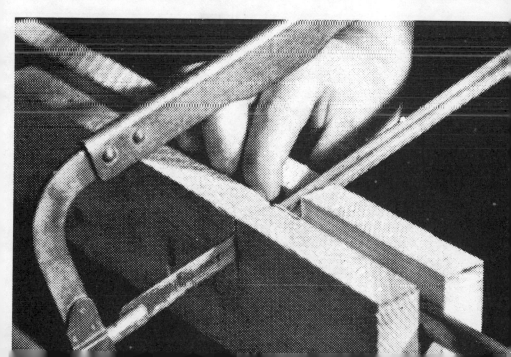

Bend a corner—Inexpensive bending spring, inserted in tubing, keeps walls from collapsing when you have to make a short-radius bend near an end. If spring sticks inside, tap tubing with a mallet to jar it loose for easy removal.

Hook it up—To join copper pipe to regular galvanized-steel plumbing, use an adapter fitting that has standard pipe threads on one end and copper joint on other. Fittings come with flare or solder joints and male or female threads.

figure on using the standard angle fittings, which probably won't take any longer to solder on than it would to make bends. If you have a lot of corners to turn, you can always insert a length of soft tubing, making the bends in it, even where the rest of the plumbing is of the rigid type.

Pick the Right Weight

Both hard and soft tubing come in two different weights, called K and L, that are commonly used in home plumbing:

Type K, a thick-walled, heavy-duty tubing, is best for exposed lines that might become dented and is only a little more expensive than the lighter weight. It's also used for underground lines that are subject to strain, for gas service lines, and for the very best plumbing and heating systems.

Type L is a lighter weight that's used for most home-plumbing and radiant-heating work. It's fine for all average indoor lines that are reasonably well protected.

What Size To Use

If you buy small-size tubing at an auto-supply store for your car, you'll find it sold according to its outside diameter. In all other cases, though, copper tubing is classified according to its nominal inside diameter, just as steel pipe is, and this is what you ask for at plumbing shops.

For homes with normal water pressure, use a ¾" copper branch line if it supplies two or more fixtures; ⅝" tubing to sill cocks; ½"

1. To make strong joint, copper must be thoroughly clean. Rub outside of tubing and inside of fitting with fine abrasive cloth. Remove burrs inside pipe with a round file.

How To Make a Soldered Connection

2. Apply thin coat of non-corrosive soldering flux to outside of tubing and inside of fitting. Then slip the tube into the fitting and wipe off excess flux around the joint.

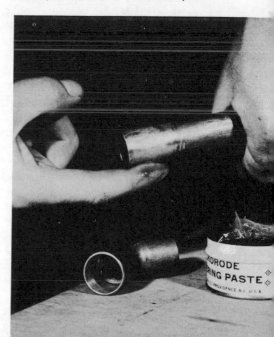

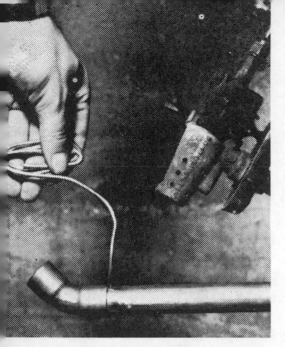

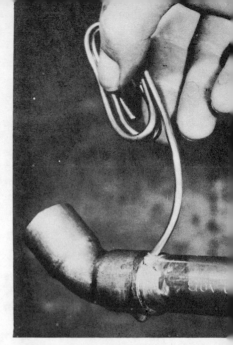

3. Play flame of blowtorch over fitting and tubing to heat both evenly. When copper is hot enough, solder flows freely when you touch joint. Capillary action draws solder in.

4. Keep feeding solder into joint, removing the blowtorch each time solder is applied. The connection is complete when a bright ring of molten solder shows all around the joint.

tubing to individual bathroom or kitchen fixtures. As a rule of thumb, it's safe to use tubing one size smaller than the galvanized pipe you'd otherwise put in.

5. Brush off excess solder with old paintbrush. This will also show if solder has completely filled joint. If not, add more. Don't move joint until solder has become cool and hard.

Fittings Make It Easy

Two types of connectors give you a choice of soldering or not. A soldered-on fitting can be used on both hard and soft tubing, while the solderless kind, called a flare fitting, is recommended only for the soft.

Use the solder joint for neat, permanent jobs. Flare fittings are more expensive, but are good for temporary lines or installations that may have to be disassembled since they are easily taken apart and re-used. They may also be a lifesaver in tight spots where the use of a blowtorch for soldering might be

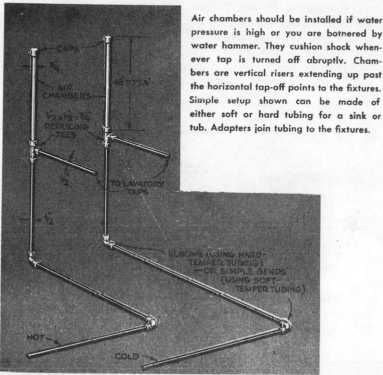

Air chambers should be installed if water pressure is high or you are bothered by water hammer. They cushion shock whenever tap is turned off abruptly. Chambers are vertical risers extending up past the horizontal tap-off points to the fixtures. Simple setup shown can be made of either soft or hard tubing for a sink or tub. Adapters join tubing to the fixtures.

difficult or dangerous.

Both types come in a complete line of Ts, elbows, couplings, reducers, valves, sill cocks and other fittings. You can also buy combination fittings that have standard pipe threads on one end and either a flare or solder connection on the other.

Installation

Whenever possible, keep cold- and hot-water lines at least 6″ apart to reduce sweating. If you are providing for an automatic washer or if water pressure is high, it's a good idea to put in air chambers at fixtures to cushion water hammer— the noisy shock when a tap is turned off suddenly. A sketch shows how this is easily done.

Install all horizontal water lines with a slight pitch, about ¼″ per foot, to allow complete draining when necessary. Soft tubing should be supported by straps every 6′ to prevent sagging, hard tubing every 10′ or at most 12′.

If you're burying an underground line, don't put a cinder fill in the trench. When the ground becomes wet, sulfur compounds in the cinders will corrode the tubing.

When you're tapping into existing plumbing, especially for hot water, make sure it's one of the domestic lines and not part of the heating system—often an easy mistake to make. Trace the lines carefully back so you are sure where they come from. Besides shutting off the main water supply, close off any intermediate valves that will reduce the amount of water that will drain from a cut line.

There's another good thing about copper tubing. While it's slightly more expensive than steel pipe, it can't rust or clog and if properly treated will last indefinitely.

Incorrect flaring of copper tubing will cause a solderless connector to leak. Here are three examples of improper flaring.

  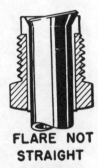

| FLARE TOO SHORT | FLARE TOO LONG | FLARE NOT STRAIGHT |

How To Make a Flared Connection

1. Solderless joint requires two-part fitting that clamps tubing in between. To make flare, slip sleeve nut on pipe first, then hammer flaring tool into end to roll edges outward.

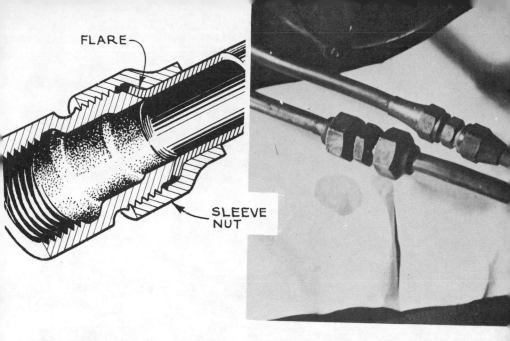

FLARE

SLEEVE NUT

2. When sleeve nut is slipped up against flare and screwed to other half of fitting, the two parts squeeze the tubing tightly between them. Such joints withstand 3,000 lb. per sq. in.

3. After joints are made, be sure to check for any slow leaks. Slide sheet of paper under joints and leave overnight. Any drippings will show up as spots on the paper.

4. Flare fittings make it easy to disconnect lines on equipment that must be disassembled from time to time, like this oilburner unit. Draw nuts up tight, but don't twist joints.

5. You can fix your car, too, with S.A.E. flare couplings that fit automotive parts. Using soft tubing, you can replace fuel and other lines that have become worn or broken.

Room Divider

A large room may be utilized more fully by dividing it into two separate areas. A full partitioning wall of wallboard could be installed to reach from floor to ceiling. However, in modern houses this idea is fast being abandoned, and semi-partitioning is being used more freely in order to give the illusion of space even though the room is divided.

There is no fixed rule about the height, width, or design of a room divider. It could reach to the ceiling, and be either a closed cabinet, or shelves which have a wallboard or plywood backing in one room with the exposed shelves facing into the other room. Or it may be open shelves which allow for viewing through the two rooms, yet act as a divider between the two areas. A room divider often is only half as

Rooms can be divided in many different ways. One simple way to do this is by installing a curtain on a traverse rod attached to the ceiling. Here, the kitchen is separated from the working kitchen by merely pulling the ceiling-to-floor drapery across the opening.

high, more or less, as the height of the room. Especially between a kitchen and dining nook the divider is kept low, so that its top acts as a counter surface.

A divider could be a simple wood trellis, over which ivy or other trailing foliage plants are trained, the plants themselves in heavy pots which stand on the floor and are painted the same color as the divider.

Types of Room Dividers

Many different materials can be

used to make a room divider. Even the same material can be handled in different ways to produce attractive room settings. Among the materials that can be used are: plywood, hardboard, perforated hardboard, perforated metal, corrugated plastic fiberglass, glass blocks, dowels, fine wire mesh; in fact, practically any standard building material.

Before you make a divider, consider all the possibilities and then use the one best suited for your needs. Among the room dividers that you can make are:

• A large double closet with sliding doors on either side of the

divider in order to make one bedroom suitable for two children.

• A drapery hung on a traverse rod attached to the ceiling can set off part of the room when you wish to conceal it.

• Accordion-fold doors or screens can be attached to a ceiling

Corrugated plastic fiberglass can be used to product attractive room dividers. These panels are translucent so that they do not block out the light; yet, they assure you of privacy in either part of the room. It is easy to make room dividers of this material by setting it into wood frames.

Photograph courtesy of Filon Industries, Inc.

track and used to separate two parts of a large room.

• Corrugated plastic fiberglass can be set within a wooden framework—it will permit light to pass through and yet you can have the required privacy.

• Jalousie windows with transparent standard glass, transluscent glass or even opaque glass can be used depending upon your needs.

• Wire mesh or wire screening can be stretched within a wooden frame to produce an "open" room divider.

• Perforated steel can likewise be nailed within a wooden frame.

• A canvas awning cloth can be tied with a running loop or through screw-eyes attached to a wooden frame to produce an unusual room divider—it is colorful, easy to remove to launder.

• 1″ or larger poles (as dowels over ⅞″ are called) can be set into a wooden frame with suitable spacing between the poles to produce a carnival or circus room divider.

• An attractive piece of furniture can be built with storage sections to serve as a divider between two parts of a room.

There is an almost unlimited number of ideas you can use to make a room divider. In this section you will find ideas and plans for several different types. If you are adventurous and design your own, you can check with various sections within this encyclopedia for how-to instructions and working details for specific materials.

This divider made of a jalousie window with translucent glass permits the shutting off of the kitchen from the dining area when desired. On the other hand, a few turns of the handle and the glass louvers open so that the view is unobstructed.

Photograph courtesy of Sun-Sash, Inc.

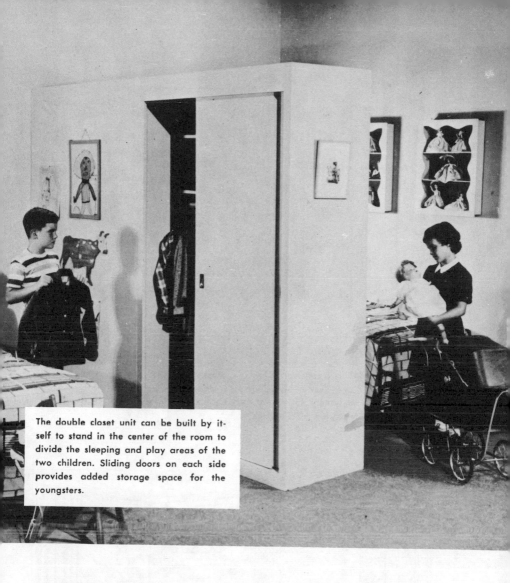

The double closet unit can be built by itself to stand in the center of the room to divide the sleeping and play areas of the two children. Sliding doors on each side provides added storage space for the youngsters.

Room Divider— Closet for Two

The problem of housing a boy and a girl in the same room may be solved by constructing a modern storage wall—a large double closet. This technique can be used in other rooms as well.

The closet-wall room divider features a divider desk, built-in drawers, lighting, closet storage space and a sliding door to close off one part of the room from the other.

The plans shown here are for a room about 10'x16' and can be adapted for use in any other size room. However, when making the unit, the closets should be at least 18" deep although it is better to have them 27" deep as noted in this plan.

The delux room-divider closet with desks and drawers. A sliding door is hung between the two closet sections so one part of the room can be closed off from the other. Note that the unit also provides shelf space along the wall for books and built-in desk lamps.

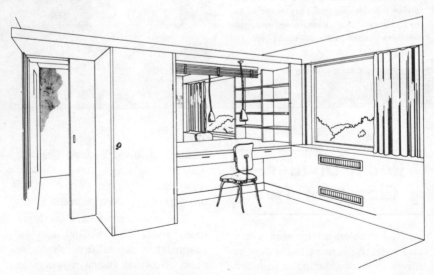

View of the closet room-divider from one of the two parts of the room. Below the desk surface are a series of drawers, and shelves have been added along the wall over the radiator enclosure unit. Of course, you can modify the plans to meet your own requirements and build it without the radiator enclosure.

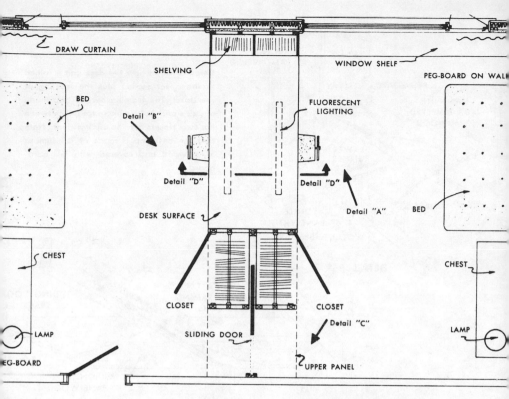

DRAW CURTAIN

SHELVING

WINDOW SHELF

PEG-BOARD ON WALL

BED

Detail "B"

FLUORESCENT
LIGHTING

Detail "D"

Detail "D"

Detail "A"

BED

DESK SURFACE

CHEST

CHEST

CLOSET

CLOSET

Detail "C"

LAMP

LAMP

PEG-BOARD

SLIDING DOOR

UPPER PANEL

Room plan showing the location of the closet room-divider with the two closets, sliding door, desks and shelves. For details on how to install the sliding door, see **Sliding Doors.**

Photograph and sketches courtesy of
Masonite Corp.

Detail A shows the construction of the radiator enclosure along the window wall, the shelf unit and how the desk top is tied into both. The framing is made of 2x2's and 2x4's as shown and then covered with tempered hardboard.

EXISTING
PLASTER

MASONITE
3/16" PANELWOOD

3/4" WOOD
SHELVING

MASONITE
1/8" TEMPERED
PRESDWOOD

2" x 4"

2" x 2"s

WINDOW SHELF

SILL

EXISTING
PLASTER

RADIATOR
VENTS
(FRAME OPENING)

EXISTING STUDS

MASONITE
1/4" TEMPERED
PRESDWOOD

1' - 0"

DETAIL A

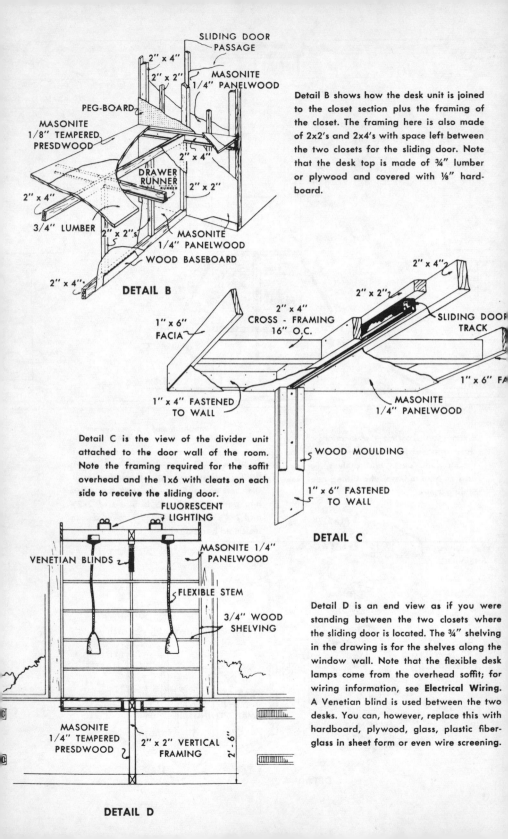

SLIDING DOOR PASSAGE

2" x 4"

2" x 2"

MASONITE 1/4" PANELWOOD

PEG-BOARD

MASONITE 1/8" TEMPERED PRESDWOOD

2" x 4"

DRAWER RUNNER

2" x 2"

2" x 4"

3/4" LUMBER

2" x 2"s

MASONITE 1/4" PANELWOOD

WOOD BASEBOARD

2" x 4"

DETAIL B

Detail B shows how the desk unit is joined to the closet section plus the framing of the closet. The framing here is also made of 2x2's and 2x4's with space left between the two closets for the sliding door. Note that the desk top is made of ¾" lumber or plywood and covered with ⅛" hardboard.

2" x 4"

2" x 2"

1" x 6" FACIA

2" x 4" CROSS - FRAMING 16" O.C.

SLIDING DOOR TRACK

1" x 6" FA

1" x 4" FASTENED TO WALL

MASONITE 1/4" PANELWOOD

WOOD MOULDING

1" x 6" FASTENED TO WALL

Detail C is the view of the divider unit attached to the door wall of the room. Note the framing required for the soffit overhead and the 1x6 with cleats on each side to receive the sliding door.

DETAIL C

FLUORESCENT LIGHTING

VENETIAN BLINDS

MASONITE 1/4" PANELWOOD

FLEXIBLE STEM

3/4" WOOD SHELVING

Detail D is an end view as if you were standing between the two closets where the sliding door is located. The ¾" shelving in the drawing is for the shelves along the window wall. Note that the flexible desk lamps come from the overhead soffit; for wiring information, see **Electrical Wiring**. A Venetian blind is used between the two desks. You can, however, replace this with hardboard, plywood, glass, plastic fiberglass in sheet form or even wire screening.

MASONITE 1/4" TEMPERED PRESDWOOD

2" x 2" VERTICAL FRAMING

2' - 6"

DETAIL D

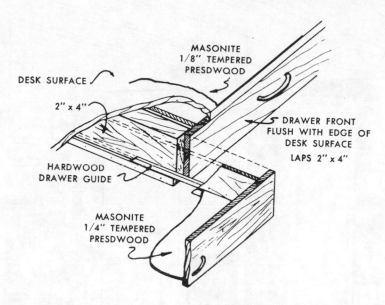

MASONITE
1/8" TEMPERED
PRESDWOOD

DESK SURFACE

2" x 4"

DRAWER FRONT
FLUSH WITH EDGE OF
DESK SURFACE
LAPS 2" x 4"

HARDWOOD
DRAWER GUIDE

MASONITE
1/4" TEMPERED
PRESDWOOD

Drawer details should be followed carefully. Use 1x6 tongue-and-groove boards or plywood for the desk top and cover the wood with ⅛" hardboard. Fasten the 2x4's to which the drawer guides are attached with countersunk screws before applying the hardboard top. For details on how to make the drawers, see section on **Drawers.**

Sketches courtesy of Masonite Corp.

Room Divider— Entry Wall

Island entry closet is a free-standing unit which sets the front door off from the living room area. There's plenty of storage space with this room divider.

Storage space for living room and entry hall is provided in this free-standing island entry closet. It also serves to define the living and entry areas without confining either. Because it replaces the conventional wall needed to screen the living room from the front door, this modern built-in room divider more than pays for itself.

On the entry hall side is a roomy clothes closet and deep sections for bulk storage. On the other side are cabinets and a built-in counter.

Materials Needed:

FIR PLYWOOD

NUMBER	SIZE	GRADE	WHERE USED
3 panels	4'x8'x¾"	PlyPanel (A-D)	Bottom, shelves, mirror back, counter top
5 panels	4'x8'x¾"	INTERIOR A-A	Doors, partitions, sides, shelves, top
1 panel	4'x'8x¼"	INTERIOR A-A	Closet and cabinet backs, drawer bottoms
1 panel	4'x8'x⅜"	INTERIOR A-A	Trays

LUMBER

SIZE	QUANTITY	WHERE USED
2x2	20'	Framing
1x2	66'	Counter and shelf cleats, drawer guides, misc.
1x6	36'	Face trim at top, base
1x3	135'	Face trim, tray slides, track and miscellaneous
½" quarter round	36'	Base and mirror
⅜" dowel	1'	Sliding doors
¾"x2⅛"	22'	Crown molding
1¼" clothes pole	4'	Coat closet

HARDWARE AND MISCELLANEOUS

ITEM	QUANTITY	WHERE USED
Sheave rollers	2 pair	Sliding doors
Steel tracks 4'	2	Sliding doors
Flush pulls	3	Doors
Metal pulls	6	Doors
Metal adjustable standards, 28" long	4	Shelves
Metal adjustable standards, 36" long	4	Shelves
3"x1½" butt hinges	6 pair	Doors
Bullet catches	6 sets	Doors
Mirror (size to suit)	1	Over counter

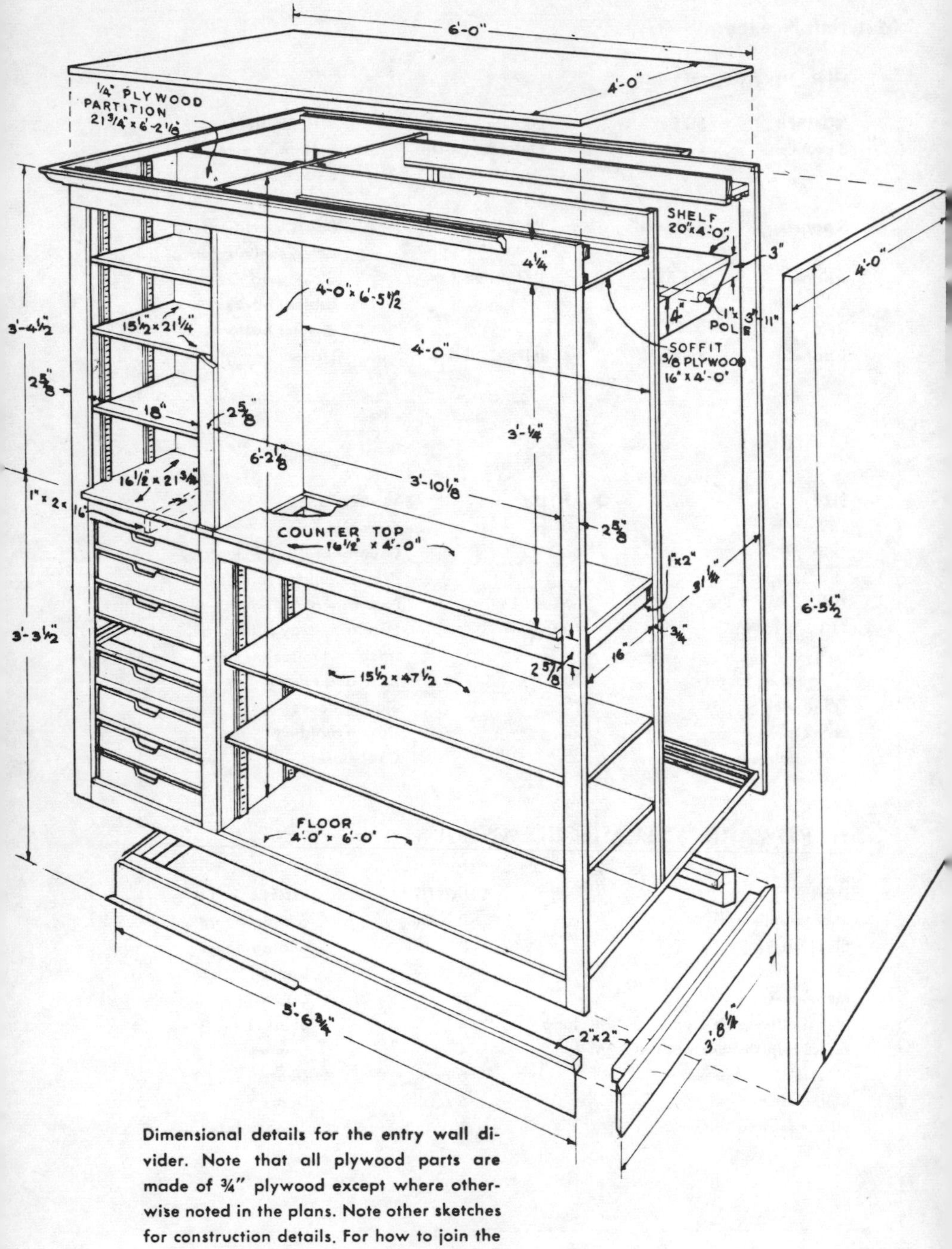
6'-0"
4'-0"
1/4" PLYWOOD PARTITION 21 3/4" x 6'-2 1/8"
SHELF 20" x 4'-0"
3"
4 1/4"
4'-0" x 6'-5 1/2
4"
1" x 3'-11" POLE
15 1/2 x 21 1/4
4'-0"
SOFFIT 3/8 PLYWOOD 16" x 4'-0'
3'-4 1/2
2 5/8
18"
2 5/8
3'-1/4"
6'-2 1/8
16 1/2 x 21 3/4
3'-10 1/8
1" x 2 x 16"
COUNTER TOP 16 1/2" x 4'-0"
2 5/8
1"x2"
3' 1/4"
6'-5 1/2"
3'-3 1/2"
3/4
16"
2 5/8
15 1/2 x 47 1/2
FLOOR 4'-0" x 6'-0'
5'-6 3/4"
2"x2"
3'-8 1/4"

Dimensional details for the entry wall divider. Note that all plywood parts are made of ¾" plywood except where otherwise noted in the plans. Note other sketches for construction details. For how to join the sections, see **Built-Ins** and **Furniture Plans.**

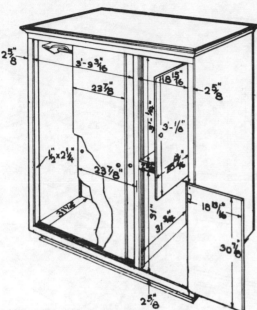

Additional details of entry closet viewed from the entry side.

Sketches courtesy of Douglas Fir Plywood Assoc.

Dimensional details of closet viewed from the living room side.

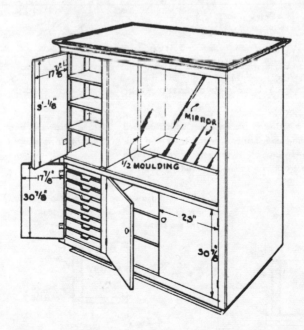

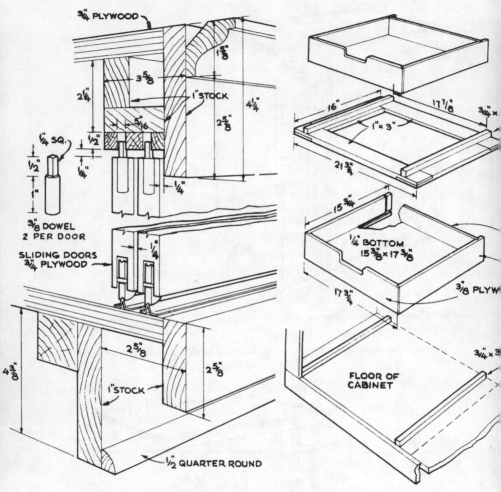

¾" PLYWOOD

1 ⅜"

3 ⅝"

1"STOCK

2¼"

4¼"

5/16"

2 ⅝"

½"

¼"

¼"

¼" SQ.

½"

1"

⅜" DOWEL
2 PER DOOR

SLIDING DOORS
¾" PLYWOOD

¼"

4⅜"

2⅝"

2⅝"

1"STOCK

½ QUARTER ROUND

16"

1" × 3"

17⅞"

¾" ×

21¾"

15¾"

¼ BOTTOM
15⅜" × 17⅜"

17¾"

⅜ PLYW

¾" × 3

FLOOR OF
CABINET

How to install sliding doors with standard
sliding door hardware—top track and rollers—by use of ⅜" dowels. If you wish to
use track and rollers, see **Sliding Doors**.

How drawers and guide units are assembled; note end lap joints for guides.

Additional drawer details. For step-by-step
how-to instructions on drawer construction, see **Drawers**.

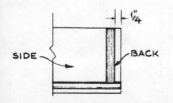

¼"

SIDE

BACK

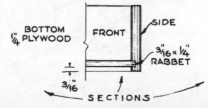

BOTTOM
¼" PLYWOOD

FRONT

SIDE

3/16 × ¼"
RABBET

⅛"

3/16

SECTIONS

¼ QUARTER-
ROUND

ALTERNATIVE

A wood folding door can be used as a room divider. Individual panels, ⅜" thick and 3⅝" wide, fold like an accordion when the doors are opened. This divider produces an attractive wood wall when closed.

Photograph courtesy of Rolscreen Co.

Room Divider— Folding Screen

It is possible to make a room divider out of an attractive wooden folding screen that rides in a track mounted on the ceiling. The individual panels are ⅜" thick and 3⅝" wide, joined by a continuous spring hinging. When folded, the door takes only 6" of space and yet when opened, occupies the same space as a standard door between two rooms.

These wood folding doors are available in pine, oak, mahogany or birch veneer and come painted, clear varnished or unfinished.

It is simple to install a wood folding door. You need a screwdriver, a hammer, saw and a small hand drill or an electric drill. Use a ⁵⁄₆₄" bit for hardwood and a ¹⁄₁₆" bit for softwood.

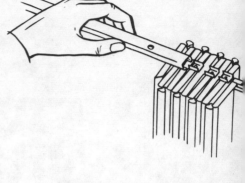

1. Draw a line down the center at the top of the opening. Center the metal track on this line and mark the screw holes. Drill holes for the screws.

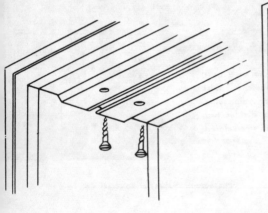

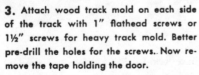

2. Slip the track over the slides at top of the Pella Door. Lift door into opening and fasten the track with 1" screws. Don't remove the tape from the door until track is in place.

3. Attach wood track mold on each side of the track with 1" flathead screws or 1½" screws for heavy track mold. Better pre-drill the holes for the screws. Now remove the tape holding the door.

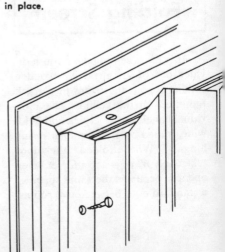

4. Fasten door to side of opening. The last panel of the door has countersunk holes for attaching ¾" long screws. Outside edge of panel should line up with the bottom edge of track mold.

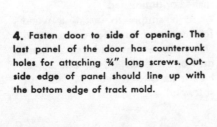

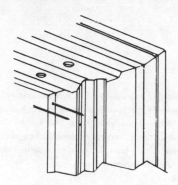

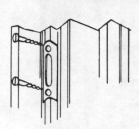

5. Attach side mold to the other side of door opening with 1" nails. If mold is too large, do not trim off the top. Make certain that mold is parallel to the sides of the door opening.

6. Attach the metal latch plate over the cut-out portion of the side mold. Be sure latch plate is in line with ridge on side mold. Drill holes for screws and use ¾" screws to hold latch plate.

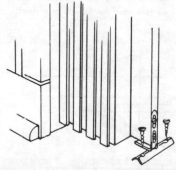

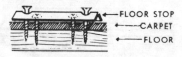

FLOOR STOP
CARPET
FLOOR

7. Fasten metal floor stop with ¾" screws to floor. Fold door back and mark line on floor directly under front edge. With front edge on the floor stop, drill screw holes and fasten in place. If the catch does not engage the floor stop, loosen the screws which hold it to the end post and lower it enough to engage the floor stop.

8. If the floor stop is installed on a carpet or rug, two 1½" round-head screws should be placed under the floor stop to raise it up high enough to engage the catch. Then use 1½" flathead screws to hold the floor stop in position. Now install the other door if you use twin-doors as a room divider.

Sketches courtesy of Rolscreen Co.

- - - - - - - - - - - - - - - - - - - -

Room Divider— Jalousie

If you have a window with a view you'd rather not see too often, this jalousie is just the answer. Of course, it can be used as a room di- vider, too, depending upon your requirements.

Jalousies make unusually attractive room dividers and permanent screens. The painted wood frame houses individual panels of a material such as Novoply. These panels, which swing on metal pins, have an attractive texture that adds an unusual touch in the room's decor.

Attractive jalousie divider can be adjusted to permit the breeze to come through and yet conceal the view from one section to another. Here, redwood Novoply has been given a two-tone finish and mounted in a painted wooden frame.

Photograph and sketches courtesy of
United States Plywood Corp.

Plans for the jalousie room divider. These three views show how the metal pin and flange are attached to the top and bottom of each panel to permit it to pivot. Cut each of the panels 1' wide and as high as you need for the room divider.

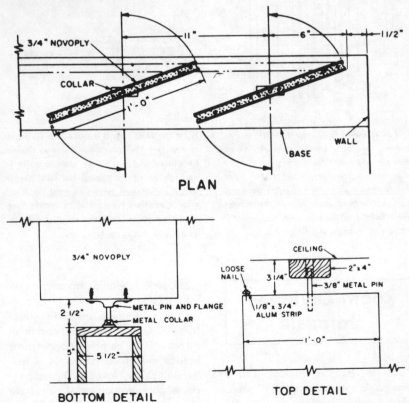

3/4" NOVOPLY

COLLAR

11"   6"   1 1/2"

1'-0"

WALL

BASE

PLAN

3/4" NOVOPLY

2 1/2"

METAL PIN AND FLANGE
METAL COLLAR

5"   5 1/2"

BOTTOM DETAIL

CEILING

LOOSE NAIL

3 1/4"

2"x4"

3/8" METAL PIN

1/8" x 3/4" ALUM STRIP

1'-0"

TOP DETAIL

Room Divider—Storage Cabinet

This room divider, designed by William Pahlman, is a handsome piece of furniture with many uses. It makes an excellent support for a TV set. Its three roomy cabinets (with

Handsome storage cabinet room-divider is made of birch plywood. Designed by William Pahlman, the unit can be made with a curved or straight valance, depending upon the rest of the furnishings in the room.

Photograph and sketches courtesy of United States Plywood Corp.

doors opening from either side) provide extra storage space at a convenient place. The decorative top shelf is suitable for plants, ornaments or books.

There is a choice of valances with this unit so that you can use either the curve-cut valance or the alternate straight valance which will give your room divider a contemporary look. Mr. Pahlman suggests that long Lumiline electric lights be placed under the lower shelf where they will be concealed by the valances.

The room divider as shown here was built from lumber core birch plywood, but there are many other beautifully grained panels from which to choose. Complete step-by-step plans for this attractive unit are available from a plywood company which commissioned Mr. Pahlman to design it, but here are several detail drawings to help the more advanced handyman in planning and building his own room-divider storage cabinet.

Materials Needed:

2 hardwood plywood panels—lumber core—4'x8'x¾"—one panel should be good on both sides
20' of ¾" square hardwood for cleats
10 #10 flathead screws, 1½" long
84 #10 flathead screws 1¼" long
6 continuous brass hinges, 1¼" (open) by 4⅜" long
1 gross of #4 flathead brass screw
1 gross of #4 flathead brass screws, ⅝" long
8 adjustable shelf-pins
6 cabinet knife-catches
4 single-pin ¾" glides for the feet
6 brass cabinet knob pulls
Glue for joining the pieces
Paint and paint roller or plywood tape to veneer edges of plywood
2 quarts of clear finish such as Satinlac
Paste furniture polish

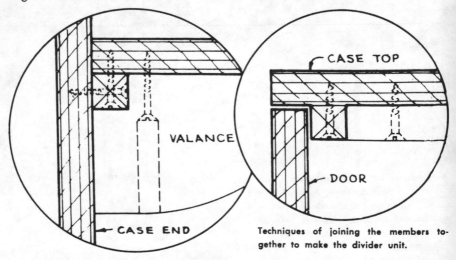

Techniques of joining the members together to make the divider unit.

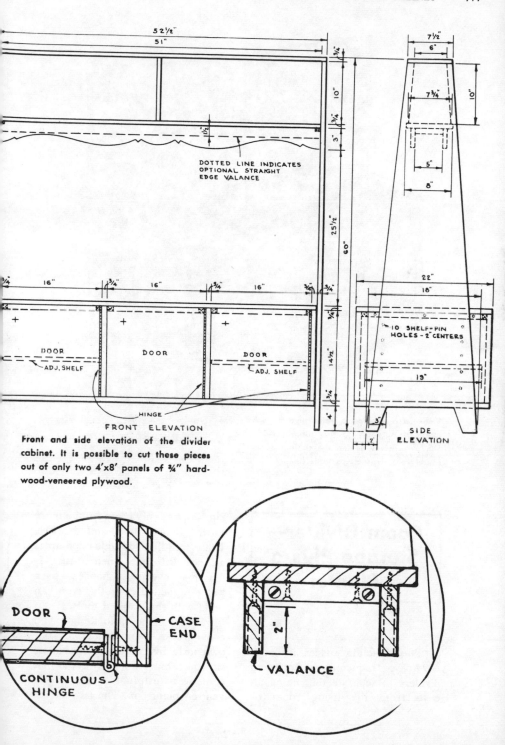

DOTTED LINE INDICATES
OPTIONAL STRAIGHT
EDGE VALANCE

10 SHELF-PIN
HOLES - 2" CENTERS

DOOR
ADJ. SHELF

DOOR

DOOR
ADJ. SHELF

HINGE

FRONT ELEVATION

SIDE ELEVATION

Front and side elevation of the divider
cabinet. It is possible to cut these pieces
out of only two 4'x8' panels of ¾" hardwood-veneered plywood.

DOOR

CASE
END

CONTINUOUS
HINGE

VALANCE

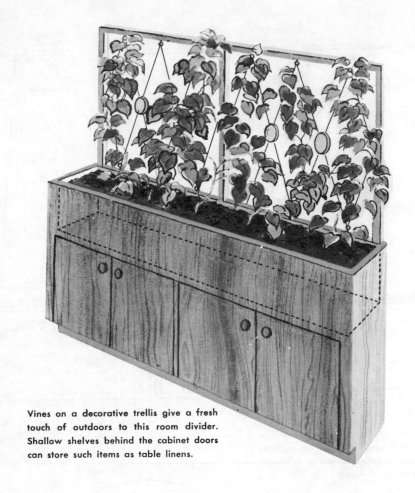

Vines on a decorative trellis give a fresh touch of outdoors to this room divider. Shallow shelves behind the cabinet doors can store such items as table linens.

Room Divider— Storage Plus a Planter

Dual-function spaces in modern homes frequently call for room dividers to separate the dining alcove from the living room or kitchen, a family room from a more formal living room, and the like, These well-lighted, wide-open areas are not disturbed—their attractiveness may even be enhanced—by a well-designed divider that you can build with the simplest tools.

Following a basic design, you can make a room divider to your own taste by combining a shallow storage cabinet and plant stand that contains a rustproof copper or galvanized plant box. The lady of the

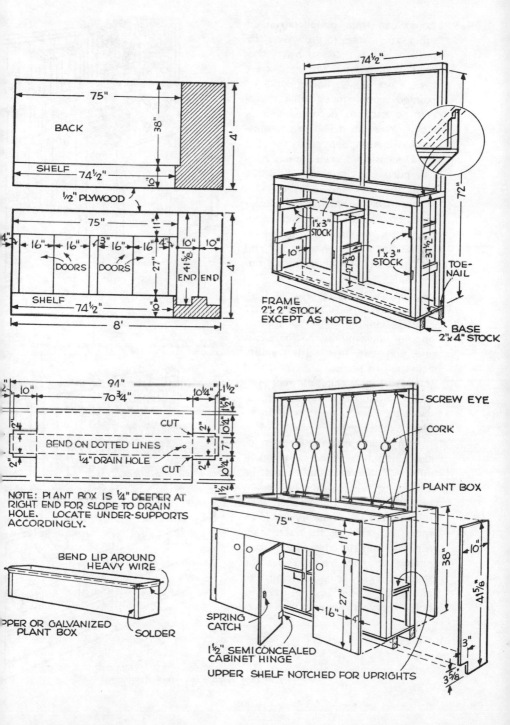

BACK

75"

SHELF   74½"

½" PLYWOOD

38"

4'

75"

16" 16" 3" 16" 16" 4"   10" 10"

DOORS   DOORS

11"

27"

41⅝"

END END

SHELF   74½"

8'

4'

74½"

FRAME
2"x 2" STOCK
EXCEPT AS NOTED

1"x 3"
STOCK

10"

1"x 3"
STOCK

2"x 8"

37½"

31½"

72"

TOE-
NAIL

BASE
2"x 4" STOCK

91"

70¾"

10"

10¼" 1½"

CUT

BEND ON DOTTED LINES

¼" DRAIN HOLE

CUT

2"

2"

7"

10¼" 10¼"

NOTE: PLANT BOX IS ¼" DEEPER AT
RIGHT END FOR SLOPE TO DRAIN
HOLE.   LOCATE UNDER-SUPPORTS
ACCORDINGLY.

BEND LIP AROUND
HEAVY WIRE

COPPER OR GALVANIZED
PLANT BOX

SOLDER

SCREW EYE

CORK

PLANT BOX

75"

11"

38"

27"

16" 4"

10"

41⅝"

3"

3⅝"

SPRING
CATCH

1½" SEMICONCEALED
CABINET HINGE

UPPER SHELF NOTCHED FOR UPRIGHTS

house can train philodendron or other hardy vines to grow over the trellis which is made of heavy colored cord strung through screw eyes. Cork floats, bottle corks or painted spools among other things can be used to decorate such a trellis. You can make up an unusual trellis with paper clips.

Dimensions shown are not critical, but were chosen to allow the front and back and two shelves to be cut from two standard 4′x8′ plywood boards. If greater length is required for your room, you can increase that dimension up to 10″ and still have sufficient stock to cut out the ends.

The 2x2 frame is heavier than that ordinarily required for similar construction, but it gives an appearance of substantiality to the trellis and may add that extra stability necessary to prevent the household tragedy of an upset. You may even find it desirable to attach the separator to the floor and wall with unobtrusive metal angles.

Any plant box requires drainage. This may be achieved by punching a ¾″ hole near one end of the bottom to take off surplus water, and tilt the box toward that end. Punch from the inside to provide a spout that will keep the water from running along the edges, and place a pitcher or other vessel under the spout at least during watering. Put pieces of broken flowerpot over the hole to prevent clogging; then cover

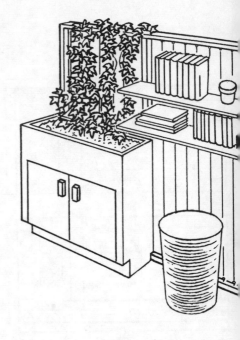

Basic design can be varied as you wish.

Drawers in case require increased depth.

the bottom with 1" of coarse drainage material.

You may prefer to purchase a metal box having a false bottom and special provisions for drainage, in which case change the dimensions to suit.

You will find ½" interior A-B plywood for the faces of sufficient thickness to add strength to the toe-nailed joints supporting the rear uprights on the base. It has one finished side that will take paint. If your room is wallpapered, you may wish to cover the inside of the doors with a matching paper, or a fabric may be glued on. Hardboard would be equally satisfactory, or you can make the faces of redwood, cypress or cedar.

Since your separator very likely will be used with one end against a wall, the facepiece is eliminated at that end. The frame should be cut to fit if it is to go against a baseboard.

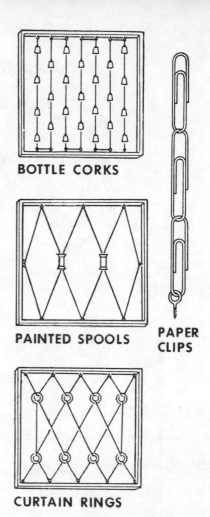

BOTTLE CORKS

PAINTED SPOOLS

PAPER CLIPS

CURTAIN RINGS

GRASS CONDITIONS						
	Good Drainage	High Fertility	Shade	Sun	High Moisture	Drought Hardy
Kentucky Blue	√	√		√	√	
Red Fescue	√		√			
Bermuda	√	√		√		
Centipede	√	√				
Grama	√			√		√
Buffalo	√			√		√
Crested Wheat	√	√		√		√
Bent		√		√		
St. Augustine			√			
Zoysia				√		√
Carpet				√		

Homeowners' Guide To Pliers

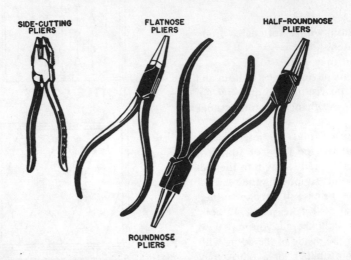

SIDE-CUTTING PLIERS

FLATNOSE PLIERS

HALF-ROUNDNOSE PLIERS

ROUNDNOSE PLIERS

First Aid for Pliers

AILMENT	REMEDY
Badly rusted	Soak in kerosene for at least 24 hours; then clean with steel wool. Use penetrating oil to work the joint loose. Dry and polish with oil.
Loose jaws or rivet	Close jaws of the pliers and set with broached side* on anvil or metal block. Hit top half of the rivet with flat head of a ball pein hammer.
Tight jaws or rivets	Open pliers to first tight spot and set with broach side down over a hole in a metal block. Hit the rivet squarely with the flat head of a ball pein hammer.
Dull, won't grip	Stroke a checking file across the inside of the jaws, particularly of a long nose pliers.
Dull cutting edge	Place pliers open in a vise with the head flat. Use an India stone to stone out the imperfections and then sharpen with the India stone.

* The rivet through the pliers has two sides—one is round and the other is broached; that is, somewhat star-shaped, a circle with four points.

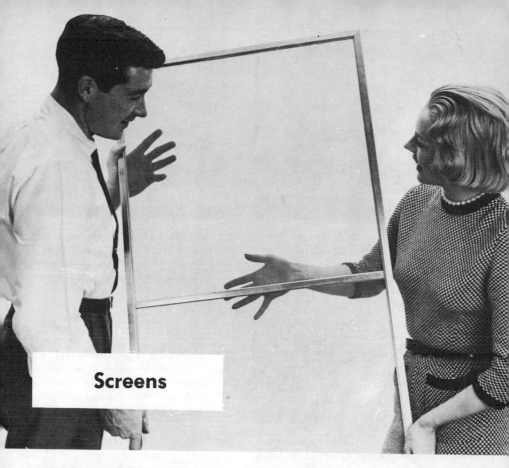

Screens

Screen doors and windows require attention at least twice a year. They should be renovated and put on in the spring, and removed and prepared for storage in the fall. If a good grade of screening has been used and the screens have been well cared for, the work involved will not be great.

Replacing the Screening

If a screen is badly damaged and the entire piece of screen must be replaced, you can follow any of the three methods shown here. First, however, you must prepare the wood frame. To do this, you should:

(a) use a flooring or glazier's chisel to remove the moldings, taking care not to split or crack them

(b) scrape and scrub out any corrosion left by the old screening

(c) paint or varnish any wood that will touch the screening

(d) make accurate measurements to determine how much screening you will need for the job

(e) get aluminum tacks to use with aluminum screening; steel are second best, but don't use brass or copper.

How To Re-Screen a Single Frame

If you have a wood frame with a tack-on molding, you can follow this technique. All you need is a magnetized tack hammer, two C clamps and two 1″ boards, and two 2″ boards to use for supports.

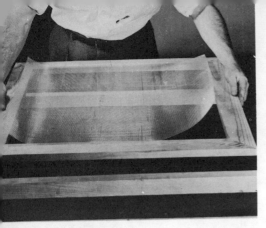

1. Cut the screening to size so that it overlaps the frame sufficiently to be covered by the molding afterwards. Set frame over two 2″ boards with the screen side up as shown.

2. Under the top and bottom edges of the wooden frame, lay 1″ boards—any scrap lumber will do for this job—so that the 1″ boards rest on the 2″ boards as shown.

3. Tack screening in place across top of frame with tacks or staples, if you wish. Then clamp the frame to the 2″ boards with C clamps set at the center of the frame to bend the frame down.

Photographs courtesy of Aluminum Company of America.

4. Pull the aluminum screening taut and tack along the bottom. Continue to exert pressure during the tacking process to keep the screening taut.

5. Remove the clamps and then tack the sides of the screening to the frame. Finally, replace the moldings and nail them into place; counterset the nails slightly. Trim off any surplus screening.

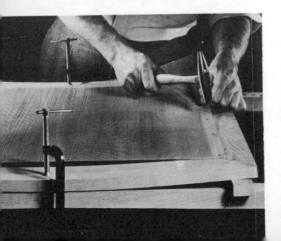

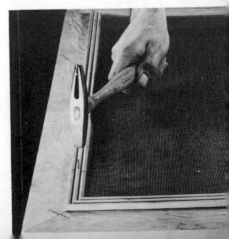

1. Butt the edges of the screens together. Lay 2" boards along the outer edge as shown. Then set a piece of cut screening over both.

2. Tack screening at one raised edge. Pull the screening taut and tack at opposite edge of the other frame.

How To Re-Screen Multiple Frames

If you have more than one screen to cover, you can follow this technique. All you need is the new screening, a hammer, tacks and two 2" boards—any scrap will do—to use as supports. Don't forget to prepare the wooden frames before you start to apply the screening to them.

Photographs courtesy of Aluminum Company of America.

3. Remove the boards and press butted frame flat. Tack both frames along the butted edge. Note position of the tacks through the screening.

4. Cut the screens apart. Trim and finish tacking the edges. Then replace the molding on each of the two wood frames and cut off surplus screening.

1. Cut screening to exact outside measurements of the opening left when you have removed the molding.

2. Cut a perfectly square notch at each corner, to inside edge of the slots, but not beyond.

How To Roll-In Screening

Possibly you have purchased or made screens for your home with roll-in screening. To replace the screening you will need the screen cloth, a screen wheel, a tool butt and a hammer. Work carefully to be assured of a professional-like job.

3. Hold the top edge of the screening in place. Run a screen wheel, in short hitches, along the entire length of the top rail.

4. Now use the wheel to insert the spline. If you're careful, a nail punch or nail set can be used in place of the wheel.

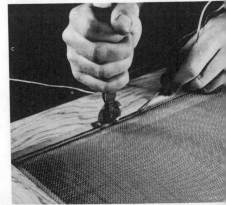

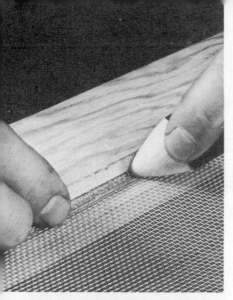

5. Run tool butt along inside of frame to crease screening flat. Do not crease at the edge of the frame. Both the wheel and tool butt are available in many hardware stores.

6. Repeat the procedure at bottom of frame and then at the sides in that order. Now, you can tack molding in place.

Photographs courtesy of Aluminum Company of America.

Lifts and Reinforcing Angles

Many sliding window screens have no pulls or handles with which to raise the screen, and the screens are usually opened by pushing upward on the upper rail. This pressure tends to pull the frame apart.

Handles or pulls that are obtainable at slight expense should be screwed to the lower sash rails. Handles provide an easy method for raising the screens and relieving the pressure on sash rails.

The screen frame may be reinforced and made more rigid by means of small angle irons screwed into each inside corner of the frame or by attaching flat metal pieces across each corner on the face of the frame. If the frames have butt or mitered joints, and if there are no nails to interfere, they can be reinforced by driving metal corrugated fasteners across the corners into the face of the frame.

The following tools and materials are needed: Hand drill, screwdriver and hammer, two handles or lifts for each sliding screen, four small angle irons, flat metal pieces or metal corrugated fasteners for each screen, and a sufficient quantity of small screws.

Protection for Screen Doors

Where screen doors are likely to be damaged by small children or pets jumping against them, it is advisable to have extra protection for the lower half of the door. Doors may be purchased which are already equipped with guards but, if they are not obtainable, a protective screen of heavy, large-mesh wire called hardware cloth may be applied over the regular screen wire in the lower portion of the frame.

The following tools and material are needed: Claw hammer, heavy screen wire sufficient to cover the

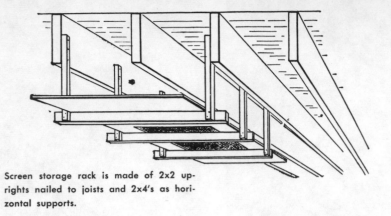

Screen storage rack is made of 2x2 uprights nailed to joists and 2x4's as horizontal supports.

lower portion of the screen-door frame, and small staples to fasten screen wire to frame.

To Close Screen Doors Tightly

The following tools and materials are needed: Screwdriver and light hammer, screen-door spring or door check. Screen doors that slam are annoying and doors that do not close tightly are a source of trouble. To eliminate these difficulties, door closers and other devices that are inexpensive and easy to apply may be obtained from hardware dealers or mail order houses. Instructions furnished by the manufacturer should be carefully followed in making the installation.

A simple but effective way to deaden the sound of screen-door slamming is to tack three small square pieces of felt cloth or rubber to the main door frame at points of contact. One piece should be placed near the top, another near the bottom, and the third midway between.

Hinges and Closing Devices

Screen-door hinges are generally of two types: Spring, and loose-pin butt hinges.

Since, with ordinary spring it is necessary to remove the screws and plug up the holes when the door is taken down, butt hinges with removable pins may be preferred. If butt hinges are used or if spring hinges have lost their pulling power, the door may be made to close tightly by fastening a slender coil spring (obtainable from a hardware dealer) between the screen-door frame and the main door jamb. The spring should be so placed that there will be sufficient pull to close the door tightly when it is released.

To accomplish this, one end should be attached to the door jamb with a small screw hook 3″ to 5″ away from the screen door, as space permits; the other end should be attached to the middle cross rail of the screen door by means of a similar hook at a point where the spring will be under enough tension to keep the door closed. If the hook on the door jamb is too near the screen door, the spring will exert too little pull or closing force and the door will remain slightly open.

If the door jamb is too narrow to permit the use of the sort of spring described, a short heavy coil spring may be used on the outside face of the screen door. It should be placed at a point between the hinges

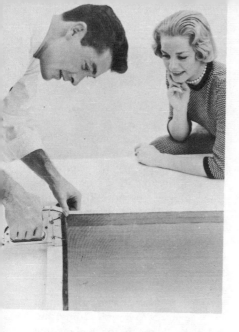

When making or repairing screens, you can hold the screen cloth to a wooden frame by using staples. Drive staples about 2″ apart.

and diagonally across the crack between the screen door and the main door jamb. The ends of the spring should be fastened with wood screws to the frame of the screen door and to the front of the main door jamb.

Sagging Screen Door

If joints in the frame of a screen door become loosened, allowing the lower half of the door to sag and the bottom edge to drag on the threshold, a metal rod equipped with a turnbuckle may be used to raise the bottom rail clear of the floor. One end of the rod should be fastened to the face of the frame at the center of the intersection between the bottom rail and the outer vertical stile, and the other end should be fastened as high up as it will reach on the face of the vertical stile that carries the hinges.

When the two ends of the rod have been screwed on firmly, the turnbuckle may be turned to shorten the rod and lift the bottom rail.

Storing Screens

Screens will last longer if they are taken down in the fall and stored in a dry place for the winter. A good plan, if the basement has no finished ceiling, is to suspend them from the ceiling in a corner on a framework made of wood. The hangers that hold the screens should be nailed to the floor joists about 2′ apart and hung at an elevation that will permit the screens to lie perfectly flat. This can be achieved by laying two

The screen cloth can also be held to a wooden frame by tacks spaced about 1½″ apart. The exposed edge of the screen cloth, whether tacks or staples are used, is covered with a wood molding.

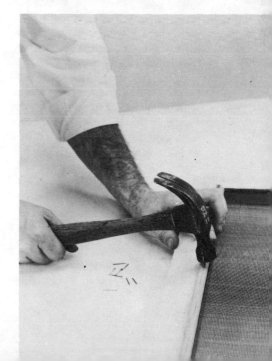

or three boards under the screens to form a shelf.

Screen doors may be placed on the hangers first and the window screens laid on top of them, with lath between to keep the doors and screens separated. They should be covered with paper or canvas to protect them from dust. This method of storage keeps screens free from accidental harm, in a place where they will not gather floor dampness, where they have the advantage of free air circulation, and where they are not likely to become warped. The screens and window frames should be numbered to correspond to each other so that they can be readily matched. They may be inconspicuously marked in Roman numerals with a small chisel or with numbered nails resembling thumb tacks. The nails are furnished in duplicate and can be applied to screens, window frames, or window sills. For example, one tack numbered 3 may be fastened to the screen and another with the same number to the corresponding window frame or sill.

The following tools and materials are needed: Screw driver to remove doors, numbered nails resembling thumb tacks, claw hammer, saw, a few lengths of boards, and sufficient nails to build the hanging frame to the screen-storage rack.

"Knock-Down" Window Screens

Knock-down wooden screen frames which are easy to assemble may be purchased at reasonable prices, and a variety of kits and materials are available for making aluminum screens (see *Screens—Aluminum Frame Screens*).

The wooden sets include everything but the screen wire, leaving the purchaser free to select the grade he desires. They usually include four pieces of wood making up the two sides, the top, and the bottom. These pieces are usually notched at one end to insure a firm joint. The other end is left square, to be sawed to the proper length to fit the window. In the case of sliding screens, grooves are already cut in the side pieces to permit sliding, and provision is made for tacking the screen wire and attaching the molding.

Knock-down frame sets also include four pieces of molding to be tacked over the edges of the screen wire, two slides to be attached to the sides of the window frame, and a metal lift or handle for raising the screen. Sufficient nails and tacks are provided to complete the job. To make the frame hold its rigidity and remain square, small flat angle irons may be screwed into each corner. If the wooden joints are mitered and nails do not interfere, steel corrugated fasteners may be driven into the face of the frame across the corners to make the frame more rigid. The joints should be coated with waterproof glue before nailing, the nails countersunk, and the nail holes filled with putty to make a neat job. A priming coat of paint and one or two finishing coats in the desired color will complete the work.

The following tools and materials are needed for assembling wooden screen kits: Saw, claw ham-

With Fiberglas screen cloth, it is also possible to attach the screening to a wood frame with ordinary household cement.

Photographs courtesy of Owens-Corning Fiberglas Corp.

Patching the Fiberglas screen cloth is done with an electric iron. Just cut the patch, set it in place and use a thin sheet of paper between the patch and a moderately warm iron. The heat seals the patch in place.

mer, nail set, and small flat paint brush; complete screen frames, screen wire, small tacks, paint, and small quantity of putty and glue; four angle irons with screws for each frame, if desired.

Inside Screens

In summer cottages, and sometimes in permanent homes, it may be desirable to have screens placed inside of the windows. Inside screens are necessary if there are casement windows which open outward.

In the case of double-hung windows, it is possible to use half-length screens. They can be made to slide up and down on runners placed just inside the lower window sash. The screens should be placed

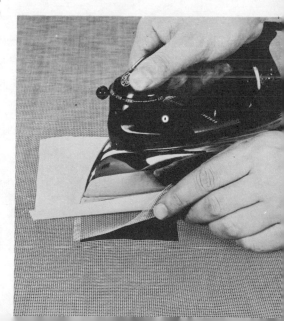

How To Patch a Screen

Trim the break to a square or rectangle shape with a pair of tin snips or old scissors. Then snip out a patch from a piece of scrap wire. Make the patch big enough so that it overlaps the screen cutout about ½" on each side. With the patch in hand, pull out two cross wires on each of ifs four sides. Using a mallet and a block of wood, bend the exposed wire ends outward at right angles.

Carefully place the patch over the cut-out so the bent wires can be pressed through the screen. In doing this, apply the patch on the screen surface that will be inside the house. Then, backing up the patch with the wood block, use the mallet on the opposite side of the screen to bend over the wire ends. For a neat appearance, bend the wire inward toward the center of the patch. As the final step, paint the patch to prevent rust and blend it with the rest of the screen.

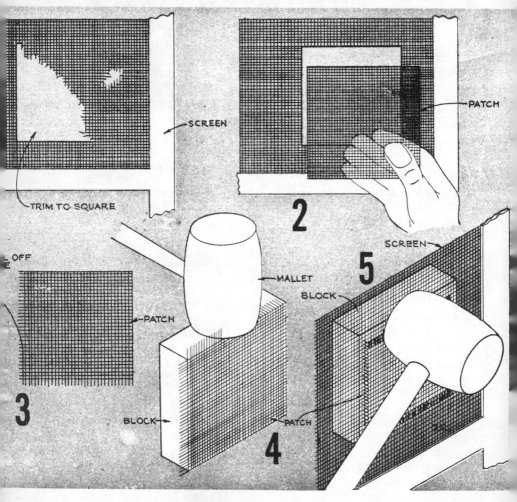

as close to the window sash as possible, so that space will not be left between the meeting rail of the sash and the screen frame for insects to enter.

Full-length screens, suitable for either out-swinging casement or double-hung windows, may be made in two vertical sections, each section being half the width of the window opening. The sections may be made to slide past each other horizontally by placing them on separate runners laid side by side on the window sill and along the top of the window frame. In this case also, care should be taken to avoid leaving cracks between the frames. Roll screens also are available for full-length inside protection.

Interior screen frames may be painted or enameled on the inside to match the woodwork, and on the outside to match or harmonize with the outside window trim.

Inside screens are protected from the weather when windows are closed and should last longer than outside ones. They usually slide easier, since they are not so likely to warp from exposure.

Painting Screens

For directions on how to paint the screen wire, refer to the section on *Painting*.

Screens— Aluminum Frame

Aluminum can be used to make your own window screens. You can purchase aluminum screen kits, made in a number of sizes and adjustable to fit practically any size window, or you can purchase Do-It-Yourself Aluminum and make your own frame and add the screening.

The aluminum screen kits— available in 5 sizes in the full screen and 4 sizes in the half screen—come with their own miter box. This enables the buyer to saw the aluminum framing members to exact size. The kits also come with Fiberglas screen cloth and splines to fasten the screening into the frame.

The Homeshield aluminum screen frame is mechanically assembled very quickly. Once the top, sides and bottom have been cut to exact size, they are joined by special slip-in corner braces.

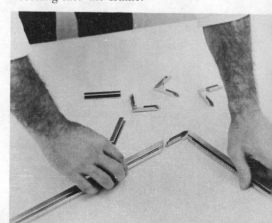

The Fiberglas screen cloth is cut to size and laid over the frame. It is secured within the frame by tapping a spline (a long thin aluminum strip, in this case) into a groove on the frame. The excess screen cloth can be cut off with a razor blade.

Screens—
Wood, Home-Made

If you're in a new house with odd-size windows a complete set of screens can put quite a dent in your pocketbook. Building them yourself, you can have them at a fraction of the retail price.

If you've got screens to repair, you'll find it almost as cheap and easy to build new ones as to repair the old set.

Measuring Windows

To start with, measure the width and height of your exterior window frames carefully. Plan your screen frame, if you are using wood, to be about ¼" bigger in both directions so that you can plane it to an exact fit.

Good stock to use is select-grade white pine 1¼" or ⅛" thick. Be sure there are no warped pieces. The two vertical side members, the horizontal top member and the horizontal middle piece are all 2" wide. The horizontal bottom rail is 3" wide. These are the dimensions by which you will buy your lumber, but the actual finished dimensions will be more like 1¾" for the narrow pieces and 2¾" for the bottom rail.

Corner Joints

One of the best corner joints for assembling the screen frames is the doweled and glued one shown in the accompanying photographs. Use a waterproof glue intended for outdoor work.

Two alternative methods, however, involve less work and are adequate for small screens, such as needed on basement windows. A

mitered corner joint can be glued and fastened with corrugated fasteners or so-called Chevrons that will hold the two pieces together under pressure while the glue dries.

A nailed butt joint reinforced with a metal bracket is another method for small screens. Smear the end of one piece with glue, then hold it upright in your vise while you nail the other piece onto the end with two long finishing nails. Then screw a metal angle bracket on each corner, using 1" flathead screws.

Finishing Frames

Whatever joining method you use, you'll save yourself a lot of work if you fit and paint the frames before covering them with wire. Plane them to a snug but not a tight fit. Don't forget to bevel the lower edge of the bottom rail to match the slope of the window sill. Then, with numbering tacks, number frames and windows in pairs so that you can tell where each screen goes. Fasten your screen hangers in place at the top. Then from the inside, screw in hooks and eyes to hold the bottom rail of the screen to the window sill.

Fastening Screening

For the screening, it is best to use a material such as aluminum wire or one of the many plastic screen fabrics now available. These types are easy to stretch into place, and you need never worry that rust or corrosion will cause unsightly stains on the adjoining woodwork. While this screening can be fastened

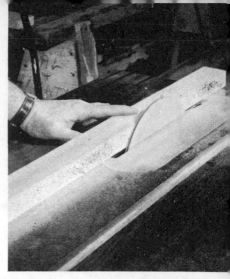

1. Two vertical pieces should be clamped together and run through saw at same time to make sure they are of identical length. Use a miter box if you have no power saw.

2. Sand all pieces smooth. Sanding disk of type that mounts on saw arbor will give pieces a satiny finish, as will a conventional belt and disk sander. Use fairly fine paper.

with regular carpet tacks, it is much faster and easier to do the job with a stapling-gun. If you do not own one you can probably rent one from a local building-supply dealer.

As a final step, countersink all

nail heads slightly and fill the remaining holes with putty. After the entire screen is done, these little spots and any other marks in the paint can be easily touched up with the same paint.

3. Plane a flat along one side of dowel, held in vise, to provide escape slot for glue. One or two light strokes does it. Ten ⅜" dowels, each 4" long, are needed for each screen.

4. Taper end of dowel by holding it against sanding disk and spinning it lightly in your hand. All dowels should be cut and prepared before you start to assemble frames.

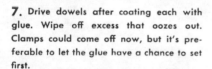

5. Assembly. It's easier to glue the frame together and then put it in the dowels. A pair of long clamps, such as the adjustable pipe type shown, will speed this operation.

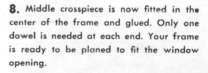

6. Now drill two ⅜" dowel holes a little more than 4" deep in each corner joint. Be careful to get holes true—a jig made by boring one hole in a small block will help.

7. Drive dowels after coating each with glue. Wipe off excess that oozes out. Clamps could come off now, but it's preferable to let the glue have a chance to set first.

8. Middle crosspiece is now fitted in the center of the frame and glued. Only one dowel is needed at each end. Your frame is ready to be planed to fit the window opening.

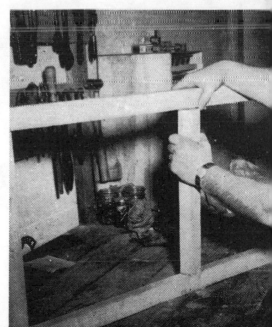

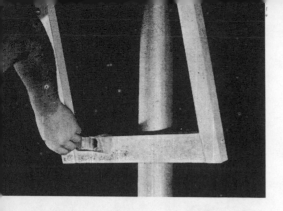

9. Paint all your frames before covering them. Give the frames a coat of exterior primer first. Allow this to dry for two or three days, then apply a coat of trim paint.

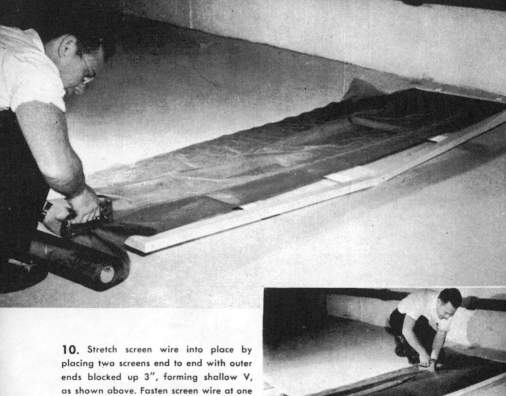

10. Stretch screen wire into place by placing two screens end to end with outer ends blocked up 3″, forming shallow V, as shown above. Fasten screen wire at one end, then pull it across and fasten it to far end of other screen. Now remove the blocks and let the frames fall back onto the floor, as at right, putting the screen under tension. Complete the tacking around the other three sides, lapping wire onto wood about ½″ all around. Then cut screens apart and trim off waste wire.

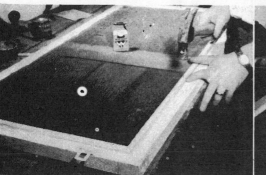

11. Cover exposed edges of wire with ½" half-round molding. Paint molding first and then nail in place with 1" brads. It's not much more work to miter the corners.

12. Nail a batten strip, ¼" by 1¾", instead of half-round molding, across the center rail. This covers up wire over the center crosspiece for a neat job.

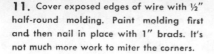

Screens, Folding

These may be large or small, highly decorative or functionally simple. The movable screen serves as a partition when you want to divide a section of the room; it acts as a cover-up in front of any part of the room which you don't want to have exposed; and it is an excellent way to deflect drafts from open win-

Unusual folding screen is covered with rubber tiles. You can make this unit out of ½" plywood and then cover the panels with tiles. This screen is covered with red, black and gray tiles in a perspective pattern, designed by George Schlining, repeating the random pattern rubber flooring design. This pattern was suggested as a decorating device which greatly increases the illusion of depth in a small room.

Photograph courtesy of Rubber Flooring Division of the Rubber Manufacturers Association.

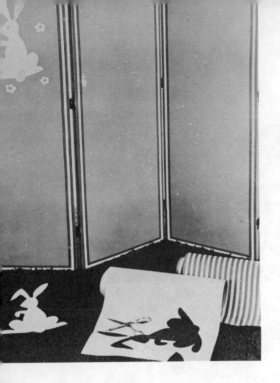

Another unusual treatment of a folding screen is shown here. A cutout of a floppy-eared bunny highlights this nursery screen decorated with self-adhesive contact plastic fabric. The plastic comes in many solid colors as well as patterns and wood grains. Just put your imagination to work.

This basket-weave screen is made of a wood frame with dowels and woven in tempered hardboard. The sides "A" are made of 1x2's, the top "B" is 1x4 stock and the bottom "C" is 1x6 stock. Join the corners with glue and dowels. Before the parts are assembled, however, add the 3/8" dowels as noted in the sketch. The 1/8" tempered hardboard is cut into strips 3¾" wide and 53" long and woven between the dowels.

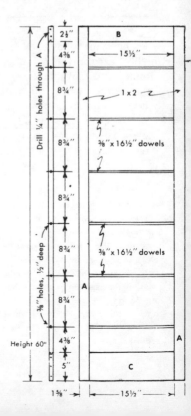

dows or doors, especially in a room where a baby's crib is kept.

The screen may be built of solid pieces of plywood, hinged together. Buy ¾ ", cut the sections (or leaves) the height and width you desire (usually 3 or 4 pieces are used). Smooth the edges with sandpaper. You may want to paint over the plywood; or perhaps cover it with wallpaper; or more originally with interesting maps, posters, magazine covers, or blown-up photographs.

A screen may be made of wood frames, each section a separate frame. Cut the wood strips the height and width desired, and put the frame together at the corners with any wood joint. Over or inside these frames you may nail any plain or designed fabric you desire, or wallboard (later painted over), or perhaps corrugated plastic glass which you can buy by the square foot and cut to fit.

Another attractive folding screen is made with louvered wood shutters formerly used on a window. You may have some unused shutters, or buy them the desired size at a lumber dealer. They may be painted to harmonize with the walls, or left as natural wood if you prefer.

Whichever you choose—solid, frames, or shutters—the leaves of the screen are put together with hinges, one near the top, one at the bottom. Usually a double-acting hinge is used, so that the leaves of the screen may go in either direction. However, if you use a single hinge, make sure to reverse the direction at consecutive joinings of the leaves, in order to have the screen fold together properly when closed.

If you use the screen often, and move it from one place to another, you could attach casters at the bottom (at the outer edge of the two end leaves, and at the folds) to make moving easier.

How To Store an Electric Power Mower

1. Clean all the exposed parts—the housing around the electric motor, the handles, the cutting blades and the top shield protecting the cutting blades as well as the underside of the unit.

2. Apply a thin film of oil or grease to the underside of the mower and the cutting blades to prevent rusting.

3. Examine the electric cable for nicks and frayed ends as well as the plug itself. Repair any parts or replace them if the damage is marked.

4. Check the on-off switch to see that it clicks instantly. If there's any doubt, it's best to replace it. See *Electrical Wiring*.

5. Follow those storage steps outlined for a gasoline-power mower that also apply to an electric-power mower.

Storage

There are many different ways to obtain increased storage space in any home. And there are few homes where additional storage is not desired. Examine your home and check through the following idea list to see where you can add storage to your home:

2. Maybe you have "waste" space in the attic. For how to make a closet or chest under-the-eaves, see *Attics*.

1. Make full use of the space in your closets. For ideas and how-to, see the following sections: *Built-Ins* and *Kitchen*.

3. Full storage walls are becoming increasingly popular. It is possible to convert an entire wall into storage space. For different types of wall units and the how-to, see *Built-Ins*.

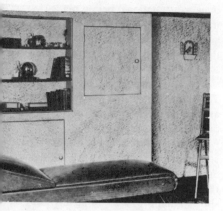

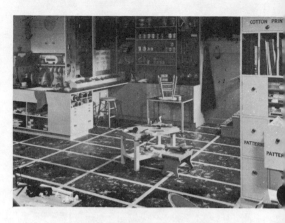

4. Outdoor storage is often a problem, especially with garages just big enough to hold the family car.

5. Cabinets and chests are convenient for added storage space. For plans and several different styles of chests and cabinets, see sections on *Built-Ins* and *Furniture*.

Storm Door

A storm door is an extra outside door used in the winter to keep the interior of the home warmer. It creates an air pocket between it and the regular door of the home and this air pocket serves as an insulator. Furthermore, by having two doors, it reduces any possible draft that might be caused by the poor fitting of the regular door.

Storm doors can be purchased ready-made and then cut to fit your door perfectly and hung with hinges like the conventional door. A storm door, however, is hinged so that it opens outward. Some storm doors are available as combination models; the inside glass panel can be removed in the summer and replaced with a screen.

Storm Windows

Storm windows and doors materially reduce heat losses, and in cold regions the less expensive types will, in time, pay for themselves in reduced fuel bills. They are extensively used in cold climates for reasons of comfort as well as fuel savings, and to avoid excessive frosting of single-glass windows.

once, installations being made by the dealer or by the adept home handyman. In this type of frame, the glass panes are replaced by screens by slipping out the storm sash and inserting the screen sash. The sash frames are not very thick and, therefore, occupy a minimum of storage space.

In the conventional aluminum storm-screen unit, the frame has double or triple tracks along which the glass panes and screen panel slide so that they are completely self-storing.

Another type of combination storm window and screen permits the screens to roll up automatically on rollers hidden in the window frame when the storm windows are in use, and permits the lower half of the window to be raised when screening only is needed. This type also presents no storage problem because neither pane nor screen is removed when not in use.

When storing storm windows, you can label them by attaching a self-adhesive tape on which you can write. The special finish on the label prevents the writing from blurring or coming off.

When properly installed, storm windows provide a still-air space which reduces heat conduction to the outside and to some degree prevent infiltration of cold air. Storm windows reduce frosting of inside windowpanes by protecting them from the low outdoor temperatures that cause condensation. If it is impossible to provide storm windows for all window openings, they should be installed on windows on the sides of the house that face prevailing winter winds. To be most effective, storm sash should fit tightly. There are two types in general use: those that are installed permanently, and those that can be put up and taken down as the seasons change.

There are several types of permanent storm sash frames in which storm window or screen sections can be inserted. They may be of wood or metal and are installed but

WEST WINDOW

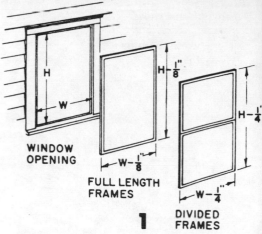

WINDOW OPENING

FULL LENGTH FRAMES

H—$\frac{1}{8}$"

W—$\frac{1}{8}$"

H—$\frac{1}{4}$"

W—$\frac{1}{4}$"

1

DIVIDED FRAMES

A third type of automatic window disappears info the wall at the flip of a switch, carrying the screen into place as it moves. Double-glazed, it can be installed in old or new homes and requires no storage space.

Removable wood storm sash may be installed in the same manner as full window screens. They may be suspended from the top or side of the casing on hinges or other hangers to swing outward for ventilation or other purposes. They may also be fastened with ordinary wood screws, hooks and eyes, or other devices, and sometimes are provided with sliding openings in the bottom rail to admit air when desired. If the sash is hung, rather than fastened in place with screws, care should be taken to obtain a good fit on all sides of the sash. They may be held open, when desired, by means of long hooks inserted in screw eyes or by special devices which are available for the purpose. If storm sash is placed flush with the window casing, it may be supported by loose-pin butt hinges. This will allow removal of the sash by pulling the pin of the hinge. If ordinary hinges will not fit, there are special storm-window hinges designed for any type of frame. Consult your

1. Measure window opening just outside the blind stop around the frame. Storm sash, when completed, should fit against the face of the blind stop. When making divided frames, you may divide the height equally or you may construct your storm sash so that the joining line matches the meeting line of the window rails.

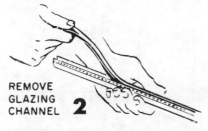

REMOVE GLAZING CHANNEL **2**

2. Pull the plastic channels out of the glazing channels and set them aside for the moment.

3. Mark ends of frame members to length, using the measurements obtained in step 1. Either scribe 45° angles with a combination square at each end of frame members for miters or make a small miter box to aid in mitering the ends.

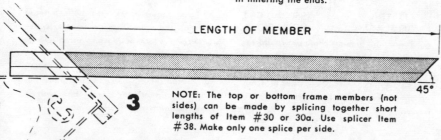

LENGTH OF MEMBER

45°

3

NOTE: The top or bottom frame members (not sides) can be made by splicing together short lengths of Item #30 or 30a. Use splicer Item #38. Make only one splice per side.

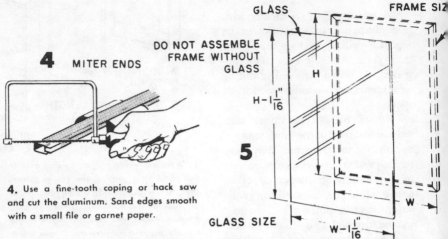

4 MITER ENDS

DO NOT ASSEMBLE FRAME WITHOUT GLASS

GLASS

FRAME SIZE

H

$H-1\frac{1}{16}''$

5

GLASS SIZE

$W-1\frac{1}{16}''$

W

4. Use a fine-tooth coping or hack saw and cut the aluminum. Sand edges smooth with a small file or garnet paper.

5. The width of the glass frame should be $1\frac{1}{16}''$ less than the outside width of the frame and the height should likewise be $1\frac{1}{16}''$ less than the height of the frame. Use single-strength glass for small panes, up to 6 square feet, or double-strength glass for large panes, over 6 square feet.

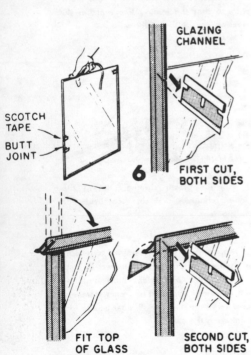

GLAZING CHANNEL

SCOTCH TAPE

BUTT JOINT

6 FIRST CUT, BOTH SIDES

FIT TOP OF GLASS

SECOND CUT, BOTH SIDES

6. Stretch the glazing channel around the edges of the glass, using tape to hold the plastic edging in place. Let the glazing overlap at the corners. Then, using a razor, cut the pieces so that a perfect miter is formed.

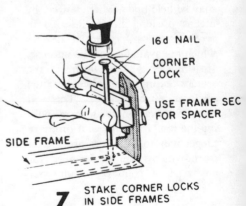

16d NAIL

CORNER LOCK

USE FRAME SECT FOR SPACER

SIDE FRAME

7 STAKE CORNER LOCKS IN SIDE FRAMES

7. Push corner locks into both mitered ends of the side frame members. Stake these corners locks in place by using a large nail (16d size) as a punch. Use a scrap piece of the sash section for a spacing guide. Nail should pierce the metal just behind the edge of the corner lock web to keep the joint from working loose.

hardware dealer as to the type of fastening best fitted for use on your house.

Summer Storage?

Storm windows and doors, if of wood, should be kept well-painted and stored in a dry place when not in use. In some cases, it may not be feasible to suspend a wood rack from the basement ceiling to store windows and doors during the winter. To avoid stacking them, ready-made metal storage racks may be procured which hang from first-floor joists in the basement. They have adjustable hooks on which to hang the window sash, which they engage directly without extra screws or other holding gadgets, fixing them securely and firmly. The sash may be hung sidewise or lengthwise, whichever is most convenient.

How To Make Aluminum Storm Sash

The new Do-It-Yourself Aluminum makes it possible for the handyman to make his own aluminum storm sash. Special formed sections are available and the entire unit can be assembled with ordinary hand tools. If your window area is 9

square feet or less, you can use single full-length storm sash, but with larger windows, it is better to divide the window into two panels.

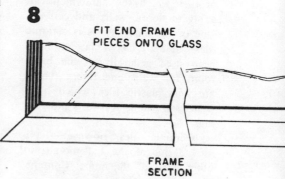

FIT END FRAME
PIECES ONTO GLASS

FRAME
SECTION

8. Assemble end frame members over top and bottom ends of the glass pane and glazing channel. Be sure to center end frame member between edges of glass pane so it will match with side members.

Sketches courtesy of Reynolds Metals Co.

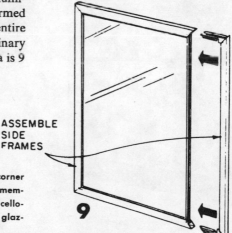

ASSEMBLE
SIDE
FRAMES

9. Add side frame members with corner locks already in place to end frame members. With a razor blade, cut off any cellophane tape protruding beyond the glazing channel.

Tiles

There are many different types of tiles which, the handyman can apply to floors, walls and ceilings. One of the oldest types is ceramic tile—these are baked clay and have been used generally in the bathroom for walls and floors. There are also plastic tiles which have been used mainly for walls and ceilings.

Ceramic tiles, however, have moved out of the bathroom into other parts of the home. Contemporary homes often have kitchen counter work tops and sometimes even living room walls made of ceramic tile. These tiles can be applied with special waterproof adhesive to any suitable smooth surface. No longer is it necessary to apply wire lath and cement to set the tiles in place.

Plastic tiles, which have gained in popularity since the end of World War II, are available in many different colors, sizes and patterns.

Tiled bathrooms have long been common in most homes. However, tile is "growing up" and moving into other rooms of the house.

There are basically two types of plastic tiles. The rigid ones are made of polystyrene; the flexible tiles are usually made of vinyl. Both are applied in somewhat the same manner, although some flexible tiles come already glued. All that is necessary is to moisten the adhesive backs of these self-adhesive tiles and they can then be applied to the wall or floor.

Metal tiles of various kinds also are available. One of the most recent developments is an aluminum tile to which a ceramic coating is bonded at a temperature of from 900° to 1000° F. It can be cut easily and even bent if necessary. The tile is applied with mastic.

For additional information on tiles, see sections on *Ceiling Tiles* and *Floor Tiles*.

Living room walls of textured tile blend perfectly with period or contemporary furnishings. Here striated molded wall tiles are being applied to a living room wall with a special adhesive.

Photograph courtesy of Monsanto Chemical Co.

Ceramic Tile

Ceramic tile is one of the oldest building materials known to man. Its history dates back centuries ago when it was first discovered that clay baked at high temperatures turns into a hard, durable material which is both waterproof and fireproof.

But tile is one of the most modern of materials, too. It is easy for the average handyman to install and will afford a lifetime of constant, rugged use without deterioration. Real tile—that is, tile made from baked ceramic materials—is a per-

manent installation. Its colors never fade. Because of its durability and the absence of any upkeep or remodeling, real tile constitutes a significant economy.

Today, ceramic tile is available to the homemaker in an amazing variety of sizes, shapes, colors, and textures. With a good waterproof adhesive, tile can be readily installed on walls, floors, and countertops.

Technically, there are two main divisions of tile: wall and floor tile. Wall tiles in popular use range from 4¼″ square to 6″x9″ rectangles. They come in either a high glaze or a matt glaze which is a somewhat softer-looking surface.

Floor tiles go from "dots" (11⁄32″ squares) to 9″ squares. Commonly used nominal sizes, though, are the 2″ square, the 1″ square, and the 1″x2″ rectangle. Floor tiles are generally unglazed.

Floor tiles can be broken down into three subdivisions:

• *Ceramic mosaics* are less than six square inches in facial surface.

• *Pavers* are those unglazed floor units measuring six square inches or more in facial surface.

• *Quarries* are made to resist especially severe conditions of weather and wear. They have a strong, dense body which can withstand extremes in temperature.

Technique of Handling Tile

Here are simple instructions for installing ceramic wall and floor tiles.

Virtually all common home surfaces which are true, level, free from moisture and foreign matter are suitable for receiving tile. In any area affected by steam or water, the base surface should be covered with two coats of primer, the second applied at right angles to the first.

All joints and apertures, such as those for bathroom fixtures, should be sealed off with a waterproof tape.

To begin tiling, install the bottom row first. Establish a level line for it. If the floor is not level, make cuts in the bottom row of tiles. If this is done, the top row of the wainscot will be level.

CUTTING

Simply draw a pencil line over the glazed surface parallel to the raised bars on the back of the tile, take an ordinary glass cutter and score the surface along the line. Then place the tile, glazed side up, over a nail and press on either side of the scored line. The tile will part cleanly down the line.

For special cutting, such as around fixtures, use pliers to nip off small chunks of the tile. Then smooth the surface with a Carborundum stone.

Tiles in the bottom row should be "buttered' individually with a small dab of adhesive and then pressed against the wall. Don't put on too much adhesive; it may ooze out of the joints between tiles.

After setting the first row, spread a thin layer of adhesive over several square feet with a saw-tooth trowel. Press the tiles firmly into place with a twisting motion of the hand. Spacing bars on the edges of wall tile will keep the pieces a uni-

Standard
WALL SIZE

and
WALL TRIM PIECES

4¼"

Wall tiles in popular use range from 4¼"x4¼" to 6"x9". They are easily installed not only in the bathroom and kitchen but in any room of the home.

form distance apart.

Once a wall has been tiled, let it set for a day or so that the volatile elements in the adhesive can escape. Then soak the joints between tiles with a wet sponge at least four times at five-minute intervals. A gallon of water is enough for about 50 square feet of tilework. Soaking —thorough soaking—is done so that the tiles will not draw water from the fine cement, called grout, used to fill the spaces between them.

GROUTING AND FINISHING

Commercial grout is a fine white powder. Mix it with water to the consistency of heavy cream. Let it stand for 15 minutes and remix. The mixture can be applied to the tile joints with a sponge, a squeegee or by hand with a pair of rubber gloves. Fill the joints completely.

Going over the job with the end of the handle of a toothbrush will give it a professional finish. It will help to force the grout into the joints, too.

Cleaning is simple. A damp sponge or cloth will remove the excess grout from the face of the tile. A dry cloth should be used for polish.

But before the final polishing, all the grouted joints should be wet down with a sponge several times in the next four or five days, so that they will set properly.

How To Tile Floors

Floor tile is set very much the same way as wall tile. The surface must first be in good condition, firm, perfectly smooth and free from moisture and foreign matter. Floor tile—the smaller unglazed units— come pasted on to paper sheets measuring 1'x2'. Sheets of the tile are pressed into the adhesive spread on the floor, with the papered side uppermost. Let the tile set an hour. Wet the paper slightly with a damp sponge and pull it off the tile. At this time, the adhesive will still be pliant so you can re-align individual tiles if necessary. If you have to walk over the floor now, do so on board or cardboard so your weight will be more equally distributed.

The floor, just like the wall, should be allowed to set for a day before grouting. But floor tile, which has little absorbency, doesn't have to be soaked before grouting.

The grout mixture here is diferent. It should consist of one part waterproof Portland cement and one part finely screened sand. A minimum amount of water should be used in mixing—just enough for workability. Spread this mixture over the floor and work it into the joints with a squeegee. Joints should be completely filled.

All excess mortar should be removed before it begins to harden. Use a burlap cloth at first and then a damp cloth. If necessary, go over it several times until all traces of grout are gone. Then polish with a dry cloth.

The floor must now be cured. Cover it and keep all traffic off it for about three days. If it's necessary to walk on it during that time, put down boards.

Where Tile Can Be Used

Fine installations of ceramic tile by the homemaker have been made

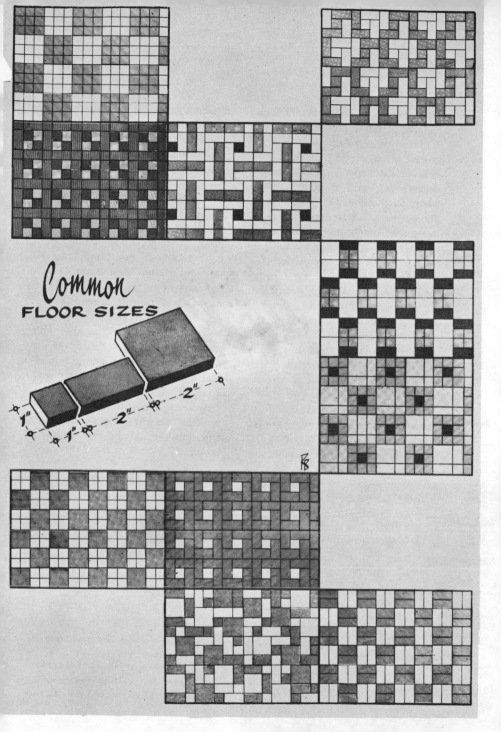

Common
FLOOR SIZES

1"   1"   2"   2"

The most commonly used ceramic floor tiles include 1"x1", 1"x2" and 2"x2". These three sizes can be combined in many different ways and in various color combinations to form an almost infinite number of patterns.

on bathroom walls, floors and countertops; in home laundries where a definitely waterproof surface is required; anywhere in the kitchen, including extensive countertops and splashbacks; and in game rooms where a durable yet permanently decorative finish is desired. Tile is being used increasingly as surfacing for living room floors and in the dining area. The most recent trend is the use of colorful tile on the exterior of homes where a decorative yet weatherproof paneling is desired, such as the exterior overlooking the outdoor terrace.

Terraces, of course, have long been made of tile—quarry tile which is also made from natural ceramic materials. Quarry comes in shades of red, chocolate and buff. Entranceways are also popular sites for quarry tile.

Smaller decorative uses of tile around the home include: fireplace fronts, hearths, windowsills where plants are set, table tops, surfaces of room dividers, radiator tops, stairways, and shelves.

Cleaning Ceramic Tile

All tile made from natural ceramic materials is easy to keep clean. A detergent is best for both floor and wall. For floors, the detergent solution should remain on the surface a few minutes before mopping. Wipe the floor and wall dry with a soft cloth. Most soap leaves a sticky film over tile. This film retains dirt and could make the floor slippery. If such a condition already exists it can be remedied with a wash of commercial scouring powder or kerosene. Waxes, plastic finishes, polishes, emulsions, nonslip coatings and the like are never required.

HOW TO INSTALL CERAMIC TILE

1. Essential material and equipment for installing ceramic tile is shown here. The average bathroom requires from 75 to 100 square feet of wall tile, about 30 square feet of floor tile, and some 50 trim pieces.

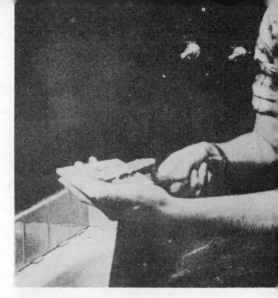

2. All walls must be primed to have waterproof backing. Shower and tub walls must receive two coats, one of which is applied at right angles to the other. Fixture openings and all corners should be sealed with waterproof tape. Cover your tub with newspapers for protection.

3. First tiles are set around the top of the tub. Keep the row level. Small pieces of cardboard can be used for this. These first tiles are "buttered" with a small daub of adhesive and then pressed firmly against the wall.

4. Adhesive is spread over a small area so it will not dry before tiles are installed. Apply only that amount of adhesive which escapes readily from between the edges of your saw toothed trowel.

5. Ceramic tiles for walls measure 4¼"x4¼". Use a twisting motion of the hand to press wall tiles in place. Most wall tiles have self-spacing bars along their edges so that uniform and straight lines are maintained.

6. All tubs need a soap dish and grab bar. This is put in after the row of tiles is installed so that straight and accurate lines are kept. Then pry two tiles loose and cut to fit around the dish.

7. Cutting tile is done with an ordinary glass cutter and a nail. Simply score the glazed surface of the tile, put the back of the tile over a long nail and then apply pressure to either side. A Carbordundum stone is used to smooth all edges.

8. Ordinary pliers can be used to cut tiles for fitting around pipes. Sketch with a pencil on the face of the tile the area to be cut out. Use your pliers to nibble away small chunks. The job doesn't have to be perfect because the flange on the fixture will hide it.

9. Straight lines are a "must." When tiling away from the tub, use a carpenter's level to establish a straight line from which you should tile downwards to the floor. In this way, all tiles that have to be cut to measure are kept next to the floor.

10. If the floor is not level, you may have to cut each bottom tile to size. This is done by marking the back of a tile and then transferring the mark to the face of another tile. Use the same technique when cutting for a corner.

11. Let tiles set for a day so that volatile elements can escape from the adhesive. Then, before grouting, soak the spaces between tiles thoroughly with water. You'll need about four gallons for the average bathroom. Soaking is done to prevent the tiles from drawing water from the grout mixture.

12. Grout is rubbed into the tile joints with a sponge, squeegee or a pair of rubber gloves. Grount can not harm the tile face. Be sure to force it deep into the joints. Excess grout is quickly washed away with water.

13. FLOOR TILE, called ceramic mosaics, comes in sheets and is installed just by pressing the sheets in place over the adhesive. Paper backs are removed by soaking with a moderately wet sponge. Because floor tile has no absorbence, it does not have to be soaked with water before grouting.

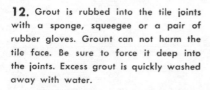

14. Cleaning grout from tile, wall or floor, is accomplished with water and sponge. Then wipe the tiles dry with a soft cloth. This will accentuate the fresh glamour of glazed tiles and the rich textured tones of floor tile.

Marble Tile

1. Adhesive is spread on the wall surface with a notched trowel, covering only the amount of wall space which can be tiled in an hour's time.

2. No adhesive is placed on the back of the tile. The Markwa marble tile is pressed into the adhesive firmly and twisted into place to prevent build up of adhesive on the edges of the tile.

Marble tiles are available to be applied to any wall surface that has been properly prepared. The marble tiles are installed in a man-

ner somewhat the same as ceramic tiles. Here is the technique of handling marble, in this case Vermont Pavonazzo.

3. A string is used to space the marble tiles correctly, row after row. The string can be removed after all the tiles are set or row by row.

4. To cut marble tiles to shape, it is advisable to use a tile setter's saw to make the straight parts of the cut.

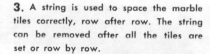

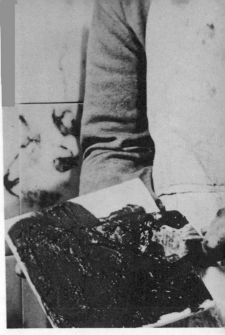

5. To complete the shaping of the tile cut, use a tile setter's clipper along the curved edges to produce an even, smooth cut.

6. It is possible to set marble tiles with mortar. In this case, each tile is buttered with mortar applied with a trowel.

Photographs courtesy of Vermont Marble Co.

7. The mortar-buttered tile is placed into position and tamped into place securely with the handle of the trowel.

8. After all the tiles have been set into place either with adhesive or mortar, all joints are filled with white Portland non-staining cement mixed with water to the consistency of thin cream and spread on with the hand.

9. The excess grouting cement is easily washed off the marble surface with a damp sponge. Do this shortly after the grout is applied and before it has had a chance to dry solidly on the face of the marble.

Plastic Tile

1. Parallel and plumb lines are as essential when installing plastic tiles as they are for ceramic tiles. In figuring a guide line for height, be sure to leave not less than a half-tile cut above the tub.

2. Spread the mastic downward with a wavy motion using a notched trowel held at right angles to the wall. Apply enough mastic for three hours' work—not more. Have mastic at room temperature.

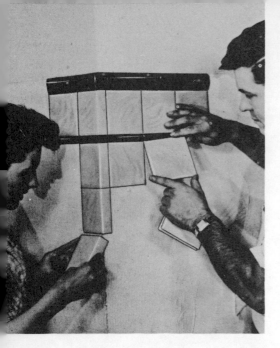

3. If there is a prominent corner in the bathroom, you can start to tile from that point. Note how corner piece is molded so that metal or rubber trim is not necessary at the corner.

4. Putting on the base tile is easy. These special cove pieces are applied over the wall tiles after spreading a layer of mastic over the bottom tiles with a notched trowel.

5. Where tile has to be cut to fit around a pipe or around the curved portion of the tub, you can draw the pattern on the tile and then cut the plastic tile with a coping saw to the exact shape.

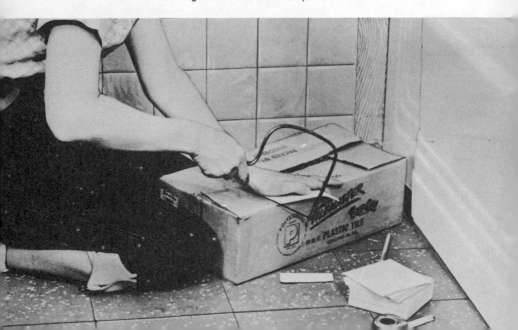

6. Inside corner trim is easy to set into place. It is installed after the rest of the tiles have been glued to the wall. Edges of corner trim are feathered so that they do not project from wall.

7. After the tile has been installed, the excess mastic is cleaned off with a soft cloth moistened with tile cleaner. Soap or detergent and water can be used in about a week or 10 days.

Photographs courtesy of Tilemaster Corp.

Vinyl Tiles

Flexible plastic tiles made of vinyl are available in a variety of colors and textures. They are made in two types: one is applied with a

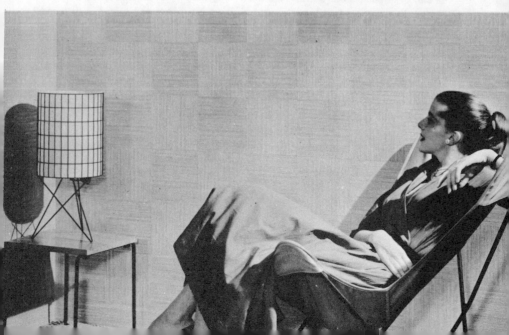

mastic or adhesive and the other is self-adhesive.

The vinyl tiles are applied with mastic and set in place in a manner similar to the rigid plastic tiles made of polystyrene. The self-adhesive type is applied as shown in the accompanying illustrations.

1. Check the walls and/or the ceiling to see that the surface is prepared for the tiles. All wallpaper, water or oil paint that is loose or scaly should be removed. Fill all holes and cracks with patching plaster and let dry.

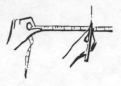

2. Find the center of the wall or ceiling by measuring as you would for floor tiles. For how-to see the sections on Ceiling Tiles and Floor Tiles in other volumes of this encyclopedia.

3. Place the tile with the adhesive side up on a stack of newspapers. Dip a brush, an old, clean paint brush will do—into a bowl of clean water and apply a thin even coat of water to the adhesive of the tile. First apply it across and then up and down; the adhesive will whiten when the water is applied uniformly.

4. Place one corner of the first tile at the center mark and position it horizontally, or diagonally if a diamond pattern is desired. Press down with a wad of cloth and make certain that all the edges as well as the rest of the tile are firmly bonded. If the tile does not grab, either too much or too little water was used. Remove it and let it dry for a few seconds; then apply fresh water and set it into place.

5. Continue to add tiles, setting the grain or texture at the desired angle. Continue to work up and down from the center mark until parts of a tile are needed to complete the job. Apply all the full-size tiles before you start to apply the pieces.

6. At the ends or edges of walls and ceilings, part tiles may be needed. Mark off on an actual tile the size needed and cut, using a straight edge to draw the line and a scissors to cut. Then apply the tiles.

7. A wall irregularity may cause hairline seams between tiles to show. You can obtain colored filler and fill in the seam between the tiles. Follow the directions on the can. Within three or four days after the tiles have been installed, you can wash the wall tiles with soap and water. That's the only maintenance they need.

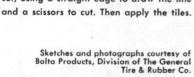

Types of Buffs and Compounds for Various Materials

MATERIAL	FOR CUTTING		FOR COLORING	
	Wheel	Compound	Wheel	Compound
Iron, Steel, Hard Metals	Spiral Sewed	Emery or Stainless	Cushion	Stainless
Brass, Copper, Aluminum, Soft Metals	Spiral Sewed	Tripoli	Cushion or Loose	Stainless or Rouge
Brass or Copper Plate		DO NOT CUT	Loose, Cushion or Flannel	Tripoli or Rouge
Solid and Plated Gold or Silver		DO NOT CUT	Flannel	Natural Rouge or Jeweler's Rouge
Nickel or Chrome Plate	Spiral Sewed	Stainless	Cushion or Loose	Stainless
Plastics	Cushion or Loose	Tripoli or Stainless	Loose	Stainless

How-To Fire Fighting Guide

SODA ACID

PUMP

GAS CARTRIDGE

FOAM

Fire Extinguisher Facts

TYPE	KINDS OF FIRE	HOW TO START	DISCHARGE
Soda Acid	Class A	Turn over	
Water Pump	Class A	Pump by hand	For 2½ gal. size
Gas Cartridge	Class A and small Class B	Turn over and pump	30'–40' 50–55 sec.
Foam	Class A and Class B	Turn over	
Carbon Dioxide	Class B	Pull pin and open valve	6'–8', about 42 sec. (15-lb. size)
	and	Turn handle, pump by hand	20'–30' 45 sec. (1-qt. size)
Vaporizing Liquid	Class C		
Dry Chemical	and sometimes Class A	Pull pin and open valve (or press lever), then squeeze nozzle valve	About 14' 22–25 sec. (30-lb. size)

Note: Do not use water-base extinguishers on electrical fires.

CARBON DIOXIDE

VAPORIZING LIQUID

DRY CHEMICAL

Upholsterer's Hammer

This is a double-pointed hammer, often with one end magnetized. The head is about 5½" long and the faces at the ends are about ½" in diameter. This small hammer is convenient to reach places where the conventional claw hammer cannot be used.

Upholstering a Chair

When the covering of a chair gets torn or worn thin, when the springs give out or the frame cracks, it's time to start an upholstery project. One of the most common upholstery jobs done in the home is making kitchen chairs look new.

Accompanying this article are two how-to series. If the padding or foam rubber is still sound, all that's needed is to add new material. Here you will find the methods to follow when using vinyl plastic or fabric.

However, if the padding is gone, it must be replaced. You can follow the technique shown here.

If the frame of the chair is damaged, it is simple to repair. For information, see section on *Furniture Finishing*.

Recovering a Kitchen Chair

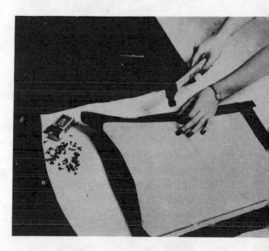

1. To recover a kitchen or dinette chair with a plastic material such as Boltaflex, remove the old covering and use this as a pattern to cut the material. Then, begin tacking in the middle of the straightest seat edge, working out to about 1" from the corners. Tacks should be placed about 1" apart and at least ¼" from the edge of the chair.

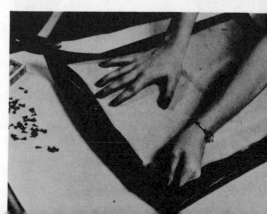

2. When all the straight edges have been tacked, fold the corners neatly and tack them down into place. Drive the tacks straight without sinking the heads into the material.

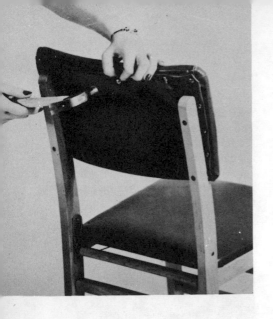

3. After finishing the seat and back, set them into place on the chair frame. The chair back is covered in a manner similar to seats. Fold the material over along the edges so that a smooth, neat edge is obtained. Use decorative tacks to hold this piece of vinyl in place.

Photographs courtesy of Bolta Products, Division of General Tire & Rubber Co.

New Look for an Old Chair

It has been said that nearly 8 million dinette chairs are reupholstered every year. Of these, more than half require new batting or padding. While latex rubber is often used, many handymen find a material such as Tufflex easy to handle. It comes in a roll ¾" thick, 16½" wide and 66" long—enough to cover four dinette chairs.

1. After unscrewing the seat and back from the chair, remove the old covering and cushioning material. An old screwdriver will do the job.

2. Use chair seat as a pattern and trace outline on Tufflex. Mark guide slightly larger to provide padding to wrap around the seat edges.

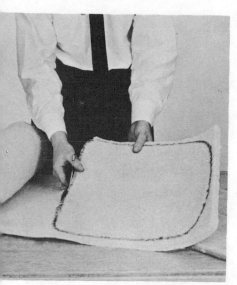

3. Ordinary household scissors can be used to cut this material. It is easy to obtain a straight and neat edge.

4. Put chair seat and cushioning material on the upholstery material; cut, leaving 4" extra on all the sides. Any material can be used.

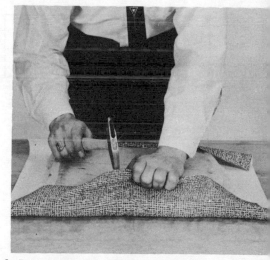

5. Place new seat covering finished side down. Center base and cushioning material and tack covering to underside of the chair base.

6. Turn chair seat to opposite side, pull covering up tightly around the edges and tack at center first.

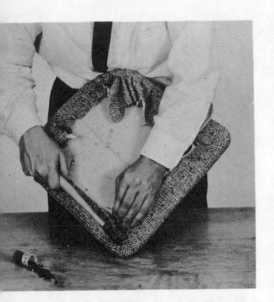

7. Tack corners last, pulling the material tight before each tack is applied for a trim appearance.

8. Make the bottom side look neat by trimming off the excess of the covering material with a scissors.

Photographs courtesy of Wood Conversion Co.

Upholstering with No-Sag Springs

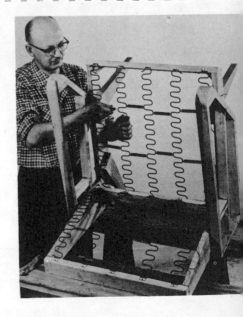

In place of conventional coil springs which require some skill and a good deal of work to tie together properly, springs of the No-Sag type are designed for easy home application or speedy commercial use. The springs come in two different sizes or gages. The 11 gage is

Cross ties are used to join the springs. If additional ties are needed, twine can be used. The springs should be covered with burlap or a strong fabric.

No-Sag springs are installed with special metal clips at each end. Note that spring forms a shallow arc between the front and back of this sofa.

used for small chair backs or dinette chairs, while the 9 gage (the heavier spring) is used for medium and large chairs as well as sofas and daybeds.

The springs are installed with a shallow arc so that the center is slightly higher than either end. The ends of the springs are held to the frame with special metal clips. Af-ter the springs are in place, cross ties—helical springs—are used to connect the springs together. Twine may also be used where necessary.

Burlap or a strong fabric is ap-plied over the springs and nailed to the frame. Over this a minimum of 2" of cotton, rubberized curled hair or foam rubber should be used as a padding.

How-To Guide To Flush Tank Repairs

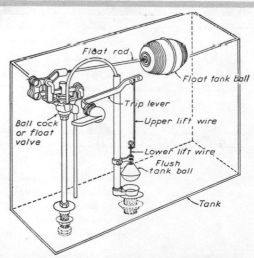

Flush valve mechanism for filling flush tank.

Vise Clamps

To protect the work from dents and scratches, false jaws are often set over the jaws of a vise. They can be made of brass, copper tempered hardboard, plastic or aluminum, and sometimes wood. Wood jaws, as a rule, are permanently attached to the vise whereas the others are easily removed and used only when needed.

How-To Join Wall Edges

Here are four of the most commonly used wall joints (left to right): butt, V joint, beveled edge joint and open bevel.

Space is left between the panels for expansion and contraction and this opening is covered. Here are four techniques you can use (left to right): batten of the same material as the wall panel, batten made of wood trim, batten of half-round and metal snap-on molding.

If you wish to try your hand at some others, here are additional ways to form a wall panel joint (left to right): wood insert, molding insert, wood inlay and a metal divider strip.

Wainscot

The paneling or lining of the interior walls to the height of a chair rail is called wainscoting. While wood is generally used, the same effect is created with wallpaper, vinyl plastic sheeting, cork, tiles or, in fact, any material. The molding at the top of the wainscoting material is called the wainscoting cap.

This method of interior wall finishing is often used not only for its decorating effect but also because of its practical value. A durable, washable material over the lower section of the wall makes it easier to maintain, especially in the kitchen or dining room.

Wallpapering

Not only are there many colors and patterns of wallpaper from which to make your selection, but there are also several basic types.

• There are special fabric-backed papers that are durable and easy to clean with a damp cloth.

• Plastic-impregnated papers are also easily cleaned and can be used in any heavy traffic area of the home.

• Textured wallpapers are available for a three-dimensional effect; they are made to resemble brick, etched wood, straw, burlap, split bamboo. They are waterproof and scrubbable.

• Ready-pasted wallpaper can be applied easily; just dip the paper into water and hang. There is no mixing or application of paste.

• Standard wallpapers are made in a variety of finishes; some are washable and some are sun- and color-fast.

Wallpaper is easily applied by the handyman or, for that matter, the handywoman. In fact, a large number of women apply wallpaper —more women apply this type of wall covering than any other material. Wallpaper can be applied over almost any old wall surface; it is necessary, however, to condition the old wall.

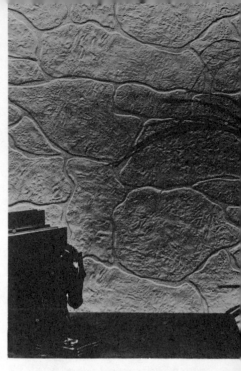

Etched wood is a three-dimensional textured wallpaper which can be painted any color you wish.

Another textured, three-dimensional wallpaper resembles fieldstone.

Washable, fabric-backed wallpapers are available in many different patterns. Here a wine basket pattern has been combined with knotty pine wallpaper to give provincial charm to the dinette.

Preparing the Walls for Paper

Here's how to condition an old wall.

• If you have old wallpaper—the old paper, if firm, makes a satisfactory base for the new. All seams must be sanded smooth. If the paper is loose, it must be removed. You can get it off by soaking with warm water and then scraping with a putty knife, or you can use special chemical wallpaper removers. Some wallpaper and hardware stores have special wallpaper steamers to help in the removal of old paper. The cleaned wall or old paper must be sized before the new paper is applied.

• Wallboard and plasterboard walls—if you have dry wall construction, all joints must be taped or filled with patching plaster. Small indentations need not be filled as the paper will cover them. The entire surface must be sized.

• Plywood walls—all joints between the plywood panels must be filled and the entire surface given a coat of shellac to keep the grain from raising. After the shellac is dry, size the wall.

• Rough plaster and interior stucco—sand the wall with coarse sandpaper and remove all the high spots. Although paper can be applied over the wall, ignoring the depressions, it is better to make the wall fairly smooth. Otherwise, the imperfect undersurface will mar an attractive papering job.

• Calcimined or whitewashed walls—it is necessary to wash the walls with warm water and a sponge to remove the calcimine or whitewash. Fill all cracks and crevices with patching plaster. Size the walls.

• Painted walls—if the walls have been painted with a semi-gloss or enamel, it is necessary to remove the gloss. This can be done chemically with special wall preparers or wash the surface with 1 part ammonia to 6 parts water; then rinse and allow to dry. Any painted wall must be sized before wallpapering.

Techniques of Wallpapering

The first job you have, after deciding upon the wallpaper you wish, is to determine how much is needed. A roll of wallpaper contains about 35 square feet. But a word of caution: some companies prepare their wallpaper in double-rolls (common with papers 18" to 20" wide), while others use triple-rolls (for paper about 28" wide).

While any dealer will help you determine how many rolls you need if you give him the length, width and height of the room measurements, here's an easy way for you to do it:

• measure the length and width of the room
• add these two figures together and then multiply by 2
• multiply this figure by the height of the room
• divide this figure by 30 to get the number of single rolls needed; this allows for normal waste in matching patterns
• count the number of windows and doors in the room and deduct 2 rolls for every 3 openings, either doors or windows
• add 1 roll for safety.

After you have prepared the wall surfaces to be papered, follow the steps shown in the accompanying photographs.

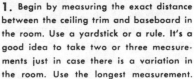

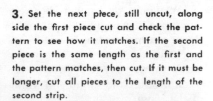

1. Begin by measuring the exact distance between the ceiling trim and baseboard in the room. Use a yardstick or a rule. It's a good idea to take two or three measurements just in case there is a variation in the room. Use the longest measurement.

2. Use a large table for cutting. If you use a solid or small pattern wallpaper add 4" to the wall measurement. Otherwise, add 8" to the room height. This is necessary to permit the proper matching of the pattern.

3. Set the next piece, still uncut, along side the first piece cut and check the pattern to see how it matches. If the second piece is the same length as the first and the pattern matches, then cut. If it must be longer, cut all pieces to the length of the second strip.

4. It is necessary to obtain a perfectly plumb line as a guide to hang the first strip. Set your guide line about 2" less than the width of the paper from any corner, door or window. Use a plumb line or a string with a screwdriver or spoon to obtain the guide line.

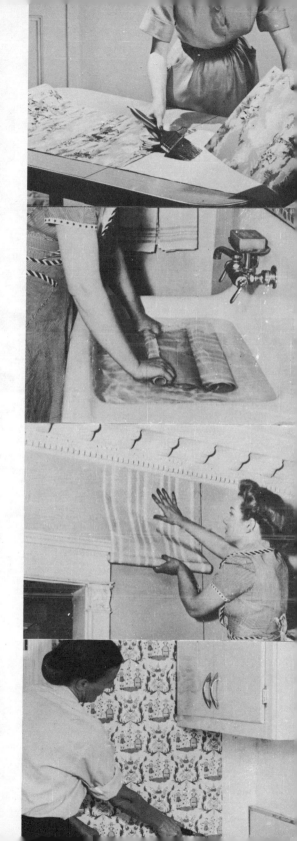

5. Center the first piece on a table (you might want to use newspapers to protect the surface) and apply the thoroughly-mixed wallpaper paste to the back of the paper with a brush. Fold back the ends as shown; this makes it easier to handle the sheet in order to set it into place.

Photographs courtesy of Standard Coated Products, Inc., The Wallpaper Council and United Wallpaper, Inc.

6. If you have purchased pre-pasted paper, use the sink, bathtub or a large basin and soak the paper in moderately warm water. Roll the sheet loosely while it's under water to make certain that all the underside with adhesive on it gets the proper amount of water.

7. Set the first strip with the top flush against the ceiling trim and with one edge along the guide line on the wall. Press the top into place by hand and then unroll or unfold the paper so that the edge continues along the guide line.

8. When it is necessary to trim the excess off along an edge because of a door or cabinet, or along the baseboard, the same technique is used. One easy way to do the job is to purchase a cutting knife that uses single-edge razor blades for cutting purposes.

9. Another way to cut off the excess is to use a pair of scissors. The first step is to score the line with the blades of the scissors. Then life the paper carefully off the wall and cut with the scissors. The razor blade method is, however, quicker and easier.

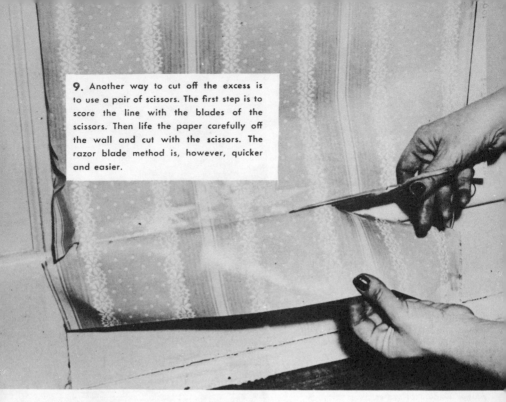

10. A smoothing brush is used to press the wallpaper flat against the wall. You can purchase this brush as part of a wallpapering kit or you may be able to rent one at the wallpaper or hardware store where you have purchased the paper.

11. After applying the paste to the second strip, hang it by aligning the pattern. It may be necessary to underlap both the ceiling and baseboard moldings to do this. However, if you have cut the strips long enough, there should be no problem.

12. For a professional-looking job, butt the edges of the paper by pressing them together. There's little need to worry about tearing the paper as you do the job.

13. Around the tops of doors and windows, use short strips—the actual height plus the amount of paper necessary to match the pattern. However, always allow about 3" to 4" extra so that you can obtain a perfect seam along the top and bottom.

14. The excess of the small strips is cut in the same manner as the long strips along the baseboard. With a razor-cutting tool, this is a one-step operation and it is possible to get a straight, smooth line along the bottom and top edges.

15. If you have electrical switch or outlet boxes in the wall, the covers should be removed before the paper is applied. After the paper is brushed on, the box will project through the paper. Tear or cut off the excess paper around the box

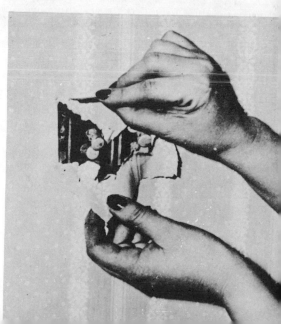

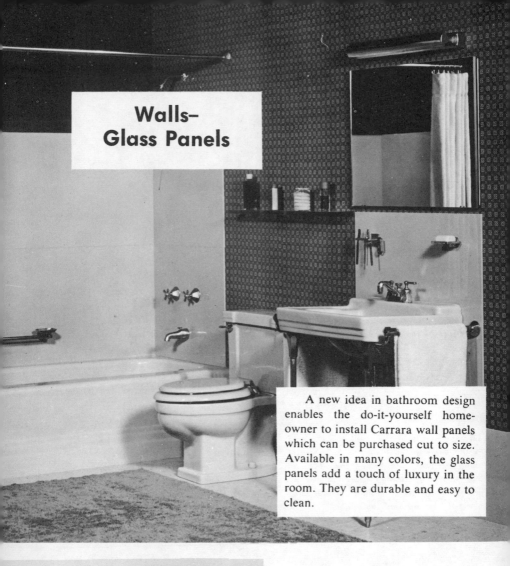

Walls–
Glass Panels

A new idea in bathroom design enables the do-it-yourself home-owner to install Carrara wall panels which can be purchased cut to size. Available in many colors, the glass panels add a touch of luxury in the room. They are durable and easy to clean.

1. Just three steps are necessary prior to ordering the glass. Measure the back wall along the tub length, measure the base of the room and make cardboard patterns of the location of plumbing outlets. It is best to remove the plumbing fixtures when making this installation.

2. A cardboard template is made to provide a pattern for the dealer to drill holes for the tub fittings through the Carrara panel. Place template over fittings to check the hole alignment. Make a similar template for the sink fittings.

3. Using a trowel, apply the mastic or adhesive to the panels in a thin coat with serrations made by the trowel to allow for expansion when setting, or apply the mastic as strips running in both directions.

4. Apply a thick coating of the mastic along the rim of the tub. Then, place the bottom back Carrara panel against the back wall. Apply pressure against the glass to give proper adhesion between the glass and the wall. Use a level to make certain that the panel is plumb.

5. Before installing the end panel, the edge which butts against the back panel should be buttered with pointing compound to insure a waterproof seal.

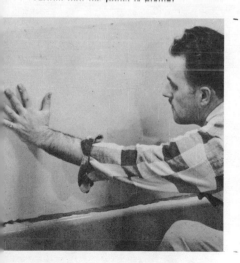

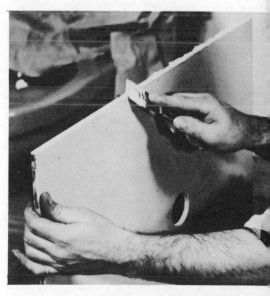

6. Set the end panel into place in the same manner as the back panel, remembering to apply a thick coating of mastic along the rim of the tub.

7. After buttering the ends of the upper back glass panel, set it into place over the lower panel. The upper end panels are installed in a similar manner with pointing compound along the edges.

8. The base panels along the floor in the bathroom are applied after coating the back of the panel with mastic. Always use a level to make certain that the panels are plumb.

9. Mounting plates for the fixtures are fastened with machine screws to small threaded ferrules inserted in the glass at the dealer's shop. The soap and grab fixture is attached to the mounting plate with screws.

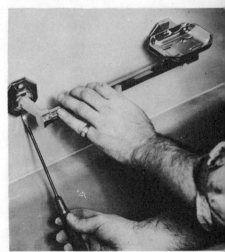

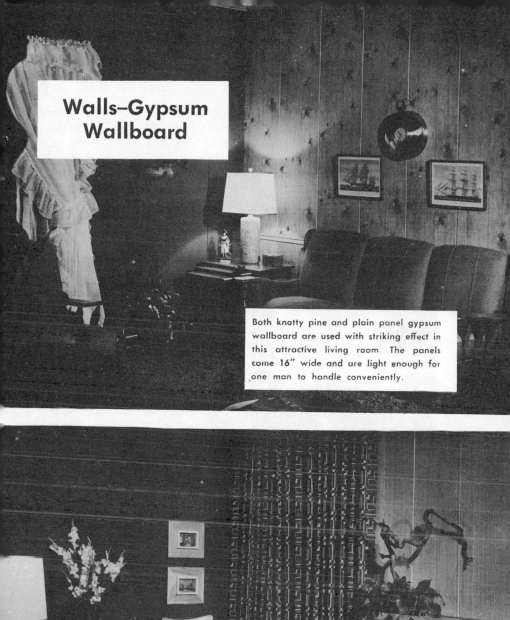

Walls–Gypsum Wallboard

Both knotty pine and plain panel gypsum wallboard are used with striking effect in this attractive living room. The panels come 16" wide and are light enough for one man to handle conveniently.

One of the most widely used wall materials today is gypsum wallboard. The newer panel type appeals to handymen because of its application and because it does not require joint treatment. The panels, ⅜" thick, are 16" wide and come in lengths of 8', 9' and 10'. Furthermore, the panel gypsum wallboard is available in simulated wood grain as well as a striated pattern; neither of them requires any additional decoration.

In any remodelling project, the gypsum panels can be applied over old surfaces of gypsum wallboard or plaster or nailed directly to the studs. The techniques of working with gypsum panels are shown in the accompanying photographs. The handyman working with gypsum for the first time will find that he will obtain better results in a shorter time if he uses these 16" panels instead of the conventional 4'x8' panels.

Two different types of spreaders are used to apply Perf-a-Tape cement to Sheetrock panels. One is a three-notch spreader used for the 16" panels and the other is a one-notch spreader used to apply cement to panels less than 16" in width.

Photographs courtesy of United States Gypsum Co.

1. Plan the layout of the 16" panels before you start to work. In all cases, joints in the face layer must occur between the underlying supports. If a large window, door or fireplace is a wall feature, center the panels or the joints so that as balanced an effect as possible is achieved.

2. On the other hand, if the wall does not have an opening to feature, arrange the gypsum panels so the two end panels are approximately the same width. Try to avoid narrow strips because they may be difficult to install. It is a good idea to measure and plan each of the walls before you apply the panels.

3. To start the job, remove all trim along baseboard and ceiling. Then remove the wrapping from all panel bundles and place each panel face down in a neat pile. You can set them on the floor but it's easier to work at sawhorse height. Keep the work in the center of the room; it's easier to reach all four walls.

4. The panels can be applied with cement which should be mixed in a clean metal container—a 5-gallon paint can will do. Use about 22 pints of water for 25 lbs. of cement. Mix vigorously until mixture is smooth and lump-free. You need about 60 lbs. of cement for each 1,000 square feet of wall.

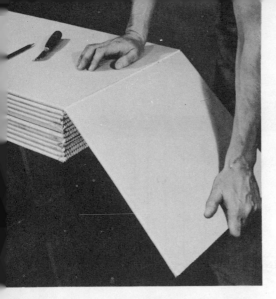

5. To cut panels, cut the face paper and edges with a sharp knife. Then snap the board as shown, breaking the core. Then cut paper on the underside and snap board up for a clean break. Extra pressure on the knife is necessary for cutting paper of wood-grained panels. Use straight edge as guide when cutting.

6. To spread the cement, place the three-notch spreader at the end of the top panel. Fill spreader about half full with cement. Using the little finger of your left hand as a guide on the edge of the panel, draw the spreader blade to within 12" of the other end of the panel, leaving 3 sharp, firm ridges of cement.

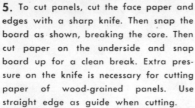

7. Without moving the spreader, shove the top panel back about 10" and then continue to spread the cement on the top board and off onto the underlying board, as shown. The top panel is now ready for application. Then spread cement on second panel, reversing the direction of the spreader.

8. On panels narrower than 16" it is best to use the one-notch spreader. One ribbon of cement is sufficient on sizes up to 6" in width. For panels from 7" to 10" in width, two ribbons of cement should be applied to the back edge of the panel. Above 10", you can treat in the same manner as the full panel.

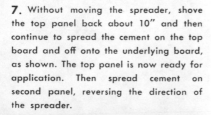

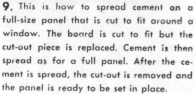

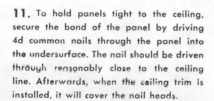

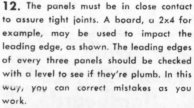

9. This is how to spread cement on a full-size panel that is cut to fit around a window. The board is cut to fit but the cut-out piece is replaced. Cement is then spread as for a full panel. After the cement is spread, the cut-out is removed and the panel is ready to be set in place.

10. Having determined the layout and corresponding width of the first panel, start the wall application by placing the first panel at the corner. Plumb the wall first with a carpenter's level. Press panel lightly against the undersurface to assure an even adhesion of the panel to the wall.

11. To hold panels tight to the ceiling, secure the bond of the panel by driving 4d common nails through the panel into the undersurface. The nail should be driven through reasonably close to the ceiling line. Afterwards, when the ceiling trim is installed, it will cover the nail heads.

12. The panels must be in close contact to assure tight joints. A board, a 2x4 for example, may be used to impact the leading edge, as shown. The leading edges of every three panels should be checked with a level to see if they're plumb. In this way, you can correct mistakes as you work.

13. Within 15 minutes after the panels have been applied, surfaces of all adjoining panels, except the last two applied, should be levelled by impacting the joints gently with the width of a 2x4. Over uneven surfaces, it may be necessary to nail an edge temporarily in position with 4d finishing nails, as shown.

14. For a true fit at a corner, it is advisable to scribe the corner on the piece to be cut as a pattern. Measure the width, top and bottom, and use the pattern for marking and cutting the corner panel as required. Few corners are perfectly plumb so that adjustment must be made with any wall material.

Walls
Plastic-Surfaced
Hardboard

Photographs courtesy of Armstrong Cork Co.

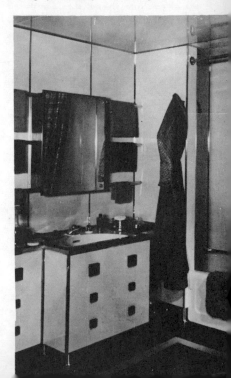

Plastic-surfaced hardboard is available in many patterns and colors. It also comes in different forms —panels, planks and squares. Because it is easily cleaned, durable and waterproof, it is highly favored in kitchens and bathrooms. The wood-grains, however, can be used anywhere in the house.

Plastic-surfaced hardboard, like Monowall, makes an attractive bathroom easy to keep clean.

This striking kitchen is finished in colorful, easy-to-clean plastic-surfaced hardboard.

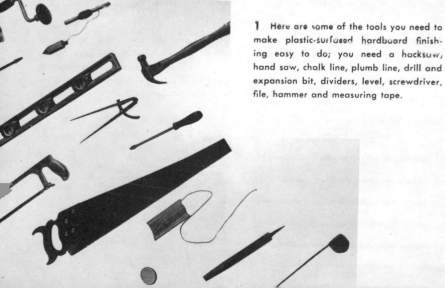

1 Here are some of the tools you need to make plastic-surfaced hardboard finishing easy to do; you need a hacksaw, hand saw, chalk line, plumb line, drill and expansion bit, dividers, level, screwdriver, file, hammer and measuring tape.

2. Start to clear the room by removing the moldings—both the baseboard and ceiling trim. For details see sections on **Baseboard** and **Ceiling Trim**. A floor or glazier's chisel and pinch bar make this an easy job.

3. If you are working in the bathroom, you'll find it convenient to remove **some** of the fixtures, like the sink. Make certain that the water is shut off before you start to work.

4. So that you will know where to place the unit after the wall material has been installed, use a plumb line and measure all distances carefully. Mark these dimensions down where they won't get lost.

5. Hardboard can be installed over walls that are reasonably level and solid. If cracked plaster is loose, better knock it out. If the surface is firm, you need take no further action.

6. Knock out the loose plaster until you come down to the lath boards or wire lath. Chip away only the loose part—do not damage the remainder of the sound wall.

7. You can use wood to shim the wall out so that it is level. It may be necessary to use several thicknesses of thin wood or combine plywood or boards until you obtain the proper surface.

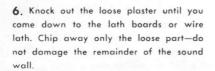

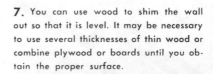

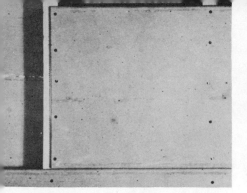

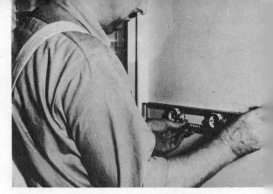

8. If you're working on a new wall, it is best to provide a base for the hardboard surfacing. Here Temlok lath is nailed directly over the studs so that Monowall can be applied.

9. Make all measurements carefully along the wall using a plumb line and a level. Plan for the most economical use of the panels whether you set the 4'x8' panels horizontally or vertically on the wall to be covered.

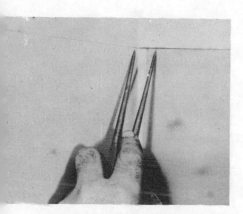

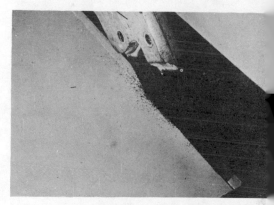

10. Most room corners are not perfectly plumb. Therefore, set a piece of the wall material next to the corner and with a pair of dividers, trace the exact outline of the corner on the wall material.

11. Cut the plastic-surfaced hardboard with a hand saw for straight lines or a compass or coping saw for irregular edges.

12. Panels are always cut with the good face up. After the panel has been cut, turn it over and trim off the rough edge with a block plane or a sharp knife.

13. If you have to fit a panel over projections in the wall, like faucet handles, paint the edges and then press the panel against the wall as if it were going into place. The wet paint will show the exact location for cut outs for the faucet handles.

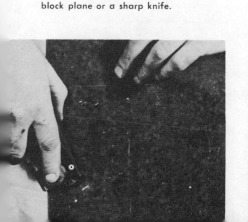

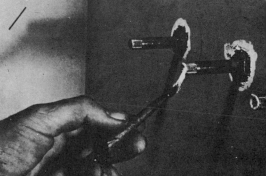

14. The painted edges will leave their mark. Through the back of the panel, drive a nail from back to front in the exact center of the mark.

15. Turn the panel with the good face up and drill the necessary holes through the panel. It is essential to make all cuts or holes with the good side of the panel up.

16. Special metal channel can be used along the edges, at corners and between the individual panels. These channels are available in chrome as well as matching the plastic-surfaced hardboards. Apply metal molding to wall with adhesive.

17. Apply a thin sealer coat of panel-board cement on the wall with a notched trowel. This technique is used where the hardboard is glued to the wall.

18. Then with a notched trowel, spread the cement on the back of the hardboard panel as shown. Apply only as much adhesive as will remain after the notches are passed over the adhesive.

19. Press the Monowall firmly against the wall, making certain that it sits inside the channel used as a base. The channel is needed around a bathtub but need not be used elsewhere.

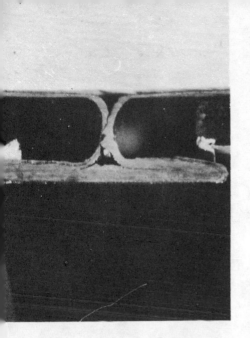

20. A connector channel should be used between two adjoining panels of Monowall. The panels should be cut ⅛" short to allow for dimensional change in the material.

21. If the hardboard panels are being applied over rough plaster, it is best to apply the cement in large globs spaced about 4" apart so that the cement will spread when the panel is pressed into place.

22. Now you can install the decorative trim to conceal the edges. Cap and base molding in matching or contrasting colors can be nailed in place.

Photographs courtesy Armstrong Cork Co.

23. With the proper wall fastener, re-install the fixtures in the room. A fiber plug in the home can be used with a screw, or special solid wall fasteners can be used instead.

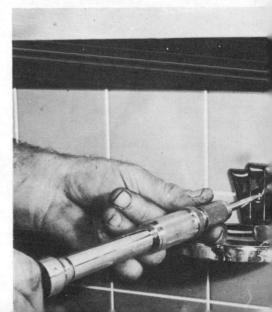

Other Techniques for Applying Plastic-Surfaced Hardboard

Plastic-surfaced hardboard is also available in planks and squares which can be attached to any solid, level wall surface with special clips.

Wood-grained pattern on these 16" square blocks can be set in a basket-weave pattern on the wall. The tongue-and-groove joints conceal the fastening clips.

Photographs courtesy of Marlite Wall Panels, Marsh Wall Products, Inc.

Also available in planks, 16" wide and 8' long, this plastic-surfaced hardboard can be installed over old walls or furring strips using special clips which are concealed by the joints.

After the planks or blocks have been installed, it's a simple job to add a baseboard and ceiling trim to produce a finished effect. Regular wood trim can be used or there are moldings made to match the plastic hardboard.

Window

There are many different types of windows used in homes today.

1. Double-hung windows— perhaps these are the most familiar type of window for they have been used for centuries in homes. Essentially, this type of window is divided into an upper and lower sash or sections that slide up and down past each other. The glass in each sash is sometimes divided by muntin bars into a number of small sections, called "lights."

2. Casement windows—these are windows in which the movable ventilators are hinged to the frame at either side and swing out or in to provide 100% ventilation.

3. Awning windows—this type of window has a series of sections that swing outward from the bottom in the fashion of an awning. They are sometimes controlled by means of a rotating crank handle. In some types, all the sections open or close at the same time; in others, the individual sections are controlled separately.

4. Projected windows—these have movable ventilators, called vents, which project outward or inward in a horizontal plane. Usually, one section swings outward while the other swings inward.

5. Horizontal sliding windows —originally designed for contem-

PROJECTED VENTS

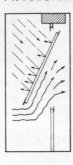

WindoWall vents swing out at the bottom and down from the top. They form protective canopies over the open window, shedding rain and snow while admitting the fresh air.

The WindoWall Unit is perfect for the living room, dining room, for enclosing a porch, or for any location where a truly modern picture window is desired. It provides both an expansive view of the outdoors and an opening portion for ventilation. The units are available in types and sizes for various requirements. Mullions may be used to combine units in extra large wall openings.

TILT-IN VENTS

Basement Window vents swing in at the top to deflect drafts upward and shed the rain.

Basement Windows are designed for use in openings of concrete or cinder block walls, as found in most of today's basements. Also fit other construction. Used over workbench in garage.

Utility Windows also swing in, deflect drafts and shed rain.

Utility Windows are used in basements (especially the high downhill side), in basement areaways, garages and farm buildings.

Sketches courtesy of Detroit Steel
Products Co.

SWINGING VENTS

Fenestra casement vents swing out on bronze bushed hinges to catch the breeze and deflect it in. Casements with two vents catch breezes from three directions —right, left and head-on.

Used in living room, dining room, kitchen, bedroom — throughout the home—wherever such conveniences and benefits as more daylight, superior weathertightness, modern design beauty and controlled fresh-air ventilation are desired. They are ideal for use over furniture or over the kitchen sink with the easily-operated sill adjuster permitting effortless opening. Ideal also as flanking windows for fixed picture windows.

PROJECTED VENTS

Projected-out vents form canopies over the openings, shedding rain. Projected-in vents shed rain while deflecting drafts upward. Window permits ventilation in bad weather.

Projected windows can be used in any room of the home. They are specially desirable for the bedroom, where they may be left open at night to furnish draft-free fresh air without worrying about the damage to walls and furnishings that would result from a sudden rainstorm. They are well suited for the kitchen, too, permitting ventilation all day, rain or shine. Excellent for breezeways, terraces.

porary ranch-type homes, sliding windows get their name from the fact that the movable sash, or glass itself in some styles, slides horizontally from side to side instead of up and down.

6. Picture windows—these are fixed glass panes covering a large area. Made of heavier glass, generally plate glass, these windows are single or double glazed; that is, have a single or double layer of glass within the frame.

7. Jalousie windows—similar to awning windows, jalousie windows are made entirely of glass and there is no sash around the individual sections. See *Jalousie*.

While window sash and frame were traditionally made of wood, steel and aluminum windows have become increasingly popular.

Window Portfolio

Conventional double-hung windows consist of an upper and lower sash that slide up and down past each other.

Casement windows are hinged at the side and when open permit 100% ventilation as compared with only 50% for double-hung windows.

Photographs courtesy of Andersen Corp.

Casement windows are also made with metal sash. Here, casement windows are used at the ends while the others are fixed in metal sash.

Photograph courtesy of Aluminum Window Manufacturers Association.

Photographs courtesy of Andersen Corp.

Sketch courtesy of Aluminum
Window Manufacturers Association.

Awning type windows blend well in a contemporary home. Because of the slope of the window, it can be kept partially open in the rain without water coming into the house.

Awning windows in metal sash are used here for an entire wall. The individual sections are controlled as a unit with a single crank handle.

These window walls are set on rollers; each of the twin sections rolls, like a sliding door, to permit opening for ventilation.

Photograph courtesy of Andersen Corp.

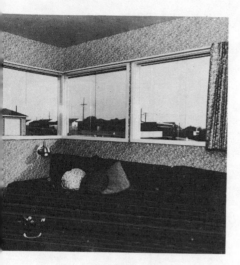

Horizontal sliding windows are easy to clean; in this model, the glass comes out. The individual glass sections slide in special grooves in the frame.

The jalousie window is also all glass. The louver action of the individual panes is controlled by a single handle.

Sketch courtesy of Sun-Sash Co.

Workbench

A good workbench is the most essential piece of equipment in the workship. There are many different types of benches from which to choose. Many handymen find that the enclosed type is more difficult to build but easier to maintain. Whether you use an open or closed bench, it should be solid and made

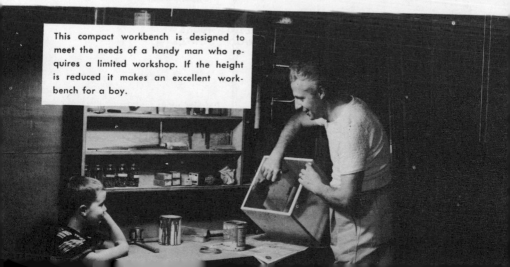

This compact workbench is designed to meet the needs of a handy man who requires a limited workshop. If the height is reduced it makes an excellent workbench for a boy.

of quality wood. Here are plans for several different types of workbenches. Select the one that fits your needs best; you can modify the dimensions according to your requirements.

Compact Workbench-Tool Cabinet

All that you need for this easy-to-make unit are:

2 panels of ¾″ fir plywood, A-D, 4′x8′

1 panel of ″¼ fir plywood, A-D, 4′x4′

32′ of 2x4

3 dozen #10 flathead screws, 3″ long

glue

4d and 6d finishing nails.

The bench itself is 23¾″x60″ and the wall cabinet is 36″x60″. Cut the plywood to the sizes noted in the sketch and join with glue and finishing nails. The bench top is made of a double piece of ¾″ plywood which is screwed to the frame.

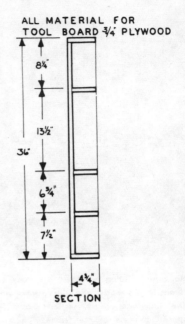

ALL MATERIAL FOR TOOL BOARD ¾″ PLYWOOD

8¼″

13½″

36″

6¾″

7½″

4¾″

SECTION

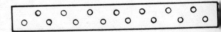

TOOL SHELF PLAN

SIZE, SPACING, AND NUMBER OF HOL TO BE DETERMINED BY TOOLS TO STORED

Photograph and sketches courtesy of Division, Rubber Manufacturers Association

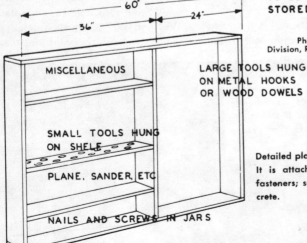

60″

36″

24″

MISCELLANEOUS

LARGE TOOLS HUNG ON METAL HOOKS OR WOOD DOWELS

SMALL TOOLS HUNG ON SHELF

PLANE, SANDER, ETC

NAILS AND SCREWS IN JARS

Detailed plans for making the tool cabinet. It is attached to the wall with special fasteners; see section on **Anchors for Concrete.**

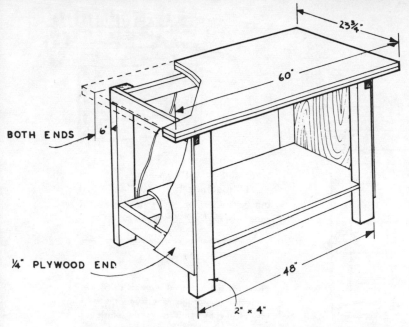

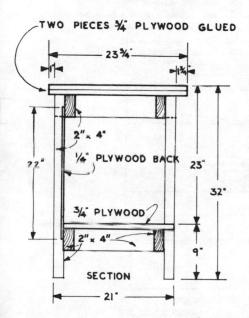

BOTH ENDS 6"

23¾"

60"

¼" PLYWOOD END

2" x 4"

48"

TWO PIECES ¾" PLYWOOD GLUED

23¾"

1"   1¾"

2" x 4"

¼" PLYWOOD BACK

22"   23"

32"

¾" PLYWOOD

2" x 4"

9"

SECTION

21"

Detailed plans for making the workbench. Glue and nail all joints; attach the double plywood top with flathead screws into the frame.

Plans for a Sturdy Workbench

This 30"x60" workbench is exceptionally strong. It is as suitable for use in an apartment as in a basement workshop. It's tough enough to withstand any rough treatment, yet small enough to fit almost any location.

If possible, use maple for your workbench. It's an exceedingly hard, durable wood. When you buy the lumber, get D4S lumber, that is, dressed four sides. In this way, all surfaces will be smooth, there will be less chance of splinters and you'll have a finished-looking bench.

To build the bench illustrated in these plans, you will need the following materials:

1 piece of 2x8 12' long and another piece of 2x6 12' long for the workbench top,

1 piece of 2x4 12' long for the legs,

1 piece of 2x4 10' long for the top rails and a piece of 2x6 10' long for the bottom rails,

a piece of 1x12 6' long for the tool rack, and the following hard-

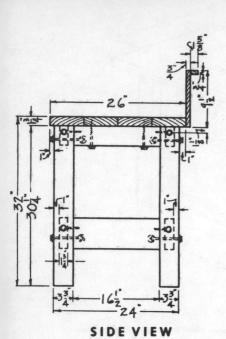

SIDE VIEW

ware and accessories—

16 machine bolts (⅜"x6"), 10 lag screws (⅜"x5") and several pieces of ⅜" or ½" dowels.

Workbench plans courtesy of Stanley Tools.

Sketches courtesy of Stanley Tools.

Plans for a traditional workbench. A convenient tool storage rack forms the back rest of the bench. This sturdy bench can be made larger or, if space permits, make a double bench using a double base but making the top in one piece 10' long.

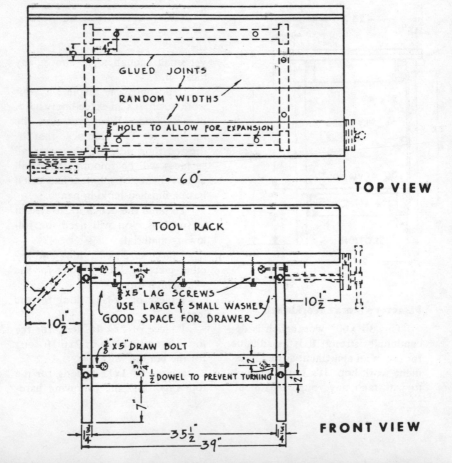

GLUED JOINTS

RANDOM WIDTHS

⅝" HOLE TO ALLOW FOR EXPANSION

60"

TOP VIEW

TOOL RACK

⅜"X5" LAG SCREWS
USE LARGE & SMALL WASHER
GOOD SPACE FOR DRAWER

⅜"X5" DRAW BOLT

½" DOWEL TO PREVENT TURNING

10½"

10½"

5¼"

7"

3¾"   35½"   3¾"
          39"

FRONT VIEW

Wall Workbench

If space is limited, you can make this drop-leaf workbench. It is designed for use in a utility room in a basementless house or in the garage. There is always enough space for this type of a bench for it is compact and has no legs.

The bench is made by notching two 2x4's to fit another 2x4 bolted to the wall; they serve as the slanting legs. Two planks, 1x10's or preferably 1¼ x 10's, are fastened to three 2x4's to form the base of the work-

bench top. For a tough working surface, nail a piece of ¼" tempered hardboard over the planks. The wall edge of the top is secured to a 2x4 fastened to the wall. The notched 2x4 legs are fastened to the outside edge of the top. By nailing a couple of 1x2's across the slanting legs, you create a handy place for storing short pieces of lumber and hardboard. You can make a drawer (see section on *Drawers*) to fit under the workbench top.

Sketches courtesy of Masonite Corp.

Wall workbench can be used where space is limited.

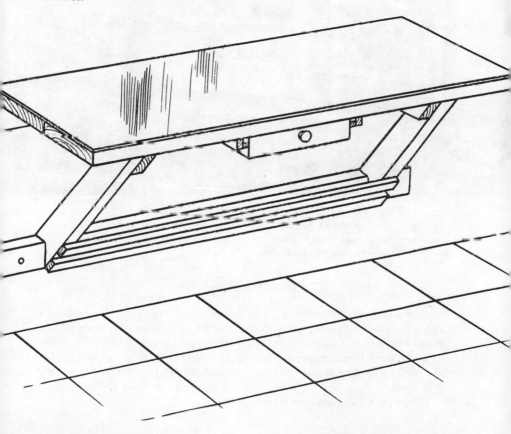

This fold-a-way workbench is ideal for apartment house use where space is limited. Plans with step-by-step instructions are distributed by a manufacturer of portable power tools.

Photographs courtesy of Cummins of John Oster Manufacturing Co.

Fold-a-Way Workbench

For the handyman with limited space, as in an apartment, this workbench can be folded away and stored in a closet. It is recommended for use with a multi-purpose electric drill shop.

The bench folds up into a storage cabinet hung on the door. All the hand tools can be hung on the perforated board used as the cabinet back. In addition, there is a catch-all basket attached near the bottom of the door for convenient storage.

Wall cabinet storage is an ideal addition to any workshop bench. Make the cabinet of fir plywood and mount the doors with strong hinges so that the inside of the doors can also be used for storage space.

Photographs courtesy of Stanley Tools.

If you don't wish to make a cabinet for the tools, hang them on a perforated board (see section on **Perforated Wallboard**). Some tool collections, like the one shown here, come already mounted on the board, or the board can be purchased separately.

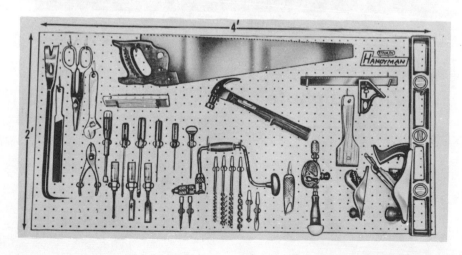

Yoke

The top horizontal member of a window frame is sometimes referred to as a yoke, when the word is used in its architectural sense.

Zig-Zag Rule

A zig-zag rule is one type of folding rule and can be made of wood or metal. Generally, made in 6″ sections that open up to as much as 8′, this rule gets its name from the manner in which it is opened and closed.

Zinc Sulphate

Manufactured by dissolving scrap zinc in sulphuric acid, zinc sulphate is used as a drier for linseed oil and as a preservative for wood.

INDEX

Special HOW-TO GUIDES for Homeowners Handymen